EQUITY

EQUITY

A COURSE OF LECTURES

BY

F. W. MAITLAND

Edited by A. H. CHAYTOR & W. J. WHITTAKER

REVISED BY

JOHN BRUNYATE, M.A.

*Formerly Fellow of Trinity College, Cambridge,
and of Gray's Inn, Barrister-at-Law*

CAMBRIDGE
AT THE UNIVERSITY PRESS
1936
REPRINTED
1969

CAMBRIDGE UNIVERSITY PRESS
Cambridge, New York, Melbourne, Madrid, Cape Town,
Singapore, São Paulo, Delhi, Tokyo, Mexico City

Cambridge University Press
The Edinburgh Building, Cambridge CB2 8RU, UK

Published in the United States of America by Cambridge University Press, New York

www.cambridge.org
Information on this title: www.cambridge.org/9780521176507

© Cambridge University Press 1909, 1936

First edition 1909
Reprinted 1910, 1913, 1916, 1920, 1926, 1929, 1932
Second edition, revised 1936
Reprinted 1969
First paperback edition 2011

A catalogue record for this publication is available from the British Library

ISBN 978-0-521-07777-4 Hardback
ISBN 978-0-521-17650-7 Paperback

PREFACE TO FIRST EDITION

As the Downing Professor of the Laws of England Maitland lectured on Equity at Cambridge over a period of some eighteen years, and for the last time in the spring and summer of 1906. He said himself, "The practising lawyer distrusts the professor of law, and rightly". We venture to hope that these lectures may lessen that distrust. Those who heard them delivered—amongst whom we are—with all Maitland's gaiety, and with all his charm of manner and his power of making dry bones live, will not easily forget either the lectures or the lecturer. Equity, in our minds a formless mystery, became intelligible and interesting; and as for the lecturer, well, there were few things that his hearers would not have done, or attempted, to please F. W. Maitland.

These lectures were written for his students, but when urged to publish them, a few years ago, he said to one of us that although he had no time to do so yet they were in such a form that they could readily be published later on. We think that our successors at Cambridge will be glad to have this book, and that the Common Lawyers, a great and growing body wherever English is spoken, may find here some clear and trustworthy, if brief, account of the famous system of Equity.

Though Maitland had written out these lectures very fully, yet of late years he used the MS. chiefly as a scheme for his oral lecture, making a great many marginal notes, and comments on later cases. We have to thank Mr Roland Burrows, of the Inner Temple, who heard these lectures delivered in 1906, for the use of his notebooks, which have enabled us in many instances to see how Maitland himself had treated and had expanded these later notes. No doubt in our incorporation of them into his text there must be errors, errors that Maitland would have avoided, and without doubt he would have entirely re-written many passages, but the blame for any mistakes must be ours, and we shall be grateful to those who will point them out in order that they may be corrected in the future.

To the twenty-one lectures on Equity we have added seven lectures upon the Forms of Action at Common Law, in order to present at the same time Maitland's account of the development of the two systems which grew up side by side. Here was the structure upon which rested the whole common law of England, and, as Maitland says, "the forms of action we have buried but they still rule us from their graves". The evasion of the burden of archaic procedure and of such barbaric tests of truth as battle, ordeal and wager of law, by the development of new forms and new law out of criminal or quasi criminal procedure and the inquest of neighbour-witnesses has never been described with this truth and clearness. He makes plain a great chapter of legal history which the learners and even the lawyers of to-day have almost abandoned in despair. The text of the chief writs is given after the lectures and a paged analysis of the seven lectures has been printed at the end of the book.

In the editing of these latter lectures Mr E. T. Sandars, of the Inner Temple, also one of Maitland's pupils, has given us much invaluable help, and he has also prepared the Index and the Table of Cases. For him, as for us, the work has been a labour of love.

Amongst the cases given as references in the footnotes Equity lawyers may miss certain authorities to which they frequently refer, but as the lectures were intended, at least primarily, for the student, we have often preferred to give, by way of reference, some modern case reported in the Law Reports series, and for that reason more accessible and more useful to the student. We have referred in the notes to the chief cases decided since Maitland's death upon the points dealt with in the text.

A. H. C.
W. J. W.

LONDON
August 1st 1909

PREFACE TO THE SECOND EDITION

MAITLAND'S *Equity* has not been revised since its first publication under the editorship of A. H. Chaytor and W. J. Whittaker in the year 1909, and even at the present date surprisingly little revision has been found necessary. The reason no doubt is that the greater part of the book deals with the basic rules of equity which were well established at the time when Maitland wrote the book and have not materially changed since that date. The main change has of course been the passing of the Property Acts of 1925 and most of the revision is concerned with these Acts.

The text of the lectures themselves, which were Maitland's own work, has been left unchanged, except that two passages on pp. 63 and 85 have been omitted. These passages, which were both highly technical, dealt with certain questions arising on the Statute of Uses and with the devolution of trust estates; both passages have been rendered obsolete by the Acts of 1925 and it was thought preferable that the student should no longer be burdened with them. The footnotes to the original text, which were not Maitland's work, have where thought desirable been added to and altered. In addition five longer notes have been added at the end of the appropriate chapters dealing with matters which could not conveniently be covered by a footnote. The lectures on Forms of Action which have hitherto been included with Maitland's *Equity* have been excluded from this edition and will be published separately.

The book is in form a series of lectures rather than a text-book. For this reason it does not cover the ground as closely as would an ordinary text-book. The general principles of equity are more fully discussed, but a number of points are omitted altogether, as for example the doctrine of a clog on the equity of redemption, and there is nowhere any attempt to collect the whole of the cases on a particular point. Such a form has great advantages and I have attempted to preserve it by not unduly burdening the book with notes and authorities, even at the risk of omitting certain authorities that might be considered important. Two of the longer notes which have been added, namely those on Restrictive Covenants and Trusts, go beyond the original scope of Maitland's text. On restrictive covenants it appeared to me that Maitland's text covered only part of the ground that a student would wish to cover and that the discussion of other aspects of restrictive covenants would add to the value of Maitland's own work. The reason for adding the Note on Trusts was to elaborate a rather wider conception of the trust and also to deal with a number of points in various parts of the book which could best be treated together.

Perhaps the hardest question which faces a person revising Maitland's *Equity* is the question what to say about his treatment of equitable rights as rights *in personam* and not rights *in rem*. His views on this point pervade the book and are of the essence of it. To deal with them satisfactorily would require an elaborate criticism of Maitland's main thesis. After much consideration I have come to the conclusion that such criticism is not within the functions of a reviser and that the student should look to other books written from a different standpoint to find the presentation of the opposite point of view, for example to the authorities which are referred to and discussed in Hanbury's *Modern Equity*, chapter III. I have therefore not included any note upon this point.

JOHN BRUNYATE

LINCOLN'S INN
June 1936

CONTENTS

TABLE OF CASES

Table of Cases

TABLE OF STATUTES

LIST OF LORD CHANCELLORS AND LORD KEEPERS

(Since Henry VII with dates of taking the seal)

Hen. VIII.	Warham, Abp Canterbury	1509
	Wolsey, Abp York	1515
	Sir T. More	1529
	Sir T. Audley	1532
Edw. VI.	Wriothesley	1544
	St John	1547
	Rich	1547
	Goodrich, Bp Ely	1551
Mary.	Gardiner, Bp Winchester	1553
	Heath, Abp York	1556
Eliz.	Sir Nic. Bacon	1558
	Sir T. Bromley	1579
	Sir Chris. Hatton	1587
	Burleigh and others	1591
	Sir J. Puckering	1592
Jac. I.	Ellesmere	1596
	Bacon	1617
Car. I.	Williams, Bp Lincoln	1621
	Coventry	1625
	Finch	1640
	Lyttleton	1641
Car. II.	Clarendon	1660
	Sir Orlando Bridgeman	1667
	Shaftesbury	1672
	Nottingham	1673
Jac. II.	Guilford	1682
	Jeffreys	1685
Wm. III.	Somers	1693
	Sir Nathan Wright	1700
Anne.	Cowper	1705, 1714
	Harcourt	1708
Geo. I.	Macclesfield	1718
	King	1725
Geo. II.	Talbot	1733
	Hardwicke	1737
Geo. III.	Northington	1760
	Camden	1766
	Bathurst	1771
	Thurlow	1778
	Loughborough	1793
Geo. IV.	Eldon	1801, 1807
	Erskine	1806
Wm. IV.	Lyndhurst	1827, 1834, 1841
	Brougham	1830
Vict.	Cottenham	1836, 1846

Vict.	Truro	1850
	St Leonards	1851
	Cranworth	1852, 1865
	Chelmsford	1858, 1866
	Campbell	1859
	Westbury	1861
	Cairns	1868, 1874
	Hatherley	1868
	Selborne	1872, 1880
	Halsbury	1885, 1886, 1895
	Herschell	1886, 1892
Edw. VII.	Loreburn	1905
Geo. V.	Haldane	1912, 1924
	Buckmaster	1915
	Finlay	1916
	Birkenhead	1919
	Cave	1922, 1924
	Hailsham	1928, 1935
	Sankey	1929

LECTURE I

THE ORIGIN OF EQUITY (I)

DURING the present term I intend to give a course of lectures
of an elementary character upon some of the main doctrines of
Equity. I intend to speak of Equity as of an existing body of
rules administered by our courts of justice. But for reasons
which you will easily understand a brief historical prelude seems
necessary. For suppose that we ask the question—What is
Equity? We can only answer it by giving some short account of
certain courts of justice which were abolished over thirty years
ago. In the year 1875 we might have said 'Equity is that body
of rules which is administered only by those Courts which are
known as Courts of Equity.' The definition of course would not
have been very satisfactory, but now-a-days we are cut off even
from this unsatisfactory definition. We have no longer any courts
which are merely courts of equity. Thus we are driven to say
that Equity now is that body of rules administered by our
English courts of justice which, were it not for the operation of
the Judicature Acts, would be administered only by those courts
which would be known as Courts of Equity.

This, you may well say, is but a poor thing to call a definition.
Equity is a certain portion of our existing substantive law, and
yet in order that we may describe this portion and mark it off
from other portions we have to make reference to courts that are
no longer in existence. Still I fear that nothing better than this
is possible. The only alternative would be to make a list of the
equitable rules and say that Equity consists of those rules. This,
I say, would be the only alternative, for if we were to inquire
what it is that all these rules have in common and what it is that
marks them off from all other rules administered by our courts,
we should by way of answer find nothing but this, that these
rules were until lately administered, and administered only, by
our courts of equity.

Therefore for the mere purpose of understanding the present

state of our law, some history becomes necessary. I will try to tell the main story in a few words but you should read it at large in the books that I have just mentioned—Story, Lewin, Ashburner, Strahan, Holdsworth—or in other books such as Spence's *Equitable Jurisdiction*.[1]

In Edward I's day, at the end of the thirteenth century, three great courts have come into existence, the King's Bench, the Common Bench or Court of Common Pleas and the Exchequer. Each of these has its own proper sphere, but as time goes on each of them attempts to extend its sphere and before the middle ages are over a plaintiff has often a choice between these three courts and each of them will deal with his case in the same way and by the same rules. The law which these courts administer is in part traditional law, in part statute law. Already in Edward I's day the phrase 'common law' is current. It is a phrase that has been borrowed from the canonists—who used '*jus commune*' to denote the general law of the Catholic Church; it describes that part of the law that is unenacted, non-statutory, that is common to the whole land and to all Englishmen. It is contrasted with statute, with local custom, with royal prerogative. It is not as yet contrasted with equity, for as yet there is no body of rules which bears this name.

One of the three courts, namely, the Exchequer, is more than a court of law. From our modern point of view it is not only a court of law but a 'government office', an administrative or executive bureau; our modern Treasury is an offshoot from the old Exchequer. What we should call the 'civil service' of the country is transacted by two great offices or 'departments'; there is the Exchequer which is the fiscal department, there is the Chancery which is the secretarial department, while above these there rises the king's permanent Council. At the head of the Chancery stands the Chancellor, usually a bishop; he is we may say the king's secretary of state for all departments, he keeps the king's great seal and all the already great mass of writing that has to be done in the king's name has to be done under his supervision.

---

[1] For the titles of these books, which had been mentioned before the lecture began see the note at p. 11.

He is not as yet a judge, but already he by himself or his subordinates has a great deal of work to do which brings him into a close connexion with the administration of justice. One of the duties of that great staff of clerks over which he presides is to draw up and issue those writs whereby actions are begun in the courts of law—such writs are sealed with the king's seal. A man who wishes to begin an action must go to the Chancery and obtain a writ. Many writs there are which have been formulated long ago; such writs are writs of course (*brevia de cursu*), one obtains them by asking for them of the clerks—called Cursitors—and paying the proper fees. But the Chancery has a certain limited power of inventing new writs to meet new cases as they arise. That power is consecrated by a famous clause of the Second Statute of Westminster authorizing writs *in consimili casu*. Thus the Chancellor may often have to consider whether the case is one in which some new and some specially worded writ should be framed. This however is not judicial business. The Chancellor does not hear both sides of the story, he only hears the plaintiff's application, and if he grants a writ the courts of law may afterwards quash that writ as being contrary to the law of the land.

But by another route the Chancellor is brought into still closer contact with the administration of justice. Though these great courts of law have been established there is still a reserve of justice in the king. Those who can not get relief elsewhere present their petitions to the king and his council praying for some remedy. Already by the end of the thirteenth century the number of such petitions presented in every year is very large, and the work of reading them and considering them is very laborious. In practice a great share of this labour falls on the Chancellor. He is the king's prime minister, he is a member of the council, and the specially learned member of the council. It is in dealing with these petitions that the Chancellor begins to develop his judicial powers.

In course of time his judicial powers are classified as being of two kinds. It begins to be said that the Court of Chancery, 'Curia Cancellariae'—for the phrase is used in the fourteenth century—has two sides, a common law side and an equity side, or a Latin side and an English side. Let us look for a moment at the origin of these two kinds of powers, and first at that which concerns us least.

(1) Many of these petitions of which I have spoken seek for justice not merely from the king but against the king. If anybody is to be called the wrong doer, it is the king himself. For example, he is in possession of land which has been seized by his officers as an escheat while really the late tenant has left an heir. Now the king can not be sued by action—no writ will go against him; the heir if he wants justice must petition for it humbly. Such matters as these are referred to the Chancellor. Proceedings are taken before him; the heir, it may be, proves his case and gets his land. The number of such cases, cases in which the king is concerned, is very large—kings are always seizing land on very slight pretexts—and forcing other people to prove their titles. Gradually a quite regular and ordinary procedure is established for such cases—a procedure very like that of the three courts of law. The proceedings are enrolled in Latin—just as the proceedings of the three courts of law are enrolled in Latin (hence the name 'Latin side' of the Court of Chancery)—and if a question of fact be raised, it is tried by jury. The Chancellor himself does not summon the jury or preside at the trial, he sends the question for trial to the King's Bench. All this is by no means unimportant, but it does not concern us very much at the present time.

(2) Very often the petitioner requires some relief at the expense of some other person. He complains that for some reason or another he can not get a remedy in the ordinary course of justice and yet he is entitled to a remedy. He is poor, he is old, he is sick, his adversary is rich and powerful, will bribe or will intimidate jurors, or has by some trick or some accident acquired an advantage of which the ordinary courts with their formal procedure will not deprive him. The petition is often couched in piteous terms, the king is asked to find a remedy for the love of God and in the way of charity. Such petitions are referred by the king to the Chancellor. Gradually in the course of the fourteenth century petitioners, instead of going to the king, will go straight to the Chancellor, will address their complaints to

him and adjure him to do what is right for the love of God and in the way of charity. Now one thing that the Chancellor may do in such a case is to invent a new writ and so provide the complainant with a means of bringing an action in a court of law. But in the fourteenth century the courts of law have become very conservative and are given to quashing writs which differ in material points from those already in use. But another thing that the Chancellor can do is to send for the complainant's adversary and examine him concerning the charge that has been made against him. Gradually a procedure is established. The Chancellor having considered the petition, or 'bill' as it is called, orders the adversary to come before him and answer the complaint. The writ whereby he does this is called a subpoena —because it orders the man to appear upon pain of forfeiting a sum of money, *e.g. subpoena centum librarum*. It is very different from the old writs whereby actions are begun in the courts of law. They tell the defendant what is the cause of action against him—he is to answer why he assaulted and beat the plaintiff, why he trespassed on the plaintiff's land, why he detains a chattel which belongs to the plaintiff. The subpoena, on the other hand, will tell him merely that he has got to come before the Chancellor and answer complaints made against him by A. B. Then when he comes before the Chancellor he will have to answer on oath, and sentence by sentence, the bill of the plaintiff. This procedure is rather like that of the ecclesiastical courts and the canon law than like that of our old English courts of law. It was in fact borrowed from the ecclesiastical courts, not from their ordinary procedure but from the summary procedure of those courts introduced for the suppression of heresy. The defendant will be examined upon oath and the Chancellor will decide questions of fact as well as questions of law.

I do not think that in the fourteenth century the Chancellors considered that they had to administer any body of substantive rules that differed from the ordinary law of the land. They were administering the law but they were administering it in cases which escaped the meshes of the ordinary courts. The complaints that come before them are in general complaints of indubitable legal wrongs, assaults, batteries, imprisonments, disseisins and so forth—wrongs of which the ordinary courts take cognizance, wrongs which they ought to redress. But then owing to one thing and another such wrongs are not always redressed by courts of law. In this period one of the commonest of all the reasons that complainants will give for coming to the Chancery is that they are poor while their adversaries are rich and influential—too rich, too influential to be left to the clumsy processes of the old courts and the verdicts of juries. However this sort of thing can not well be permitted. The law courts will not have it and parliament will not have it. Complaints against this extraordinary justice grow loud in the fourteenth century. In history and in principle it is closely connected with another kind of extraordinary justice which is yet more objectionable, the extraordinary justice that is done in criminal cases by the king's council. Parliament at one time would gladly be rid of both—of both the Council's interference in criminal matters, and the Chancellor's interference with civil matters. And so the Chancellor is warned off the field of common law—he is not to hear cases which might go to the ordinary courts, he is not to make himself a judge of torts and contracts, of property in lands and goods.

But then just at this time it is becoming plain that the Chancellor is doing some convenient and useful works that could not be done, or could not easily be done, by the courts of common law. He has taken to enforcing uses or trusts. Of the origin of uses or trusts you will have read and I shall have something to say about it on another occasion. I don't myself believe that the use came to us as a foreign thing. I don't believe that there is anything Roman about it. I believe that it was a natural outcome of ancient English elements. But at any rate I must ask you not to believe that either the mass of the nation or the common lawyers of the fourteenth and fifteenth centuries looked with disfavour upon uses. No doubt they were troublesome things, things that might be used for fraudulent purposes, and statutes were passed against those who employed them for the purpose of cheating their creditors or evading the law of mortmain. But I have not a doubt that they were very popular, and I think we may say that had there been no Chancery, the old courts would have discovered some method of enforcing these fiduciary obligations. That method however must have been a clumsy one. A system of law which will never compel, which will never even allow, the defendant to give evidence, a system which sends every question of fact to a jury, is not competent to deal adequately with fiduciary relationships. On the other hand the Chancellor had a procedure which was very well adapted to this end. To this we may add that very possibly the ecclesiastical courts (and the Chancellor you will remember was almost always an ecclesiastic) had for a long time past been punishing breaches of trust by spiritual censures, by penance and excommunication. And so by general consent, we may say, the Chancellor was allowed to enforce uses, trusts or confidences.

Thus one great field of substantive law fell into his hand—a fruitful field, for in the course of the fifteenth century uses became extremely popular. Then, as we all know, Henry VIII— for it was rather the king than his subservient parliament—struck a heavy blow at uses. The king was the one man in the kingdom who had everything to gain and nothing to lose by abolishing uses, and as we all know he merely succeeded in complicating the law, for under the name of 'trusts' the Chancellors still reigned over their old province. And then there were some other matters that were considered to be fairly within his jurisdiction. An old rhyme[1] allows him 'fraud, accident, and breach of confidence'—there were many frauds which the stiff old procedure of the courts of law could not adequately meet, and 'accident', in particular the accidental loss of a document, was a proper occasion for the Chancellor's interference. No one could set any very strict limits to his power, but the best hint as to its extent that could be given in the sixteenth century was given by the words 'fraud, accident and breach of confidence'. On the other hand he was not to interfere where a court of common law offered an adequate remedy. A bill was 'demurrable for want of equity' on that ground.

In the course of the sixteenth century we begin to learn a

---

[1] 'These three give place in court of conscience,
    Fraud, accident, and breach of confidence.'

little about the rules that the Chancellors are administering in the field that is thus assigned to them. They are known as 'the rules of equity and good conscience'. As to what they have done in remoter times we have to draw inferences from very sparse evidence. One thing seems pretty plain. They had not considered themselves strictly bound by precedent. Remember this, our reports of cases in courts of law go back to Edward I's day—the middle ages are represented to us by the long series of Year Books. On the other hand our reports of cases in the Court of Chancery go back no further than 1557; and the mass of reports which come to us from between that date and the Restoration in 1660 is a light matter. This by itself is enough to show us that the Chancellors have not held themselves very strictly bound by case law, for men have not cared to collect cases. Nor do I believe that to any very large extent the Chancellors had borrowed from the Roman law—this is a disputed matter, Mr Spence has argued for their Romanism, Mr Justice Holmes against it. No doubt through the medium of the canon law these great ecclesiastics were familiar with some of the great maxims which occur in the *Institutes* or the *Digest*. One of the parts of the *Corpus Juris Canonici*, the Liber Sextus, ends with a bouquet of these high-sounding maxims—*Qui prior est tempore potior est jure*, and so forth, maxims familiar to all readers of equity reports. No doubt the early Chancellors knew these and valued them—but I do not believe that we ought to attribute to them much knowledge of Roman law or any intention to Romanize the law of England. For example, to my mind the comparison sometimes drawn between the so-called double ownership of England, and the so-called double ownership of Roman law can not be carried below the surface. In their treatment of uses or trusts the Chancellors stick close, marvellously close, to the rules of the common law—they often consulted the judges, and the lawyers who pleaded before them were common lawyers, for there was as yet no 'Chancery Bar'. On the whole my notion is that with the idea of a law of nature in their minds they decided cases without much reference to any written authority, now making use of some analogy drawn from the common law, and now of some great maxim of jurisprudence which they have borrowed from the canonists or the civilians.

In the second half of the sixteenth century the jurisprudence of the court is becoming settled. The day for ecclesiastical Chancellors is passing away. Wolsey is the last of the great ecclesiastical Chancellors, though in Charles I's day we have one more divine in the person of Dr Williams. Ellesmere, Bacon, Coventry, begin to administer an established set of rules which is becoming known to the public in the shape of reports and they begin to publish rules of procedure. In James I's day occurred the great quarrel between Lord Chancellor Ellesmere and Chief Justice Coke which finally decided that the Court of Chancery was to have the upper hand over the courts of law. If the Chancery was to carry out its maxims about trust and fraud it was essential that it should have a power to prevent men from going into the courts of law and to prevent men from putting in execution the judgments that they had obtained in courts of law. In fraud or in breach of trust you obtain a judgment against me in a court of law; I complain to the Chancellor, and he after hearing what you have to say enjoins you not to put in force your judgment, says in effect that if you do put your judgment in force you will be sent to prison. Understand well that the Court of Chancery never asserted that it was superior to the courts of law; it never presumed to send to them such mandates as the Court of King's Bench habitually sent to the inferior courts, telling them that they must do this or must not do that or quashing their proceedings—the Chancellor's injunction was in theory a very different thing from a mandamus, a prohibition, a certiorari, or the like. It was addressed not to the judges, but to the party. You in breach of trust have obtained a judgment— the Chancellor does not say that this judgment was wrongly granted, he does not annul it, he tells you that for reasons personal to yourself it will be inequitable for you to enforce that judgment, and that you are not to enforce it.[1] For all this, however, it was natural that the judges should take umbrage at this treatment of their judgments. Coke declared that the man who obtained such an injunction was guilty of the offence denounced

[1] Cf. *Ellerman Lines* v. *Read* [1928] 2 K.B. 144.

by the Statutes of Praemunire, that of calling in question the judgments of the king's courts in other courts (these statutes had been aimed at the Papal curia). King James had now a wished-for opportunity of appearing as supreme over all his judges, and all his courts, and acting on the advice of Bacon and other great lawyers he issued a decree in favour of the Chancery. From this time forward the Chancery had the upper hand. It did not claim to be superior to the courts of law, but it could prevent men from going to those courts, whereas those courts could not prevent men from going to it.

Its independence being thus secured, the court became an extremely busy court. Bacon said that he had made 2000 orders in a year, and we are told that as many as 16,000 causes were pending before it at one time: indeed it was hopelessly in arrear of its work. Under the Commonwealth some vigorous attempts were made to reform its procedure. Some were for abolishing it altogether. It was not easily forgotten that the Court of Chancery was the twin sister of the Court of Star Chamber. The projects for reform came to an end with the Restoration. Still it is from the Restoration or thereabouts—of course a precise date can not be fixed—that we may regard the equity administered in the Chancery as a recognized part of the law of the land. Usually, though not always, the great seal is in the keeping of a great lawyer—in 1667 Sir Orlando Bridgman, the great conveyancer, has it; in 1673 Sir Heneage Finch, afterwards Lord Nottingham, who has been called the father of equity; in 1682 Sir Francis North, afterwards Lord Guilford; in 1693 Sir John Somers, afterwards Lord Somers, a great common lawyer. I think that Anthony Ashley, Earl of Shaftesbury, the famous Ashley of the Cabal, was the last non-lawyer who held it, and he held it for but one year, from 1672 to 1673. Then during the eighteenth century there comes a series of great Chancellors. In 1705 Cowper, in 1713 Harcourt, in 1725 King, in 1733 Talbot, in 1737 Hardwicke, in 1757 Northington, in 1766 Camden, in 1778 Thurlow, in 1793 Loughborough, in 1801 Eldon. In the course of the century the Chancery reports improve; the same care is spent upon reporting the decrees of the Chancellors that has long been spent on reporting the judgments of the judges in the courts of common law. Gradually, too, a Chancery bar forms itself, that is to say, some barristers begin to devote themselves altogether to practising before the Chancellor, and do not seek for work elsewhere. Lastly, equity makes its way into the text-books as a part, and an important part, of the law of the land. By far the greatest text-book of the century is, I need hardly say it, Blackstone's *Commentaries*—it comes to us from the middle of the century—but of Blackstone's view of equity I must speak next time.

Note. Before beginning this course of lectures Professor Maitland used to recommend various books to his students. The list in 1906 appears to have been the following:

Story, *Equity Jurisprudence* (1892).
Lewin, *Law of Trusts* (1904).
Ashburner, *Principles of Equity* (1902).
Strahan and Kenrick, *Digest of Equity* (1905).
Holdsworth, *History of English Law*. Vol. 1 (1903).
Digby, *History of the Law of Real Property* (1898).

LECTURE II

THE ORIGIN OF EQUITY (II)

WE have brought down our brief sketch of English Equity to the time of Blackstone. Let us now look at the matter through the eyes of the great commentator. He is concerned to show that the so-called equity of the Court of Chancery is in reality law, and he also considers himself concerned to show that the so-called law of the three old courts is in a sense equity. I shall read a somewhat long excerpt from him because it contains some valuable illustrations. He begins by asserting that every definition or illustration which draws a line between the two jurisdictions, by setting law and equity in opposition to each other, will be found either totally erroneous, or erroneous to a certain degree.

1. 'Thus in the first place it is said that it is the business of a court of equity in England to abate the rigour of the common law. But no such power is contended for. Hard was the case of bond-creditors, whose debtor devised away his real estate; rigorous and unjust the rule which put the devisee in a better condition to the heir: yet a court of equity had no power to interpose. Hard is the common law still subsisting, that land devised, or descending to the heir, shall not be liable to simple contract debts of the ancestor or devisor...and that the father shall never immediately succeed to the real estate of the son: but a court of equity can give no relief; though in both these instances the artificial reason of the law, arising from feudal principles, has long ago entirely ceased.' He gives other instances of hard and antiquated rules, for the rigour of which equity has no mitigation.

2. 'It is said that a court of equity determines according to the spirit of the rule and not according to the strictness of the letter. But so also does a court of law. Both for instance are equally bound and equally profess to interpret statutes according to the true intent of the legislature'....

3. 'Again, it hath been said, that fraud, accident and trust are

the proper and peculiar objects of a court of equity.' But, he urges, all frauds are equally cognizable by a court of law and some are only cognizable there. Many accidents are relieved against in courts of law. And, though it is true that the courts of law will not take notice of what is technically called a trust—created by a limitation of a second use—still it takes notice of bailments and a bailment, *e.g.* a deposit, is in fact a trust.

4. 'Once more; it has been said that a court of equity is not bound by rules or precedents, but acts from the opinion of the judge founded on the circumstances of every particular case. Whereas the system of our courts of equity is a laboured, connected system governed by precedents, from which they do not depart, although the reason of some of them may perhaps be liable of objection. Thus the refusing a wife her dower in a trust estate, yet allowing the husband his curtesy'—and he gives several other illustrations of rules which are but questionably just—'all these, and other cases that might be instanced are plainly rules of positive law.'

He sums up: 'The systems of jurisprudence in our courts both of law and equity are now equally artificial systems, founded in the same principles of justice and positive law; but varied by different usages in the forms and mode of their proceedings: the one being originally derived (though much reformed and improved) from the feudal customs, as they prevailed in different ages in the Saxon and Norman judicatures; the other (but with equal improvements) from the imperial and pontifical formularies, introduced by their clerical chancellors.'[1]

You will see what this comes to. Equity is now, whatever it may have been in past times, a part of the law of our land. What part? That part which is administered by certain courts known as courts of equity. We can give no other general answer. We can give a historical explanation. We can say, for example, that the common law is derived from feudal customs, while equity is derived from Roman and canon law (Blackstone, I think, greatly overrates the influence of Roman and canon law in the history of equity), but in no general terms can we describe either the field of equity or the distinctive character of equitable

---

[1] Blackstone, III, 429 *et seq.*

rules. Of course we can make a catalogue of equitable rules, and we can sometimes point to an institution, such as the trust strictly so called, which is purely equitable, but we can make no generalization.

We will come back to this point by and by. Meanwhile let us carry our hurried sketch to an end. The first three quarters of the nineteenth century saw an enormously rapid development of the equitable jurisdiction. Remember this, that until 1813 there were only two judges in the Court of Chancery. There was the Lord Chancellor, and there was the Master of the Rolls, and it was but by degrees that the latter had become an independent judge; for a long time he appears merely as the Chancellor's assistant. In 1813 a Vice-Chancellor was appointed. In 1841 two more Vice-Chancellors. In 1851 two Lords Justices of Appeal in Chancery. When the Court was abolished in 1875 it had seven judges. Cases in the first instance were taken before the Master of the Rolls, or one of the three Vice-Chancellors, and then there was an appeal Court constituted by the Chancellor and the two Lords Justices; but the Chancellor could sit as a judge of first instance if he pleased and sometimes did so. I need hardly say that every Chancellor has been a great lawyer—some like Brougham, Campbell, Herschell, Halsbury, have been by origin common lawyers, others like St Leonards, Westbury, Hatherley, Selborne, Cairns, equity lawyers. There was a large body of practitioners who never, or only on the rarest occasions, went into courts of law, just as there was another large body of practitioners who never saw the inside of a court of equity, and who would have very frankly admitted that of equity they knew next to nothing.

There came great reforming statutes which recast the procedure of both courts. Some of their provisions we may now regard as prophetic, that is to say, they paved the way for that fusion of the two procedures which was accomplished in 1875. Thus, for example, the Court of Chancery was enabled in certain cases to give damages,[1] and the courts of law were enabled in certain cases to grant injunctions:[2] formerly the in-

---

[1] The Chancery Amendment Act 1858 (Lord Cairns's Act), s. 2.
[2] The Common Law Procedure Act 1854, ss. 79 and 82.

junction had been characteristic of the Court of Chancery, while the judgment for damages had been characteristic of the court of law. Again the statutes which enabled the parties to an action and other interested persons to give evidence in courts of law did something towards bridging over the gulf.[1] At last came the Judicature Acts of 1873 and 1875,[2] which took effect in the latter year. The old courts were abolished, Chancery, Queen's Bench, Common Pleas, Exchequer, also the Court of Probate, the Court of Divorce, and the Court of Admiralty. In their place was put a High Court of Justice with a Court of Appeal above it. This High Court of Justice was divided into five divisions, Chancery, Queen's Bench, Common Pleas, Exchequer—that makes four—the fifth being Probate, Divorce and Admiralty. But you should understand that the divisions of the High Court are utterly different things from the old independent courts. Certain particular business was assigned to each division. Thus for example to the Chancery Division was assigned (among other things) 'the execution of trusts charitable or private', 'the redemption and foreclosure of mortgages', and so forth. But this is now to be regarded as a mere matter of convenience: the distribution of business might at any time be changed without any act of parliament merely by rules made by the judges, and even the divisions of the High Court can be abolished or changed without any act of parliament by an order in council, and indeed the Common Pleas and Exchequer Divisions were abolished by an order in council of 16 December, 1880. But this is not all, for in the second place we must note that every judge, to whatever division he may belong, is bound to administer in any case that comes before him whatever rules our law—taking the term 'law' in its widest meaning—has for that case; be those rules rules of common law or rules of equity. It is no longer possible for a judge to say to a litigant 'You are relying on a trust and this court can take no notice of a trust', or 'This is a matter of pure common law and

---

[1] 6 & 7 Vic. c. 85, s. 1 (1843) (interest); 14 & 15 Vic. c. 99, s. 2 (1851) (parties).

[2] Now for the most part replaced by the Supreme Court of Judicature (Consolidation) Act 1925.

not within the cognizance of a court of equity.' It is no longer necessary for a man to institute a suit in equity in order to obtain evidence that he wants to use in an action at law. It is no longer possible for him to obtain an injunction from equity restraining his adversary from taking proceedings at law.

Then as to procedure there was a great change. Practically we have now what might well be called a Code of Civil Procedure. It is to be found partly in the Judicature Acts, partly in a large body of Rules of Court made by the judges in exercise of rule-making powers given to them by statute. This code of procedure is supposed to combine all the best features of the two old systems, the system of the common law, and the system of equity.

Then as to substantive law the Judicature Act of 1873 took occasion to make certain changes. In its 25th section[1] it laid down certain rules about the administration of insolvent estates, about the application of statutes of limitation, about waste, about merger, about mortgages, about the assignment of choses in action, and so forth, and it ended with these words:

'Generally in all matters not hereinbefore particularly mentioned, in which there is any conflict or variance between the rules of equity and the rules of the common law with reference to the same matter, the rules of equity shall prevail.'

Now it may well seem to you that those are very important words, for perhaps you may have fancied that at all manner of points there was a conflict between the rules of equity and the rules of the common law, or at all events a variance. But the clause that I have just read has been in force now for over thirty years, and if you will look at any good commentary upon it you will find that it has done very little—it has been practically without effect. You may indeed find many cases in which some advocate, at a loss for other arguments, has appealed to the words of this clause as a last hope; but you will find very few

---

[1] This section, excepting paragraph 2, is repealed by the Supreme Court of Judicature (Consolidation) Act 1925. Most of the provisions repealed are to be found re-enacted in the Property Acts of 1925. Paragraph 11, which is the provision on a 'conflict or variance' quoted in the text, is now contained in s. 44 of the Supreme Court of Judicature (Consolidation) Act 1925.

cases indeed in which that appeal has been successful. I shall speak of this more at large at another time, but it is important that even at the very outset of our career we should form some notion of the relation which existed between law and equity in the year 1875. And the first thing that we have to observe is that this relation was not one of conflict. Equity had come not to destroy the law, but to fulfil it. Every jot and every tittle of the law was to be obeyed, but when all this had been done something might yet be needful, something that equity would require. Of course now and again there had been conflicts: there was an open conflict, for example, when Coke was for indicting a man who sued for an injunction. But such conflicts as this belong to old days, and for two centuries before the year 1875 the two systems had been working together harmoniously.

Let me take an instance or two in which something that may for one moment look like a conflict becomes no conflict at all when it is examined. Take the case of a trust. An examiner will sometimes ʋe told that whereas the common law said that the trustee was the owner of the land, equity said that the *cestui que trust* was the owner. Well here in all conscience there seems to be conflict enough. Think what this would mean were it really true. There are two courts of co-ordinate jurisdiction—one says that A is the owner, the other says that B is the owner of Black-acre. That means civil war and utter anarchy. Of course the statement is an extremely crude one, it is a misleading and a dangerous statement—how misleading, how dangerous, we shall see when we come to examine the nature of equitable estates. Equity did not say that the *cestui que trust* was the owner of the land, it said that the trustee was the owner of the land, but added that he was bound to hold the land for the benefit of the *cestui que trust*. There was no conflict here. Had there been a conflict here the clause of the Judicature Act which I have lately read would have abolished the whole law of trusts. Common law says that A is the owner, equity says that B is the owner, but equity is to prevail, therefore B is the owner and A has no right or duty of any sort or kind in or about the land. Of course the Judicature Act has not acted in this way; it has left the law of trusts just where it stood, because it found no conflict, no variance even, between the rules of the common law and the rules of equity.

Other instances might easily be taken. As a remedy for a breach of contract a court of law could give damages; as a remedy for a breach of contract a court of equity could grant a decree for specific performance. In many cases it would happen that a man would have his choice between the two remedies— he could go to law for damages, he could ask the Court of Chancery to compel his adversary to do just what he had promised to do. In many other cases he had no choice, the one remedy open to him was an action for damages; equity would give him no help. In yet other cases the converse was true, he had no action for damages, but he could none the less obtain a decree for specific performance. Here again there is no conflict. There is nothing absurd, nothing contradictory in the statement 'You are entitled to damages for the breach of this contract, but no court will compel your adversary to perform it specifically'; nor in the statement 'You can not obtain damages for the breach of this contract, and yet you may have a decree for specific performance'. There is here no room for the play of these words in the Judicature Act about the prevalence of equity.

Or take a case of tort, a case of nuisance. There is no absurdity, no self-contradiction in this statement: 'X by building that wall has done you a wrong for which he can be compelled to pay you damages, but all the same the case is not one in which he ought to be enjoined to pull the work down on pain of going to prison.'

No, we ought to think of equity as supplementary law, a sort of appendix added on to our code, or a sort of gloss written round our code, an appendix, a gloss, which used to be administered by courts specially designed for that purpose, but which is now administered by the High Court of Justice as part of the code. The language which equity held to law, if we may personify the two, was not 'No, that is not so, you make a mistake, your rule is an absurd, an obsolete one'; but 'Yes, of course that is so, but it is not the whole truth. You say that A is the owner of this land; no doubt that is so, but I must add that he is bound by one of those obligations which are known as trusts'.

We ought not to think of common law and equity as of two rival systems. Equity was not a self-sufficient system, at every point it presupposed the existence of common law. Common law was a self-sufficient system. I mean this: that if the legislature has passed a short act saying 'Equity is hereby abolished', we might still have got on fairly well; in some respects our law would have been barbarous, unjust, absurd, but still the great elementary rights, the right to immunity from violence, the right to one's good name, the rights of ownership and of possession would have been decently protected and contract would have been enforced. On the other hand had the legislature said, 'Common Law is hereby abolished', this decree if obeyed would have meant anarchy. At every point equity presupposed the existence of common law. Take the case of the trust. It's of no use for Equity to say that A is a trustee of Blackacre for B, unless there be some court that can say that A is the owner of Blackacre. Equity without common law would have been a castle in the air, an impossibility.

For this reason I do not think that any one has expounded or ever will expound equity as a single, consistent system, an articulate body of law. It is a collection of appendixes between which there is no very close connexion. If we suppose all our law put into systematic order, we shall find that some chapters of it have been copiously glossed by equity, while others are quite free from equitable glosses. Since the destruction of the Star Chamber we have had no criminal equity. The Court of Chancery kept very clear of the province of crime, and since the province of crime and the province of tort overlap, it kept very clear of large portions of the province of tort. For example, before 1875 it would grant no injunction to restrain the publication of a libel, for normally the libel which is a tort is also a crime and it was thought, and rightly thought, that such a matter should not be brought before a court where a judge without any jury tried both fact and law. Indeed if you will look at your books on tort you will find that on the whole—if we except the province of fraud—equity has had little to do with tort, though it has granted injunctions to restrain the commission of nuisances and the like. The law of contract has been more richly provided with equitable appendices. The power of the Chancery to compel specific performance, and its power to decree the cancellation or rectification of agreements brought numerous cases of contract before it, and then it had special doctrines about mortgages, and penalties, and stipulations concerning time. Property law was yet more richly glossed. One vast appendix was added to it under the title of trusts. The bond which kept these various appendixes together under the head of Equity was the jurisdictional and procedural bond. All these matters were within the cognizance of courts of equity, and they were not within the cognizance of the courts of common law. That bond is now broken by the Judicature Acts. Instead of it we find but a mere historical bond—'these rules used to be dealt with by the Court of Chancery'—and the strength of that bond is being diminished year by year. The day will come when lawyers will cease to inquire whether a given rule be a rule of equity or a rule of common law: suffice it that it is a well-established rule administered by the High Court of Justice.

Certainly I should have liked at the outset of my course to have put before you some map, some scheme of equity. But for the reasons that I have endeavoured to state I do not think that such a map, such a scheme can be drawn. Attempts at classification have been made, but they have never been pushed very far and are now of little, if any, service to us. The scheme adopted by the great American judge, Story, and which found very general acceptation, was this—Equity is (1) exclusive, (2) concurrent, (3) auxiliary. You see the basis of this scheme—it is one on which we can no longer build. Equity has an exclusive cognizance of certain subjects, *e.g.* trusts, a cognizance that is exclusive of courts of law. Then it has a concurrent jurisdiction, a jurisdiction that is concurrent with the jurisdiction of courts of law over certain other subjects, *e.g.* fraud. Finally men sometimes go to equity merely in order to obtain its assistance in proceedings which they are taking or are about to take in courts of law, *e.g.* the plaintiff in an action at law goes to the Chancery in order that he may obtain discovery of the documents on which his opponent will rely. Here equity exercises an auxiliary jurisdiction. Then under each of these titles Story and other writers will give a string of sub-titles. Thus the concurrent jurisdiction deals with account, mistake, actual or positive fraud, constructive fraud, administration, legacies, confusion of boundaries, dower, and so forth. But you will at once see that this string is a mere string and not a logical scheme—observe for example the leap from legacies to boundaries, and from boundaries to dower. I am not complaining of Story's procedure; on the contrary it seems to me the only procedure open to him. In my opinion he had to deal not with a single connected system, but with a number of disconnected doctrines, disconnected appendixes to or glosses on the common law. And you will observe that such classification as he could make is no longer useful. It presupposes that there is one set of courts administering law, another set administering equity. That is no longer the case in England. No court, no division of a court, can now say these or those rules are my exclusive property; for every division of the High Court is capable of administering whatever rules are applicable to the case that is before it, whether they be rules of the common law or rules of equity.

When some years ago the new scheme for our Tripos was settled, we said that candidates for the second part were to study the English Law of Real and Personal Property and the English Law of Contract and Tort, with the equitable principles applicable to these subjects. It was a question whether we ought not to have mentioned equity as a separate subject. I have no doubt however that we did the right thing. To have acknowledged the existence of equity as a system distinct from law would in my opinion have been a belated, a reactionary measure. I think, for example, that you ought to learn the many equitable modifications of the law of contract, not as part of equity, but as part, and a very important part, of our modern English law of contract. And books such as those of Anson and Pollock enable you to do so. I should consider a book on Contract extremely imperfect if it gave no account of the equitable doctrine of part performance, the equitable doctrine of undue influence, the equitable remedy of rectification, and the like. For all this however it has seemed to me possible that certain important provinces of equity, in particular the great province of trust, may not be fully dealt with by other lecturers. Hence these lectures. At the end of my course I hope to speak once more of the modern relation between equity and law and of the prevalence which is assured to equity by the Judicature Act of 1873.

In my view equity has added to our legal system, together with a number of detached doctrines, one novel and fertile institution, namely the trust; and three novel and fertile remedies, namely the decree for specific performance, the injunction, and the judicial administration of estates. Round these, as it seems to me, most of the equitable rules group themselves. Of course I do not intend to speak of all or nearly all equitable rules, but I mean to deal at some length with trusts and then to speak of certain other matters in an order that I shall endeavour to explain from time to time.

LECTURE III

USES AND TRUSTS

OF all the exploits of Equity the largest and the most important is the invention and development of the Trust. It is an 'institute' of great elasticity and generality; as elastic, as general as contract. This perhaps forms the most distinctive achievement of English lawyers. It seems to us almost essential to civilization, and yet there is nothing quite like it in foreign law. Take up for instance the Bürgerliches Gesetzbuch—the Civil Code of Germany; where is trust? Nowhere. This in the eyes of an English practitioner is a big hole.

Foreigners don't see that there is any hole. 'I can't understand your trust', said Gierke to me. We must ask why this is so. Well, the trust does not fit easily into what they regard as the necessary scheme of jurisprudence.

Let me explain a little; for this will be of service in practical consideration of the nature of equitable rights.

Jurists have long tried to make a dichotomy of Private Rights: they are either *in rem* or *in personam*. The types of these two classes are, of the former, *dominium*, ownership; of the latter the benefit of contract—a debt.

Now under which head does trust—the right of *cestui que trust* —fall? Not easily under either. It seems to be a little of both. The foreigner asks—where do we place it in our code—under Sachenrecht or under Obligationenrecht?

The best answer may be that in history, and probably in ultimate analysis, it is *jus in personam*; but that it is so treated (and this for many important purposes) that it is very like *jus in rem*. A right primarily good against *certa persona*, viz. the trustee, but so treated as to be almost equivalent to a right good against all—a *dominium*, ownership, which however exists only in equity. And this is so from a remote time.

The modern trust developed from the ancient 'use'. Therefore we must speak briefly of uses and of the famous Statute of Uses, not for antiquarian purposes, but in order to throw light on the juristic nature of the modern trust.

First as to words. The term 'use' is a curious one; it has, if I may say so, mistaken its own origin. You may think that it is the Latin *usus*, but that is not so; it is the Latin *opus*. From remote times—in the seventh and eighth centuries in barbarous or vulgar Latin you find 'ad opus' for 'on his behalf'. It is so in Lombard and Frank legal documents. In Old French (see Godefroy)[1] this becomes *al oes, ues*. In English mouths this becomes confused with 'use'. In record Latin it remains *ad opus*. If I hold land *ad opus Johannis*, this of course means that I hold it on behalf of John. Sometimes you get *ad opus et ad usum Johannis*, and sometimes a pedantic re-introduction of the Latin 'p'—'*oeps*' and '*eops*'. If the sheriff seizes land *ad opus domini Regis* this means that he seizes land on behalf of the king, that he is acting as the king's agent. Now this phrase thus used we can trace back far in our legal history—certainly it appears in Domesday Book; one man is constantly doing things, *ad opus* another man. In particular the sheriff is always making seizures *ad opus Regis, as os le Roy*. Thus from 1224 we get this phrase,[2] *commisit terram suam custodiendam Wydoni fratri suo ad opus puerorum suorum*—he committed his land to his brother Guy to be kept to the use of his children. So also we can trace back into the thirteenth century the conveyance of villain land by surrender and admittance. The seller comes into court and surrenders the land *ad opus*, to the use (we must say) of the purchaser. There is as yet no law, no equity of 'uses'; but in many cases this term *ad opus* points to a legal relationship. In the fourteenth century (which for us is the important time) it has long been used currently to describe cases of agency and bailment. My agent receives money to my use. This leaves its mark in such phrases as 'convert to his use'—'goods received to his use'. If I seize land to your use, or to the use of the king, that means that I have acted as your agent or the king's agent. Then again we find the same phrase employed in cases which

---

[1] *Dictionnaire de l'Anc. Langue Française.*
[2] Bracton's Note Book, pl. 999.

are more akin to those which beget the law, or rather the equity of uses at a later day. Already in the thirteenth century a landowner will sometimes want to make a settlement. Perhaps he is tenant in fee simple and desires to become tenant in tail. In order that this may be accomplished—for he cannot enfeoff himself—he will enfeoff some friend to the use (*ad opus*) that the friend shall re-enfeoff him in tail. The law will enforce such a bargain for as yet the use, if we may already so call it, can be regarded as a condition: to enfeoff X. Y. to the use that he shall make a feoffment is the same thing as enfeoffing him upon condition that he shall make a feoffment.

So far as I am aware however the first occasion on which we find that land is being permanently held by one man to the use (*ad opus*) of another man, or rather, by one set of men to the use of another set is this. In the second quarter of the thirteenth century came hither the Franciscan friars. The rule of their order prescribes the most perfect poverty: they are not to have any wealth at all. They differ from monks. The individual monk can own nothing, but a community of monks, an abbey, a priory, may own land and will often be very rich. On the other hand, friars' priories are not to have property either individually or collectively. Still, despite this high ideal, it becomes plain that they must have at least some dormitory to sleep in. They have come as missionaries to the towns. The device is adopted of having land conveyed to the borough community to the use of the friars. Thus in a MS. at Oxford Ricardus le Muliner *contulit aream et domum communitati villae Oxoniae ad opus fratrum.*[1] Very soon in various towns in England a good deal of land is held thus. Attention was directed to this case by the outbreak of the great dispute as to Evangelical Poverty, the quarrel between the Franciscans and Pope John XXII.

But in the fourteenth century this old phrase is being used to express a substantially new relationship in connexion with the holding of land.

We find the landowner conveying his land to his friends *ad opus suum.* Why? Unquestionably the main reason is in order that he may in effect make a will. He will have the benefit and

---

[1] See *History of English Law*, 2nd edition, vol. II, pp. 237, 238.

the profits while he lives, and after his death his friends will convey the land according to his direction.

Remember that as regards freehold land every germ of testamentary power is stamped out in the twelfth century (except as to burgage tenures).

Note in passing that a device of this kind is not new. The power to make a will of chattels was acquired in this way among the Germanic tribes. The institution of an executor was originally a transaction *inter vivos*—a conveyance of goods by a dying man to friends who will execute his wishes. But the revived Roman law (in the eleventh century) plays upon this, and the will of chattels becomes a true testament, revocable, ambulatory—but with the executor keeping his place.

History in some sort is repeating itself. In the fourteenth century (we may say) we see an attempt to do in the case of land what had long ages before been done in the case of chattels.

Why was the power to make a will of land desired? In order to increase the fund applicable for the good of the soul, and in order to provide for daughters and for younger sons.

Further, the law bore hardly on the dying landowner—with its reliefs, wardships, marriages, escheats. Can these be evaded? Yes, by a plurality of feoffees. Here joint tenancy comes to his aid (trustees, as you know, are always joint tenants). There will be no inheritance and no relief, wardship, marriage. By keeping up a wall of joint tenants, by feoffment and refeoffment, he can keep out the lord and can reduce the chances of reliefs and so forth to nothing. During the fourteenth century landowners begin to discover that a great deal can be done by means of this idea. A landowner will convey land to a friend, or rather to a party of friends, for his own use (*ad opus suum*). There is a bargain between them that he is to have the profits and the enjoyment of the land, while the feoffees are to be the legal owners. Many objects can be gained by such a scheme. (1) One may thus evade the feudal burdens of wardship and marriage. Of course if you had a single feoffee and he left an heir under age, the scheme would break down, for the lord would claim a wardship of this infant heir. But the plan was, as I have said, to enfeoff, not a single friend, but a party of friends—sometimes

as many as ten—as joint tenants, and as these feoffees died off
fresh feoffees could be put in their places so that the lord's
chance of a wardship could be reduced to nil. The lord could not
look behind the feoffees; they were his tenants; it was nothing
to him that they were allowing another person to enjoy land
which by law was theirs. (2) So too the law of forfeiture for
treason and escheat for felony could be evaded. The king and
the lord could not look behind the feoffees to the feoffor who
had no longer any rights in the land, while that every one of
seven or eight feoffees should commit treason was hardly to be
expected. (3) The Statutes of Mortmain might be evaded. If I
choose to allow the members of a religious house to enjoy the
proceeds of my land, this is no breach of the Statutes. That house
is not the owner of the land for I am the owner. (4) One might
defeat one's creditors in this way. I incur debts; my creditors
obtain judgment, they obtain a writ of elegit; they come to seize
my land; they find that I have not got any land to seize, and you
must not seize the land of X, Y and Z, because A owes you a
debt. (5) Lastly, by means of this device one could give oneself
the power of making something very like a will of lands. My
feoffees undertake to carry out any testamentary disposition that
I may make of the land which has been conveyed to them. Why
should they not do so? I do not attempt to devise land by my
will, I merely request certain people to deal in a certain way
with land which belongs to them, not to me.

You will see that the success of this scheme would have been
marred if the courts of law had compelled the feoffees to fulfil
the honourable understanding by virtue of which they had
acquired the land. If they had begun to say 'After all this land
is the feoffor's land; the feoffees are a mere screen, or the
feoffees are merely the feoffor's agents', then the whole scheme
would have broken down—wardships, marriages, forfeitures,
escheats would have followed as a matter of course. But the
common law was not prepared to do this. It had no forms of
procedure, no forms of thought, which would serve for these
cases. They could not extend the law of conditional feoffments
to meet these uses, for the uses were too vague. The feoffees are
not enfeoffed upon condition that they shall do just some one

definite act; a prolonged course of conduct active and passive is required of them. But you may say—Why at all events should not the courts of law treat this bargain as a contract? An agreement there certainly is. In consideration of a conveyance made by A to X, Y, Z, the said X, Y, Z agree that they will hold the land for the behoof of A, will allow him to enjoy it and will convey it as he shall direct. Now I think it very right that we should observe how a use, or in modern terms, a trust generally has its origin in something that we can not but call an agreement. The feoffee to uses did agree, the modern trustee does agree that he will deal with the land or the goods in a certain way. If therefore in the fourteenth century our law of contract had taken its modern form, I think that the courts of law would have been compelled to say 'Yes, here is an agreement; therefore it is a legally enforceable contract, and if it be broken an action for damages will lie against the infringer.' This might well have been done if the feoffee had covenanted by deed to observe the confidence that was reposed in him; and in case there was no deed any difficulty arising from a want of 'consideration' might have been evaded by a little ingenuity. But then we have to remember that in the fourteenth century—and that in the present context is the important century—the common law had not yet begun to enforce 'the simple contract'—it had not yet evolved the action of assumpsit out of the action of trespass. If A conveys land to X, Y and Z and they promise to hold the land for his behoof and to obey his directions, this is as yet an unenforceable promise unless it be made by a document under seal. In the fifteenth century the courts of common law acquired the action of assumpsit and it may be a little difficult for us to understand why they did not then begin to enforce the agreements—for agreements they are—in which uses have their origin. The answer, I think, is that by this time they had missed their opportunity once and for all—the Chancellor was already in possession, was already enforcing uses by means of a procedure far more efficient and far more flexible than any which the old courts could have employed. Besides, as I have already said, the objects which men were seeking to obtain by means of uses could hardly have been attained if the courts of common law had begun to ascribe any legal effect to the use. Some of those objects may have been discreditable enough—men ought not to defraud their creditors—but others of those objects had the spirit of the time in their favour. Feudalism had ceased to be useful; it had become a system of capricious exactions—it was very natural and not dishonourable that men should attempt to free themselves from the burdens of reliefs and wardships and marriages, from the terribly severe law of forfeiture and escheat for crime, that they should wish to make wills of land or go very near to making them. Do not be persuaded that the common lawyers looked with disfavour upon uses—the great Littleton himself had land held in use for him.

Meanwhile the Chancellor had begun to enforce these bargains. Why should he do so? Why should he not do so? Let me repeat once more—I shall have to come back to this over and over again—that use, trust or confidence originates in an agreement. As to the want of valuable consideration for the trustee's promise, it might, I think, fairly be said that even if there is no benefit to the promisor, the trustee, there is at all events detriment to the promisee, the trustor, since he parts with legal rights, with property and with possession. Men ought to fulfil their promises, their agreements; and they ought to be compelled to do so. That is the principle and surely it is a very simple one. You will say then that the Chancellor begins to enforce a personal right, a *jus in personam*, not a real right, a *jus in rem*— he begins to enforce a right which in truth is a contractual right, a right created by a promise. Yes, that is so, and I think that much depends upon your seeing that it is so. The right of *cestui que use* or *cestui que trust* begins by being a right *in personam*. Gradually it begins to look somewhat like a right *in rem*. But it never has become this; no, not even in the present day.

This I hope to explain at length in some future lecture. At present let us notice that during the fifteenth century uses of lands became very common—already in the fourteenth the practice has begun among the great and we find the famous John of Gaunt disposing by his will of lands which are held to his use by feoffees. We find that Henry of Bolingbroke, afterwards Henry IV, is a *cestui que use* and Gascoigne C.J. is one of his feoffees. He provides for Thomas, John and Joan Beaufort, his illegitimate children, with remainder over to his right heirs. About the first will of land purporting to be held to the use of the testator is in 1381 and is that of William, 4th Lord Latimer —the hero of the first parliamentary impeachment.[1] Immediately there was a rapid spread of the new institution, and about the year 1400 the Chancellor has interfered between the *cestui que use* and the feoffees. It is a little strange that he (the prime minister as it were) should interfere. For the king (always lord) is losing on all hands. The interests of the great lords are divided, for they are both lords and tenants. There is need here for further investigation. Perhaps we may suppose a scandalous case; and intervention by the Chancellor without much reflection, urged by a shock to public morality. Henry V had land held to his use.[2]

Did the Chancellor ask himself what sort of right he was giving, whether *in rem* or *in personam*; did he ask himself under what rubric this new chapter would stand? Probably not. As between the feoffor (*cestui que use*) and the original feoffees the case is plain—it is scandalous dishonesty if the feoffees disregard the trust.

It might have been regarded as a breach of contract. But this was not done, perhaps because breach of contract was a matter for the common law. At any rate the language of contract was not used—there was no formal promise exacted from the feoffees, no '*obligo me*', etc. It seems to be felt from the first that contract is not what is wanted—that contract won't do.

There is one strong reason against treating it as a contract, the feoffor (who is *cestui que use*) has then a chose in action and this would be inalienable. But our landowner did not mean to exchange ownership of land for the (inalienable) benefit of a promise.

No, there is no 'obligatory' language: all is done under cover of 'use'; a little later of 'confidence' and 'trust'.

[1] The will of Lord Latimer, 1381, Test. Ebor. Surtees Society Publications, vol. IV, p. 113; that of John of Gaunt, *ib.* p. 223—Feb. 3, 1398.
[2] For the earliest known instances of application for the Chancellor's interference see *Select Cases in Chancery*. Selden Society's Publications, vol. x, pp. 48, 69, *et al.*—between 1396 and 1403.

Secondly, we see this at an early time: the remedy is given not to the trustor but to the *destinatory*. In the earliest instances the trustor and the *cestui que trust* (or *use*) are the same person—still it is as destinatory, not as 'author of the trust' that he has the remedy. This marks it off from contract. Refer to John of Gaunt's will; consider the disposition in favour of the Beauforts —it would not do to give the remedy to John of Gaunt's heir: he is the very person who is interested in breaking the will.

This principle runs through our law of equity to the present day—the destinatory, beneficiary, *cestui que trust* has the remedy. (It is an unfortunate term, '*cestui que trust*', with an obscure history. It suggests a falsehood at this point.)

Thirdly, as regards estates and interests the common law of land is to be the model—*aequitas sequitur legem*—see, *e.g.*, the estates tail with remainders given to the Beauforts by John of Gaunt. We shall have to speak of this afterwards in connexion with the modern law of trusts. The new class of rights is made to look as much like rights *in rem* (estates in land) as the Chancellor can make them look—that is in harmony with the real wish of the parties who are using the device. They also are taking the common law as their model. Thus we get a conversion of the use into an incorporeal thing—in which estates and interests exist—a sort of immaterialized piece of land. This is a perfectly legitimate process of 'thing making' and one that is always going on. For an old example you may take the advowson; new examples are patent right, copyright: goodwill is now in the very process.

But (fourthly) the Chancellor can not create new rights *in rem*. So to do would be not to supplement but to overrule the common law. Besides, if he had made this attempt the whole scheme of obtaining quasi-testamentary power would have broken down. Once say *cestui que trust* is really owner, it follows that he can not make a will, and on his death reliefs, wardships and so forth must follow.

Here perhaps is the reason why the courts of law did nothing for *cestui que use*. If they had allowed *cestui que use* any sort of right the whole scheme might have broken down. A great question of policy would be opened—if wills of land are to be made then the king should be compensated. Men prefer to live from hand to mouth rather than open big questions. The great Littleton had made a will (Litt. ss. 462–3).

Fifthly, the greatest question remains—against whom is a trust enforceable? This is the line of development—as regards purchasers all is to depend on conscience. If you buy with notice, then in conscience it is my land. In the modern sense it depends on notice actual or constructive. We shall come to the actual rules hereafter; in the meanwhile we may contrast statements such as that of Salmond in his *Jurisprudence*, who speaks, at p. 278, of the *cestui que trust* as 'the real owner',[1] and of the right of property of the trustee as 'fictitious', with the treatment of their respective rights by Professor Langdell in the *Harvard Law Review*, vol. I, at p. 59.

Some have thought that this new jurisprudence of uses was borrowed from the Roman law; that the English use or trust is historically connected with the Roman *fidei commissum*. I do not myself believe in the connexion. One reason for this disbelief I will at once state because it leads on to an important point. From the first the Chancellors seem to have treated the rights of the *cestui que use* as very analogous to an estate in land. They brought to bear upon it the rules of the English land law as regards such matters as descent and the like. The *cestui que use* may have an estate in the use, it may be an estate in fee simple descendible to heirs general, an estate in fee tail descendible to heirs of the body, an estate for life, or it may be a chattel interest, a term of years in the use. As regards all these matters the maxim was that equity should follow the law. It was not a rule without exceptions, for, as you are aware, it was possible to make certain limitations of the use which could not be made of the legal tenancy of the land—there might be springing uses and shifting uses whereas the common law allowed the creation of no future estate that was not a true remainder. But still the rule was very generally observed. The use came to be conceived as a sort of metaphysical entity in which there might be estates very similar to those which could be created in land, estates in

---

[1] Salmond, *Jurisprudence or the Theory of the Law*. The reference is to the 1st edition, 1902. See 8th edition, pp. 284–9.

possession, remainder, reversion, estates descendible in this way or in that.

Uses seem to have become so common that the Chancellors were able to introduce even the doctrine of resulting uses. A enfeoffs X and there is no consideration for the feoffment, it is presumed (so common have uses become) that A does not intend that X shall enjoy the land; it is presumed that X is to hold to the use of A. If A really wishes to make a gift of the land to one who is not his kinsman he must declare that the feoffment made to X and his heirs is made to the use of X and his heirs. This I say is so if X be not a kinsman of A. The law of consideration is yet in its infancy. It is being evolved contemporaneously in the courts of common law in connexion with simple contracts, and in the Court of Chancery in connexion with trusts—and the Court of Chancery holds that blood relationship, though not a valuable consideration, is, as the phrase goes, a good consideration to raise a use. That doctrine, as I understand, still holds good in our own day. A makes a grant unto X and his heirs, saying nothing about a use. If there be no valuable consideration, and if X be not a kinsman of A, the use results which, at the present day, means that nothing passes from A to X,[1] but it is otherwise if there is a tie of blood between A and X; for this, though it be not a valuable consideration, though it would not support a parol promise, is a good enough consideration to raise a use.

I shall have more to say of resulting uses by and by; I was led to mention them because the doctrine about them shows that feoffments to uses had become extremely common, insomuch that it is assumed as a general rule that if a man gratuitously parts with his land he intends to keep the use to himself and does not mean that the feoffee should profit by the gift.

More than once the legislature had to take notice of uses. A statute of 15 Ric. II, c. 5, prevented religious and other corporations from evading the Statutes of Mortmain by means of uses. Other statutes from the first half of the fifteenth century provide that in certain cases a *cestui que use* in possession of land may for

---

[1] This refers to the law before 1926. See now Law of Property Act 1925, s. 60.

certain purposes be treated as the legal owner of it. The practice of enfeoffing to uses, as I have said, spread rapidly downwards among the people. The feoffor in possession had become extremely common, and a statute of Richard III shows both the prevalence of the institution and the difficulties that arose under it. This statute—1 Ric. III, c. 1—the first act of a king with a shaky title, recited that 'Forasmuch as by privy and unknown feoffments great unsurety, trouble, costs and grievous vexations daily grow among the king's subjects, insomuch that no man that buyeth any lands tenements...&c., nor women that have jointures or dowers in any lands tenements or other hereditaments, nor men's last wills to be performed, nor leases...nor annuities...be in perfect surety nor without great trouble and doubt of the same, because of the said privy and unknown feoffments.' Observe the words favourable to last wills. The statute then in effect enacted that every estate made by any person should be good not only against him but against all persons seised or claiming to the use of him or his heirs. That would prevent the feoffee acquiring merely a estate by wrong or no estate at all. Henceforth both feoffee and *cestui que use* can make an estate. In effect it gave a sort of statutory power of alienating the legal estate.

At last there comes the famous Statute of Uses (1535, 27 Hen. VIII, c. 10).[1] A long preamble states the evil effects of the system and legal writers of a later day have regarded the words of this preamble as though they stated a generally admitted evil. As a matter of historical fact this is not true. The Statute of Uses was forced upon an extremely unwilling parliament by an extremely strong-willed king. It was very unpopular and was one of the excuses, if not one of the causes, of the great Catholic Rebellion known as the Pilgrimage of Grace. It was at once seen that it would deprive men of that testamentary power, that power of purchasing the repose of their souls, which they had long enjoyed. The king was the one person who had all to gain and nothing to lose by the abolition of uses.

You may read the Statute of Uses at length in Digby's *History of the Law of Real Property*. The important clause in this statute

---

[1] The Statute of Uses was repealed by the Law of Property Act 1925.

is the first. It is long and verbose; but when we have rejected what is unnecessary it reads thus—Where any person or persons shall be seised of any lands or other hereditaments to the use, confidence, or trust of any other person or persons, in every such case such person and persons that shall have any such use confidence or trust in fee simple, fee tail, for term of life or for years or otherwise shall stand and be seised deemed and adjudged in lawful seisin, estate and possession of and in the same lands and hereditaments in such like estates as they had or shall have in the use.

Now I am not going to pronounce an exhaustive commentary on this section, for I only wish to speak of uses in so far as this is absolutely necessary in order that I may speak of the modern law of trusts. But there are a few points which you will of course remember.

1. This statute abolished the power of devising a use which men had heretofore enjoyed. The use was now the legal estate and the legal estate of freehold could not be devised except by special local custom. Then, as you will remember, a statute of 1540, 32 Hen. VIII, c. 1,[1] which was followed by an explanatory act of 34–5 Hen. VIII, c. 5, gave a certain power of devising freehold land. It however drew a distinction between lands held by knight's service and land held by socage, which was maintained until the statute 12 Car. II, c. 24 (1660),[2] abolished the military tenures.

2. It introduced two new methods of conveying freehold; it put the covenant to stand seised and the bargain and sale by the side of the feoffment. If A, having the legal estate, had covenanted that he would stand seised to the use of B, this before the statute had given B a use in the land. After the statute it passed the legal estate to B. If A for valuable consideration agreed to sell the land to B this mere agreement—there was no need for a deed, there was no need for a writing—had, before the statute, given B the use of the land—the bargainor became seised to the use of the bargainee. After the statute such a bargain and sale would have the effect of conveying the legal estate

---

[1] Known as the Statute of Wills.
[2] Known as the Statute of Tenures.

to B. Then, as you know, in the same year another statute provided that every bargain and sale of an estate of inheritance should be by deed enrolled (27 Hen. VIII, c. 16). But this Statute of Inrolments did not extend to bargains and sales for terms of years, and then, as you know, the mode of conveyance by lease and release was invented—and men succeeded in conveying freehold without livery of seisin and without an enrolled document which would be open to the eyes of the public.

3. The statute had the effect of enabling men to make certain limitations of the legal estate which they had not previously been able to make. This effect is often described in picturesque language.[1] The use had been more flexible than the legal estate, and now the use imparted its flexibility to the land. The only future estates that a man could create at common law were remainders strictly and properly so called—but as regards the use the Chancellors had disregarded some of the ancient rules—and now the legal estate went along with the use. Executory limitations of the use, and therefore of the legal estate, became possible—legal estates could be made to 'spring' and to 'shift' by means of springing and shifting uses.

But all this lies rather within the province of a lecturer on real property law than in the province of a lecturer on trusts. However, it is absolutely impossible for one to speak of trusts, even at the present day, without speaking first of uses. For one would of course like to answer the question—How can a trust be created?—and this unfortunately we cannot do without touching the learning of uses. A document is put before us. Does it or does it not create a trust? That often is a question which involves an interpretation of the Statute of Uses. Thus—to put a very simple case—a testator says, I devise and bequeath all my freeholds, copyholds and leaseholds, and also all my personal estate unto A in trust for B. Is there here a trust? Must we distinguish the freeholds from the copyholds and the chattels? It is from this point of view that I must say a few words about the statute.[2]

---

[1] The allusion apparently is to *Chudleigh's Case*, 1 Co. Rep. at p. 124a, and Challis, *Law of Real Property*, 2nd edition, p. 352.

[2] Since the repeal of the Statute of Uses the question here discussed can hardly arise except in connexion with titles commencing before 1926.

1. The statute has no word about chattels personal, and does not affect the law or the equity which concerns them in any way.

2. The statute does not in any way affect the law, the equity or the customs by which copyholds are governed.

3. It is often said that the statute does not apply to leaseholds, to terms of years. This is true, but it requires explanation. In order that the statute may be applicable it is essential that we should find one person (A) seised to the use of another person (X). Now seisin implies freehold. Therefore, if we find that A has merely a chattel interest in the land, the statute has nothing whatever to say to the case. On the other hand, suppose we find that A is seised to the use of X, then the statute does apply albeit that X has been given a mere term of years in the use. If you will read the statute you will see that it expressly meets this case. If one person (A) be seised to the use of another person (X) then such person (X) as shall have any such use 'in fee simple, fee tail, for term of life, or for years or otherwise' is to be deemed and adjudged in lawful seisin and possession of the land for the same estate that he had in the use. Therefore, suppose that I, being tenant in fee simple, convey land unto A and his heirs to the use of or upon trust for X for the term of 1000 years, here we have a case expressly provided for by the statute: the term of years given to X will be a legal term of years.

But then—for we will go on with the story—suppose that X, having this term of years, assigns it to B to the use of Y,—this case is outside the statute, for X is not seised, B will not be seised, and the statute does not find any person seised to the use of Y. Therefore, it is true to say that the statute does not apply to the conveyance or assignment of a term of years when once that term has been created. But it may well apply to the creation of a term of years. In settlements of real estate it is common for the settlor to create by means of uses not only freehold estates, but also terms of years. These terms of years are given to trustees in order that they may raise portions for younger children, and the like, and they are legal terms. Thus, on my marriage, I convey land to X and Y and their heirs to the use of myself for life, and after my death to the use of T and T' for a term of 1000 years, and, subject to that term, to the use of my first and other sons successively in tail male. The Statute of Uses will take effect not only as regards the freehold estates given to me and my sons but also as regards the term of years given to T and T'—it will be a legal term, for X and Y are found seised to the use of T and T'—and wherever one person is seised to the use of another, there the statute steps in. That is the true test. Do you or do you not find one person seised to the use of another?

4. The statute applies wherever one person is seised 'to the use, confidence or trust' of another. These three words are used as synonyms. To convey to A upon trust for X, this has precisely the same effect as conveying to A to the use of X. And no doubt there are other expressions which will do as well. The words 'use' and 'trust' are not sacramental terms. But the statute only applies where there is a simple use, trust or confidence—it does not apply where there is an active trust. I convey land unto A and his heirs, to the use that they shall sell the land and divide the proceeds among my children, or upon trust that they shall so sell and divide. The statute has nothing to say to this case. You do not find one person seised in trust for another person—you find A seised upon trust to make a sale.

The line which divides the simple use, trust or confidence, which is within the statute, from the active trust, which is not within the statute, is often a very fine one. The test seems to be this, Does the instrument before us merely tell A that X is to have the enjoyment of the land, or does it impose upon A some more special duty? Thus I convey unto A and his heirs upon trust to permit X to receive the profits of the land during his life. This is a simple use, trust or confidence—I am only saying in effect that A is to hold for X's benefit. The statute operates, and X has a legal estate. On the other hand, I convey to A and his heirs upon trust to collect the rents and profits of the land and pay them to X during his life. Here I impose an active duty on A, he is to collect rents and pay them to another. Here the statute does not come into play, and the legal estate remains in A.

Very difficult cases have arisen where the formulas have been run together—thus 'in trust to pay the rents and profits to X or to permit him to receive the same', or 'in trust to permit X to receive the rents or to pay them to him'. Courts of law have attempted to meet these cases by saying that in a deed the first phrase is the important one, while in a will the last phrase prevails. Thus in a deed the words 'in trust to pay the rents and profits to X or permit him to receive the same' will leave the legal estate in A, while in a will these same words will carry the legal estate to X. I do not wish to go into these cases of interpretation—but just note that the statute only applies where you have a use or trust which, either in terms or in effect, is just simply a use or trust for X. If the instrument in question leaves any discretionary power to A—if, for example, he is to divide the income between X, Y and Z in such shares as he shall think proper, that of course is a ground for holding that he is and they are not to have the legal estate.

Let us take as examples two cases, *Baker* v. *White* and *Van Grutten* v. *Foxwell*; and in the latter case you ought all to read Lord Macnaghten's famous judgment on the origin and history of the Rule in *Shelley's Case*.

In *Baker* v. *White*, L.R. 20 Eq. 166 (1875), there was a devise of freeholds and copyholds to A and B to hold the same to A and B their heirs, executors, administrators and assigns, upon trust, during the life of J, to receive the rents thereof and pay them to J for life or otherwise to permit J to receive them; followed by a devise after J's decease to the use of the heirs of his body. The testator appointed A, B and J executors and declared that the receipt of the trustees and executors for any money payable under the will should be a sufficient discharge:

It was held by Sir George Jessel, then Master of the Rolls, that J took a legal estate tail in the freeholds and an equitable estate for life in the copyholds.

In *Van Grutten* v. *Foxwell* [1897] A.C. 658, the limitations—applicable to the case which happened, of an only child—were these: a devise to X and Y in trust to receive the rents and profits for the use and benefit of the testator's daughter, B, and to apply them in the maintenance and education of B while under age, and after majority to permit and suffer B to take the rents and profits for her life and after B's death X and Y are to stand seised in trust for the heirs of the body of B. 'Such lands to be legally conveyed to such heirs.'

The main question was whether the rule in *Shelley's Case*[1] was applicable in this case, since there were abundant expressions in the will which showed that to apply that rule would defeat the testator's intention.

The will might have been read as giving the trustees the legal estate only during the minority and again after the death of the tenant for life. It was held, however, that the legal estate vested in the trustees throughout, that the rule in *Shelley's Case* applied, and that B took an estate tail.

Lord Herschell, at p. 662, said 'It is well settled that if the estate taken by the person to whom the lands are devised for a particular estate of freehold and the estate limited to the heirs of that person are not of the same quality, that is to say if the one be legal and the other equitable, the rule in *Shelley's Case* has no application. If they are either both legal or both equitable the rule applies. Although the legal estate is in the present case vested, in the first instance, in the trustees, there is no doubt that the language of the will by which the trustees are to permit and suffer his child to receive the rents and profits for her sole use and benefit is sufficient, if those words stood alone, to pass the legal estate to the testator's child. It is equally clear however that the trusts of the will require that prior to his child attaining twenty-one the legal estate should be in the trustees, and that it should again be in the trustees after his child's death. Where there are such dispositions as are to be found in the present case, I think the true view is that the legal estate remains throughout in the trustees and that the estate of the beneficiaries is equitable only.'

Lord Davey, at p. 683, said 'It is admitted that during the minorities of the testator's children the purposes of the will require that the trustees shall take the legal estate. It is also admitted that after the death of the children the trustees must take the legal estate in order to enable them to convey to the heirs of the children, at twenty-one, and in the mean time to

[1] The rule in *Shelley's Case* was abolished by the Law of Property Act 1925, s. 131.

receive the rents, issues and profits, and provide for the maintenance and education of "such heirs". But it is said that the words of gift to the children after attaining majority are such as to give them the legal estate during their lives. The words applicable, in the event which has happened, are "If I have only one child, then to permit and suffer such one child to have receive and take the said rents &c.... during her life". No doubt the words "permit and suffer" are sufficient to pass the legal estate; but it is not an absolute rule and the words are not inconsistent with the legal estate remaining in the trustees, though they have no duties to perform. It is a convenient rule that where there are recurring occasions for the exercise of active duties by the trustees and no repeated devises to them to enable them to perform their duties, the legal estate, if once in the trustees, is to be deemed to be vested in them throughout, notwithstanding the duration in the mean time of what would but for the recurring duties be construed as uses executed in the beneficiaries.'

5. It is commonly said that the main result of the Statute of Uses is to add three words to every conveyance. The story is told thus: Shortly after the statute, in *Tyrrell's Case*, 1557,[1] a Court of Common Law holds that there can not be a use upon a use. This is often regarded as a purely unreasonable decision for which far-fetched explanations must be sought—*e.g.* that the phrase 'no use upon use' was a well-known phrase importing prohibition of compound interest. This dogma being propounded, it is supposed that the Chancellor at once sees his opportunity, and says in effect 'I will enforce these secondary uses just as I did enforce primary uses before the statute.'

Professor Ames[2] has shown that this story is not true—in two respects: first the decision in *Tyrrell's Case* is not inexplicable; and secondly the interference of the Chancellor in favour of the secondary use did not take place for about a century after the Statute of Uses.

---

[1] Dyer, 155. The case is printed also in Digby's *History of the Law of Real Property*.

[2] In an article in *The Green Bag*, IV, 81. See too Williams on Real Property, 23rd edition, at p. 187.

Mr Cyprian Williams in the latest editions of Williams on Real Property has adopted Professor Ames's theory and has given a most excellent statement of it—so excellent that I should like you to read it. It is in section iv of chapter 7 at pp. 173 to 176 of the 20th edition.

LECTURE IV

THE MODERN TRUST

WE are now to consider the main outline of the modern law of trusts. We call it law and such in the wide sense of that word it is, but remember also that technically it is all equity, and that we constantly have to distinguish the rules of equity from the rules of law.

No doubt we should like to begin our discussion with a definition of a 'trust'. But I know not where to find an authoritative definition. This is how a distinguished writer, Mr Lewin, deals with the matter:

'As the doctrines of trusts are equally applicable to real and personal estate, and the principles that govern the one will be found *mutatis mutandis* to govern the other, we cannot better describe the nature of a trust generally, than by adopting Lord Coke's definition of a use, the term by which before the Statute of Uses a trust of land was designated. A trust, in the words applied to the use, may be said to be "A confidence reposed in some other, not issuing out of the land, but as a thing collateral annexed in privity to the estate of the land, and to the person touching the land, for which *cestui que trust* has no remedy but by subpoena in the Chancery".'[1]

This definition, if definition it is to be called, comes from Coke upon Littleton, p. 272 (b); it is of interest and I shall return to it. But to say that a trust is a confidence is not very useful; for if we go on to ask what is a confidence, we shall probably be told that it is a trust. There is another objection.—This definition or description seems to involve the assertion that wherever there is what is technically called a trust, there is what in ordinary speech would be called some trust, some reliance, or confidence reposed by one person in another. Now that may be true of nine trusts in ten. If I convey land to you as a trustee for me, or as a trustee for my wife and children, there is not merely what our law calls a trust, there really is trust placed by me in you; I do trust you,

[1] Lewin on Trusts, 13th edition, p. 11.

I do place confidence, faith, reliance in you. In such a case it well may be that the *cestui que trusts* do not place any reliance or confidence in the trustee. I pay over to you a sum of money upon trust for my son, you agree to hold it upon trust for him— here I, the trustor, the author of the trust, do place confidence in you the trustee. But then I am not to be the *cestui que trust*; my son is the *cestui que trust*, and this trust may be perfectly constituted although he knows nothing about it. He perhaps is a baby in arms, or perhaps he is in Australia, or even perhaps he is unborn, for you may have a trust for an unborn person or an unascertained person. Here it can not be said that *cestui que trust* places any trust or reliance in the trustee. But further we may well have a trust although no person has in any ordinary sense of the word placed trust or reliance in the trustee. At this moment I declare to you by word of mouth that I constitute myself a trustee of this watch for my eldest daughter. There is already a perfect trust in the technical sense. So soon as my daughter has heard what has happened she can enforce the trust against me; I am a trustee; she is my *cestui que trust*—yet it is obvious that during the interval, and that interval may be several years, she has not been placing trust in me, or confidence in me; she has known nothing of my declared intention to hold the watch in trust for her.

Where judges and text-writers fear to tread professors of law have to rush in. I should define a trust in some such way as the following—When a person has rights which he is bound to exercise upon behalf of another or for the accomplishment of some particular purpose he is said to have those rights in trust for that other or for that purpose and he is called a trustee.

It is a wide vague definition, but the best that I can make. I shall comment on it by distinguishing cases of trust from some other cases.

1. The trustee is bound to use his rights in a certain way, bound to use them for the benefit of another, or for the accomplishment of a certain purpose. One is not made a trustee by being bound *not* to use one's rights in some particular manner. On every owner of lands or goods there lies the duty of not using them in various ways. The law of torts largely consists

of rules which limit the general rights of owners. I must not dig a quarry in my land so as to cause the subsidence of my neighbour's land. If I do this I commit a wrong and give my neighbour a cause of action; but of course I am not a trustee of my land for him.

2. A debtor is not a trustee for his creditor.[1] I am heavily indebted. Certainly I ought not to give away my goods and thus prevent my creditors from obtaining payment of what is due to them. If I do so a court with bankruptcy jurisdiction may punish me. What is more, conveyances or assignments of property may be set aside as being frauds against creditors. For all this I am not a trustee for my creditors. No creditor can point to a particular thing or a particular mass of rights and say, 'You were bound to use that or to retain that for me or to hand it over to me'. The creditors, unless they be mortgagees, have merely rights *in personam*; if they be mortgagees they have also rights *in rem*; but in neither case is there any trust.

3. We must distinguish the trust from the bailment. This is not very easy to do, for in some of our classical text-books perplexing language is used about this matter. For example, Blackstone defines a bailment thus: 'Bailment, from the French *bailler*, is a delivery of goods in trust, upon a contract expressed or implied, that the trust shall be faithfully executed on the part of the bailee' (*Comm.* II, 451).

Here a bailment seems to be made a kind of trust. Now of course in one way it is easy enough to distinguish a bailment from those trusts enforced by equity, and only by equity, of which we are speaking. We say that the rights of a bailor against his bailee are legal, are common law rights, while those of a *cestui que trust* against his trustee are never common law rights. But then this seems to be a putting of the cart before the horse; we do not explain why certain rights are enforced at law while other rights are left to equity.

---

[1] The distinction between a debtor and a trustee often arises in cases when an agent has received money for his principal. The agent may hold the money as his own and become a debtor to the principal for the amount of it (as is the case with a banker) or he may be a 'fiduciary agent' and hold the money as trustee for the principal. On this point see *Foley* v. *Hill*, 2 H.L. C. 28 and the note on p. 227 below.

Let us look at the matter a little more closely. On the one hand we will have a bailment—A lends B a quantity of books—A lets to B a quantity of books in return for a periodical payment—A deposits a lot of books with B for safe custody. In each of these cases B receives rights from A, and in each of these cases B is under an obligation to A; he is bound with more or less rigour to keep the books safely and to return them to A. Still we do not I think conceive that B is bound to use on A's behalf the rights that he, B, has in the books. Such rights as B has in them he has on his own behalf, and those rights he may enjoy as seems best to him. On the other hand, S is making a marriage settlement and the property that he is settling includes a library of books; he vests the whole ownership of these books in T and T' who are to permit S to enjoy them during his life and then to permit his firstborn son to enjoy them and so forth. Not unfrequently valuable chattels are thus settled so that whoever dwells in a certain mansion during the continuance of the settlement shall have the use of the pictures, books, plate, and so forth. Now here T and T' are full owners of the chattels. S and the other *cestui que trusts* have no rights in the chattels, but T and T' are bound to use their rights according to the words of the settlement, words which compel them to allow S and the other *cestui que trusts* to enjoy those things.

You may say the distinction is a fine one, almost a metaphysical one—and very likely I am not stating it well—but there are two tests which will bring out the distinction. The one is afforded by the law of sale, the other by the criminal law.

(*a*) A is the bailor, B is the bailee of goods; B sells the goods to X, the sale not being authorized by the terms of the bailment and not being made in market overt or within the Factor's Acts. X, though he purchases in good faith, and though he has no notice of A's rights, does not get a good title to the goods. A can recover them from him; if he converts them to his use he wrongs A. Why? Because he bought them from one who was not owner of them. Turn to the other case. T is holding goods as trustee of S's marriage settlement. In breach of trust he sells them to X; X buys in good faith and has no notice of the trust. X gets a good title to the goods. T was the owner of the goods; he passed his rights to X; X became the owner of the goods and S has no right against X—for it is an elementary rule, to which I must often refer hereafter, that trust rights can not be enforced against one who has acquired legal (*i.e.* common law) ownership *bona fide*, for value, and without notice of the existence of those trust rights. Here you see one difference between the bailee and the trustee.

(*b*) Then look at the criminal law. Even according to our medieval law a bailee could be capable of the crime of larceny. If before the act of taking he had done some act which, as the phrase went, determined the bailment, if for example the carrier broke bulk and then took the goods—this was larceny. And now-a-days, as you know, by virtue of a statute the bailee can be guilty of larceny though apart from the act of conversion he· has done no act determining the bailment. But to the trustee of goods who misappropriated them the common law of crime had nothing whatever to say. How could a court of common law have punished the trustee? It said that he was the owner of the goods, and a man can not steal what he both owns and possesses. Not until 1857 did it become a crime for the trustee to misappropriate goods that he held in trust—and even now the crime that he commits is not larceny and is not a felony. All this you may read at large in Stephen's *History of the Criminal Law*. I refer to it merely in order to show you that despite Blackstone's definition of a bailment there is a great and abiding distinction between a bailee of goods and a true trustee of goods. And the difference I think is this—the bailee though he has rights in the thing—'a special property' or 'special ownership' they are sometimes called—has not the full ownership of the thing; 'the general ownership' or 'the general property' is in the bailor. On the other hand the trustee is the owner, the full owner of the thing, while the *cestui que trust* has no rights in the thing. That statement that *cestui que trust* has no rights in the thing may surprise you, but I shall justify it hereafter. The specific mark of the trust is I think that the trustee has rights, which rights he is bound to exercise for the benefit of the *cestui que trust* or for the accomplishment of some definite purpose.

Cases can be conceived where it would be difficult to say

whether there was a bailment by deposit or a trust. For instance, I go abroad in a hurry and do not know whether I shall return. I send a piano to a friend, and I say to him, 'Take care of my piano and if I don't return give it to my daughter.' This may be construed both ways, as a bailment or as a trust. Perhaps the age of my daughter—a thing strictly irrelevant—would decide which way it would go.

4. An executor or administrator merely as such is not a trustee for the legatees or next of kin.[1] I say that he is not a trustee merely because he is executor or administrator; but he may very easily become a trustee for them and in a given case it may be hard to decide whether a man has been merely an executor or administrator or has also been a trustee. The question may be of great practical importance because the Statutes of Limitation draw a distinction between an action by a legatee against an executor and an action by *cestui que trust* against his trustee. Take two cases to illustrate this. *In re Davis* [1891] 3 Ch. 119, you will find the Court of Appeal saying that a certain action was an action for a legacy against an executor as such; and then *In re Swain* [1891] 3 Ch. 233, you will find Romer J. holding that a certain action, though the plaintiff was a legatee and though the defendant was an executor, was not an action brought by a legatee for a legacy against an executor as such, but was an action by *cestui que trust* against a trustee. And see *In re Timmis* [1902] 1 Ch. 176, and *In re Mackay* [1906] 1 Ch. 25.

This difficulty can I think be explained only by a piece of history. In the middle ages the proper court for a legatee who wished to sue an executor for a legacy was neither a court of common law, nor the Court of Chancery, but an ecclesiastical court, a court Christian. In course of time the Chancery stole away this jurisdiction from the ecclesiastical courts. But the legatee's action for his legacy is far older than the doctrine of trusts and has never been brought within that doctrine. I must not go into this matter at any length, but I must admit that my definition of a trust is somewhat too wide. In the case of an

[1] Since 1925 this statement is no longer true as regards the next of kin. The whole position is discussed on pp. 233 to 236 below.

executor when debts have been paid we do find one person fully owner of the goods—for undoubtedly the executor is the full owner of the goods—and yet he is bound to use his rights in a particular way, he is bound *e.g.* to hand over the testator's watch to M and his books to N—but for all this he is not a trustee for M and N. I must admit that this is so and at present can only append to my definition the remark that executors and administrators while acting merely as such are not trustees, and add that a historical explanation, though hardly any other explanation, can be given of this.

Observe however the Judicial Trustees Act 1896. Section 3 of that Act[1] enables the Court to relieve honest trustees from liability for breach of trust, in certain cases; and section 1 subsection 2 says 'The administration of the property of a deceased person whether a testator or intestate shall be a trust and the executor or administrator a trustee within the meaning of this Act.'

So again says the Land Transfer Act 1897,[2] when altering the law of inheritance and providing that realty shall pass to the personal representatives. Section 2 provides that subject to the powers and rights relating to administration given by that Act 'the personal representatives of a deceased person shall hold the real estate as trustees for the persons by law beneficially entitled thereto'.[3]

The tendency of modern statutes is to equiparate executors and administrators with trustees. Still, especially as regards the Statute of Limitations, it is necessary to say that the executor or administrator in relation to personal estate is not as such a trustee.

Note the difference between these two wills. 'I give my watch to A, the rest of my personal property to B, and I appoint C as my executor'; and 'I give all my personal property to C upon trust as to my watch for A, and as to the residue for B, and I appoint C my executor.'

---

[1] Now Trustee Act 1925, s. 61.
[2] Repealed by the Law of Property Act 1922. For the present position see note on p. 235 below.
[3] On the effect of this section see *Toates* v. *Toates* [1926] 2 K.B. 30.

5. I have spoken of the trustee as having rights which he is bound to exercise on behalf of another. In many cases those rights will be the legal estate in land or the legal ownership of moveable goods, and these cases indeed are so common that sometimes people speak as though it were essential that a trustee should have 'the legal estate'. But really this is not so. In the first place the subject-matter of the trust may not be a true proprietary right, it may not be the legal estate in land or the legal ownership of goods, it may be a mere personal right, the benefit of a contract or debt. A owes B a sum of money upon a bond or by simple contract; B on his marriage assigns this debt to T and T' upon certain trusts for himself, his wife and children. That is a not uncommon case and here the right of the trustees, the right that is put into trust, is merely *jus in personam*, the right of a creditor to be paid a certain sum of money. Then again though there may be land in the case the trustees may not have the legal estate in it. Let us say that one set of trustees is holding land upon trust for A during his life with remainder to B in fee; B is going to marry; it is possible that he will convey his rights to another set of trustees upon certain trusts for himself, his wife and children. But the rights that he can convey are themselves merely equitable rights, and the second set of trustees therefore will have merely equitable rights. It not unfrequently happens that you will find one set of trustees standing behind another set. There has been a settlement and then a sub-settlement. So again when an estate which is subject to a mortgage is put into settlement, the settlor having merely equitable rights can (unless he pays off the mortgage) convey none but equitable rights to his trustees.[1]

6. I have said that the trustee is bound to exercise his rights on behalf of some other person or for the accomplishment of some purpose. I think that these last words are necessary. We may of course have a simple trust which merely binds the trustee to hold for another person: thus T holds land in fee in

---

[1] Since 1926 this particular example fails since the mortgagor of land now has a legal estate. Note that a person may for some purposes be regarded as a trustee although he has no estate at law or in equity in the property. See the observations on fiduciary agents on p. 231 below.

trust for A in fee, or T is entitled to a sum of Consols and the whole equitable right to this sum is vested in A. Here is a simple trust for another person. But very often we cannot say that a trustee holds simply on behalf of another. Take a common case; T and T' hold land upon trust to sell it and to divide the proceeds between A, B, and C. Here if A, B, and C are all of full age and otherwise competent legal persons, they may say to the trustee 'No, we will not have the land sold, we prefer to have it kept for us', and then the trustee must obey. Still unless they all agree in giving such a direction to the trustee, his duty is to sell—that is the purpose or one of the purposes that he is bound to accomplish. And then of course we may have far more elaborate trusts, where the trustee's duty is much rather that of accomplishing a purpose than that of holding on behalf of any ascertained person. For example S transfers a sum of Consols to T and T' upon trust that they shall spend the income in giving prizes for essays on the Law of Trusts according to a scheme of regulations which he has drawn up. Here there is no one who can say 'You are holding this fund on my behalf; in equity it belongs to me.' Of such 'purpose' trusts, chiefly charitable trusts, I shall not here say much. But they are not to be left out of sight. They are often characterized by this—there is no definite *cestui que trust*. I think we may say that there is no *cestui que trust* at all. No private person can enforce them in his own name. They are enforced by means of actions brought in the name of the Attorney-General. If there be any *cestui que trust* it is the public. Their history goes back to the Act 43 Eliz. cap. 4.[1]

A very wide sense is given to the word 'charitable'.[2] The highest recent authority is to be found in the judgments delivered in the House of Lords in the case of the *Commissioners of Income Tax* v. *Pemsel* [1891] A.C. 531. The scope given to the word 'charitable' nearly equals any purpose conceived to be directly beneficial to the public or to some class of the public.

---

[1] This Act was 'An Act to redress the mis-employment of lands goods and stocks of money heretofore given to certain charitable uses'.

[2] See for example *In re Lopes* [1931] 2 Ch. 130, where the Zoo was held to be a charity.

But where is the line to be drawn? It certainly is far from clear. Take, for instance, *In re Scowcroft* [1898] 2 Ch. 638. The vicar of a parish devises to the vicar for the time being a building to be used as a village club and reading room to be maintained for the furtherance of conservative principles and religious and mental improvement and to be kept free from intoxicants and dancing. This was held to be a charitable purpose.

Then take *In re Nottage* [1895] 2 Ch. 649. That was the gift of a sum of money with a direction that the interest was to be expended in providing a cup to be given for the encouragement of yacht racing. Held to be not a charitable purpose.

But compare *In re Macduff* [1896] 2 Ch. 451 and *Blair v. Duncan* [1902] A.C. 37. In the former case the Court of Appeal held that 'philanthropic purposes' were not necessarily charitable; and in the latter case the House of Lords held that a gift 'for such charitable or public purposes as my trustee thinks proper' was void for uncertainty. And see *Hunter v. Attorney-General* [1899] A.C. 309. There, Lord Davey, at p. 323, said 'Where charitable purposes are mixed up with other purposes of such a shadowy and indefinite nature that the Court cannot execute them (such as "charitable or benevolent", or "charitable or philanthropic" or "charitable or pious" purposes), or where the description includes purposes which may or may not be charitable (such as "undertakings of public utility") and a discretion is vested in the trustees, the whole gift fails for uncertainty'.[1]

Remember that charitable trusts, provided that they are limited to commence within the time allowed by the rule against perpetuities, are valid though their objects are perpetual.

In a few cases 'Purpose' trusts which are not charitable are upheld—*e.g.* trusts for the maintenance of a tombstone. But they must comply with the rule of perpetuities.

Read *In re Dean*,[2] 41 Ch. D. 552, in which there was a trust

---

[1] Recent cases illustrating the same point are *Houston v. Burns* [1918] A.C. 337 and *Attorney-General v. National Provincial Bank* [1924] A.C. 262. The objection of uncertainty does not apply where the trust is charitable (cf. *Weir v. Crum Brown* [1908] A.C. 162).

[2] But query whether the trust in this case ought not to have been held bad for perpetuity. A better example is *In re Hooper* [1932] 1 Ch. 38.

for the maintenance of dogs and horses. It was held to be valid though not enforceable—there was no *cestui que trust*—but there was no resulting trust for the heirs or the next of kin of the testator.

But it is questionable at present how far this principle goes. In Ireland trusts for masses for the repose of the soul are upheld.[1]

On the other hand—if there is a special trust solely for the benefit of one person—a trust that a trustee shall do something for his benefit—then this *cestui que trust* being *sui juris* can put an end to this purpose trust at any moment that he pleases—*e.g.* a gift of £1000 in trust to purchase an annuity for C. D. In this case C. D. can demand that the fund shall be paid over to him instead of being used to buy the annuity.[2] Or take a trust of a fund to accumulate until C. D. attains the age of 24 years and then to pay the accumulated fund to him. Here C. D. on reaching the age of 21 can stop the accumulation and demand that the fund shall be paid over to him forthwith.

It is necessary however as these instances show to take notice of purpose trusts in any definition of a trust.

This I fear is all that I can say at present about the definition of a trust. Some points will become clearer to us as we go along.

Our next question must be How is a trust created? And here we come upon a classification of trusts which turns upon the mode by which they are created. Trusts are created (1) by the act of a party, (2) by the operation of law. I do not think that these terms are unexceptionable, still they are well known and useful. A further classification has been made:

		Express
	By act of a party	
Trusts		Implied
		Resulting
	By act of the law	
		Constructive

[1] Trusts for masses have now been held charitable in England; *In re Caus* [1934] 1 Ch. 162.

[2] And even where the annuitant dies before the annuity can be purchased his estate is entitled to such a sum as the annuity would have cost. See *In re Robbins* [1907] 2 Ch. 8.

Now I should say that the normal means by which a person becomes bound by a trust is a declaration made by him by words or implied in his conduct to the effect that he intends to be so bound. As I have already hinted this morning, the creation of a trust may be a perfectly unilateral act—there may not be more than one party to it—and we may fail to find in it any element that could in the ordinary use of words be called trust or confidence. I declare myself a trustee of this watch for my son who is in India. If afterwards I sell that watch, although my son has never heard of the benefit that I had intended for him, I commit a breach of trust and my son has an equitable cause of action against me.

But though this be so the commonest origin of a trust is a transaction between two persons. This we may for a while treat as typical. Here S conveys land, or moveable goods, or Consols, or a debt, to T upon a trust, and T consents to execute that trust. We have here an agreement between S and T, and since that agreement is a binding one—since it can be enforced by that part of our law which is called equity, we well might say that there is a contract between S and T. Indeed I think it impossible so to define a contract that the definition shall not cover at least three quarters of all the trusts that are created. For my own part I think that we ought to confess that we can not define either agreement or contract without including the great majority of trusts and that the reasons why we still treat the law of trusts as something apart from the law of contract are reasons which can be given only by a historical statement. Trusts fell under the equitable jurisdiction of the Court of Chancery and for that very reason the Courts of Law did not enforce them. Just now and again they threatened to give an action for damages against the defaulting trustee—but they soon abandoned this attempt to invade a province which equity had made its own. Therefore for a very long time to come I think that we shall go on treating the law of trusts as something distinct from the law of contracts—we shall find the former in one set of books, the latter in another set. Only let us see that in the common case a trust originates in what we can not but call an agreement. S transfers land or goods or debts to T upon a trust; T promises,

expressly or by his conduct, that he will be bound. If you please
you can analyse the transaction into a proposal and an acceptance
—Will you hold this land, these goods, in trust for my wife and
children? Yes, I will.

You will find it laid down as an elementary rule that no one
can be compelled to undertake a trust. Until a man has accepted
a trust he is not a trustee. You, without my knowledge, convey
land unto and to the use of me and my heirs upon trust for X.
When I hear of that conveyance I can renounce the rights and
the duties that you have attempted to cast upon me. If I am
prudent I shall very likely execute a deed saying that I renounce
the estate; but now-a-days it is clear that even a freehold estate
(there used to be doubt about this) may be renounced by parol.
I do not think that in strictness any active renunciation can be
expected of me any more than I can be compelled to answer a
letter in which you propose to sell me a horse. If, when I hear
of the trust I simply do nothing, then I am no trustee, I thereby
disclaim the estate. *In re Gordon*, 6 Ch. D. 531, an estate had
been devised to E. A. upon certain trusts; three years afterwards
he died, and the question was raised whether he had accepted
or rejected the legal estate and the trust. Jessel M.R. said
' I think that there was sufficient evidence of disclaimer.... In
the first place we have this, that he never acted; that is a very
strong circumstance, a man lives three years and does not act at
all. It is a strong proof that he does not intend to act. Of course
it is not in itself conclusive, but it is evidence that he does not
intend to act.' *In re Birchall*, 40 Ch. D. at p. 439, Lindley L.J.
said ' Formerly it was held that the legal estate in freeholds could
not be disclaimed except by record; but that doctrine was given
up, and it was held that the disclaimer could be by deed. Since
that time the law has been carefully considered, and it is now
established that a man's assent to a devise is presumed unless he
disclaims, which may be by conduct, as well as by record or by
deed.'[1] Upon principle, as it seems to me, the law cannot throw

---

[1] For an interesting case of disclaimer by a grantee in trust and a decision
that the settlement was not rendered inoperative but that the trust was imposed on the settlor see *Mallott* v. *Wilson* [1903] 2 Ch. 494. See too *In re
Clout and Frewer's Contract* [1924] 2 Ch. 230.

on a man the burden of either accepting or rejecting the trust: if he does absolutely nothing that can be construed as an acceptance of the trust, this should be enough. But in practice it would not be very safe to rely upon this doctrine, for one may very easily do something or say something that can be regarded as an acceptance of the trust. If in any way one assumes the rights that are to be conferred on the trustee, one thereby assumes also all the duties of the trust, and when once those duties are assumed they cannot be easily got rid of, as we shall see when we speak of the ways in which men cease to be trustees. Therefore if you hear that any one has been conveying property to you as a trustee, and you do not wish to be burdened with a trustee's duties, you will be wise in repudiating in some emphatic manner the rights and the duties which were to have been thrust upon you.

Now as regards the formalities necessary to the constitution of a trust, there is extremely little law—trusts have not been hedged about by formalities. I believe that I may state the matter thus: Subject to one section of the Statute of Frauds and to the Wills Act, a trust can be created without deed, without writing, without formality of any kind by mere word of mouth; and subject to certain established rules of construction no particular words are necessary. This proposition I intend to develop next time.

CREATION OF A TRUST

W E ended with this: Subject to a certain section of the Statute of Frauds and to the Wills Act, a trust can be created without deed, without writing, without formality of any kind by mere word of mouth; and subject to certain established rules of construction no particular words are necessary. We will now develop this proposition.

In the old days no deed, no writing, was necessary to create a use, trust or confidence. I enfeoff you, and by word of mouth I declare that you are to hold to the use of X.[1] You must hold to the use of X. As to trusts this still is law, except in so far as it has been altered by the Statute of Frauds.

By that Act, 29 Car. II, c. 3, s. 7, 'All declarations of or creations of trusts or confidences of any lands, tenements or hereditaments shall be manifested and proved by some writing signed by the party who is by law enabled to declare such trust, or by his last will in writing, or else they shall be utterly void and of no effect.'

§ 8. 'Provided always that where any conveyance shall be made of any lands or tenements by which a trust or confidence shall or may arise or result by the implication or construction of law, or be transferred or extinguished by an act or operation of law, then, and in every such case, such trust or confidence shall be of the like force and effect as the same would have been if this statute had not been made, anything hereinbefore contained to the contrary notwithstanding.'

I will read also the next section in order that you may contrast it: it will come before us at a later time.

---

[1] The trusts could apparently be declared by signs only. Cf. from the recitals of the Statute of Uses (3) '...the hereditaments of this realm have been conveyed...by fraudulent feoffments...craftily made to secret uses intents and trusts; (4) and also by wills and testaments sometime made by *nude parolx* and words, sometime by signs and tokens, and sometime by writing, and for the most part made by such persons as be visited with sickness, in their extreme agonies and pains...'.

§ 9. 'All grants and assignments of any trust or confidence shall likewise be in writing signed by the party granting or assigning the same, or by such last will or devise, or else shall be utterly void and of none effect.'[1]

1. The 7th section speaks of declarations and creations of trusts or confidences, the 9th section of grants and assignments of trusts or confidences.

2. The 7th section relates only to trusts and confidences of lands, tenements and hereditaments. The 9th relates to all grants and assignments of any trust or confidence, whether of hereditaments, of moveable goods, or of choses in action or of what you will.

At this point I may remark that the words 'lands, tenements and hereditaments' in the 7th section include copyholds and chattels real, but they have been held not to include a debt due upon mortgage of real estate.[2]

3. The 9th section requires that every grant or assignment of a trust shall *be in* writing, signed by the party granting or assigning the same. The 7th section merely requires that the declaration of trust shall be *manifested and proved* by some writing signed by the party who is by law enabled to declare such a trust. Your attention will have been drawn to a similar point when you were studying the two yet more famous sections of the statute, the

---

[1] Sections 7, 8 and 9 of the Statute of Frauds were repealed by the Law of Property Act 1925, and re-enacted with alterations by section 53 of that Act, which is as follows:

'53. (1) Subject to the provisions hereinafter contained with respect to the creation of interests in land by parol—

'(*a*) no interest in land can be created or disposed of except by writing signed by the person creating or conveying the same, or by his agent thereunto lawfully authorised in writing, or by will, or by operation of law;

'(*b*) a declaration of trust respecting any land or any interest therein must be manifested and proved by some writing signed by some person who is able to declare such trust or by his will;

'(*c*) a disposition of an equitable interest or trust subsisting at the time of the disposition, must be in writing signed by the person disposing of the same, or by his agent thereunto lawfully authorised in writing or by will.

'(2) This section does not affect the creation or operation of resulting, implied or constructive trusts.'

[2] *Benbow* v. *Townsend*, 1 M. and K. 506.

4th and the 17th, which are important in our law of contract. To satisfy the 7th section the writing may be posterior to the creation of the trust. 'The statute will be satisfied if the trust can be manifested and proved by any subsequent acknowledgment by the trustee, as by an express declaration by him or by a memorandum to that effect, or by a letter under his hand, or by a recital in a deed executed by him; and the trust, however late the proof, operates retrospectively from the time of its creation' (Lewin).[1] Thus if I convey land to you and it is agreed between us that you are to hold it upon trust for X, but nothing about this be said in the conveyance or in any other writing, the trust for X can not be enforced; but should you write and sign a letter admitting that the conveyance was made to you in trust for X, then not only will the trust be enforceable against you for the future, but you will be treated as having been all along a trustee for X, and will be accountable as such.

4. You will observe that neither section requires a deed.

5. You will observe that unlike the two famous sections, the 4th and the 17th, neither of these sections (7th and 9th) says anything about signature by an agent.[2] The one requires the signature of the party who is by law enabled to declare the trust, the other requires the signature of the party granting or assigning the trust.

6. You will observe that a proviso to the 7th section (this proviso constitutes the 8th section) protects the doctrine of trusts which arise or result by the implication or construction of law. The requirement of writing is not to destroy this doctrine. On the other hand the 9th section requires signed writing for the grant or assignment of a trust, no matter whether that trust has arisen by declaration or by the construction of law.

7. Observe that Courts of Equity have dealt boldly with section 7, saying that the Statute of Frauds is not to be made a cover or cloak for fraud. Take this declaration of the Court of Appeal. 'It is further established by a series of cases, the pro-

---

[1] See now Lewin on Trusts, 13th edition, p. 49.

[2] Section 53 (1) (c) of the Law of Property Act 1925, which replaces section 9 of the Statute of Frauds, expressly permits signature by an agent who is authorized in writing.

priety of which cannot now be questioned, that the Statute of
Frauds does not prevent the proof of a fraud; and that it is a
fraud of a person to whom land is conveyed as a trustee, and
who knows it was so conveyed, to deny the trust and claim the
land himself.' *Rochefoucauld* v. *Boustead* [1897] I Ch. 196. This
doctrine deprives the statute of a good deal of its efficacy. In
time past Courts of Equity in construing statutes were apt to
read into every statute a proviso to the effect that the law was not
to serve as a shield for fraudulent people.

This, I think, is the sum and substance of our law relating to
the formalities necessary for the creation of trusts by act *inter
vivos*. A trust may also be declared and transferred by will. You
will have observed that the 7th and 9th sections of the Statute
of Frauds admit and declare this rule. As to the formalities
necessary for the execution of a valid will we have now to go to
the great Wills Act of 1837, 1 Vic. c. 26. I need say nothing
about these formalities save this, that you can not create a trust
by any instrument of a testamentary character that is not a valid
will—I use the term will so as to include codicil. This may seem
a little more obvious to you than really it is, so I will dwell on
it for a moment.

Suppose that by my will I devise land to T and his heirs 'upon
trust', but do not specify the particular trust. Then by a paper
signed only by one witness I declare my intention to be that T
shall hold in trust for X. When I die the beneficial interest in
the land that I have devised to T will descend to my heir at law,
or if my will contains a residuary devise it will go to my residuary
devisee. But you may say 'Granted that paper attested by but
one witness is not a valid will or codicil; is it not a valid declaration of trust, for the 7th section of the Statute of Frauds does
not require two witnesses; it does not require any witness?'
Or put another case. By my will I bequeath a horse to T 'upon
trust', but do not specify the trust, and by word of mouth I
declare that T is to be a trustee for X. Is there not here a valid
declaration of trust, for the Statute of Frauds does not even
require writing where a trust is declared of a personal chattel?
The answer in both cases is that I am trying to make what
in truth is a testamentary disposition without observing those

formalities which the law requires in the case of all testamentary dispositions.

If, therefore, I make a devise to T saying nothing of any trust and I then make a declaration that T is to hold in trust for X, but this declaration is not made with the formalities required by the Wills Act, and is not communicated to and assented to by T during my lifetime; then on my death T will take the land beneficially, unburdened by any trust. If on the other hand I devise to T 'upon trust', but do not mention what trust, and then by some paper which is not a valid will declare that the trust is for X, then on my death my heir at law, or my residuary devisee, if I have one, will be equitably entitled to the land that I devised to T. X can not establish the trust, and T can not retain the beneficial interest for himself, for I have made clear on the face of my will that I did not intend him to have it.[1] The former of these doctrines, however, undergoes a qualification if during my lifetime I communicate to T my intention that he should hold merely as a trustee for X and T assents to hold in that character. A man, it is said, must not profit by his own fraud, and Courts of Equity have made even the provisions of the Wills Act yield to this maxim. Mr Lewin lays down the rule thus, 'If a testator devise real estate or bequeath personal estate to A, the beneficial owner upon the face of the will, but upon the understanding between the testator and A, that the devisee or legatee will, as to a part or even the entirety of the beneficial interest, hold upon any trust which is lawful in itself in favour of B, the Court, at the instance of B, will affect the conscience of A, and decree him to execute the testator's intention'.[2]

Read *In re Boyes* (1884), 26 Ch. D. 531 (Kay J.). A makes a will leaving all to his solicitor B, whom he appoints sole executor. It is agreed between them that B shall dispose of the property as A shall direct. No direction comes to B during A's life. After A's death two letters to B are found among his papers, telling B

---

[1] A secret trust can however sometimes be established even though the existence of some trust appears on the face of the Will. See *Blackwell* v. *Blackwell* [1929] A.C. 318.

[2] 13th edition, p. 57.

to hold for X—B must hold in trust for A's next of kin. A could not give himself the power to make an informal will. If the direction had been communicated in A's lifetime, and B had assented to it, there would have been a trust for X.

In re Stead [1900] 1 Ch. 237 is an interesting case—a gift to A and B jointly. A is told, but B is not told, of the trust. A is bound as to an undivided moiety. Is B bound? Yes, if the trust was told to A before the making of the will; no, if it was only told to A afterwards. This distinction rests on no sound reason, as, indeed, Farwell J. points out. You must accept it as the result of two lines of cases—the one set asserting a rule that no person can claim an interest under a fraud committed by another, whilst the other set was decided in the opposite way lest otherwise one beneficiary might be enabled to deprive the rest of their benefits by setting up some secret trust communicated to himself alone.

In the quotation just made from Lewin you may have noticed the words 'upon any trust which is lawful in itself'. What Mr Lewin is thinking of is a doctrine which has come into play chiefly in relation to certain trusts which are stigmatized as superstitious, and therefore unlawful. I devise or bequeath property to T as though T were to be the beneficial owner, but T has agreed with me that he will spend the property in paying for masses for my soul. My heir at law, or my residuary devisee, or my next of kin, as the case may be, can go to the Court, and in an action against T can oblige him to say whether or no there was this secret trust, and if the trust be proved against him, then it being plain on the one hand that he was not intended to enjoy the property beneficially, and on the other hand that the trust is one which is unlawful, he will have to hold it for my heir, my residuary devisee or legatee, or my next of kin, as the case may be. So also until 1891[1] one could not leave to a charity realty, or personalty that, as the phrase went, 'savoured of the realty'. If then I devised all my freeholds to T, and there was an arrangement between us that T should convey the land to a charity, my heir at law if he could prove that secret and unlawful trust could compel T to convey to him. The practical moral of this is that if you wish to have masses said for your soul at the cost of your

[1] Mortmain and Charitable Uses Act 1891.

estate, leave your estate to some one who is of your way of thinking, but be extremely careful not to tell him what you want done. If he is a good friend of yours very likely the masses will be duly said—there is nothing unlawful in saying masses, and nothing unlawful in paying for masses—but do not constitute a secret trust unless you are very sure of your kinsfolk.[1]

I have been led into this digression by a wish to show you how the law concerning the creation of trusts is affected by the law of wills.

So much as to the formalities necessary when a trust is declared. You will notice that there is little to be said about this matter. Equity has been characterized by a certain disregard for forms. Then as to the necessary words—we can only say that subject to certain rules of construction any words will do which adequately express the intention of creating a trust.[2]

*   *   *   *   *   *

It is one of the most important and most unyielding rules of construction that technical words will be understood to have their technical meaning. But in this context it is common to introduce a contrast between two classes of trusts. Trusts it is said are either 'executed' or 'executory'. One may regret that no better words have been found to express this distinction, for 'executed' and 'executory' have, as you know, hard enough work to do in connexion with the law of consideration in contract. The distinction becomes important in the construction of wills. A testator may either himself make a settlement or may sketch out a settlement that is to be made after his death. Well, the rule comes to this that in the latter case you will have a little more latitude in considering what the testator really meant than you will have in the former. Often enough the cause of this distinction has been the rule in *Shelley's Case*.[3] That rule applies to wills as well as to acts, *inter vivos*; it applies to equitable as well as to legal estates. If I devise unto and to the use of T and his heirs in trust for X for life with remainder to the heirs of the

---

[1] As an illustration of the limits of the doctrine of secret trusts see *In re Pitt-Rivers* [1902] 1 Ch. 403.

[2] In the 1st edition there followed here a passage concerned with the Statute of Uses which has been omitted as being obsolete.

[3] Now abolished by the Law of Property Act 1925, s. 131.

body of X, here X has an equitable estate tail. But if I leave money to trustees, direct them to purchase land and settle it upon X for life with remainder to the heirs of his body, then in the case of this executory trust there may be more question as to whether the Shelley rule is to be brought into play. If by some other phrase I show that my real intention is that X shall have but a life estate with remainder to his first and other sons successively in tail—if for example I say that X is to hold without impeachment of waste—the Court may be able to say: 'The testator has not made a settlement, he has only sketched out a settlement; we can see what he really meant, and the sketch being but a sketch, we will not catch at technical phrases and defeat what we believe to be his intention.' If this be so with executory trusts in wills it is still more so with executory trusts in marriage articles. John and Jane are going to marry: they cannot wait for the preparation of an elaborate settlement; they execute a brief agreement and may be they say that all John's freehold land shall hereafter be settled on John for life and then, subject to a jointure of £500 a year for Jane, on the heirs of the body of John. Here a Court will be somewhat ready to say that the rule in *Shelley's Case* is not to be applied to this brief and executory instrument. It is pretty evident that if the land be settled in just those terms which were written down in the agreement the intention of the parties will be defeated. Here the Court has this to go upon—the object of the agreement must be that of providing for the children of the marriage, but if the husband is to have an estate tail this will be no provision for the children; the husband could bar the estate tail to-morrow, sell the land and squander the proceeds. No, we must suppose that in this merely executory agreement 'heirs of the body' means 'first and other sons'. Thus in addition to the rules of construction for executed trusts we have another body of rules of construction for executory trusts, or rather two more sets of rules, one for executory trusts in wills, the other for executory trusts in marriage articles. *In re Johnston* (1884), 26 Ch. D. 538.

Even in deeds where the trust is of the executed kind, the Court takes a greater liberty of looking at the whole instrument where merely equitable interests are being dealt with than where the interests are legal; *e.g.* an equitable fee has been held to be given by deed without words of limitation or the words 'in fee simple'. *In re Tringham* [1904] 2 Ch. 487. *In re Oliver* [1905] 1 Ch. 191. If you would know more of this matter then I will send you to Lewin chap. VIII, but we must not delay long over mere rules of construction.[1]

Technical words are to be technically construed, but a trust can be created by the most untechnical of words. This is seen very clearly in the treatment of wills. In the past the Court of Chancery seems to have been eager to catch at any phrase which could possibly be twisted into an expression of trust. A testator leaves property to T and expresses a wish, a hope, that T will use it in a certain way, or for a certain purpose. If that way, that purpose, be at all definite, the Court will see in this a declaration of trust, to use a phrase often used, a precatory trust. Here are some of the terms which have been held sufficient: 'desire', 'will', 'request', 'entreat', 'beseech', 'recommend', 'hope', 'do not doubt', 'am well assured', 'well know', 'confide', 'of course he will', and so forth. Often the testator has been leaving his property to his wife, and then he has said 'I hope, I believe that she will maintain our children'—or 'of course she will provide for our children'—here the Court has been very ready, even eager to see a trust. Just of late years there has been a marked reaction against the more extreme applications of this doctrine of precatory trusts. Still it is highly imprudent for a testator to express in his will any sort of wish, or hope, or expectation unless he desires that this should become a binding trust.[2] If ever you have to put into a will any such expression of wish, hope, or expectation and the testator does not intend to

---

[1] *In re Tringham* was overruled in *In re Bostock* [1921] 2 Ch. 469. *In re Oliver* was explained as being a case of an executory trust. Unless the instrument is executory the same principles of construction are applied whether the interests dealt with are legal or equitable. Since 1926 a fee simple, whether legal or equitable, can be given without the use of any technical terms (Law of Property Act 1925, s. 60). On the difference between executed and executory trusts see Lewin on Trusts, 13th edition, chap. IV.

[2] Maitland does not go far enough. If the testator does wish to create a binding trust he would equally be highly imprudent to rely on words such as 'wish', 'hope' or 'expectation'. He should in fact state explicitly whether or not he intends to create a binding trust for otherwise there will have to be an application to the Court to construe the will.

create an enforceable duty, you will do well to say in the strongest terms, 'But this is not to be deemed a trust, it is not to be deemed a duty enforceable by the courts'.

In re Williams [1897] 2 Ch. 12 is a good illustration of the modern limit, as Rigby L.J. differs from Lindley and Smith L.J.J. The testator gives the residue of his estate to his wife, her heirs, executors, administrators and assigns absolutely 'in the fullest trust and confidence that she will carry out my wishes in the following particulars'. She was to keep up a policy on her own life (which policy was her own property) and by her will she was to leave the moneys payable under that policy and also the moneys payable under a policy on the testator's life (which was his property) to his daughter Lucy. Lindley and Smith L.J.J. held that the wife took the residue unfettered by any condition or trust. This case is the highwater mark of the reactionary doctrine. But in the case of *Comiskey* v. *Bowring-Hanbury* [1905] A.C. 84, the House of Lords held that a precatory trust was established, under a will not easy to distinguish from that in the case that I have last cited.

Of course even before the modern reaction the courts have sometimes had to say 'No, this really is too vague, we can't enforce it.' For example, a testator gives property to his wife and desires her 'to use it for herself and her children and to remember the Church of God and the poor'—this is too vague. Still I think you would be surprised at the looseness of some of the phrases in which the Court of Chancery was able to discover a definite and enforceable trust.

I now come to a rule of very great importance; it draws a line between the trust that is created for valuable consideration and the voluntary trust. Mr Lewin approaches the subject thus: 'Where there is a valuable consideration and a trust is intended to be created, formalities are of minor importance, since if the transaction cannot take place by way of "trust executed", it can be enforced by a Court of Equity as a contract.'[1] Let us see what this means. I agree with you that if you marry my daughter I will convey Blackacre Farm to trustees, named or unnamed, upon certain trusts for the benefit of you, her, and

---

[1] 13th edition, p. 61.

the issue of the marriage. This agreement is put into writing, that writing I sign. You marry my daughter. Now we can put the transaction in one of two ways and it matters not very much in which way we put it. (1) Here is a contract and one of which a Court of Equity will enforce the specific performance. (2) Here is already a declaration of trust: true that the legal estate has not yet been conveyed to those persons who are to be in the end the trustees of it; but there is a fundamental rule of equity that a trust shall never fail for want of a trustee—I myself am already a trustee for you, your wife, the issue of your marriage. I say it does not matter very much in which way we state the case, for it is another rule of equity that the vendor of land so soon as the agreement for sale is signed can for very many purposes be treated as a trustee for the purchaser. In this case now before us you, your wife and the children of the marriage are in very much the same position as that in which you would be had I already conveyed Blackacre to the trustees and made a formal settlement. You can enforce the trusts against me, if I die you can enforce the trusts against my representatives, if I dishonestly give Blackacre to X for no valuable consideration, you can enforce the trusts against X, if I dishonestly sell and convey Blackacre to Y, you can enforce the trusts against Y, unless indeed he purchased without notice express or implied of those trusts.[1] Well, if the estate had been duly conveyed to trustees you would be able to do no more. The chance that the legal estate may come to the hands of a *bona fide* purchaser for value without notice of your equitable rights is—as we shall observe at length hereafter—a chance which every *cestui que trust* must run. I do not say that you ought not to require the execution of a formal settlement. There are several reasons why you ought to do so, for so long as the legal estate is in me and there is no formal conveyance to trustees it is somewhat easy for me to commit a fraud and pass the legal estate to a *bona fide* purchaser who having no notice of your equitable rights will laugh at them. Still here there is a trust already created, I am your trustee.

Far otherwise would it be were there no valuable considera-

[1] Such an agreement, if made after 1925, would not bind a purchaser unless registered as an estate contract under the Land Charges Act 1925.

tion for my promise. In writing I promise to convey certain land to trustees upon trust for you, because you have been a good friend to me, or because you have already married my daughter, though before the marriage I made no promise to do anything for you. Now here of course there is not any enforceable contract, we have but a voluntary promise which is not enforceable either at law or in equity. Let us go one step further, let us suppose that my promise is made by deed, by covenant. Here is a promise enforceable at law by an action for damages, for promises under seal are valid though made without valuable consideration. So if I break my promise you may get damages. But you will not get specific performance, for it is a rule of equity that specific performance of a voluntary promise will not be enforced even though that promise be under seal. You have a bare, personal, contractual right. Equity will do absolutely nothing for you. I have not declared a trust for you, I have merely promised to convey to a trustee for you. You say 'True, but still you have promised'—I reply 'Yes, but the promise, even though it be under seal, is not one which equity will enforce.'

Thus where there is a valuable consideration it is often unnecessary for us to distinguish the promise to constitute a trust from the constitution of a trust. But otherwise is it if the transaction be voluntary, for then this distinction is vital.

In the classical case of *Ellison* v. *Ellison* (6 Ves. 656, and White and Tudor L.C. vol. II, p. 782 (9th edition)) Lord Eldon laid down the rule thus: 'I take the distinction to be, that, if you want the assistance of the court to constitute you *cestui que trust* and the instrument is voluntary, you shall not have the assistance for the purpose of constituting you *cestui que trust*,—as upon a covenant to transfer stock, &c., if it rests in covenant and is purely voluntary, this court will not execute that voluntary covenant. But if the party has completely transferred stock, &c., though it is voluntary, yet the legal conveyance being effectually made the equitable interest will be enforced by this court.'

As regards voluntary transactions therefore we have to distinguish clearly between the promise to constitute a trust, which is unenforceable, and the constitution of a trust. And this as we shall see more fully next time is not always a very easy feat.

LECTURE VI

TRUSTS IMPLIED, RESULTING
AND CONSTRUCTIVE

I HAVE to-day to add a little to what has been already said about
the constitution of voluntary trusts. We have this rule, a voluntary trust if perfectly created is valid and enforceable. Of course,
as you know, there are statutes which make important exceptions
to this rule, statutes which invalidate certain voluntary transactions. In particular there are the two statutes of Elizabeth—
the statute of the 13th year in favour of creditors, the statute of
the 27th year in favour of purchasers[1]—also there is the bankruptcy law to be considered. But these invalidating statutes
apart, the voluntary trust, if perfectly created, is valid. On the
other hand a promise to create a voluntary trust can not be
enforced. As Lord Eldon said—if you are a volunteer you shall
not have the help of a Court of Equity to make you a *cestui que
trust*.

What then is meant by the perfect creation of a voluntary
trust? Well, the settlor must intend to do one of two things.
Either he must intend that some other person shall hold the
property in question upon certain trusts, or he must intend to
make himself a trustee, to retain the property in question but to
hold it henceforth upon the designated trusts.

We will look first at the former alternative. The settlor does
not mean to become a trustee, he means that some other person
shall be the trustee. Here the question becomes this—Has he
done all that it was in his power to do to transfer the property to
that trustee and declare a trust of it? About this matter we have
however some subordinate rules.

1. If the subject-matter of the intended trust be some legal
estate or legal rights vested in the settlor, and that estate or those
rights be transferable at law, then the settlor must do all that the
law requires in order that he may transfer that estate or those

[1] Both these Acts are repealed by the Law of Property Act 1925 and re-
enacted with alterations by sections 172 and 173 of that Act.

rights to the trustee. If for example the settlor be legal tenant in fee simple he must execute a deed transferring his legal estate to the trustee. If he be the legal owner of moveable chattels such as plate or books he must pass the property in them to the trustee, and this he can do by deed or by delivery. If he wishes to settle Government stock now standing in his name, this must be transferred into the name of the trustee. If in any way he fails to perfect the legal transfer, equity will give no help whatever. Thus for example suppose him to be the tenant of a copyhold whose name appears on the rolls of the manor, a mere covenant to surrender it to the trustee is no complete transfer; there must be a surrender and admittance. So long as the matter rests in covenant equity will give no help. The covenant, being a covenant, is valid in a court of law, the trustee may be able to get damages out of the settlor if he will not surrender the copyhold, and if the trustee gets any damages he will have to hold the money upon the trusts—but equity will give no help—it will not compel the specific performance of a voluntary promise even though it be under seal.

2. Until lately it might frequently happen that the rights which the intending settlor proposed to settle were rights of a legal kind, but rights incapable of legal transfer. Some one owed him a debt, either a bond debt or a simple contract debt, and he wished that the benefit of this debt should be held in trust for his wife and children. But the debt being a chose in action could not, as you know, be assigned so as to give the assignee a legal right to sue for it. Here if equity had said—You must execute a legal transfer of your rights—it would have required an impossibility and said in effect—You cannot make a valid voluntary settlement of such rights as these except by constituting yourself a trustee. After some hesitation it conceded that if the settlor made a written assignment of the chose in action to the trustee—this, though inoperative at law, was a sufficient transfer within the meaning of the rule that we are now considering.[1] However under section 25 sub-section 6 of the Judicature Act of 1873 this class of cases has perhaps dis-

---

[1] See *e.g. Fortescue* v. *Barnett*, 3 M. and K. 36, *Kekewich* v. *Manning*, 1 De G. M. and G. 176.

appeared, for the person who is entitled to a legal chose in action can now make a legal assignment of it. Then does this case now fall into our first class? We have a man with legal rights capable of legal transfer. Very well, if he wishes to make a valid voluntary settlement, without making himself a trustee, he must, it may be said, execute a legal transfer of his rights to the trustee in the form prescribed by the Judicature Act. But this is at least dubious. In the case of *In re Griffin* [1899] 1 Ch. 408, Byrne J. seems to have thought that the completed formalities under the Judicature Act were not necessary to validate the voluntary assignment of a chose in action.

3. The subject-matter of the proposed settlement may itself be purely equitable. For example T holds land in trust for S, or he holds stock upon trust for S; S wants to settle his estate or interest. Well, here he has no legal estate to transfer. One mode of effecting his purpose will be to direct the old trustee to hold the land or the stock upon a new trust, another mode will be to execute an assignment of his equitable right to some new trustee T' upon the new trust. Here, as there is no legal estate in the case, no deed is necessary, an assignment in writing to the new trustee will be enough.

4. We have said that a man intending to make a voluntary settlement may do so by making himself a trustee. If he plainly declares that he holds himself to be a trustee for certain purposes of certain rights legal, or it may be merely equitable, which are vested in him—this is enough. If the rights in question are rights in lands or hereditaments then—because of the Statute of Frauds—the declaration must be proved by signed writing. In other cases word of mouth will be enough. But here we come upon a rule of some importance—An imperfect gift will not be construed as a declaration of trust.

I have a son called Thomas. I write a letter to him saying 'I give you my Blackacre estate, my leasehold house in the High Street, the sum of £1000 Consols standing in my name, the wine in my cellar.' This is ineffectual—I have given nothing— a letter will not convey freehold or leasehold land, it will not transfer Government stock, it will not pass the ownership in goods. Even if, instead of writing a letter, I had executed a deed

of covenant—saying not I do convey Blackacre, I do assign the
leasehold house and the wine, but I covenant to convey and
assign—even this would not have been a perfect gift. It would
be an imperfect gift, and being an imperfect gift the Court will
not regard it as a declaration of trust. I have made quite clear
that I do not intend to make myself a trustee, I meant to give.
The two intentions are very different—the giver means to get
rid of his rights, the man who is intending to make himself a
trustee intends to retain his rights but to come under an onerous
obligation. The latter intention is far rarer than the former.
Men often mean to give things to their kinsfolk, they do not
often mean to constitute themselves trustees. An imperfect gift
is no declaration of trust. This is well illustrated by the cases of
Richards v. *Delbridge*, L.R. 18 Eq. 11, and *Heartley* v. *Nicholson*,
L.R. 19 Eq. 233. It may be illustrated by cases in which the rule
seemed to act with great hardship. A husband might often wish
to make a present to his wife of some chattel, for example a
piano. But before the Married Women's Property Act of 1882,
there was a great difficulty in his way. He might do one of two
things: he might give the piano to a trustee upon trust for his
wife's separate use, or he might declare himself to be a trustee of
it for his wife's separate use. But one thing he could not do. He
could not transfer the legal ownership of the chattel to his wife.
Suppose that he said 'I give you this piano, or this brooch', and
let us say he delivered the things into his wife's keeping, and she
wore the brooch. Well, some judges, impressed by the hardship
of the case, were willing to say that this imperfect gift—a
perfect gift being impossible—might be regarded as a declaration of trust; the husband must be taken to have made himself
a trustee for his wife's separate use (*Baddeley* v. *Baddeley*, 9 Ch.
D. 113)—but I believe that this charitable doctrine was of
doubtful authority (see *In re Breton's Estate*, 17 Ch. D. 416).
However the Married Women's Property Act of 1882 removed
this particular difficulty. Still the rule that I have been en-
deavouring to explain is an important one. Imperfect gifts are
not to be construed as declarations of trust.[1] Once more let me

---

[1] There is a curious qualification to this rule established in *Strong* v. *Bird*,
L.R. 18 Eq. 315. A purports to release a debt owed to him by B but does not

remind you that where there is valuable consideration all is otherwise, because the mere promise for value to create a trust is (except where the Statute of Frauds stands in the way) a promise that can be specifically enforced, and thus it is already, in effect, the creation of a trust. Before passing on, notice the curious doctrine that the issue of a marriage are within the marriage consideration—are not volunteers. This may be important upon the question of enforcing an imperfect gift. Take an agreement in consideration of marriage to convey land to be held in trust for the children of the marriage. No conveyance is made. This agreement is enforceable at the suit of a child. Contrast the position of a child of a previous marriage. It is difficult to say that the child of the marriage gives consideration; and the case should be treated as exceptional; a relic of the time when the doctrine of consideration was not fully thought out. Notice also that a voluntary assignment though by deed and absolute in terms is not enforceable either at law or in equity if the subject-matter is a mere expectancy (*spes successionis*)—*In re Ellenborough* [1903] 1 Ch. 697; a case of voluntary assignment by deed of expectations under the intestacy of relatives of the assignor. But an agreement for value to assign such expectancies is valid and enforceable in equity—see *Tailby* v. *Official Receiver*, 13 App. Cas. 523, where Lord Macnaghten, at p. 543, points out that these, as well as future property and mere possibilities, are assignable for value in equity.[1]

I have said now what I have to say about the creation of trusts by the act of a party. Lewin and other text-writers divide trusts

perfect the release. Then A dies having appointed B his executor. Held that A's property being vested at law in B (as executor) and B's equity arising out of the imperfect release being as good as the equity of the legatees under the Will, the release of the debt is, as against the legatees, made perfect. The same rule applies where an imperfect gift is made to a person who subsequently becomes the donor's executor; *In re Stewart* [1908] 2 Ch. 251.

There is a further minor exception to the general rule in a case where land is conveyed to an infant after 1925. Since 1925 an infant cannot hold a legal estate in land, but by section 27 of the Settled Land Act 1925, a conveyance to an infant, although voluntary, will operate as a contract for valuable consideration to create a settlement on the infant in the proper form and as such can be specifically enforced.

[1] The effect of a promise, voluntary or for consideration, to create trusts is well illustrated by the cases on the Statutes of Limitations discussed on p. 232.

4

thus created into express and implied. It is difficult to draw the line, for since no formal words are necessary for the creation of a trust and since whenever the trust is created by the act of a party there almost of necessity will be some words used—even if a deaf-mute created a trust by 'talking on his fingers' there would be words used—the distinction comes to be one between clear and less clear words, and clearness is a matter of degree. Thus Lewin, under the head of 'Implied Trusts', treats of cases in which a testator creates a trust by such words as 'I desire', 'I request', 'I hope'. No firm line can be drawn—'I desire' is nearly as strong as 'I trust', and 'I trust that he will do this' is almost the same as 'Upon trust that he will do this'. I do not therefore think that the distinction is an important one and very often you will find that the term 'Express Trust' is given to all trusts created by act of a party, *i.e.* by declaration, while 'Implied Trust' stands for what Lewin calls a trust created by act of the law. When studying the law of contract your attention will have been drawn to a very similar, a parallel, ambiguity—sometimes 'Implied Contract' stands for a true contract constituted rather by acts than by words, sometimes it stands for a 'Contract implied by law', or '*Quasi* Contract', an obligation which is no true contract but which is treated for many or most purposes as though it was a contract. Turning now to trusts 'created by operation of law', we might similarly call them '*Quasi* trusts'; but that term is not in use.

The distinction between Express Trusts and trusts that are not Express, is thrust upon our notice by a rule of equity which is often stated thus, namely that to an action based upon the breach of an Express Trust the Statutes of Limitation are no bar.[1] In this context it seems plain that the term Express Trust is used in a different and a larger sense. The cases touching this rule about the Statutes of Limitation (or the protection given by Courts of Equity on the analogy of the Statutes of Limitation) are however intricate and some of them can hardly be reconciled with others. The main recent authority is to be found in the judgments of the Court of Appeal in *Soar* v. *Ashwell* [1893]

---

[1] The question of trusts and the Statute of Limitations is discussed at greater length in the note on p. 227 below.

2 Q.B. 390. There a trust fund was committed by trustees to a solicitor for investment—the solicitor was held not to be entitled to the protection of the Statutes of Limitation—he was held to be an express trustee or for this purpose in the position of an express trustee, either for the trustees of the settlement or for the *cestui que trusts* of the settlement. This is a case worth study if you desire to see the difficulty of drawing the line between express and other trustees. Bowen L.J. in that case said (at p. 397) 'It has been established beyond doubt that a person occupying a fiduciary relation who has property deposited with him on the strength of such relation is to be dealt with as an express and not merely a constructive trustee of such property'. And compare *North American Co.* v. *Watkins* [1904] 1 Ch. 242, where the defendant was held to be an 'express trustee', for this purpose, merely as being an agent with wide discretion to whom the plaintiffs had remitted money to make purchases of prairie lands. The judgment was affirmed in the Court of Appeal, but on another view of the facts—[1904] 2 Ch. 233.

Lewin carries his classification further. Trusts created by operation of law are (1) Resulting, (2) Constructive. 'Resulting trusts may be subdivided thus: (*a*) Where a person being himself both legally and equitably entitled makes a conveyance, devise or bequest of the legal estate and there is no ground for the inference that he meant to dispose of the equitable interest. (*b*) Where a purchaser of property takes a conveyance of the legal estate in the name of a third person, but there is nothing to indicate an intention of not appropriating to himself the beneficial interest.'[1]

1. (*a*) Resulting trusts where there is a disposition of the legal but not of the equitable interest. The general rule is that wherever upon a conveyance, devise or bequest it appears that the grantee, devisee or legatee was intended to take the legal estate merely, the equitable interest, or so much thereof as is left undisposed of, will result, if arising out of the settlor's realty, to himself, or his heir, and if out of his personal estate to himself or his personal representatives.

---

[1] See now Lewin on Trusts, 13th edition, chap. VI.

The intention of excluding the person invested with the legal estate from the enjoyment of the property may be expressed or it may not be expressed. We will deal first with cases in which it is expressed.

I convey land unto and to the use of A and his heirs upon trust, but I declare no trust. Here the use does not result, for a use is declared in favour of A and therefore A gets the legal estate. But I have by the words 'upon trust' declared my intention that A is not to enjoy the land for his own behoof—on the other hand I have not saddled him with any particular trust. Here a trust results for me. So by my will I give all my realty unto and to the use of A and his heirs upon trust and all my personalty unto A upon trust. A trust of the realty will on my death arise for my heir at law, a trust of my personalty for my next of kin. Such cases as these would of course be very rare, for here I am supposing myself to do an extremely foolish thing—to give upon trust, and declare no trust at all. But it is an extremely common thing that I should give upon trust and then declare trusts which do not exhaust all the interest that I have given to my trustee. Thus by will I give all my property to a trustee absolutely upon trust to pay the rents and income to my wife for life and I omit to say what is to be done after my wife's death—here, subject to my wife's life interest, there will be a resulting trust for my heir or next of kin. Still commoner is it that a testator gives his property upon trust, declares trusts which in certain events would exhaust the beneficial interest, but owing to some events that he has not foreseen, premature deaths or the like, some of these trusts fail—then the interest undisposed of will result. So again it is not uncommon that a testator should in declaring trusts contravene some rule of law, attempt to do what the law will not suffer him to do, for example he tries to infringe the rule against perpetuities. Here some of his trusts will fail and the beneficial interest that is thus set free will result —will result to his heir or next of kin, or will pass to other persons under a residuary devise or bequest. At all events a person who has been declared a trustee of the whole interest given him can not—unless indeed he happens himself to be heir or next of kin to the testator—claim any beneficial interest. Lewin lays down the rule thus: 'Where a trust results to the settlor or his representatives not by presumption of law but by force of the written instrument, the trustee is not at liberty to defeat the resulting trust by the production of extrinsic evidence by parol.'[1] I devise land unto and to the use of A and his heirs upon certain trusts. These trusts fail in my lifetime, A will not be allowed to produce witnesses to show that I meant him to enjoy the land in case the trusts failed. I have made A a trustee for somebody, and a trustee he must be—if for no one else then for me or my representatives.

We pass to the cases in which there is no expressed declaration of intention that A, the grantee, devisee, legatee shall be a trustee. Well, if by will I give to A and declare no intention of making him a trustee, then he is not a trustee; and if *inter vivos* and for valuable consideration I convey or assign to A so as to vest the legal estate or interest in him and declare no intention of making him a trustee, then a trustee he is not. But otherwise is it of a voluntary conveyance or assignment *inter vivos*. For no valuable consideration I convey land unto and to the use of A and his heirs. Here the use does not result, for a use has been declared in A's favour, so A gets the legal estate—but in analogy to the law of resulting uses, the Court of Chancery has raised up a doctrine of resulting trusts. If without value by act *inter vivos* I pass the legal estate or legal rights to A and declare no trust, the general presumption is that I do not intend to benefit A and that A is to be a trustee for me.[2] However this is only a presumption in the proper sense of that term and it may be rebutted by evidence of my intention. You see the difference between this case and the one lately put—if I convey to A 'upon trust' and

[1] 13th edition, p. 165.

[2] This is a point on which there has been much diversity of opinion. The authorities on the point will be found in White and Tudor L.C. vol. II, p. 762 (9th edition). In regard to voluntary conveyances of land made after 1925 it would appear to be settled by section 60 (3) of the Law of Property Act 1925, that no resulting trust for the grantor is implied. It appears also to be settled that on a voluntary transfer of stock by A into the joint names of A and B a resulting trust in favour of A will be implied (*Standing* v. *Bowring*, 31 Ch. D. 282, 287). Apart from these two cases the law remains doubtful. In practice however there will nearly always be evidence of the transferor's intention and the matter is not likely to rest on a bare presumption of law.

declare no trust, A can not produce evidence that I did not mean to make him trustee—but if there is no talk of trust at all in the instrument which gives A his legal rights, then he may produce evidence to show that I really intended him to enjoy the property.

Such is the general rule—upon a voluntary conveyance *inter vivos* the presumption is that a trust results for the giver. But then we have a sub-rule. Upon a voluntary conveyance to a wife or child the presumption is the other way—the presumption is, to use a common phrase, that there is an 'advancement', a real benefit intended for wife or child.[1] You will remember the parallel doctrine about resulting uses—blood relationship it is said is consideration enough for a use. In this case however we have merely a presumption. If I convey land unto and to the use of my son, the presumption is that I intend that he shall enjoy the land, and that no trust results in my favour; but this presumption may be rebutted.

1. (*b*) We must now take up the second class of resulting trusts. The cases with which we have as yet been dealing are cases in which there is a gift and the question is whether the donee takes beneficially or merely as a trustee. We now turn to cases in which a person buys something but the conveyance of it is at his instance made not to him but to some one else—cases of 'purchases in the name of third persons'. I buy a fee simple estate, and I say to the vendor 'I want you to convey it not to me but to X'—so he conveys the land unto and to the use of X.

Now here equity has drawn a distinction turning on the relationship which exists between me and X. Briefly stated the rule is this—that if X is my wife or my child the presumption is that I intend a benefit for X and therefore that there is no

---

[1] See for example *Batstone* v. *Salter*, L.R. 10 Ch. 431, where a lady transferred stock into the joint names of herself, her daughter and her daughter's husband and continued to receive the income on the stock until her death. Held that the daughter's husband, who survived the other two, took the stock absolutely and not subject to a resulting trust. The decision might be different at the present day so far as concerns the daughter's husband since, as a result of the Married Women's Property Acts, it is not now necessary, as it then was, that a transfer intended to benefit the daughter should be made in the name of her husband as well as herself.

resulting trust for me, though this presumption may be rebutted by parol evidence—on the other hand if X is a stranger there is a presumption, though a rebuttable presumption, that I do not intend to benefit him but intend that he shall hold as a trustee for me.

As regards strangers, Eyre C.B. stated the rule thus: 'The clear result of all the cases, without a single exception, is that the trust of a legal estate whether freehold, copyhold, or leasehold, whether taken in the names of the purchaser and others jointly, or in the name of others without that of the purchaser, whether in one name or several, whether jointly or successive, results to the man who advances the purchase money; and it goes on a strict analogy to the rule of the common law, that where a feoffment is made without consideration the use results to the feoffer' (*Dyer* v. *Dyer*, 2 Cox. 92).[1]

A special application of this is that if A and B join in purchasing an estate and the estate is conveyed to them and their heirs (which makes them in law joint tenants of it) then there is no presumption against their being joint tenants in equity as well as at law. It may be shown that they did not intend to become joint tenants of the beneficial interest, and in particular if they be partners buying land for the business of their firm, they are, in the absence of proof to the contrary, accounted to be tenants in common—*jus accrescendi inter mercatores locum non habet*. Still in general if two men pay the purchase money in equal shares there is no presumption that they intend to be other than what the conveyance will make them, namely joint tenants. But suppose that A finds two-thirds and B one-third of the purchase money then, although the conveyance makes them joint tenants in law, a trust arises. A and B as joint tenants hold in trust for A and B as tenants in common, as to two undivided thirds for A, and as to the residue for B.

But the presumption is turned the other way round where a purchase is made in the name of the purchaser's wife or child. Here the presumption is in favour of a benefit, 'an advancement' it is often called. This rule has been extended to the case of an

---

[1] It is well settled that the rule in *Dyer* v. *Dyer* applies also to personalty, see *e.g. The Venture* [1908] P. 218.

illegitimate child. Apparently it is somewhat wider, but it is usually spoken of as applying only to wife and child.[1]

Whichever way the presumption may be it is rebuttable. In the case of the stranger you may prove that a benefit to him was intended; in the case of wife or child you may prove that benefit was not intended, and this by oral evidence of the purchaser's acts and declarations. This is so even in the case of land and other hereditaments. The 7th section of the Statute of Frauds which says that a declaration of trusts of any hereditaments must be manifested and proved by signed writing, is followed by the 8th which says that this is not to apply to trusts which result by implication or construction of law. So no written declaration by the purchaser is necessary either to prove or to disprove the trusts with which we are now dealing.

2. We turn now to Constructive trusts. Under this head Mr Lewin treats of but one grand rule. It is this: that wherever a person clothed with a fiduciary character gains some personal advantage by availing himself of his situation as a trustee, he becomes a trustee of the advantage so gained. The common illustration of this is the renewal by a trustee of a lease that he holds on trust. A leaseholder, in the leading case *Keech* v. *Sandford*, White and Tudor, vol. II, p. 648 (9th edition), bequeathed a leasehold to a trustee for an infant. The lease was running out. The trustee, doing his duty, asked that it might be renewed; this application was refused; the landlord did not want an infant tenant. The trustee then obtained a new lease in his own name. It was held that this new lease must be held upon trust for the infant. Lord King said 'I very well see that if a trustee on the refusal to renew might have a lease to himself, few trust estates would be renewed to a *cestui que use*. This may seem hard that the trustee is the only person of all mankind who might not have the lease; but it is very proper that the rule should be strictly pursued and not in the least relaxed.' You see how far the doctrine goes. The landlord was under no duty to

---

[1] The extent of the rule is far from clear. One would expect that the presumption of advancement would exist whenever the purchaser stood 'in loco parentis' to the nominee (cf. the presumption against double portions, p. 240 below). This view was however rejected in *Tucker* v. *Burrow*, 2 H. and M. 515, where the earlier authorities are given.

renew this lease and neither the trustee nor his *cestui que trust* had any right to demand its renewal—but an old tenant has, if I may so speak, a sort of goodwill with his landlord. If a trustee has this advantage, even though the trust does not bind him to use it, still if he does use it he must use it for his *cestui que trust* and not for himself. But though this is a good illustration of the rule you must not suppose that it relates only to the renewal of leaseholds—far from it, if by reason of his position that trustee acquires any advantage of a valuable kind, he must hold it upon trust, he is constructively a trustee of it.

The rule includes persons who are not trustees properly so called, but all those who stand in what is called a fiduciary position. My land-agent, for instance, is not a trustee for me, for he holds no rights, no property, upon trust for me; but if he takes advantage of his position as my agent to get some benefit from a third person then he is a trustee of that benefit for me. I am not here speaking of cases of dishonesty which may come within the cognizance even of a court of law and give rise to an action of fraud—but it is a general principle of equity that if an agent acquire any pecuniary advantage to himself from third parties by means of his fiduciary character, he is accountable to his employer as a trustee for the profit that he has made. A good example of this is the following—A was a landowner, B was his attorney and also his heir presumptive; A had made a will in favour of C; A then contracted to sell part of his land; B advised that in order to carry out this contract A should levy a fine of the whole of his land; the effect of levying a fine was to revoke A's will. It was held that after A's death B, who as heir became entitled at law to such part of A's land as had not been sold, must hold it upon trust for C the devisee who had been disappointed by the advice which B had given to A. 'You,' said Lord Eldon, 'whether you meant fraud, whether you knew that you were the heir at law of the testator or not, you who have been wanting in what I conceive to be the duty of an attorney, if it happens that you get an advantage by that neglect, you shall not hold that advantage, but you shall be a trustee of the property for the benefit of that person who would have been entitled to it if you had known what as an attorney you ought to have known, and not knowing it you shall not take advantage of your own ignorance.' *Bulkley* v. *Wilford*, 2 Cl. and F. 102, at p. 177. And the scope of this doctrine is very fully explained in the judgment of Romer L.J. *In re Biss* [1903] 2 Ch. 40.[1]

But the doctrine of constructive trusts is really a very wide one. It constantly operates in cases which we are apt to think of as being otherwise explained. Put this case—T holds land in fee simple upon trust for S in fee simple; T in breach of trust sells and conveys the land to X; X at the time of the sale knew of the trust. Now of course we hold that S's rights as *cestui que trust* have not been destroyed by this sale and conveyance—they are valid against X. But why? You may perhaps say because S was in equity the owner, tenant in fee simple, of the land. That is one way of putting it, but as we shall see hereafter a somewhat dangerous way, for it may suggest that S's equitable rights are rights *in rem*, rights which cannot possibly be destroyed by any dealing that takes place between T and other persons. The more correct and the safer way of stating the matter is that X having bought and obtained a conveyance of the subject-matter of the trust knowing that the trust exists is made a trustee for S. The result would have been the same if X though he did not actually know of the trust for S ought, in the opinion of a court of equity, to have known about it; in this case also X though he obtains the legal estate by conveyance from T becomes a trustee for S. What is meant by this phrase that X 'ought in the opinion of a court of equity to have known of the trust' I shall endeavour to explain on another occasion. Here I am only concerned to point

[1] See, for recent instances, *Griffith* v. *Owen* [1907] 1 Ch. 195 and *Lloyd-Jones* v. *Clark-Lloyd* [1919] 1 Ch. 424. As is explained in *In re Biss*, there are really two different rules involved. First there is a very strict rule that no trustee or person in a fiduciary position can make a profit out of the trust; as to the persons who come within this rule see the note on p. 227 below. Secondly, there is a rule applicable both to trustees and to many persons who do not stand in a fiduciary position—*e.g.* tenants for life, joint tenants, mortgagees and partners—that in certain circumstances property acquired by such person is to be deemed an accretion to the property in which he has a partial interest. Thus in the case of renewals of leases by tenants for life the principle is that 'the renewal must be looked upon as an accretion to or graft upon the original term arising out of the goodwill or quasi-tenant right annexed thereto and that their rights to such accretion are those which they have in the term and no greater and terminate with their own life'. This rule is less strict than that applicable to trustees.

out that though a trust may have been created expressly and by way of contract, the person, or one of the persons, against whom we see it enforced has never consented to become a trustee. In the cases that I have just put, X does not consent to become a trustee for S; on the contrary his hope has been that he will be allowed to enjoy as beneficial owner the land that he has purchased from T. If then he is made a trustee this is not because he has agreed or consented to become one, but the result is produced by some rule of equity which, will he, nill he, makes him a trustee.

The rules of equity to which I refer might I think be stated thus—Any one who comes to the legal estate or legal ownership as the representative (heir, devisee, executor or administrator) of a trustee, or who comes to it by virtue of a voluntary gift made by a trustee, or who comes to it with notice of the trust, or who comes to it in such circumstances that he ought to have had notice of the trust, is a trustee. It is not usual in such a case to call the trust a constructive one, still I want you to see that the man in question gets bound by a trust without desiring to become a trustee and even although he has every wish to escape such an obligation. Put a simple case, T is trustee in fee simple for A in fee simple; T dies; formerly (as I shall explain next time) the legal estate would have descended to T's heir or passed under his will to a devisee, now-a-days it will pass to T's executor or administrator, his personal representative. Now the personal representative, Q let us call him, is undoubtedly bound by the trust. Why so? Because he has consented to accept it. No; it is very possible that when he proved T's will or took out letters of administration to T's estate he knew absolutely nothing of the trust. Still he is bound by it. Why is he bound? Because he comes to it as the trustee's representative.

Now it is usual and I think very proper to deal with the rules about this matter in a context other than the present. They come in answer to the question 'What are the nature of the *cestui que trust's* rights—against what persons or classes of persons can these equitable rights be enforced?' Still I want you to see that really they might also be treated from our present point of view. If you are going to enforce the rights of a *cestui que trust* against any person, X, you must be prepared to show that in one way or another X has become a trustee for that *cestui que trust*. That is why you cannot enforce the trust against the *bona fide* purchaser for value who has no notice, express or implied, of the trust, and who obtains the legal estate. Still I must admit that these rules will come in better when we are considering the nature of the rights of the *cestui que trust*. They presuppose that somehow or another a trust has been validly created, and they deal with the question who, when such a trust has once been created, is bound by it. In the present lecture and previous lectures we have been discussing the original nature of the trust—How does a trust first come into being? The further question 'Who is bound by it?' still remains open.

LECTURE VII

THE RIGHTS AND DUTIES OF TRUSTEES

This morning we are to speak very briefly of the rights and duties of a trustee.

1. (a) Of his rights. It is common to speak of the trustee's rights as though they were always legal rights, but of course this is not always the case. For example S is tenant in fee simple, but his estate is subject to a mortgage; on his marriage he makes a settlement; or conveys what he has to convey unto and to the use of T and T'. Now S had no legal estate—the legal estate is in the mortgagee—what therefore he conveys to trustees cannot be the legal estate, but is a merely equitable estate.[1] So also it is common enough to find, if I may so speak, one settlement behind another. Under the marriage settlement of my father and mother I am entitled to one-third share of certain stocks held by T and T', the trustees of that settlement, but my interest is subject to the life interests of my parents. I am going to marry, I assign what I can assign to U and V upon trusts for myself, my wife and children. Here, of course, the trustees of this second settlement, this sub-settlement, do not at law become entitled to my share of the trust fund. My rights are merely equitable rights, and what I assign to U and V are equitable rights. When my father and mother are both dead then it will be the duty of my trustees, U and V, to make themselves the legal owners of my third share; they must call upon T and T' to pay cash or transfer stock to them to the amount of one-third of the fund; but so long as either my father or my mother lives the rights of my trustees must be merely equitable. Therefore do not say that a trustee holds the legal estate of land or the legal interest in personalty. This may or may not be the case.[2]

*   *   *   *   *   *

[1] This of course refers to the position of the mortgagor before 1926.

[2] The 1st edition here contained a discussion of the devolution of a trust estate on the death of the trustee. The questions discussed cannot now arise except in connexion with old titles. The following is a summary of the old law:

(1) If one of several trustees died no difficulty would in general arise. The

(*b*) I have been speaking of the devolution of the trust estate on the death of a trustee. But during his lifetime the trustee can pass his rights to another. I shall have much more to say of this matter hereafter when we are considering the nature of the rights of a *cestui que trust*. But let us put a simple case. T holds

trustees would be joint tenants and on the death of one the trust property would remain vested in the survivors.

(2) When however a sole or last surviving trustee died difficulties arose. Apart from statute law the legal estate in the trust property would devolve on the death of the trustee in the same way as the trustee's own property. So far as the trust property was personalty it would pass to the personal representatives of the trustee. So far as it was land it would pass to the person to whom it was devised by his will, or, if he had died intestate or had not devised the particular land by his will, it would pass to his heir-at-law or in the case of copyholds his customary heir.

(3) The heir-at-law might be an infant or a married woman or there might be a number of co-heiresses who would take as co-parceners. In such cases there would be difficulty in selling the trust property. There might also be difficulty in knowing whether a general residuary devise in which the trust estates were not specifically mentioned, did or did not carry the trust estates.

(4) To avoid such difficulties it became the custom for a testator to include in his will an express devise of all property which he held as trustee (or mortgagee) to his personal representatives.

(5) To meet this situation statute law was enacted. Passing by section 5 of the Vendor and Purchaser Act 1874 (which was repealed in the following year) and section 48 of the Land Transfer Act 1875 (which was repealed in 1881), we come to section 30 of the Conveyancing Act 1881. That section provided that freehold land vested in a sole trustee should pass on his death to his personal representatives as though it had been a chattel real and this notwithstanding any devise of the trust property. Since 1881 such a devise is wholly inoperative as regards freeholds. The Act did not however apply to copyholds, as regards which the common law position remained until 1925.

(6) The person on whom the trust property devolved, whether the personal representative, heir-at-law or devisee, would be bound by the trust to this extent, that he could not deal with the property in breach of trust. It did not however follow that he could exercise the powers and discretions given to the trustees. His duty was primarily to hold the trust property until new trustees were appointed and then to transfer it to them. This however was an inconvenient position and a well drawn trust instrument would provide that all the powers and discretions of the trustees should be exercisable by the trustees for the time being and the personal representatives of the last surviving trustee.

(7) Since 1925 the position is as follows: Copyholds are of course abolished. On the death of a sole or last surviving trustee all the trust property, whether land or personalty, devolves upon his personal representatives. The personal representatives have power to appoint new trustees, unless there is some other person having power to do so (Trustee Act 1925, s. 36), and until a new trustee is appointed the personal representatives can exercise all the powers conferred by the trust instrument or by law on the trustees (Trustee Act 1925, s. 18).

land in fee simple upon trust for S in fee simple; T has the legal estate. Now T is fully capable of conveying that legal estate *inter vivos*; of doing this voluntarily, or doing it for valuable consideration; of doing this in accordance with the trust, or doing it in breach of the trust. We will suppose that he does it in breach of trust. He conveys the land unto and to the use of X and his heirs either gratuitously or for value. Now this is not a nugatory act. It does pass legal rights to X; the legal rights which T had have passed to X. T has committed a breach of trust, and will be liable for all harm that follows. In many—though in by no means all—cases X will have to hold that land subject to the trust. But still we cannot possibly treat this case as though nothing had been done, or as though T had merely attempted to convey away what did not belong to him. He has conveyed away what did at law belong to him, and this conveyance may have the most important results. Of those results I shall speak at another time. But I want you to distinguish two different questions—(1) Has the trustee conveyed away the estate that was vested in him? (2) Was he committing a breach of trust in so doing? Sometimes we muddle up these two questions by our use of the word 'can'. If T is holding land simply in trust for S, in one sense he *can not* sell and convey it without the consent of S—that is to say by selling and conveying it he will be guilty of a breach of trust. But in another and a more exact sense he can sell and convey it, and the sale and conveyance will not be nugatory. A man can do many things that it is unlawful for him to do, and a man can do lawfully (in the narrower sense of that word) many things that equity forbids him to do. At law the trustee has all those powers of alienating *inter vivos*, mortgaging and so forth, that he would have were there no trust in existence.[1]

An attempt to speak briefly of the duties of trustees is something like an attempt to speak briefly of the duties of contractors. In the case of contract one has to content oneself with saying very little more than that the contractor must fulfil his contract, or else one must go through all the various kinds of contract, sale, lease, mortgage, loan, bill of lading, charter party

[1] See *e.g. Boursot* v. *Savage*, L.R. 2 Eq. 134.

and so forth. In the case of trusts the difficulty is almost greater, for imperfect as must be any classification of all the contracts which our English law enables men to make, our classification of trusts is likely to be yet more imperfect. Within very large limits, such as are set by the rule against perpetuities, and the rules laid down by the Thellusson Act, and again by somewhat vaguer rules which condemn immoral trusts and trusts contrary to public policy, a man may create what trusts he pleases. Settlors make a very large use of this liberty, and the consequence is that trusts are almost infinitely various. We can do no more than notice a few very general rules, and notice further that even these few are for the more part but rules of construction, rules which will easily give way if the testator has expressed any intention contrary to them.

In the case of private trusts our law and our equity does not recognize any power in the majority of a body of trustees to bind a minority. Thus suppose that a testator has devised his land to trustees upon trust to sell: they all must join in the conveyance—a majority of them can not pass the estate that is vested in them all. But further, in equity a trustee can not shelter himself by saying that he was outvoted, that though he consented to the sale and took part in the conveyance, he was not satisfied with the price, but gave way to a majority. So let the question be about a change in the investment of a trust fund—the change can not be made unless all the trustees consent, and if it be a breach of trust no one of them will be able to say that he was bound by a resolution of the majority. Of course, however, a settlor may give power to a majority, but in the case of private trusts this is but seldom done.

The case of co-trustees is different from the case of co-executors. Each executor taken singly has a very large power of administering the personal estate of his testator, collecting debts, giving valid receipts, selling and assigning portions of the estate. On the other hand, unless the settlor has said something very unusual, one out of several co-trustees has no similar powers. Therefore, *e.g.*, in paying money that is due to trustees you should obtain a receipt from them all.

It is a very general rule that the office of trustee can not be delegated. Trustees can not shift their duties on to the shoulders of others; if they purport to do this they still remain trustees and are liable as such. If a trustee confides the application of a trust fund to another, whether that other be one of his co-trustees or a stranger, he will be personally answerable for any loss that ensues. Of course there is a great difference between attempting to delegate a trust and obtaining professional help in the exercise of a trust, the help for example of a solicitor or counsel or of a broker, banker, land-agent, valuer, auctioneer. As regards the obtaining of such professional assistance the only general rule is that, in the absence of an expressed intention to the contrary, a trustee may obtain such assistance wherever, regard being had to the ordinary course of business, it is reasonably necessary that he should do so. And he may pay for it, what it is reasonably necessary that he should pay, out of the trust property. It is even reasonably necessary in some cases that the trustee should allow trust property to come under the control of agents thus appointed. In this respect, however, the Court of Chancery has not dealt very liberally with trustees; for example, a trustee for sale was not in general justified in directing that the purchase money should be paid to a solicitor. The Trustee Act 1888, s. 1, now the Trustee Act 1893, s. 17, has made a considerable difference in this respect.[1] In some cases it empowers a trustee to direct that payment shall be made to a solicitor or to a banker. I must

[1] These sections are now replaced by section 23 of the Trustee Act 1925. Under that section trustees are authorized (briefly):

(a) To employ professional agents such as solicitors, bankers and stock-brokers and to allow them to receive and pay money.

(b) To employ agents for conducting the affairs of the trust in regard to property outside the United Kingdom.

(c) To allow a solicitor and in some cases a banker to have custody of documents against delivery of which money is to be handed over (*e.g.* a deed conveying land) for the purpose of collecting the money.

In none of the above cases is the trustee liable if the agent defaults unless for some further reason. He may become liable if he leaves money unduly long in the hands of the agent or presumably if he is negligent in choosing the agent. On the general effect of section 23 see *In re Vickery* [1931] 1 Ch. 572.

Under section 25 of the Trustee Act 1925, a trustee who intends to go abroad for more than a month is empowered (subject to certain restrictions) to appoint an attorney to act for him in the matter of the trust, but in this case he will be liable for all breaches of trust committed by his attorney.

not speak in detail about this matter, but on the whole the rule that a trustee cannot delegate his office, even to a co-trustee, has been rigorously maintained. To justify a partial delegation there must, said Lord Hardwicke, be a case of necessity, physical necessity or moral necessity. 'Moral necessity' he added 'is from the usage of mankind, if the trustee acts as prudently for the trust as he would have done for himself and according to the usage of business.' (*Ex p. Belchier*, Amb. 219.) This matter has been very fully discussed of late in the great case of *Speight* v. *Gaunt* (9 App. Cas. 1) before the House of Lords. That house there held that a trustee had been justified in employing a stock-broker and in paying large sums of trust money to him which he was to invest, and which he untruly purported to have invested in the purchase of stock. I will read a few sentences from the judgment to the same effect that was delivered in the Court of Appeal by Bowen L.J., 22 Ch. D. at p. 762.

'Now with regard to the law it is clear that a trustee is only bound to conduct the business of the trust in such a way as an ordinary prudent man of business would conduct his own.... A trustee cannot, as everybody admits, delegate his trust. If confidence has been reposed in him by a dead man he cannot throw upon the shoulders of somebody else that which has been placed upon his own shoulders. On the other hand, in the administration of a trust a trustee cannot do everything for himself, he must to a certain extent make use of the arms, legs, eyes and hands of other persons, and the limit within which it seems to me he is confined has been described throughout, both in the cases which have been referred to and the judgments which have preceded me, to be this: that a trustee may follow the ordinary course of business, provided that he run no need-less risk in doing so.' So far Bowen L.J. There should be no needless risk run. Now if a man has to purchase stock he must almost of necessity employ a stockbroker and pay the price to that stockbroker. The Court of Appeal and the House of Lords held that a trustee in doing this was following the ordinary course of business, and was running no needless risk.

Compare the case of *In re De Pothonier* [1900] 2 Ch. 529, where securities with coupons attached, and payable to bearer, were deposited with a banker in order that he might detach the coupons and thus collect the interest as it fell due, and this was held to be justified.[1]

A trustee is not entitled to any remuneration. He is allowed his expenses out of pocket. He may charge against the trust estate all costs, charges and expenses which have been reasonably incurred; thus, *e.g.*, he may charge his travelling expenses if reasonably incurred. He is generally entitled to employ a solicitor for any legal business, such as that which solicitors usually perform.[2] Costs, charges and expenses, those properly incurred, become as against the *cestui que trust* a first charge on the trust property. On the other hand, a trustee is allowed nothing for his trouble unless the creator of the trust has thought fit to say something to the contrary. Even though the trustee be a solicitor he will not be allowed to charge anything for his time and trouble. Of course, however, a settlor may arrange the matter otherwise, and it seems that a person before he accepts the office of trustee may bargain with the *cestui que trust* and say 'I will not be a trustee unless you agree to pay me a salary', but such bargains are closely scrutinized by the Court, and may somewhat easily be brought under the head of undue influence. But normally the trustee can claim nothing for his pains.[3]

A trustee must not profit by the trust. This rule includes that which we have just been stating but it goes much further. If the trustee gets any valuable advantage, any property, by reason of his office, that becomes part of the trust property. We may treat

---

[1] Note that since 1926 a trustee who invests in bearer securities not only can but in general must deposit them at a bank: Trustee Act 1925, s. 7.

[2] See now Trustee Act 1925, s. 23.

[3] The following are the cases in which a trustee can obtain remuneration:

(*a*) Where the terms of the trust so provide.

(*b*) Where all the *cestuis que trust* are *sui juris* and agree to his being remunerated.

(*c*) Where the Court authorizes him to charge, which it will do in certain cases, *e.g.* when the trust is unusually burdensome (*In re Freeman*, 37 Ch. D. 148) or where the Court is appointing a trust corporation to be trustee.

(*d*) The Public Trustee is authorized by the Public Trustee Act, 1906, to charge.

(*e*) A solicitor can obtain his profit costs when he acts in litigation on behalf of himself and his co-trustees except in so far as the costs are increased by his being a party: *Cradock* v. *Piper*, 1 Mac. and G. 664, *In re Corsellis*, 34 Ch. D. 675.

as an offshoot of this general principle the important rule that a trustee is absolutely disqualified from purchasing the trust property—even though it be by public auction. This is an absolute rule, it does not say merely that if the trustee gives less for the property than might otherwise have been obtained, he must pay the full value of what he bought and not merely the price that he agreed to pay for it; it says that however fair, however advantageous to the *cestui que trust* the purchase may be, the *cestui que trust* is at liberty to set it aside and take back the property. The trustee may not buy the trust property from himself on his own behalf; nor may he buy it as the agent of another person. On the other hand, a trustee may sometimes buy the trust property from his *cestui que trust*—buy that is the beneficial interest. There is no absolute rule against this. But equity requires in this case that the *cestui que trust* should fully understand that he is selling to the trustee and that the trustee should make a full disclosure of all that he knows about matters which affect the value of the property. Purchases by the trustee from the *cestui que trust* are not forbidden; but they are closely watched and the trustee may be called upon to show the utmost good faith. The ground of this rule is obvious—the trustee has had an opportunity of knowing, and it is his duty to know all the circumstances affecting the value of the property.

THE DUTIES OF TRUSTEES[1]

I AM speaking of the duties of trustees. So various are trusts that the only general rules that we can lay down about them are few and very general.

(i) A trustee is bound to do anything that he is expressly bidden to do by the instrument creating the trust. (ii) A trustee may safely do anything that he is expressly authorized to do by that instrument. (iii) A trustee is bound to refrain from doing anything that is expressly forbidden by that instrument (of course I am supposing that the provisions of the instrument in question are in no wise invalid or unlawful). Within these limits a trustee must (iv) play the part of a prudent owner and a prudent man of business. That is the standard by which his conduct will be judged. We can say little more without descending to particulars. When we get down to particulars, when we come to trusts of this class or that class, then we are likely to find some more specific rules. You will remember that in the development of equitable rules trial by jury has played no part. Consequently Equity has taken, if I may so speak, a somewhat different shape from that which has been assumed by some portions of our Common Law, notably the law of torts. In the law of torts there is constant reference to an ideal standard of conduct, the conduct of the man of average prudence and intelligence; but this man, we may say, is represented by the jury. Often enough a judge has to say 'Gentlemen, it is not for me to say whether the defendant acted negligently or whether he behaved as a prudent man would behave—I must leave that to you.' The verdicts which jurors give in answer to this question are no precedents. On the other hand, a judge in the Court of Chancery sitting alone has had to decide every question whether of fact or of law. He has not been able to escape the duty of deciding that a trustee in doing this or

[1] The various Acts relating to trustees which are referred to in this chapter are now repealed and replaced by the Trustee Act 1925. Reference is made in footnotes to the main alterations introduced by the 1925 Act.

that—let us say in paying trust money to a stockbroker for investment—was or was not acting as a prudent man of business would have acted. His decision is reported and it becomes a precedent. In the next case of a similar kind counsel will argue that the point is covered by authority. And so many rules about the conduct of the prudent man of business get established. Still they are somewhat dependent rules, and you will find that generally they are not hard and fast rules—they will admit of exceptions. A judge will say from time to time 'That is a sound general rule, but after all it must give way before the yet more general one that a trustee acting within the terms of his trust may do what would be done by a prudent man of business, and in the circumstances of this particular case I think that the minor rule might be disregarded.'

As is well observed by Mr Strahan in his *Digest*: 'To cite authorities, as is often done, to show what amounts to reasonable care, prudence, or intelligence, is, it is submitted, a misleading and dangerous practice. It is an attempt to decide a point of fact, not by evidence but by authority, and tends to the establishment of a doctrine of "constructive" want of care, etc., similar to the venerable but exploded doctrine of "constructive" fraud.'[1]

I will try to illustrate this matter by reference to one class of trusts—a very common class—trusts for investment. Almost every settlement throws upon the trustees the duty of investing money. And even if there is no express declaration that money is to be invested still it is a general rule that if trustees have money in their hands and are not bound at once to apply it in some other way, *e.g.* in paying it over to the beneficiaries, they ought to invest it and so make it profitable; if they retain it uninvested for a longer time than is reasonable then this will be a breach of trust.

Now we may start with our paramount rules. A trustee is bound to do what he is expressly bidden to do by the terms of the trust, supposing that to be lawful and possible. He is told to invest the fund in government securities. Subject to the provisions of certain Acts of Parliament which I shall mention by and by, he

---

[1] Strahan and Kenrick, *Digest*, at p. 94.

is bound to do this. He may safely do what he is expressly authorized to do. He is, for example, authorized to make investments of a highly hazardous nature such as prudent men do not ordinarily make—he may do it. He is authorized to lend the trust fund to one of the *cestui que trusts* taking merely a promissory note—well, lending money without taking security is of course hazardous; still he has been told that he may do it, and do it he may. He may not do what he has been expressly forbidden to do. The testator had a capricious and unreasonable dislike to some of the very safest securities, and he expressly prohibited any investment in them. This prohibition binds the trustee; if he invests upon those prohibited securities he will be answerable for any loss that occurs. Within the limits thus laid down, the rule is that the trustee must act like a prudent man of business.

Long ago however the Court of Chancery came to an opinion as to what the prudent investor does. He invests in the three per cent. Consolidated Bank Annuities. This became the rule. In the absence of express powers created by the settlement trustees ought to invest in these Annuities. There was at one time some doubt about mortgages of real estate, but I believe that the better, certainly the safer, opinion was that a trustee not expressly empowered to do so should not invest in these. The one investment open to him was the three per cent. Consols. When this doctrine was established the number of possible investments was very small. In course of time many new modes came into being, and almost every will or settlement contained a long clause giving the trustee a choice of investments, sometimes a narrow, sometimes a very wide choice. Then Parliament began to interfere, to say by statute that trustees unless expressly forbidden so to do might invest in this way or in that. I think that we are absolved from discussing these statutes for in 1889 a very comprehensive Act was passed, the Trust Investment Act of 1889, which was made applicable even to existing trusts. This Act is now replaced by the Trustee Act of 1893. Section 1 of the Act of 1893 says: 'A trustee may, unless expressly forbidden by the instrument (if any) creating the trust invest any trust funds in his hands in'—one of fifteen different ways. I will not read the

long list of permissible investments. It is a liberal list and the
Colonial Stock Act of 1900 adds yet another class to that list.[1]
On the whole I should imagine that prudent settlors will hardly
desire to give their trustees a wider choice; indeed I think it
possible that they will be concerned rather to restrict than to
enlarge the power of selection that the law gives to trustees.
And this you will observe they can do; the statute does not
interfere with our rule that a trustee must not do what he is
forbidden to do by the instrument of trust.

But now I would have you observe that these statutes merely
extend the number of the modes of investment which shall not
be unlawful for trustees. They do not say that a trustee may
safely invest in any security which can be brought under one of
the fifteen or sixteen heads. Thus, to take one example, the
Consolidated Stock of the London County Council is included.
Now suppose a trustee acting under an instrument which tells
him to invest in Consols, but does not expressly forbid him to
invest in stock of the London County Council. If he invests in
the latter this mere fact standing by itself will not be a breach of
trust; still in the circumstances of some particular case such an
investment may be a breach of trust. Suppose it notorious that
this stock is becoming worthless, the statute would not save a
trustee who invested in it. Within the limits of what is authorized
the trustee must act prudently.

This is best seen in the case of an investment upon what are
called real securities. In trust deeds and wills it has been very
usual to say that the trustees may invest upon real securities in
England or Wales. And now in the list of securities authorized
by the Acts of 1889 and 1893 we find 'real or heritable securities
in Great Britain or Ireland'.[2] But the Court has long ago come

---

[1] The statutory list of investments is now contained in section 1 of the
Trustee Act 1925, which includes a few more investments than the previous
Act. It is perhaps more common nowadays than in Maitland's time for the
settlor to insert a wider power of investment and it is rare to find the statutory
power restricted.

[2] Now: 'real or heritable securities in the United Kingdom' (which does
not include the Irish Free State). A power to invest in 'real securities' allows
the trustee to invest on a mortgage of freehold land, but does not permit the
actual purchase of land. Mortgages of leaseholds are not in general 'real
securities' but in certain cases are permitted by section 5 (1) of the Trustee
Act 1925.

to a doctrine about the liberty given to trustees by such a phrase as this. Thus it has established a rule about the amount of money that should be advanced on a mortgage. Trustees should not, it is generally said, advance more than two-thirds of the actual value of the estate if it be freehold land—*i.e.* if it be an agricultural estate, nor more than one-half if it be freehold house property. This rule is not applied with strict arithmetical rigour, but it is supposed to formulate pretty accurately the limit that prudence sets. Then again the trustee who is lending money on mortgage ought to insist upon having a valuation made by some expert, some independent expert—that is some one who is acting for him and not for the mortgagor. Then again a trustee should not lend upon a second mortgage. For a reason which I hope to give on another occasion second mortgages are never very safe. I do not know that this is a quite absolute rule, that the mere fact of lending on second mortgage is of itself a breach of trust, but undoubtedly the trustee who lends on such a mortgage ought to be able to show some very special reason for doing so. And thus about investments on 'real securities' we have a whole group of rules; some of them more stringent, some of them less stringent, but all of them pointing to this, that even though the trust deed or the Act of Parliament authorizes the trustee to choose a security of this class, he is bound to take all reasonable precautions before he lends money upon mortgage. Now this is dealt with by the Trustee Act 1893, s. 8,[1] which protects the trustee against several of his former risks, and in particular where he has advanced to the extent of not more than two-thirds of a valuation made for him by a competent surveyor or valuer.

I will choose one other illustration of the law's dealings with trustees. This also has been affected by recent statutes. Often enough a trustee is under the duty of selling land. Often enough this duty was a very difficult one. Before he offered the land for sale he had to consider the conditions under which the sale should be made. He had to consider two different things. On

---

[1] Now Trustee Act 1925, s. 8. Note also s. 9 of the 1925 Act, the effect of which is that a trustee who lends more money than he should on a mortgage which would be a proper investment for a smaller sum is liable for breach of trust only to the extent of the excess.

the one hand if he did not make the conditions stringent enough, the purchaser would be able to put the trust estate to great cost by insisting on his right to a sixty years'[1] title and on strict proof of the matters of fact involved in the title; and then after all when the cost had been incurred perhaps the purchaser would raise some small and yet valid objection and so slip out of the contract. On the other hand if he made the conditions extremely stringent, this might frighten away purchasers and the land might be sold below its true value. Well, I do not know that any more definite general rule could be laid down than that reasonable conditions were permissible and that unreasonably stringent conditions were not permissible. Certainly however the Court's standard of reasonableness was a high one. It considered that he would be right in taking legal advice, in having the title perused and the conditions drawn by a lawyer, and if he did not do this he acted at his peril. For the conveyancer it was (and still is) often a delicate task to advise a trustee who was selling. There were certain rules about divers conditions of sale which have a certain validity—it was generally understood that this or that condition was one which a trustee might use—but all these rules might give way in a given case, for they were but emanations (if I may use that phrase) of the one great rule that a trustee ought to insert all reasonable but no unreasonable conditions.

Of late Parliament has given us some help. The Vendor and Purchaser Act of 1874 laid down certain rules which were to prevail between vendors and purchasers in the absence of any stipulation to the contrary—rules much more favourable to vendors than the old unenacted rules had been. And then it said that 'trustees who are vendors or purchasers may sell or buy without excluding the application' of these rules. This policy was carried much further by the Conveyancing Act of 1881. A much larger body of rules favourable to vendors was laid down as applicable wherever not excluded by express stipulation. And then (s. 66)[2] it was said in effect that trustees might treat these rules as being reasonable. Finally the Trustee Act of 1888 and

---

[1] Now 30 years.
[2] Now Law of Property Act 1925, s. 182.

the Trustee Act of 1893, s. 14,[1] have done yet more for those who buy from trustees. A sale by a trustee is not to be impeached upon the ground that it was made under depreciatory conditions unless it shall appear that the consideration for the sale was thereby rendered inadequate. After conveyance the sale can not be impeached as against the purchaser on the ground that the conditions were depreciatory unless it shall appear that the purchaser was acting in collusion with the trustee. This however is rather a protection for the person who buys from the trustee than for the trustee himself, and subject to the two earlier Acts we still may have the question arising—Was the trustee justified in inserting or in omitting a condition of this or that kind? I know no general answer to this save that he ought to use such conditions as a prudent vendor would use and to avoid such conditions as a prudent vendor would avoid.

We may notice in this place the Judicial Trustee Act of 1896. Section 3[2] says in brief that the Court may relieve from personal liability for breach of trust a trustee who has acted honestly and reasonably and ought fairly to be excused for that breach. This statute in effect declares that trustees may, according to the existing law, be guilty of breaches of trust not only if they act honestly, but if they act reasonably. I do not think that Courts of Equity would have admitted that this was so, though in truth they had (so to speak) screwed up the standard of reasonableness to what many men would regard as an unreasonable height. If this was so, then it was for Parliament to lower the standard. That however is not what Parliament has done. What but for the Act would have been a breach of trust will be one still; but the Court is to have a discretionary power of 'relieving' the trustee from the legal consequences of his act. The consequence is that (as the law reports show) the Courts have now before them the difficult task of defining a second and lower standard—a standard of excusable breaches of trust. This, it is already evident, will be a difficult and prolonged task. For my own part I can not think that in the civil, *i.e.* non-criminal, law there should be any place for discretionary mercy. If the act is

---

[1] Now Trustee Act 1925, s. 13.
[2] Now Trustee Act 1925, s. 61.

one for which a trustee 'ought fairly to be excused' then it ought not to be stigmatized as a breach of trust. For a good example of the considerations which may disentitle the trustee to relief under this Act you should read the case of *In re Stuart* [1897] 2 Ch. 583, and also the case of *National Trustees Company of Australia* v. *General Finance Company of Australia* [1905] A.C. 373.[1] The case of *Perrins* v. *Bellamy* [1899] 1 Ch. 797 is a good instance of the granting of relief to trustees who have honestly and reasonably committed a clear breach of trust.

We have considered how men become trustees; we have now to consider how they cease to be trustees. But here we must draw a distinction. In one sense a trustee may cease to be such by wrongfully alienating those rights which he has been holding upon trust. Thus if T be holding land or goods upon trust for A and he conveys the land or the goods to X, he, T, will no longer be holding anything upon trust. It may be that in certain cases he will still have a right and a duty to recall this wrongful alienation, to get back the property and again hold it upon trust. But it may be that he can not do this; he can not do it if he has passed the legal estate or legal property to one who purchased *bona fide*, for value and without notice of the trust. In that case he no longer holds the land or the goods in trust and he is unable to get them back. Still even in this case if the money that he received from the purchaser is still in his hand, or if it can still be traced into any investment, then he holds this money or the fund into which it has been converted upon trust. Of this tracing of trust funds I should like to speak at another time. But even this may not be the case; the money that he received may no longer be traceable, and he may be insolvent. Here then he will be holding nothing upon trust. I do not think that we can in strictness call such a man a trustee; it is true that he is liable for his breach of trust; but then a man who has been lawfully discharged from the office of trustee may still be liable to an action in respect of some past and perhaps as yet undiscovered breach of trust.

At any rate we must distinguish this wrongful destruction of

[1] A decision of the Judicial Committee of the Privy Council on a Victorian statute in the same terms as section 3 of the Judicial Trustee Act, 1896.

the trust from a lawful ending of it. How can a man lawfully cease to be a trustee?

(1) By death. This requires no commentary. But his estate may be liable; and his representatives may be trustees if he be a sole or the sole surviving trustee.

(2) By duly winding up the trust by conveying the trust property to those who have become lawfully entitled to receive it and to give him a valid receipt for it. T held a fund upon trust to pay the income to the widow of S, and divide the capital among the children of S. The widow is dead. All the children are of full age. T assigns to each child his share. The trust is at an end and T is no longer a trustee.

(3) With this is closely connected another mode. T holds property upon trust for several people; they are all of full age and under no disability. If all of them agree in directing T to do something with the property and T does it and thereby divests himself of the property, the trust is at an end and he is no longer trustee. T, for example, held a fund upon trust to pay the income to the widow of S for life, and then to divide the capital among the children. The children are all of full age but the widow is still living. Now if the widow and children tell T to transfer the property to K, or to divide it among them, and T does this, the trust is at an end and T is no longer a trustee. Here of course it can not be said that T has obeyed to the letter the instrument of trust, for that bade him go on paying the income to the widow as long as she should be living. The principle is this: No *cestui que trust* who consents to a breach of trust, being of full age and under no disability, can afterwards complain of it—so if it be clear that T is a trustee for A, B, C and D, and that no other person has or can have an interest in the property, and A, B, C and D being of full age and under no disability agree in desiring T to divest himself of the property in this way or in that way, T is safe in doing it, and by doing it will bring the trust to an end. Not only is he safe in doing it but he is bound to do it. T, let us say, holds property upon trust for me for life and, subject to my life interest, upon trust for you absolutely. You and I agree that we would like to have the capital divided between us now, that I am to have a quarter and you three-quarters, or

we agree that the property should go to a charity, T will be safe in carrying out our declared wishes and is bound to carry them out. And so all the beneficiaries being competent persons they can at any time put an end to the trust. Of course if there be infants among the beneficiaries, or if the trust comprehends unborn children, it can not be thus brought to an end.[1]

(4) By virtue of a power given by the settlement or by Act of Parliament the trustee may resign his office and divest himself of the trust property by passing it on to some new trustee. Apart from powers given expressly by the settlement or by certain modern statutes the trustee can not resign his office, and he can not lawfully appoint a new trustee; to do so would be to delegate the trust. It was usual therefore in every well drawn instrument of trust to insert a power for the appointment of new trustees, and this power was expressly made applicable to a case in which a trustee desired to retire from his office. However it was common enough to find that no such power had been inserted. In that case it used to be necessary to institute a suit and to have new trustees appointed by the Court. Then an Act of 1860, known as Lord Cranworth's Act (23 & 24 Vic. c. 145), gave a certain general power of appointing new trustees. This was a useful power and reliance was often placed upon it. But we need not discuss it now, for it has been replaced by certain sections of the Conveyancing Act 1881, which deals with trusts created either before or after the Act. This is now represented by Part II of the Trustee Act 1893, which is a Consolidation Act.[2] It gives a power to appoint a new trustee. This power is exercisable where a trustee either original or substituted is dead, or remains out of the United Kingdom for more than twelve months, or desires to be discharged, or becomes unfit to act or incapable of acting.[3] The power is to be exercised by the person or persons nominated for this purpose by the instrument creating the trust,

---

[1] Or equally if any beneficiary is a married woman subject to restraint upon anticipation. In practice too the trustee will often have to retain funds to meet death duties which may arise on the death in the future of a beneficiary.

[2] Now Part III of the Trustee Act 1925.

[3] Or refuses to act or is an infant or, being a corporation, is dissolved; see Trustee Act 1925, s. 36.

or if there be no such person or none who is able and willing to act, then by the surviving or continuing trustees or trustee, or the personal representative of the last surviving or continuing trustee. The power must be exercised by writing—not necessarily by deed. It is, you will see, possible for the creator of the trust to nominate in the instrument creating the trust the person who is to exercise this statutory power. Thus suppose a man making a will in favour of his wife and children in the common form, he will probably say 'And I declare that during my wife's lifetime she shall have the power of appointing new trustees.' And in a marriage settlement one will probably say 'And it is hereby agreed that the husband and wife during their lives and the survivor of them during his or her life shall have the power to appoint new trustees.' These simple clauses have taken the place of the old lengthy forms. If there be no person nominated and able and willing to exercise the power, then the surviving or continuing trustees or trustee, or the representative of the last survivor, will have the power to appoint. Thus it is generally possible now-a-days for a trustee to retire lawfully from his office, and divest himself of the trust property in favour of a new trustee.

(5) These powers, however, will not meet all cases.[1] Formerly, as I have said, it was very common to find that there was no power to appoint new trustees. In these cases a suit was necessary. A suit was an expensive affair. The Trustee Act of 1850 (13 & 14 Viv. c. 60) gave the Court of Chancery a power to appoint new trustees whenever it was found inexpedient, difficult or impracticable so to do without the assistance of the Court; and a summary procedure, something much cheaper and more rapid than a suit, was instituted for the purpose. This power will still be useful in some cases, and in late days the procedure has again been simplified. This statutory power is now contained in section 25 of the Trustee Act 1893.[2]

You will observe, however, that the various Acts of Parlia-

---

[1] For example, a case where there is no person nominated by the trust instrument as having the power to appoint and the sole surviving trustee has disappeared and cannot be traced.

[2] Now in Part IV of the Trustee Act 1925.

ment that I have been mentioning contemplate only an appointment of new trustees; they do not contemplate a trustee retiring unless there be some one ready to perform the trust. And I believe I may say that a sole trustee has no right to retire so long as a new trustee can not be found. He has accepted the trust, and he is bound to perform it—even the Court can not relieve him of it unless he can produce a fit and proper person willing to take his place.[1]

(6) A trustee may be removed from his office against his will. You will have observed for example that the Conveyancing Act of 1881 (now the Trustee Act of 1893, s. 10) allows the appointment of a new trustee if an old trustee remains for twelve months out of the United Kingdom.[2] A settlor might provide for other cases in the same way. But apart from such powers the Court will remove a trustee who has shown himself an unfit person for the office. Thus if a trustee becomes bankrupt or commits a breach of trust proceedings may be taken by the beneficiaries, and he can be removed from his office even though (as sometimes happens) he is desirous of continuing to be a trustee.

And now there are two distinctions that we ought to take,

(i) We distinguish between the appointment of new trustees and the transfer of the trust property from the old trustees to the new. Put a case: T is trustee of all manner of property; he goes to reside abroad; A is tenant for life under the settlement, and has been given a power of appointing new trustees. He appoints K. At common law this appointment can not transfer to K the rights that are vested in T—the legal fee simple in lands, a legal term of years, a sum of Consols and the like. In order that these may pass from T to K, T must execute the acts appropriate for transferring the various rights—convey the fee simple, assign the lease, transfer the stock and so forth. In some cases such a transfer was rendered unnecessary by the Conveyancing Act, s. 34. Now by the Trustee Act 1893, s. 12, the person appointing a new trustee has power to execute a declaration which will have the effect of taking the property out

---

[1] See Trustee Act 1925, s. 39 (replacing s. 11 of the Trustee Act 1893), under which a trustee can retire without a new trustee being appointed but only if there will remain two trustees or a trust corporation.

[2] See above, p. 102.

of the old and vesting it in the new trustee. This declaration does not transfer all kinds of property, *e.g.* legal estates in copyholds, mortgages to secure trust funds, and stocks and shares transferable only by entry in the books of a company—see s. 12 (3) of the Act of 1893. The exception of mortgages to secure trust funds from the operation of this declaration is probably due to the keen desire of conveyancers to keep the trust off the title.[1]

Other cases in which there is any difficulty about the transfer can be met by applications to the Court under the Trustee Acts of 1850 and 1853. And now under the Act of 1893, section 26 and the following sections deal with the cases where the Court has power to make what is known as a 'vesting order', vesting the property in the new trustees.[2] I must not speak at length of these matters, must only distinguish the appointment of new trustees from the transfer of the trust property.

(ii) Distinguish also between an act whereby a man ceases to be a trustee for the future, and an act whereby he obtains a release in respect of his past trusteeship. Of course the two things are very distinct, but you may come across phrases which seem to confuse them, *e.g.* the term 'discharge'. A trustee may be discharged from all future duties under the trust—the property may no longer be vested in him, and he will be no longer a trustee—yet for all this he may remain liable to the *cestui que trust* for what he has done in the past; he has not been released from the consequences of his past breaches of trust.[3]

---

[1] Section 12 of the Trustee Act 1893 is now replaced by section 40 of the Trustee Act 1925. No vesting declaration is now necessary, since if not expressed it will be implied. The only assets which require to be specifically transferred are leaseholds which contain a covenant against assignment without the lessor's consent, stocks and shares and mortgages. In the case of stocks and shares and mortgages there will usually be nothing on the title to the mortgage or the register of the Company to show that the mortgage or stocks or shares are trust property as distinct from the private property of the trustees and this being so an automatic transfer would produce confusion.

[2] See now Trustee Act 1925, ss. 44–56. The commonest case in which a vesting order is needed is where the old trustee is a lunatic and therefore unable to transfer the property.

[3] The Trustee Act 1925 gives a number of new powers to trustees and to the Court. Attention should be given in particular to section 57 of the Trustee Act 1925, a very useful section which in effect gives the Court power to authorize any transaction by a trustee which apart from such authority would be a breach of trust. A corresponding provision applicable to settled land is contained in the Settled Land Act 1925, s. 64.

THE NATURE OF EQUITABLE ESTATES
AND INTERESTS (I)

This is a topic which, as it seems to me, is insufficiently explained in some of our elementary text-books. Language is there used about one person being the owner at law while another is the owner in equity in which there is no harm, provided it be properly understood; but it does not explain itself and is liable to lead to serious mistakes, not merely to unsound theories but to practical blunders.

By way of illustration I take a passage from Austin's *Jurisprudence*, I, 388. He has been explaining the difference between *jus in personam* and *jus in rem*. Then he says 'By the provisions of that part of the English law which is called equity, a contract to˙ sell at once vests *jus in rem*, or ownership, in the buyer, and the seller has only *jus in re aliena*. But according to the conflicting provisions of that part of the English system called peculiarly law, a sale and purchase without certain formalities merely gives *jus ad rem*, or a right to receive ownership, not ownership itself: and for this reason a contract to sell, though in equity it confers ownership, is yet an imperfect conveyance, in consequence of the conflicting pretensions of law. To complete the transaction the legal interest of the seller must be passed to the buyer in legal form.'

Now as a piece of speculative jurisprudence this seems to me nonsense, while as an exposition of our English rules, I think it not merely nonsensical but mischievous. Suppose that A, an owner of land, has agreed to sell land to X, but that the transaction has not yet been perfected by a conveyance. Is it really true that while law, as distinguished from equity, says that A is still the owner, equity holds that X is the owner? Is it true that in the year 1874 there was this conflict between law and equity? Think for a moment what such a conflict would have meant, one court saying that A is owner, another that X is owner—it would simply have meant anarchy. And supposing that this was so in 1874, what are we to say now-a-days when the Judicature Act of 1873, by section 25,[1] has declared that when there is a conflict or variance between the rules of equity and the rules of the common law, the rules of equity shall prevail? If the contract passes ownership, why be at the expense of a conveyance? Is it either law or equity at the present moment that a mere contract to sell land passes the ownership in land, passes a *jus in rem* from the vendor to the purchaser?

No, the thesis that I have to maintain is this, that equitable estates and interests are not *jura in rem*. For reasons that we shall perceive by and by, they have come to look very like *jura in rem*; but just for this very reason it is the more necessary for us to observe that they are essentially *jura in personam*, not rights against the world at large, but rights against certain persons.

I need not here repeat how in the fifteenth century it became common for landowners to enfeoff their friends to the use of them, the feoffors, or describe the reasons why this was done— to evade the Statute of Mortmain, to evade feudal dues and forfeitures, to evade the rights of creditors, to acquire a power of disposing of lands by will; nor need I say how the Chancellors enforced these uses, how a statute of 1535 (27 Hen. VIII, c. 10)[2] tried to put an end to the system, or how the old use reappeared under the newer name of trust. Rather let us notice that from the very first the Chancery began to adopt the rules of common law as a model in its dealings with the rights of those for whom lands or chattels were held in use or trust—let us say for the rights of 'beneficiaries'. The beneficiary was treated as having an estate in fee simple, or in fee tail or for life in the use or trust, an equitable estate; or as having a term of years in the use or trust. These estates and interests were to devolve and be transmitted like the analogous estates and interests known to and

---

[1] The Judicature Act came into operation on Nov. 1st, 1875. The provision of section 25 referred to is now contained in section 44 of the Supreme Court of Judicature (Consolidation) Act 1925.

[2] The Statute of Uses.

protected by the common law. The equitable fee simple would descend to heirs general, the equitable estate tail to heirs in tail, equitable chattel interests would pass to the executors or administrators. In all such matters the analogies of the common law prevailed; the Chancery moulded equitable estates and interests after the fashion of the common law estates and interests.

The equitable estate or interest could be conveyed or assigned *inter vivos*. Until the Statute of Frauds (29 Car. II, c. 3) it could be conveyed or assigned by word of mouth. The 9th section of that Act[1] says that all grants and assignments of any trust or confidence ['any' you will observe—whether the subject-matter of the trust be land or personal property] should be in writing signed by the party granting or assigning the same [observe, nothing about an agent], or by his last will, or otherwise should be utterly void and of none effect. That is the law now-a-days. Observe that a deed is not required even for the conveyance of an equitable fee simple.

Then again equitable estates or interests, if they are of such a kind that they do not expire with the death of the *cestui que trust*, can be devised or bequeathed by him. Exactly the same solemnities are required of a will that is to pass such an estate or interest as of a will that is to pass the legal estate in land or the legal ownership of goods.

The best because an extreme application of this principle, that equity follows the law, is perhaps to be found in the treatment of equitable estates tail. Legal estates tail could be barred by fictitious proceedings known as common recoveries. How were equitable estates tail to be barred? After some fluctuations of opinion, it was decided, though not I think until about the beginning of the eighteenth century, that the analogies of the common law must be strictly pursued:—there must be an equitable recovery; the beneficiary having the first equitable estate of freehold must make an equitable tenant to the praecipe, and thus equitable estates tail and the equitable remainders

---

[1] Now Law of Property Act 1925, s. 53 (1) (c). The section is printed on p. 58 above. Signature by an agent authorized in writing is now sufficient.

dependent on them might be barred.[1] Even in its fictions and its archaic mysteries the common law was to be the model.

There were, however, some exceptions, and a few words about these will make the point clearer.

(1) In the matter of courtesy equity followed the law. When the law gave curtesy of a legal estate, equity gave curtesy of a corresponding equitable estate. It even gave curtesy when the fee simple was settled to the separate use of the married woman. But after some hesitation it refused to create equitable dower. The reason, I take it, was that dower had become an intolerable nuisance; when once dower had attached it could not be got rid of without a fine. This exception was abolished by the Dower Act of 1833 (3 & 4 Will. IV, c. 105); it gave equitable dower of equitable estates; but at the same time it utterly altered the whole nature of dower.[2]

(2) As regards equitable contingent remainders, if such they ought to be called, equity did not adopt the corresponding legal rules, and does not now adopt them. This point is still of some importance and I hope to speak of it on another occasion.[3] The rules of the common law about this matter had long ago ceased to be reasonable, and there was a good excuse, as we shall see hereafter, for refusing to extend them to a new and substantially different class of rights.

(3) There was no escheat of equitable estates. Suppose land conveyed unto and to the use of T and his heirs in trust for E and his heirs; E dies without having disposed of his estate and without an heir. Nothing escheated to the lord; he had a tenant T and he was entitled to no more; T might now hold the land beneficially, the trust was gone and he was simply owner. However it took a great case (*Burgess* v. *Wheate*, 1 Eden, 177) to decide this point and it was decided against the opinion of Lord Mansfield, who was for carrying out the legal analogy.

---

[1] See Lewin on Trusts, 13th edition, pp. 679 *et seq*. All estates tail are of course now equitable.

[2] Dower and courtesy are now abolished as regards persons dying after 1925 except in one or two special cases; Administration of Estates Act 1925, s. 45.

[3] Since 1925 there can not be a legal contingent remainder and the matter has ceased to be of much importance.

And now the Intestates Estates Act of 1884 has removed this exception: there can now be escheat of equitable estates; the trustee may have to hold in trust for the feudal lord.[1]

These exceptional cases, two of which have been abolished and the third of which—that about contingent remainders—has no longer its old importance, will be sufficient to illustrate the wide generality of the rule that equity has permitted the creation of equitable estates and interests which so far as regards their transmissible and inheritable quality are copies of legal estates and interests.

And so again as to the rights of creditors legal analogies have been pursued. Gradually—but I do not think that this goes back beyond the Restoration—it was established that the creditor of a beneficiary might get at the equitable estate or interest by means of *fi. fa.* or *elegit*. Having got his writ of *fi. fa.* or *elegit* he might go into the Chancery and there attack the equitable rights of his debtor. But the legal analogies were strictly pursued. Before a statute of 1838 (1 & 2 Vic. c. 110, s. 12) the judgment creditor had no means of getting at stock in which the debtor had a legal interest, for stock could not be seized under a *fi. fa.*; even so he was denied a means of getting at stock in which the debtor had a merely equitable interest. So the *elegit* would enable him only to get at a moiety of the land in which the debtor had an equitable estate.

We may well say therefore that a *cestui que trust* has rights which in many ways are treated as analogous to true proprietary rights, to *jura in rem*. But are they really such?

We must begin with this that the use or trust was originally regarded as an obligation, in point of fact a contract though not usually so called. If E enfeoffs T to his (E's) use the substance of the matter clearly seems to be this that T has undertaken, has agreed, to hold the land to the use of E.

To my mind it is much easier to understand why the Chancellors of the fifteenth century should have enforced such a compact than why the courts of law should have refused a

---

[1] Escheat is now abolished as regards deaths after 1925; Administration of Estates Act 1925, s. 45. As regards the right of the Crown to claim equitable interests as 'bona vacantia' see *In re Wells* [1933] 1 Ch. 29.

remedy. Why should they not have given an action of *assumpsit*?
(See on this question, Pollock, *Land Laws*, Note E.) The action
of *assumpsit* was just being developed when uses were becoming
fashionable. It would I think be found that the Chancellors
were beforehand in this matter and, by giving a far more perfect
remedy than the common law courts could give, made any
remedy in those courts unnecessary. All that the *cestui que use*
could have obtained from them would have been an action for
damages; the Chancellor compelled the feoffee not only to
answer any complaint on oath but also to perform his duty
specifically on pain of going to prison. Anyhow a *cestui que use*
or *cestui que trust* never got an action at common law against his
trustee; but all the same it seems utterly impossible for us to
frame any definition of a contract which shall not include the
acts by which ninety-nine out of every hundred trusts are
created, unless we have recourse to the expedient of adding to
our definition of contract a note to the effect that the creation of
a trust is to be excluded. This is excellently explained by Sir
Frederick Pollock.[1] We are, as I think, obliged to say that though
our definition of contract will include almost every act creating
a trust, for historical reasons which still have an important influence on the whole scheme of our existing law, trusts are not
brought within all, or even perhaps the larger part, of the great
principles which form the Law of Contract, but have rules of
their own. Thus, to give one example, though as I have just said
ninety-nine out of a hundred trusts begin in a transaction which
must fall within our definition of an agreement, the hundredth
will not; for I can make myself a trustee for a person, and so
create a trust, without his knowing anything about it, by a
declaration that I hold lands or goods in trust for him. Certainly
as a matter of convenience it seems desirable to keep the Law of
Trust apart from the Law of Contract, though as a matter of
principle it is necessary to see, as we shall see hereafter, that
there are important analogies between the two.

However our present point must be that the Law of Trusts
(formerly Uses) begins with this, a person who has undertaken
a trust is bound to fulfil it. We have no difficulty in finding a

---

[1] *Principles of Contract*, 9th edition, pp. 222–3.

ground for this—the trustee, the feoffee to uses, is bound because he has bound himself. This is the original notion. The right of *cestui que trust* is the benefit of an obligation. This is how Coke understood the matter. 'An use is a trust or confidence reposed in some other, which is not issuing out of the land, but as a thing collateral annexed in privity to the estate of the land, and to the person touching the land...*cestui que use* had neither *jus in re* nor *jus ad rem*, but only a confidence and trust.' (Co. Litt. 272 b.)

But if this be so, why is it that the rights of *cestui que trust* come to look so very like real proprietary rights, so like ownership, so that we can habitually speak and think of him as the owner of lands and goods? Part of the answer has already been given. As regards (if I may be allowed the phrase) their internal character these equitable rights are treated as analogous to legal rights in lands or goods—I mean as regards duration, transmission, alienation. But the whole answer has not yet been given. We are examining the external side of these rights, asking against whom they are good, and we shall find that even when examined from this point of view they are like, misleadingly like, *jura in rem*.

In this development we may trace several logical stages:

(i) The first is reached when the *cestui que trust* has a remedy against the person who has undertaken to hold land or goods on trust for him.

(ii) A second step is easy. The use or trust can be enforced against those who come to the land or goods by inheritance or succession from the original trustee, against his heir, his executors or administrators, against the trustee's doweress. Such persons may be regarded as sustaining wholly or partially the *persona* of the original trustee and being bound by his obligations as regards the proprietary rights to which they have succeeded.

(iii) A third step is to enforce the trust against the trustee's creditors—*e.g.* against the trustee's creditor who has taken the land by *elegit*. There seems to have been a good deal of difficulty about this step—more than we might have supposed—and it was not taken finally until after the Restoration in 1660. Just at the same time the Court of Chancery was beginning to insist that the *cestui que trust's* creditors could attack his equitable rights. However it became well established that these rights were good against the creditors of the trustee.[1]

(iv) What shall we say of the trustee's donee, of one to whom the trustee has given the thing without valuable consideration? He has not entered into any contract with *cestui que trust* or into anything at all like a contract; he may be utterly ignorant of the trust. Nevertheless this step was taken, and as it seems at an early period. The right of *cestui que trust* was enforced against any person who came to the thing through or under the trustee as a volunteer—*i.e.* without valuable consideration, even though he had no notice of the trust. We see the *cestui que trust's* right beginning to look 'real'.

(v) A fifth step was taken and this also at an early time. The trust was enforced even against one who purchased the thing from the trustee, if he at the time of the conveyance knew of the trust. What is the ground for this? The old books are clear about it, the ground is fraud or something akin to fraud. It is unconscientious—'against conscience'—to buy what you know to be held on trust for another. The purchaser in such a case is, we may well say, liable *ex delicto vel quasi*. He has done what is wrong; has been guilty of fraud, or something very like fraud.

(vi) Having taken this step, another is inevitable. If we stop here purchasers will take care not to know of the trust. To use a phrase used in the old reports, they will shut their eyes. The trust must be enforced against those who would have known of the trust had they behaved as prudent purchasers behave. Thus, to use the term which Holmes has made familiar,[2] an objective standard is set up, a standard of diligence. It is not enough that you should be honest, it is required of you that you should also be diligent. To describe this standard will be my object in another lecture. Here it must be enough that it was and is a high standard—the conduct of a prudent purchaser according to the estimate of equity judges. If a purchaser failed to attain this standard, to make all such investigations of his vendor's title

---

[1] See *e.g. Finch* v. *Earl of Winchilsea*, 1 P. Wms. 277.
[2] *The Common Law, passim.*

as a prudent purchaser would have made, he was treated as having notice, he was 'affected with notice', of all equitable rights of which he would have had knowledge had he made such investigations: of such rights he had 'implied notice', or 'constructive notice'. We arrive then at this result, equitable rights will hold good even against one who has come to the legal ownership by purchase for value, if when he obtained the legal ownership he had notice express or constructive of those rights.

But here a limit was reached. Against a person who acquires a legal right *bona fide*, for value, without notice express or constructive of the existence of equitable rights those rights are of no avail. I will read one passage in which James L.J. stated this in forcible terms. In the case of *Pilcher* v. *Rawlins*, L.R. 7 Ch. 259, at p. 268, he said this: 'I propose simply to apply myself to the case of a purchaser for valuable consideration, without notice, obtaining, upon the occasion of his purchase, and by means of his purchase deed, some legal estate, some legal right, some legal advantage; and according to my view of the established law of this Court, such a purchaser's plea of a purchase for valuable consideration without notice is an absolute, unqualified, unanswerable defence, and an unanswerable plea to the jurisdiction of this Court. Such a purchaser may be interrogated and tested to any extent as to the valuable consideration which he has given in order to show the *bona fides* or *mala fides* of his purchase, and also the presence or the absence of notice; but when once he has gone through that ordeal, and has satisfied the terms of the plea of purchase for valuable consideration without notice, then this Court has no jurisdiction whatever to do anything more than to let him depart in possession of that legal estate, that legal right, that legal advantage which he has obtained. In such a case the purchaser is entitled to hold that which, without breach of duty, he has had conveyed to him.'

How could it be otherwise? A purchaser in good faith has obtained a legal right. In a court of law that right is his: the law of the land gives it him. On what ground of equity are you going to take it from him? He has not himself undertaken any obligation, he has not succeeded by voluntary (gratuitous) title to any obligation, he has done no wrong, he has acted honestly and with diligence. Equity cannot touch him, because, to use the old phrase, his conscience is unaffected by the trust.

The result to which we have attained might then, as it would seem, be stated in one of two alternative ways.

(1) *Cestui que trust* has rights enforceable against any person who has undertaken the trust, against all who claim through or under him as volunteers (heirs, devisees, personal representatives, donees) against his creditors, and against those who acquire the thing with notice actual or constructive of the trust.

Or (2) *Cestui que trust* has rights enforceable against all save a *bona fide* purchaser ('purchaser' in this context always includes mortgagee) who for value has obtained a legal right in the thing without notice of the trust express or constructive.

Of these two statements the second form is now the more popular, but I should prefer the first—I should prefer an enumeration of the persons against whom the equitable rights are good to a general statement that they are good against all, followed by an exception of persons who obtain legal rights *bona fide*, for value and without notice. A statement in the former form is I think preferable because it puts us at what is historically the right point of view—the benefit of an obligation has been so treated that it has come to look rather like a true proprietary right—and it might still be rash to say positively that purchasers without notice are the only owners against whom the equitable rights are invalid. It is extremely probable that until 1834, until the statute 4 & 5 Will. IV, c. 23, equitable rights could not be enforced against a lord coming to the land by way of escheat upon the death of the trustee.[1] This curious little point is very instructive. A trustee in fee simple died intestate and without an heir; the legal estate escheated to the lord. What equity was there against the lord? He did not claim through or under the trustee, and his conscience was not affected by the trust. The point is now unimportant, because the Act just mentioned, now replaced by later Acts, provides for the continuance of the trust even though there is an escheat of the legal estate. We have already seen a statutory alteration of the converse rule which declared that of an equitable estate there was no escheat.

[1] See Challis, *Law of Real Property*, 2nd edition, p. 36.

So late as the time of Coke a corporation was not bound by a trust (and to this day it is said that a corporation cannot take to the use of another).[1]

And there were others against whom the trust could not be enforced; it could not be enforced against one who claimed the thing by title adverse to the title of the trustee. Land, let us say, was given to T upon trust for E, but P was in possession asserting a different title, asserting, let us say, that the creator of the trust was not owner of the land; E could not sue P in Chancery and enforce the trust against him; T had to recover the land at law before the trust could be carried out; E's right was not a right to obtain the land from P; but if T would not bring an action against P, then E could proceed in Chancery to compel T to assert his (T's) legal right, or he might obtain permission to bring the action in T's name. In other words, as Lewin says (*Trusts*, 11th edition, p. 275),[2] 'a disseisor is not an assign of the trustee either in the *per* or *post*, for he does not claim through or under the trustee, but holds by a wrongful title of his own'. Since the Judicature Acts we cannot have that circuitous procedure by which E went to Equity in order to compel T to enforce rights at law; but still the principle of course holds good, if the land is to be recovered from P who is in no wise bound by the trust, it must be proved that T has a superior title.

The case of *In re Nisbet and Potts' Contract* [1906] 1 Ch. 386 decides for the first time that the Court of Chancery will enforce an equitable right against a disseisor—against a squatter—who has acquired title by lapse of time. But this is a case which we shall have to consider later on.[3]

Sir Frederick Pollock says, and as I think with justice, 'The true way to understand the nature and incidents of equitable ownership is to start with the notion not of a real ownership which is protected only in a court of equity, but of a contract with the legal owner which (in the case of trusts properly so called) cannot be enforced at all, or (in the case of constructive trusts, such as that which arises on a contract for the sale of land) cannot be enforced completely except in a court of equity'.[4]

---

[1] Uses were of course abolished in 1925.   [2] See 13th edition, p. 13.
[3] See *infra*, p. 166.   [4] *Principles of Contract*, 9th edition, p. 223.

THE NATURE OF EQUITABLE ESTATES
AND INTERESTS (II)

EQUITABLE estates and interests are rights *in personam* but they
have a misleading resemblance to rights *in rem*. This resemblance
has been brought about in the following way. The trust will be
enforced not only against the trustee who has accepted it and
his representatives and volunteers claiming through or under
him, but also against persons who acquire legal rights through or
under him with knowledge of the trust—nor is that all; it will be
enforced against persons who acquire legal rights through or
under him if they ought to have known of the trust. The Court
of Chancery set up a standard of diligence for purchasers and a
high one, one so high that it certainly is difficult for a purchaser
to buy land without obtaining constructive notice of all trusts
which concern that land. Still now and again the difficulty is
surmounted, and then the true character of equitable rights
becomes apparent—a purchaser acquires a legal right *bona fide*,
for value, and without notice either actual or constructive of the
trust, and he holds the land successfully against *cestui que trust*,
and *cestui que trust* may then comfort himself with the reflection
that the land never was his.

The defence of 'legal estate by *bona fide* purchase for value
without notice' is not, you should understand, a merely personal
defence flowing from the moral merits of the purchaser and competent only to him; it is competent to all who claim through or
under him even though they have notice of the equitable rights.
Thus T holds land in trust for A; T sells and conveys to X who
purchases and obtains the legal estate *bona fide* for value and
without notice; X then sells the land to Y, and Y when he takes
the conveyance has notice of the trust. None the less Y is
protected against the trust and may ignore it. The rule is put
thus 'A purchaser with notice from a purchaser without notice
is exempt from the trust, not from the merits of the second

purchaser but of the first; for if an innocent purchaser were prevented from disposing of the' land 'the necessary result would be a stagnation of property',[1] that is to say we decide that X is legal owner, that there is no equity against him, that he is owner at law and in equity; it follows that he may convey his rights to another, otherwise A by an advertisement in *The Times* might deprive X, a legal and equitable owner, of that power of selling that is incidental to ownership. If by any chance the land comes back to T, the trustee, then A's rights in the land (if we are to call them rights in the land) revive—T is holding the subject-matter of the trust, and is bound to hold it upon the trust—*sed quaere de hoc*.[2]

I have said that the standard of diligence required of purchasers is high, so high that a purchaser without notice of equitable rights is not a very common object of the law courts.

How was this standard fixed? The starting point is here: Quite apart from any doctrine of equity, a prudent purchaser (or mortgagee) of land will investigate his vendor's (or mortgagor's) title. Further a vendor of land who contracts to sell it, contracts to show a good title. This is a legal contract enforceable at law by an action for damages.[3] If the vendor fail in his part of the contract, the purchaser is not bound to fulfil his part. Rules were evolved as to what title must be shown. For instance as to length of title, it became settled that, in the absence of any bargain to the contrary, the vendor had to show a 60 years' title. The origin of this rule may perhaps be found in the Statute of Limitation, 32 Hen. VIII, which limited 60 years as the time within which a writ of right must be brought. The rule was altered by the Vendor and Purchaser Act 1874, which substituted 40 years for 60 as the time for which good title must be shown.[4] That Act and the Conveyancing Act of 1881 made

---

[1] Lewin on Trusts, 13th edition, p. 880.

[2] *Quaere, e.g.* if T gets back the land only as trustee under some new trust, or as executor of such a trustee.

[3] But remember that these damages are narrowly limited, *Bain* v. *Fothergill*, L.R. 7 H. L. 158.

[4] The period is now reduced to thirty years by the Law of Property Act 1925, s. 44.

other changes tending to absolve the vendor who sells without special stipulations from many of the heavy obligations to which the common law subjected him—they were heavy; indeed to sell land without special conditions as to title, and evidence of title, was an act of extreme rashness. But our present point must be to notice that if there had never been any such thing as equity a prudent purchaser would have investigated his vendor's title —he would have done so in order to see that the vendor had an estate to sell, that there were no legal charges on the land, no legal rent-charges for example, for against such legal rights it would be no defence to say 'I purchased in good faith.' Now equity required of purchasers that they should make that investigation of title which a prudent purchaser would have made and which a purchaser on an open contract (*i.e.* a contract without special terms) would have been entitled to make. The purchaser was deemed to have notice of all equitable rights the existence of which he would have discovered if he had made such an investigation. The standard was high. According to the view taken by equity judges the prudent purchaser of land was one who employed a solicitor—and certainly this view was defensible. In the days of fines and recoveries a prudent purchaser would in his own interest have employed a highly trained adviser, and, even with all our modern reforms, the average man could not yet be counselled to carry through a purchase without legal aid. But in reading some of the cases about constructive notice we may be inclined to say that equity demanded not the care of the most prudent father of a family but the care of the most prudent solicitor of a family aided by the skill of the most expert conveyancer.

For some years past indeed there has been a noticeable inclination against extending and even towards contracting the range of constructive notice, and in 1882 Parliament attempted to define the doctrine.

The Conveyancing Act of 1882, s. 3,[1] said this: 'A purchaser shall not be prejudicially affected by notice of any instrument fact or thing unless—

'(i) It is within his own knowledge or would have come to his

---

[1] Now Law of Property Act 1925, s. 199 (1) (ii).

knowledge if such inquiries and inspections had been made as ought reasonably to have been made by him; or

'(ii) In the same transaction with respect to which a question of notice to the purchaser arises it has come to the knowledge of his counsel as such, or of his solicitor or other agent as such, or would have come to the knowledge of his solicitor or other agent as such, if such inquiries and inspections had been made as ought reasonably to have been made by the solicitor or other agent.'[1]

How far this altered the existing rules of equity remains to be seen. Probably it altered them in one respect of which a word may be said in passing. Of course equity held that as a general rule notice, constructive notice, to the purchaser's agent was notice to the purchaser. Of course, on the other hand, it could not go so far as to say that if a solicitor acting in one transaction gained notice of a fact, every client of his in every other transaction would be affected by notice of that fact: to have so held would have been to say in effect that no one can safely employ a solicitor or counsel in large practice, for he will have had notice of thousands of equities. But there was a small group of cases in which it had been said that the transactions might be so closely connected that notice gained by the agent in one of them might be ascribed to the principal in the other of them. Now the section before us seems definitely to strike at this particular doctrine. If notice to the agent is to be notice to the principal it must have been acquired actually or constructively in the same transaction. Having regard to the previously existing rules we must I believe regard as emphatic those words 'in the same transaction'. But, to pass from this comparatively small point, it will be seen that our legislators have not told us very much—they refer to such inquiries and inspections as 'ought reasonably' to have been made. In so doing the statute seems but to state the pre-existing law. I do not think that any equity judge would have acknowledged that he required of a

---

[1] But see Law of Property Act 1925, s. 199 (2), replacing Conveyancing Act 1882, s. 3 (2), the effect of which is that the second clause quoted in the text does not protect a purchaser from a covenant, condition, provision or restriction actually contained in an instrument under which the title is derived.

purchaser more than was reasonable. Perhaps, however, the section may serve as an excuse for rejecting some of the more extreme applications of the doctrine. As already said constructive notice has been little favoured of late.

In the case of *Bailey* v. *Barnes* [1894] 1 Ch. 25 it was said by Lord Justice Lindley (at p. 35) 'The Conveyancing Act, 1882, really does no more than state the law as it was before, but its negative form shows that a restriction rather than extension of the doctrine of notice was intended by the Legislature.'

'"Ought" here does not import a duty or obligation; for a purchaser need make no inquiry. The expression "ought reasonably" must mean ought as a matter of prudence, having regard to what is usually done by men of business under similar circumstances.'

This was approved by the Court of Appeal in the case of *Taylor* v. *London and County Banking Company* [1901] 2 Ch. 231 (see at p. 258); and at p. 259 Lord Justice Stirling, with reference to this doctrine, said 'the Conveyancing Act, 1882, has introduced very considerable modifications, to which the Court is now bound to give effect'.

You should understand that this doctrine of constructive notice had given rise to a number of sub-rules of a more or less positive kind, which were generally expressed in the form 'Notice of x is notice of y'. In a court of equity there was no jury—to whom the question of what is reasonable could be left as a question of fact. Thus every decision that A was or was not 'fixed' with notice of a trust tended to generate or define a rule, and could be regarded as a precedent. By way of illustration I may refer to *Lloyd's Banking Co.* v. *Jones*, 29 Ch. D. 221 (1885). It was so much the practice for every woman who had property to have that property settled on the occasion of her marriage, that there was some ground for a contention that if a purchaser found that the property of a married woman had been dealt with as though there had been no settlement, he was bound to inquire whether there had not been a settlement—in other words that notice of a woman's marriage would be notice of a settlement. In the case just cited counsel, not without some show of authority, tried to convince Pearson J. that this was so; but he refused to be convinced. 'I am not aware', he said, 'of any presumption of law that when a woman marries she will settle her leasehold property.'

As another illustration take *Hunt* v. *Luck* [1901] 1 Ch. 45, [1902] 1 Ch. 428, decided by Farwell J. and affirmed by the Court of Appeal, where it was held that the occupation of land by a tenant affects a purchaser of the land with notice of all that tenant's rights, but not of his lessor's title or rights.

As to a tenant's legal rights—*e.g.* in a legal term of years—absence of notice is not to the point, they stand independently of notice; but as to the tenant's equitable rights—*e.g.* under an agreement for a lease, not giving the legal term of years—here notice is all-important, and the fact that a tenant is in occupation is constructive notice of all the equitable rights that he has.

The case of *Hunt* v. *Luck* was an attempt to extend this, and to say that such occupation gives constructive notice of the rights of that tenant's lessor. The facts were these. X is buying land from A; M is in possession; M pays rent to a house agent, who pays over the rent to B in a manner inconsistent with A's title. It was held that the occupation by M does not give X constructive notice of B's equitable rights. Thus we get to a rule —Occupation by a tenant is constructive notice of all the tenant's equitable rights, but is not constructive notice of the rights of some other person to whom the tenant pays rent. The purchaser was not bound to follow up the trail through the house agent though thereby he might have come upon a fraud perpetrated by his vendor. But if he had in fact learnt that the rent was being paid to someone whose receipt was inconsistent with the title of his vendor then that would be notice to him of that person's rights.

By a curious convention it is clearly settled that the fact that people are lending money jointly is not notice that they are trustees. In fact it is pretty certain that they will prove to be so.[1]

If I agree to accept a shorter title than 40 years[2] I still get

---

[1] See p. 208 below. Under Law of Property Act 1925, s. 113, the purchaser is not concerned with a trust affecting the mortgage moneys even if he has notice of it.

[2] Now 30 years.

notice of what I should have discovered if I had fully investigated the 40 years' title. The imaginary reasonable man
never takes less than a 40 years' title. So in the case of *Patman*
v. *Harland*, 17 Ch. D. 353, it was held that a lessee got notice
of what was discoverable if the lessor's title was investigated
(and having constructive notice of a deed had constructive
notice of the contents of it). This remains so even though since
the Vendor and Purchaser Act 1874 the lessee can not, on an
open contract, ask for the lessor's title. He is treated as if he
had before the Act stipulated not to inquire into his lessor's title.[1]

There is danger in making unnecessary inquiries as is shown
by the case of *Jared* v. *Clements* [1903] 1 Ch. 428.

Though a large number of sub-rules have been thus established, rules which constitute a great part of the learning of
conveyancers, still from time to time we see that they are but
applications of a general rule, a rule which is now expressed in
the Statute Book.[2] We can see also from time to time that the
historical basis of the whole elaborate structure is the prevention
of fraud. A good illustration of this is given by *Kettlewell* v.
Watson, 21 Ch. D. 685 (1882).[3] In that case there was a question
whether a purchaser had acquired constructive notice of an
equitable right. The purchaser had indeed done very little. He
employed no solicitor of his own, but allowed the vendor's
solicitor to prepare his conveyance; he made no inquiry about
the title or the deeds. But he purchased a very small plot, and
his whole purchase money was but £42. Now if these rules
about constructive notice were rules of property law, these last
facts, the small extent of land, the small amount of the price,
could hardly be of importance. But Fry J. (p. 708) treated them
as of the greatest importance. The purchaser had done all that
could reasonably be required of him considering what he was
buying, 'the costs of an investigation of title would have been so
onerous as no doubt to have made the purchase impossible'.

---

[1] This is no longer so. *Patman* v. *Harland* has been overruled by the Law
of Property Act 1925, s. 44 (5).

[2] The conclusions reached by Maitland in the following six pages of the
text are not entirely correct as the law now stands. See note on p. 137 below.

[3] Note that Fry J.'s judgment in this case was reversed on certain points by
the Court of Appeal. See 26 Ch. D. 501.

In the same case we find the judge going back to an old classical case of *Le Neve* v. *Le Neve*[1] decided by Lord Hardwicke— 'Consider,' said Hardwicke, 'what is the ground of all this.... The ground is plainly this: that the taking of a legal estate after notice of a prior right makes a person a *mala fide* purchaser.... This is a species of fraud and *dolus malus* itself; for he knew that the first purchaser had the clear right of the estate, and after knowing it he takes away the right of another person by getting the legal estate.'... Fraud or *mala fides* is the true 'ground on which the Court is governed in the cases of notice'. And then Fry J. speaks of 'that wilful shutting of the eyes' which is treated as equivalent to fraud and he absolves the purchaser of this, in consideration of the smallness of the transaction. Now to a true proprietary right we never hear the defence 'Is it not a little one?'

The case of *Battison* v. *Hobson* [1896] 2 Ch. 403 is an illustration of the length to which the doctrine of notice was formerly carried; it was allowed practically to deprive of value the old Registry Acts for Middlesex and Yorkshire. A person who knows or ought to know of a prior charge shall not get priority over that charge by registration. Therefore he may be put to inquiry of what is not on the Register. The Yorkshire Registries Act of 1884, however, expressly declares that priority given to registered assurances by the Act shall have full effect except in cases of actual fraud. A strenuous attempt was made to induce the Court to hold that the Act had not altered the previous law but it was unsuccessful. Stirling J. said, at p. 412 of the report, '"Actual fraud" I understand to mean fraud in the ordinary popular acceptation of the term, *i.e.* fraud carrying with it grave moral blame'. He held that it would be fraudulent for a solicitor to insist on priority over his client whose interest he was bound to protect, but that it would be otherwise if there were no fiduciary relationship between the two claimants.[2]

Let us now see this difference between legal and equitable rights in its practical operation. We will put two cases which in

[1] Amb. 436 and White and Tudor L.C. vol. II, p. 157 (9th edition).
[2] The student might be interested to read *Tsang Chuen* v. *Li Po Kwai* [1932] A.C. 715, a rather curious Registry case from Hong Kong.

the eyes of the moralist may seem closely similar but between which the lawyer will see a vast difference. (1) A is tenant in fee, B is occupying his land as his tenant at will; B forges a complete set of title deeds showing that he is tenant in fee; he sells the land to X; X diligently investigates the title, finds nothing suspicious; pays his purchase money and takes a conveyance. (2) T is tenant in fee holding land in trust for S, T forges title deeds concealing the trust and showing him to be simply tenant in fee subject to no equitable liability; he sells to Y, who investigates the title; the forgery is clever and it deceives him, he pays his money and takes a conveyance. The two cases may be like enough to the moralist, but how different to the lawyer. In the first A is legal owner of the land and X has had the misfortune to buy from one who had nothing to sell, to take a conveyance from one who had nothing to convey. In the other case the purchaser is the legal owner of the land, and having come to legal ownership *bona fide* for value and without notice, actual or constructive, of S's rights, S has no equity against him; S's only remedy is against the fraudulent trustee.

Observe now that this is the effect of the legal estate. Suppose that in the second of the two cases, after the fraudulent trustee has contracted to sell, the *cestui que trust* hears of this and informs the purchaser of it before the purchaser gets the legal estate. Now the case is very different even if the purchase money has been paid. Neither purchaser nor *cestui que trust* has legal ownership; the *cestui que trust's* right is merely equitable, the purchaser's right in the land is merely equitable; the *cestui que trust's* right is the older right and it prevails. As between merely equitable interests in land the rule is '*qui prior est tempore potior est jure*'—the older equity is the better. But let the purchaser get the legal estate without notice, there is no place for this maxim. The rights concerned are, if I may so speak, rights of different orders; the purchaser is legal owner and the *cestui que trust* has no means of attacking him. One would hardly have guessed this from Austin's talk about a contract to sell land passing a *jus in rem*.

We have now come upon the main clues to the complicated labyrinth of cases about 'priorities'. It happens with unfortunate frequency that a man having title to land contrives by means of fraudulent concealment to get money from a number of different persons on the security of the land—then disappears—and the lenders are left to dispute among themselves as to the order in which they are to be paid out of the value of land which is insufficient to pay all of them. In such cases these two rules have to be held in mind. First: As between merely equitable rights the oldest prevails. Secondly: No merely equitable right can be enforced against one who has acquired a legal right *bona fide*, for value, and without notice. And if these two rules be remembered the cases will become intelligible. If on the other hand we begin thinking of equitable interests as rights in land—proprietary rights—much will be unintelligible.

A neat case is *Cave* v. *Cave*, 15 Ch. D. 639. It comes to this: T is a trustee of money for A; in breach of trust he purchases land with it and has it conveyed to himself. Stopping there, A has an equitable interest in that land, T is a trustee for him, and A could enforce his right against a purchaser from T who had notice of that right. But T mortgages to X who has no notice (in this case it is easy for him to have no notice) of A's right and the mortgage is a legal mortgage. Then T mortgages to Y who also has no notice of A's right; but the mortgage to Y can only be an equitable mortgage, for X has got the legal estate. Now in what order shall we place A, X, Y? In this order—X, A, Y. We place X first; he has the legal estate and got it for value and without notice. A cannot attack him. As between A and Y order of time settles order of right, for they have both but equitable interests.

These two are not the only rules. There are some others; for a man may lose the priority that he has got. I may illustrate this by a problem set in the Law Tripos.

A lends money to B, a solicitor, on security of a legal mortgage of freeholds and with the mortgage receives possession of the title deeds. A subsequently lends the title deeds to B on a fraudulent representation by him that he desires to prepare an abstract of title and conditions of sale in order to sell and pay off the debt. B then borrows a further sum from C depositing the deeds with him as security—and soon after absconds. The property will only suffice to pay A or C. Is A's security postponed to C's? What is the rule as to loss of priority? Would A's position be different if his mortgage had been an equitable one merely?

Now why should A's security, whether it be legal or merely equitable, be postponed to C's? The suggestion of course is that A has been guilty of some negligence or imprudence in allowing B to get the title deeds, that he enabled B to commit a fraud, that he ought therefore to be postponed to C. There have been many cases about this matter. It has often been before the Courts of late and a strong line has been drawn between the conduct which will deprive a legal charge of its priority, and that which will deprive a merely equitable charge of its priority.

To return to the case taken from the examination paper. It seems quite certain that the legal mortgagee will not lose priority by mere negligence—but he will lose it by participating in fraud. Gross negligence may be evidence of fraud.

It seems probable that the equitable mortgagee may lose priority by negligence. The old cases were this way; the opposite was held by Kay J. in *Taylor* v. *Russell*, but great doubt was thrown on this by the opinions of the law lords when that case came before them ([1892] A.C. 244).

In our case there seems nothing to show that there was participation in fraud. Within the dicta the representation was a reasonable one, *i.e.* we can hold that a reasonable man might believe it. Therefore if the mortgage to the solicitor were legal we don't postpone, for we don't infer fraud. The reasonableness of the representation—*i.e.* its believableness—here comes in to negative fraud.

But suppose the mortgage equitable. Can we acquit the mortgagee of negligence? *Semble que non.* He ought not, I think (as a matter of prudence), to let deeds get into the mortgagor's hands on any pretence—even though the pretext is such as a man might well believe to be true. I think a Court would say so. He may very properly believe what the mortgagor says. If so he will employ a solicitor who will supply the mortgagor with an abstract or copies and will at the proper time produce the originals to a purchaser—but a prudent mortgagee does not let deeds get into the hands of the mortgagor. We cannot say that a suspicion of fraud ought to have been aroused, but we can say that it is careless to part with the deeds.

As regards the postponement of a legal charge, *Northern etc. Fire Insurance Co.* v. *Whipp* (1884) 26 Ch. D. 482 is the most important modern case. It was there laid down that the Court will not postpone a legal mortgage to an equitable mortgage on the ground of any mere carelessness or want of prudence on the part of the legal mortgagee.[1] It will however postpone a legal to an equitable mortgage on the ground of fraud—it will do so (1) where the legal mortgagee has assisted in or connived at the fraud which led to the creation of the subsequent equitable estate, of which assistance or connivance the omission to use ordinary care in inquiring after or keeping the title deeds may be sufficient evidence where such conduct can not be otherwise explained; or (2) when the legal mortgagee has made the mortgagor his agent with authority to raise money and the security given for raising such money has by misconduct of the agent been represented as the first estate. In the case before us A, however careless he may have been, cannot I think be charged with conniving at a fraud. In the case just cited the Court of Appeal said that 'where the title deeds have been lent by the legal mortgagee to the mortgagor upon a reasonable representation made by him as to the object in borrowing them, the legal mortgagee has retained his priority over the subsequent equities'.[2] I think that the representation made by B in this case was within this language a reasonable representation, that is to say, a representation that a reasonable man might believe, namely that he wanted the deeds in order that he might sell the estate and pay off the mortgage.

But as to the postponement of merely equitable charges it is otherwise. Negligence is sufficient for this purpose. This has been laid down by the Court of Appeal several times within recent years. *National Provincial Bank* v. *Jackson*, 33 Ch. D. 1, *Union Bank of London* v. *Kent*, 39 Ch. D. 238, *Farrand* v. *Yorkshire Banking Co.* 40 Ch. D. 182. In this case before us,

---

[1] This is probably no longer the law. See note on p. 137 below.
[2] 26 Ch. D. at p. 492.

and according to the authorities, I think that there was quite enough negligence to postpone A to C, had A's right been merely equitable.

Here then again we get a distinction between legal and equitable rights, and this is quite intelligible, for legal estates are proprietary rights, ownership or fractions of ownership, equitable rights are not. Negligence will not deprive one of ownership.[1] It is excessively negligent for one to leave one's purse on the counter of a shop, but one shall not for that reason lose ownership. Fraud or connivance at fraud is a different matter. But as between merely equitable claimants, the Court can consider the moral merits of the parties—*qui prior est tempore potior est jure* is a natural rule where merits are equal, but negligence may be a ground for postponing an older to a younger equity.

But the Court of Chancery's respect for legal right may best be seen in the rules relating to the tacking of mortgages. A mortgages land first by legal mortgage to X, and then by equitable mortgage to Y; X now without notice of Y's right makes a further loan to A upon the security of his mortgage. X can get repayment of both his loans in priority to Y. That is one of the examples of tacking; but it is by no means an extreme one. A mortgages legally to X, then equitably to Y, then equitably to Z; Z when he made the loan had no notice of Y's right. Now if Z pays off and takes a transfer of X's mortgage he can get repayment not merely of the amount due on X's first mortgage, but also of the amount due on Z's third mortgage in priority to Y; he can, as is sometimes said, 'squeeze out the second mortgagee', and he can do this even though in the interval he has obtained notice of Y's right. That is the strange part of the doctrine, he obtains priority for his own equitable charge by obtaining the legal estate after he has obtained notice of Y's equitable charge which had priority over his. Now one might have thought that equity would have shown its respect for legal

[1] See *e.g. Farquharson Brothers* v. *King* [1902] A.C. 325, and the authorities cited by Lord Macnaghten at pp. 336 and 337. 'If a person leaves a watch or a ring on a seat in the park or on a table at a café it is no answer to the true owner' (suing a *bona fide* purchaser) 'to say that it was his carelessness and nothing else that enabled the finder to pass it off as his own.' But see note on p. 137 below.

rights sufficiently if it held that the person who took a legal estate without notice of an equitable right was protected against that right, and that no advantage should have been attainable by taking a conveyance of a legal right with notice of an equitable right. And indeed if Courts of Equity could begin again perhaps they would not carry the doctrine to this extreme. But the view taken seems to be that suggested by the phrase, *tabula in naufragio*, applied in some of these cases to the legal estate. Y and Z are both equally honest men, one of them must lose his money—here is a shipwreck—he who can lawfully come by a legal plank may save himself; the fact that Y's equitable right is older than Z's is not a sufficient reason for depriving Z of what he has obtained by his own diligence and the law of the land, namely, a true proprietary right.

This doctrine of tacking has fallen out of favour.[1] An attempt was made to abolish it by section 7 of the Vendor and Purchaser Act 1874, but the section which made the attempt was repealed in the next year by 38 & 39 Vic. c. 87, s. 39. Modern cases have put some restraints on the doctrine, which at one time seemed to go to the great length of saying that the third mortgagee—always supposing that when he made his advance he had no notice of the second mortgage—might obtain priority over the second mortgagee by obtaining the legal estate in any fashion; but now it is held that if the holder of the legal estate is bound by a trust in favour of the second mortgagee, and the third knows this, the third can get no priority by means of a conveyance of that legal estate, which conveyance would be a breach of trust.[2] However the doctrine just stated about the three mortgages holds good. I quote it here as one extreme example of the respect paid by equity to the legal estate. It warns us forcibly that legal estates and equitable estates are not rights of one and the same order; they belong to different orders; the one is a right *in rem*, the other the outcome of an obligation, a trust, and of the rule that trusts can be enforced against those who when they obtain ownership know or ought to know of those trusts.

---

[1] It is now abolished by the Law of Property Act 1925, s. 94. See p. 207 below.

[2] *Pilcher* v. *Rawlins*, L.R. 7 Ch. 259. *Harpham* v. *Shacklock*, 19 Ch. D. 207.

The case of *Taylor* v. *Russell* [1892] A.C. 244 is an excellent illustration. The facts, slightly simplified, were these: M, tenant in fee simple, gives a legal mortgage to N in fee simple: this includes, among other lands, Blackacre. But the parties seem not to have known that Blackacre was included in the mortgage, and the title deeds of Blackacre remained with M. Then M sold Blackacre to F and conveyed it to him in fee, nothing being said of the mortgage. F thus obtained the equitable fee simple in Blackacre. F determines to commit a fraud by mortgaging Blackacre twice over, to A and to X, representing to each that he gets a first mortgage. He forges title deeds by which one P conveyed Blackacre to him. This deed he produces to A's solicitor, who made no further inquiry, being satisfied that F had bought from P. A advanced his money and took a mortgage. Then F produced the true title deeds to X and got another advance, X taking a mortgage, and knowing nothing (and having no notice) of A's rights. Neither X nor A knew anything of N's legal mortgage. F vanishes, and Blackacre will not pay both A and X.

Stopping here we find that A and X both have merely equitable mortgages; A's is first in point of time, and will prevail unless we hold that A has been so careless in not investigating the forgery that he ought to be postponed to X. Kay J. who tried the action, thought that there had not been such negligence as would serve to postpone A to X. But owing to what happened it became unnecessary to decide this question. What happened was this: X heard of N's legal mortgage, represented to N that he, N, did not require the security of Blackacre since the other lands were sufficient to secure the debt owed by M to N and asked N to let him, X, have the legal estate in Blackacre. N, who does not seem to have known until now that Blackacre was included in his mortgage, consented to give up his right in it, so he reconveyed Blackacre to M in order that M might convey it to X, and M did convey it to X. Before this transaction was completed M, N and X knew of A's rights. X then had got the legal estate. Did this give him priority over A? Held by the Court of Appeal and by the House of Lords that it did—albeit he got it without giving value for it, and although when he got it he knew of A's rights. It is impossible to explain such a case unless we remember that legal and equitable rights are rights of different orders.

You should read also the case of *Bailey* v. *Barnes* [1894] I Ch. 25. The case, a little simplified, was this:

Johnson, tenant in fee simple, mortgages land to Bristowe and Robins for £6000.

Next a judgment is recovered against Johnson by the plaintiff Bailey, who obtains an order for a receiver by way of equitable execution against Johnson's equity of redemption: in other words Bailey now acquires an equitable charge.

The mortgagees took possession. On the 21st of December, 1889, they transferred the mortgages to Barnes in consideration of some £6300, the amount of principal and interest.

On the 23rd of December, 1889, Barnes purporting to exercise the mortgagee's power of sale conveyed to Hannah Midgley, for the exact sum which he had paid, free from the equity of redemption. The apparent inference is that the equity of redemption was worth nothing. In fact Barnes was a mere nominee of Midgley and there had been no real exercise of the power of sale.

On the 4th of March, 1890 (3 months afterwards), Midgley mortgaged to X for £6000.

On the 29th of July, 1890, Midgley being dead, her executor agreed to sell the equity of redemption to Lilley for £2500, and on the 13th of August he conveyed it to Lilley for that sum. (Ought not Lilley to have said to himself 'I am treating as worth £8800 odd what three months ago a mortgagee sold for £6300, can that sale have been an honest transaction, were not Midgley and Barnes colluding to deprive Johnson of an equity of redemption which was not valueless'? However, the suspicions of his solicitors were not aroused, and this even though they saw a valuation at £8700, which had been made in January, 1890.)

On the 15th of August the plaintiff Bailey begins proceedings to set aside the sale by Barnes to Midgley. Stirling J. sets aside the sale. Then at this late hour, Lilley, knowing that the sale was invalid, paid off the £6000 mortgage and took a conveyance of the legal estate.

Two questions arose: (1) Had he notice of the fraud or impropriety at the time of his purchase of the equity of redemption? (2) If not, can he at this very late moment save himself by means of the legal estate? It was held by Stirling J., and by the Court of Appeal, that the answer to the first question was No, and to the second question Yes.

Let us take the case of *Taylor* v. *London and County Bank* [1901] 2 Ch. 231. It is a very instructive case, and so let us read the whole story in the head note to the report in the Law Reports. That head note, as you see, covers more than two pages, but the bare facts are these:

In 1882 one T, a solicitor, took with his own money a mortgage by sub-demise of certain leaseholds.

In 1889, being then a trustee of the B settlement, he received and, without the knowledge of his co-trustee, fraudulently appropriated a sum of money belonging to that settlement, and by entries in his books purported to appropriate his own mortgage debt to make it good but he never communicated this to his co-trustee or to their *cestui que trusts.*

[In 1896, however, one of the *cestui que trusts* heard of the appropriation. He was a solicitor, and acted as such for the others, but though all were *sui juris* and absolutely entitled they never called for a transfer or made any inquiry as to the mortgage.]

In 1889 T was also a trustee of the T settlement.

In 1895 he had become sole trustee and N was appointed co-trustee with him. N inquired as to the trust funds. T represented the mortgage to be part thereof, and, at N's request, T drew up and executed a legal transfer of it to himself and N. N was ignorant of the B settlement, T acted as the solicitor and retained the deeds.

In 1897 T fraudulently deposited the deeds with the defendant bank as security for a debt and executed a deed-poll charging the debt on all his interest, binding himself to execute a legal mortgage, and appointing three officers of the bank as his attorneys to execute such legal mortgage on his behalf. The bank had then no notice of either settlement.

In 1898 T absconded. The bank received notice of the T

settlement, but not of the B settlement. It thereupon caused its three officers to execute a legal mortgage to the bank.

Now let us analyse the case and consider the following points:

Point 1. Do the rules as to realty apply, or those as to charges on debts or personal trust funds? If the latter rules apply notice determines priority, according to the rule in *Dearle* v. *Hall*.[1]

It was held, of course, that mortgage debts charged on land are governed by the rules as to priorities applicable to interests in land, and so notice to the mortgagor is immaterial (*Jones* v. *Gibbons*, 9 Ves. 407)—just as leaseholds are treated as real estate for this purpose.

Point 2. Is there appropriation of the mortgage to B settlement, in other words did this mortgage belong in equity to the *cestui que trusts* of B settlement? Rigby L.J. said No. Stirling and Williams L.JJ. said Yes; and I think that the previously decided cases undoubtedly support the majority, though they have done a great deal of harm by introducing a questionable doctrine: *Middleton* v *Pollock*, 2 Ch. D. 104, *Sharp* v. *Jackson* [1899] A.C. 419.

Therefore if all that had happened was T's bankruptcy, then the B *cestui que trusts* could have held the mortgage; though in this case it was not even an authorized security. But they are volunteers only; not purchasers for value.

Point 3. On the transfer of 1895 the legal estate vests in T and N. All the Lords Justices agreed that the transfer was for valuable consideration, as N had a right to sue T for the trust fund, which right he gave up when he accepted the mortgage. Such cases as *Thorndike* v. *Hunt*, 3 De G. and J. 563, and *Taylor* v. *Blakelock*, 32 Ch. D. 560, establish that a person in the position of N must be treated as a purchaser for value.

Point 4. There was no actual notice of the appropriation to the B trust to trustees of the T trust as such. Was there constructive notice? It was contended that there was, but this question was held to be concluded by section 3 (ii) of the Conveyancing Act 1882, for T did not acquire his knowledge as N's solicitor, nor in the preparation of the transfers to himself and

[1] 3 Russ. 1.

N—'not', to use the words of the section, 'in the same transaction in which a question of notice to the purchaser arises'.

Before the bank's mortgage the position therefore was that the legal estate was in the T trustees holding for value upon express trusts for the *cestui que trusts* of that settlement.

Point 5. The bank does not get the legal estate by the deed of 1897 executed by T. Later it did get a legal mortgage; the deed of 1898 executed by its three officials gave it the legal estate in an undivided moiety by severing the joint tenancy existing in T and N, the other moiety remaining vested in N. Can the bank use this legal estate in a moiety as *tabula in naufragio*?

Here the bank takes the legal estate in breach of an express trust binding on T, and it had actual notice of the trust at the time the transfer of this legal estate was executed by its officers in 1898. Where there is no such notice then the point is still open. There was of course no relation back of the legal estate to the deed of 1897, and it was held to be contrary to equity for the bank, with such notice, to get in the legal title against N or the T beneficiaries, and it was not allowed to gain any priority by virtue of having done so.

Point 6. But ought not the beneficiaries of the T settlement to be postponed for negligence—as regards the moiety of which the legal estate went to the bank—because the title deeds were left in T's possession? Probably among equities such postponement may take place upon the principles laid down in *Farrand v. Yorkshire Banking Co.*, 40 Ch. D. 182 (1888). But it was held that there had not been such negligence as will postpone in this case, since a fiduciary relationship existed between them and T, the person left in possession of the deeds, and they had no ground to suspect any want of good faith on his part, *In re Vernon, Ewens and Co.*, 33 Ch. D. 402 (1886).

The result is that as regards both moieties the bank has no priority over the T settlement, and can be compelled to give up the legal estate in the moiety obtained from T to the T trustees.

Point 7. There remains a struggle between the B settlement and the T settlement as to this moiety, the legal estate in which was thus vested in the bank.

B settlement got no declaration of trust nor any assignment of the legal estate. Its charge was first in time, and that is all that can be said on that side—but it was not obtained for value. On the other hand the T beneficiaries (by their trustee N) are purchasers for value, with an express trust in their favour; this gives them the better right to call for the legal estate, and therefore having the better right to call for the legal estate they are entitled to the benefit of the legal title under the rule laid down in *Wilkes* v. *Bodington*, 2 Vern. 599 (1707).

The result therefore was the complete triumph of the T settlement, and the bank was directed to re-convey to the present T trustees the moiety of the legal estate, and also to deliver up to them the deeds relating to the property.

NOTE ON *OLIVER* v. *HINTON* AND *WALKER* v. *LINOM*

THE law cannot now be regarded as being as simple as would appear from Maitland's text and in particular his proposition that a legal estate will not be postponed on the ground of negligence can no longer be sustained. The two cases of *Oliver* v. *Hinton* [1899] 2 Ch. 264 and *Walker* v. *Linom* [1907] 2 Ch. 104 should be read.

In *Oliver* v. *Hinton* the title deeds to land were in the hands of an equitable mortgagee. The mortgagor sold the land to a purchaser without disclosing the equitable mortgage. The purchaser, who had no actual notice of the mortgage, did not require an abstract of title or production of the deeds. Held that the purchaser ought to be postponed to the mortgagee. On the face of it the case appears to be a simple one of constructive notice but it was decided (at least by Lindley M.R.) on the ground that, apart from any question of constructive notice, the purchaser had been guilty of such negligence that he ought to be postponed to the equitable mortgagee and it has stood since as authority that a legal estate may be postponed on the ground of negligence alone and without fraud.

Walker v. *Linom* goes further. There Walker on his marriage conveyed land to the trustees of his marriage settlement. Certain deeds were handed over to the trustees but the deed conveying the property to Walker was overlooked and was allowed to remain in Walker's possession. Later Walker executed a mortgage of the land to a third party. Held by Parker J. that all the parties except Walker had acted honestly but that the trustees had been negligent in allowing the deed to remain in the hands of Walker and on that account were to be postponed to the mortgagee and that the beneficiaries under the marriage settlement, although they had not themselves been negligent, stood in no better position than their trustees. Here there is a clear case of the legal owner being deprived of his ownership by negligence in regard to the title deeds. The other point raised in the case, namely how far the beneficiaries suffer for their trustees' negligence, is a rather difficult point into which it would not be profitable to enter. The point will also be found discussed in *Lloyds Banking Co.* v. *Jones*, 29 Ch. D. 221 and *Capell* v. *Winter* [1907] 2 Ch. 376.

Since the Property Acts of 1925 and particularly the Land Charges Act 1925, difficult questions of priorities are less likely to arise and a detailed study of the cases seems hardly to be worth while. The student who is interested should however refer to two more recent cases, namely, *Grierson* v. *National Provincial Bank* [1913] 2 Ch. 18, where there was held not to be negligence sufficient to postpone the holder of a prior legal estate, and *Tsang Chuen* v. *Li Po Kwai* [1932] A.C. 715, where *Oliver* v. *Hinton* was considered and distinguished by the Privy Council.

One further observation may be made in regard to *Walker* v. *Linom*. The head note to that case and also passages in the judgment refer to the interest of the mortgagee as a 'subsequent equitable interest'. Now the position strictly was this: The trustees had the legal estate throughout and Walker had only an equitable life interest determinable on alienation. The remainder of the equitable interest in the property was vested in the other beneficiaries. Thus Walker had in effect nothing that he could convey to the mortgagee. The position was in essence the same as if, the trustees being the owners of the property, a complete stranger had purported to mortgage it. In such circumstances it is not perhaps strictly correct to say that the legal estate of the trustees is postponed on account of negligence to the subsequent equitable interest of the mortgagee, for that suggests that apart from the negligence there is an equitable interest in the mortgagee. It is more accurate to say that the mortgagee, having taken nothing under the mortgage from Walker, since Walker had nothing to give, yet has an equity against the trustees arising out of their negligence which has caused him to take an otherwise invalid mortgage. This aspect of the matter was no doubt present to Maitland's mind in writing the text. Regarding equitable interests as essentially personal rights he could readily admit the possibility that conflicting equitable interests might co-exist and that the earlier might be postponed to the later on the ground of negligence. He did not however regard it as possible to have a subsequently created interest conflicting with an earlier legal interest, since no one but the legal owner could create an interest conflicting with his own estate. Where the legal owner was fraudulent, an equity would arise out of the fraud but Maitland would not allow that negligence could give rise to such an equity. Since the decision in *Walker* v. *Linom* however we must admit that negligence and not fraud only can give rise to the equity.

THE NATURE OF EQUITABLE ESTATES
AND INTERESTS (III)

By this time we shall have convinced ourselves, if we required conviction, that it is practically unsafe to regard equitable estates and interests as rights *in rem*, as ownership or fractions of ownership. As to what I may call the theoretic question, the question of appropriate classification, I will say one word more. I do not for one minute think that it should be part of our conception of a right *in rem*, that the person who has that right can never be deprived of it save by his own act. To say nothing of cases in which the law may force a sale of it upon him—cases in which, under our Lands Clauses Act or similar provisions, he is deprived of his land in order that a railway or the like may be constructed—there are other cases in which he may lose his right by the act and the wrongful act of another. Thus is it under our common law when one who is not the owner, and who even may be a thief, sells goods in open market to a *bona fide* purchaser; the owner's ownership is gone, the purchaser becomes owner. A similar result may be brought about under the Factors Act—a Factors Act of great importance was passed in 1889 and was largely repeated in the Sale of Goods Act 1893. Some foreign codes go yet further and lay down that as regards moveables *possession vaut titre*—the *bona fide* purchaser from a possessor in general obtains ownership. Now at first sight these instances may seem analogous to the case of the person with an equitable estate who loses it when a *bona fide* purchaser acquires the legal estate for value and without notice; and I think it possible that the equitable doctrine may be historically connected with the doctrine about sales in market overt. But really there is a marked difference between the two cases—in that of the sale in market overt the buyer gets ownership, but we do not conceive that he gets it from the seller, for the seller never had ownership; while the rule about the effect of a purchase in rendering equitable rights unenforceable is based on this that the trustee has ownership, and transfers it to the purchaser, and that there is no reason for taking away from the purchaser the legal right which has thus been transferred to him.

To come to practical applications. One maxim of prudence is this: Never leave a legal estate outstanding however 'dry' it may be.[1] Often enough land is conveyed or devised to trustees who at first have some active duties to perform—there may be charges to pay, children to be educated and the like—but after awhile the whole equitable estate becomes vested in one person of full age, who is in possession of the land; the trustee now has nothing to do but to convey the land according to the directions of this *cestui que trust*; very probably the very existence of this legal estate is forgotten; on the trustee's death it passes to his devisee or heir, or since the Conveyancing Act 1881 (s. 30), to his personal representatives, and perhaps it goes on devolving from one set of representatives to another—it is as 'dry' a legal estate as dry can be—it looks like the ghost of a departed right. Nevertheless if you are buying or taking a mortgage from the *cestui que trust*, from the person who seemingly is to all intents and purposes the real and only owner of the land, do not be persuaded to leave that legal estate outstanding, but insist on having a conveyance of it. For think what will be your position if it is conveyed to someone who can say 'I have bought the land and obtained the legal estate *bona fide* for value and without notice of your merely equitable rights.'

Another practical rule is this—Have as little to do with second mortgages as possible, for think of the possibility that a charge later than yours may be tacked to the legal estate and that you may be squeezed out. Yet another rule is that if you do take a second mortgage you should at once give notice of it to the first mortgagee for this will at all events prevent his tacking a subsequent advance.[2]

[1] The transitional provisions of the Law of Property Act 1925 provided for the automatic 'getting in' of bare legal estates outstanding on 31st December, 1925, and under the new legislation bare legal estates are in future unlikely to arise.

[2] Tacking is now abolished and second mortgages can be registered under the Land Charges Act 1925. From the point of view of title therefore they

Thus far we have been dealing with land. The rules which decide the priority of equitable charges on personal trust funds are different to those which relate to charges on land.[1] As regards equitable charges on land the general rule is that they rank in order of date, but as regards charges on personal trust funds, the general rule is that they rank according to the order in which the trustees get notice of them. T holds stocks or shares in trust for E, E gives a charge on his interest to X as security for a loan, and then gives a similar charge to Y as security for a later loan; Y having at the time no notice of X's right gives notice to T before X does; Y's charge is prior to X's. The rule is the same where the subject-matter of the charge is not a trust fund but a mere debt—a creditor assigns his debt first to X and then to Y: Y when he paid his money had no notice of the previous assignment; he gives notice to the debtor before X does and so get priority. In the case of a debt we see the reason for this rule; it is a rule for the protection of debtors. A debtor is of course justified in paying his creditor until he has received notice that he ought to pay someone else; when he has received notice that he ought to pay to Y, he is justified in paying to Y; you cannot expect him to make inquiries as to secret assignments. The same rule has been applied to interests in personal funds created by trusts as well as to rights arising under what are commonly and conveniently called contracts as opposed to trusts—indeed we here see once more how like a right under a trust is to a purely contractual right—the trustee may safely pay to *cestui que trust* until he has notice of an assignment, and he may safely pay and will be bound to pay to the assignee who is the first to give him notice, even though there has been another assignment of earlier date. Therefore of course we get the practical rule—If you take an equitable assignment of a debt or trust fund give notice to debtor or trustee. The notice is not necessary to complete the equitable assignment as against the original creditor himself or his

---

can be made reasonably safe. They are still risky investments since they bear the whole of the depreciation of the mortgaged property. It is still prudent for the second mortgagee to give notice to the first mortgagee.

[1] See p. 209 below. The rule in *Dearle* v. *Hall*, which applies to personalty, has been extended to interests in land by the Law of Property Act 1925, s. 137.

representatives, including his trustee in bankruptcy, but the claims of competing assignees rank as between themselves according to priority of notice.

Let us sum up the question of priorities when the subject-matter is a chose in action or a trust fund of personalty.

Here notice to the debtor or trustee becomes important. A second assignee (mortgagee) if he has no notice of the first assignment may gain priority by being the first to give notice. The rule had its origin in *Dearle* v. *Hall*[1] and *Loveridge* v. *Cooper*,[2] both in 1823, and both decided by Plumer M.R.; and is based upon an obscure mixture of principles. They are:

(1) Protection of the debtor or trustee. The debtor may pay his original creditor until he has received notice of an assignment. He gets notice of an (equitable) assignment. What may he do then? He is not necessarily safe in paying the assignee. But if there be another earlier assignee who has not given notice he can not complain of payment to the person who has given notice.

So in the case of a trust fund. T is trustee for A. A assigns to X then to Y. Y gives notice. If before notice of X, T pays to Y, X can not complain.

Hence the rule of prudence: give notice. See *Ward* v. *Duncombe* per Lord Macnaghten [1893] A.C. at p. 394.

(2) Hence arose a sort of notion that notice was necessary to complete the title. (Lord Macnaghten at p. 392.)

(3) By the Bankruptcy Acts—the order and disposition clause —goods left in the order and disposition of a debtor with the consent of the true owner were treated in bankruptcy as the property of the estate. This idea was applied to choses in action. A owes a debt to X, X assigns to M. X goes bankrupt, the debt is part of his estate, unless M has already given notice to A. (The giving of notice is regarded as a sort of taking possession[3] —the chose in action is no longer in assignor's order and disposition.) This is not so in the modern law. In the Act of 1883 the order and disposition clause (s. 44)[4] has a proviso 'things in

---

[1] 3 Russ. 1.   [2] 3 Russ. 30.
[3] Cf. *Hill* v. *Peters* [1918] 2 Ch. 273.
[4] Now Bankruptcy Act 1914, s. 38.

action other than debts due or growing due to the bankrupt in the course of his trade or business shall not be deemed goods within the meaning of this section'.

One base of *Dearle* v. *Hall* is thus cut away, and one on which Plumer M.R. had laid great stress.

Well, it gets decided that a second assignee (if he had no notice of the prior assignment) can get priority by being first to give notice to the debtor or trustee even though before payment notice of the first assignment comes in. The rule pushed to this extent where several assignees have given notice before payment is not necessary for the protection of the debtor or trustee. But *Dearle* v. *Hall* can not be overruled for it was followed in the House of Lords in *Foster* v. *Cockerell*.[1]

But difficulties begin when there is not continuously just one trustee.

The modern cases show a tendency towards treating 'the trustees' as a sort of corporation, so that notice if once got in sticks for good and all—or like a register in which something is inscribed. But this is not yet triumphant.

Take the great case of *Ward* v. *Duncombe* [1893] A.C. 369. A is first assignee, B is second assignee. T_1 and T_2 are trustees. T_1 knows of A; T_2 doesn't. B gives notice to T_1 and T_2. T_1 dies. T_3 is appointed. In the contest A is preferred to B, though when the contest opens the trustees for the time knew of B and not of A. (You should read the judgment of Lord Macnaghten.)

Then take *In re Wasdale* [1899] 1 Ch. 163, decided by Stirling J. T_1 and T_2 are the trustees. A gives notice to T_1 and T_2. Both die or resign. T_3 and T_4 are appointed. B gives notice to them. A is preferred. This is what has been called the registration principle.

But see *In re Phillips' Trusts* [1903] 1 Ch. 183. T_1, T_2 are the trustees. A gives notice to T_1—not to T_2. T_1 dies. B gives notice to the existing trustees. B is preferred (against the registration principle), by Kekewich J., on the authority of a case[2] much doubted by Lord Macnaghten in the House of Lords.

---

[1] 3 Cl. and F. 456.
[2] *Timson* v. *Ramsbottom*, 2 Keen 35, doubted [1893] A.C. at p. 394.

This is an unsatisfactory result. The practical moral is this: give notice to each one of the trustees.

Read *In re Lake* [1903] 1 K.B. 151, a case of secret misappropriation. L was a solicitor and many times over a trustee. He executed in favour of a client and *cestui que trust*, A, whose money he had appropriated, a mortgage of some policies of life insurance. The mortgage was not communicated to A nor was any notice given to the Insurance Companies. Later L executed another mortgage of the same policies to a clerk in his own office as trustee for other defrauded clients. This second mortgagee was the first to give notice to the Insurance Companies and he prevailed.

And see *In re Dallas* [1904] 2 Ch. 385. In that case D in 1897 charged in favour of S his interest in a legacy expected from his father who was still living. In 1898 he charged the same expected legacy to B. In 1902 the father died naming D sole executor. In January, 1903, D, who had never acted, renounced probate. In March, 1903, administration was granted with the will annexed. Next day B gave notice to the administratrix and a week later S did so. Subsequently the legacy which was in Court was paid out to the administratrix. It was held by the Court of Appeal that, though S's delay was not due to any default on his part, yet B was to be preferred as he was the first to give notice when the fund came into existence and there was a person having a legal dominion. *Semble*, notice to an executor who never acts and renounces is bad; and a notice to the assignor is ineffectual.

As to the legal assignment of debts in general, this only became possible under section 25, sub-section 6 of the Judicature Act 1873.[1] To make the assignment a 'legal' one, *i.e.* to enable the assignee to sue in his own name, it must under that section (1) be an absolute assignment in writing and one which does not purport to be by way of charge only, (2) express notice in writing must be given to the debtor, and (3) it is expressly provided that the assignee's right shall be subject to all equities which would have had priority over it, if this Act had not passed. Thus the assignment will not be legal, *i.e.* will not enable the

---

[1] Now Law of Property Act 1925, s. 136.

assignee to sue in his own name, until notice in writing has been given to the debtor. The possible analogy of the rules relating to a legal estate in lands is excluded, the legal assignee may find that his assignment is treated as posterior to one which is merely equitable and of which he had no notice. For merely equitable assignments are still important.[1] Any assignment which is not absolute but conditional and any assignment which on the face of it purports to be by way of charge only can not be a legal assignment. Any agreement for value to transfer to another the benefit of the debt or chose in action is a good equitable assignment even though made by word of mouth only and not in writing; and the notice to the debtor or trustee necessary to give priority under the rules of equity was not, and is not now, required to be notice in writing.[2] Further it appears to be questionable whether an assignment of part only of a debt is within section 25, sub-section 6 of the Judicature Act 1873, or whether such an assignment can only be valid in equity and whether, therefore, the assignee must still sue in the name of the assignor.[3] In modern practice instead of suing in the name of the assignor it is usual merely to join the assignor as a co-plaintiff, or even as a defendant if he refuses to be a plaintiff. And recently in several cases where the joining of the assignor has been a mere formality in no way needed to protect the debtor the highest courts have shown a tendency to permit the equitable assignee to succeed, although the assignor has not been joined in any form.[4]

---

[1] See *Brandts* v. *The Dunlop Co.* [1905] A.C. 454. A mere direction, request or even permission given by the creditor to the debtor to pay the debt to a third person may be a valid equitable assignment which the debtor must observe upon peril of having to pay twice over. See per Lord Macnaghten at p. 462: 'All that is necessary is that the debtor should be given to understand that the debt has been made over by the creditor to some third person.'

[2] Since 1925 the notice must be in writing; Law of Property Act 1925, s. 137 (3).

[3] It is now settled that there cannot be a legal assignment of part only of a debt; *Williams* v. *Atlantic Assurance Co.* [1933] 1 K.B. 81.

[4] See *Tolhurst* v. *Associated Cement Manufacturers* [1903] A.C. 414, at pp. 420 and 424; *Brandts* v. *Dunlop Co.* [1905] A.C. at p. 462, and *Dawson* v. *Great Northern and City Railway Co.* [1905] 1 K.B. 260, per Stirling L.J. at p. 271 delivering the judgment of the Court (Collins M.R., Stirling and Mathew L.JJ.). In the first of these cases the assignor was a Company in liquidation and possibly dissolved; in the second the assignor was a bankrupt,

Finally, as regards equitable rights in moveable goods, cor-poreal chattels, we hear very much less.[1] Doubtless if I bought a piece of plate from a trustee knowing that he held it on trust for E, E might enforce his right against me, and this would be so even though I purchased in market overt. But a purchaser of moveable goods is not expected to investigate his vendor's title. Of course if he buys from one who is not owner, and the sale does not take place in market overt or fall within the rules intro-duced by the Factors' Acts he gets a bad title. But though this be so, equity has not been able to say of corporeal chattels as it has said of land and of trust funds that the prudent purchaser makes an investigation of title. Corporeal chattels are outside the realm of constructive notice. In *Joseph* v. *Lyons* (1884) 15 Q.B.D. 280, an attempt was made to apply that doctrine to goods, but the Court of Appeal would not hear of it. Cotton L.J. said 'I think that the doctrine as to constructive notice has gone too far and I shall not extend it'—and Lindley L.J. 'It seems to me that the modern doctrine as to constructive notice has been pushed too far, and I do not feel inclined to extend it.'

In leaving this particular topic I may perhaps be allowed to say that in my opinion the words that I have just quoted point out the true course for the law reformer. If our land law is to be simplified this will not be by a repetition of the partial and abortive attempt at abolishing the difference between equitable and legal estates which was made by the Vendor and Purchaser Act of 1874 in the section directed against tacking; but on the contrary by laying stress on the distinction and depriving equit-able estates of their would-be proprietary character by relaxation of the doctrine of constructive notice. Perhaps the statutory definition of constructive notice that we have now got in section 3 of the Conveyancing Act of 1882 may do something towards this end; but more thorough-going measures seem necessary.[2]

and had already been paid in error; in the last case the assignee had irre-vocable authority to give a receipt for the assignor. But compare *Performing Rights Society* v. *London Theatre of Varieties* [1924] A.C. 1 and *Williams* v. *Atlantic Assurance Co.* [1933] 1 K.B. 81.

[1] Note that an agreement conferring a right in equity to personal chattels or to a charge or security thereon is a bill of sale within section 4 of the Bills of Sale Act 1878, and requires to be registered unless it falls within one of the exceptions specified in the Act.   [2] See note on p. 206 below.

And now a few words as to the general relation between Equity and Law. A few years ago there was, if I may so speak, a visible distinction. If it was impossible to explain the distinction without a long historical discourse, still it was possible to point to the distinction as a visible matter of fact—to say to the inquirer 'Go to Westminster Hall and you will there see courts administering Common Law; then go to Lincoln's Inn and you will there see courts administering Equity.' The existence of the distinction was made emphatic in every sort of way. In the Courts of Common Law were judges hearing 'actions' begun by 'writ', carried on by 'declaration' and 'plea' with a system of procedure of which trial by jury was the central fact. In the Court of Chancery were the Chancellor, Master of the Rolls, and Vice-Chancellors hearing 'suits' begun by 'bill' with a system of procedure which made no use of a jury and differed at almost every possible point from the procedure of the Common Law. In the smallest matters one saw the difference—the same man who was a 'solicitor' of the Court of Chancery was an 'attorney at law'. If at times the differences in detail seemed unnecessarily great one had to remember that the Chancery had by the very law of its being to keep very clear of the field of common law. The mere fact that the old courts could do something was a reason why the new court should not do it.

And now all this has passed away; one can no longer say 'Here is a Court which administers nothing but common law, and there a Court which administers nothing but equity.' The task of the student is really all the harder. Let us look at the matter a little.

In the first place let us guard ourselves against the fallacy of supposing that the Chancery Division of the new High Court is the Court of Chancery under a new name, or that the old courts of common law are now called the Queen's Bench Division. This would be a great error. It is true that actions of certain kinds have been assigned to one division, actions of certain other kinds to the other, though in many cases the plaintiff has a choice. This is a convenient division of labour— the trying with a jury is done in one division, the other has a machinery adapted for taking accounts. But a rule of court might alter this assignment, and an Order in Council might abolish the existing 'divisions'—the Common Pleas Division and the Exchequer Division were thus merged in the Queen's Bench Division. And, to come to a more important point, every judge in whatever division he may be sitting is bound to apply every rule whether of common law or of equity that is applicable to the case before him. He cannot stop short and say that is a question of common law which I am incompetent to decide, or, that is a merely equitable right and I can take no notice of it.

But if this be so, if the two bodies of rules have to be administered together, have not the terms law and equity lost their meaning? Well, as terms, they are merely historical terms, and such they have been for centuries past; but they will endure for a long time yet, for they do express distinctions of the utmost importance—distinctions among the rules of substantive law—and if we had not inherited this pair of terms we should be obliged to invent others to serve the same purpose.

For the Judicature Act did not alter the substantive law—save in a few points to be hereafter mentioned—did not change the nature of rights or even give new remedies. It only made a thorough change in procedure—introducing a new procedural code, partly borrowed from that of the common law, partly borrowed from that of equity, and in part newly invented.

A few points of substantive law were expressly dealt with by section 25[1]—the 1st sub-section relates to the administration of assets; it never came into force, for the Act of 1875, s. 10, repealed it and put another somewhat similar clause in its stead —the 2nd sub-section said that no claim of a *cestui que trust* against his trustee for any property held on an express trust or in respect of any breach of such trust shall be barred by any Statute of Limitations—the 3rd sub-section related to the doctrine of equitable waste—the 4th to merger by operation of law—the 5th to the rights of a mortgagor in possession—the 6th to the assignment of choses in action—the 7th to stipulations in contracts,

---

[1] The section is repealed (except for sub-section 2) by the Supreme Court of Judicature (Consolidation) Act 1925. Most of the provisions of the section are reproduced by the Property Acts of 1925. The 11th sub-section now appears in section 44 of the Supreme Court of Judicature (Consolidation) Act 1925.

which according to the doctrines of equity are not of the essence of the contracts—the 8th to the issuing of injunctions and the appointment of receivers—the 9th to damages by collisions at sea—the 10th to the custody of infants and to a number of little miscellaneous points—then follows the 11th to which I wish to draw attention. 'Generally in all matters not herein-before particularly mentioned in which there is any conflict or variance between the rules of equity and the rules of the common law with reference to the same matter, the rules of equity shall prevail.'

Now what did this sub-section do? Did it turn equitable estates into legal estates, acting like a second Statute of Uses? Of course it did not. There was no conflict or variance here between common law and equity. The statement that T is owner but is a trustee for E is not self-contradictory. It is no more self-contradictory than the statement that A is the owner of goods but owes more debts than he can pay. Austin, we have seen, speaking of the position of one who has agreed to buy land but had not yet obtained a conveyance, talks of the conflict between law and equity, of how equity held that the contract passed a *jus in rem*. To speak thus is to take a very superficial view of the case—the right that the purchaser gets by the contract is no right *in rem*, and there is no conflict between law and equity.

So far as I am aware it never entered into the head of anyone that the Judicature Act had rendered trusts impossible. But it did enter the heads of some that this 11th sub-section had done much more than really it did. Some of the cases about this are very instructive and will help to show us what is the relation between law and equity at the present time.

Take the case of *Joseph* v. *Lyons* (1884) 15 Q.B.D. 280. The substance of the case is this. One Manning by bill of sale assigned to Joseph as security for money lent certain furniture and jeweller's stock in trade then in a certain house—'and also all the stock in trade and effects which shall at any time during the continuance of this security be brought into the said house'. After a while Manning pledged part of the jewellery which formed the stock in trade with Lyons, a pawnbroker, who took the goods without knowing of the bill of sale and in the ordinary course of his business. These things Manning had acquired after the date of the bill of sale. Joseph demanded these goods from Lyons, but Lyons claimed to hold them as security for the money that he had lent; whereupon Joseph sued Lyons.

Now of course it is a rule of common law that a man can not give to another the ownership of goods that he neither owns nor yet possesses. I assign to you my furniture now in my house, and any furniture that I may hereafter acquire and place in that house. The ownership in these hereafter to be acquired goods[1] can not pass to you—for either the things are not yet in existence, or if in existence they are not mine to give. The utmost that can be done under the common law by any would-be assignment of goods hereafter to be acquired will be to act (1) as a licence to you to seize those goods when I have acquired them, and (2) as a covenant by me that I will deliver them to you and thereby make them yours when I do acquire them. Equity was prepared to do a little more for you. If the assignment was for value and was sufficiently specific in its terms, pointing out exactly what goods it was to affect—saying, *e.g.* any stock in trade hereafter acquired by me and brought into such a shop—it would decree specific performance of this contract. This being so, as in the case of land, it would further hold that the contract could be specifically enforced against volunteers claiming under me, and even against persons purchasing the goods from me with notice of this specifically enforceable contract. This was the subject of a famous decision by a divided House of Lords in *Holroyd* v. *Marshall*, 10 H.L.C. 191. And so lawyers easily slipped into the way of saying that in equity one could make an assignment of goods hereafter to be acquired though one could not do so at law. This was a compendious way of putting the matter and was not likely to deceive any equity lawyer.

It seems however to have deceived Huddleston B., who (his reasons are not given) held that Joseph could recover the goods or their value from Lyons. In the Court of Appeal Joseph's counsel boldly stated the propositions that he had a valid equitable title to the after acquired goods, and that as the Judicature Acts had abolished the distinction between legal and equitable

[1] Or 'future goods' as they are called in the Sale of Goods Act.

interests, he had also a valid legal title. The answer to this
argument lies in the question: But what was meant by a valid
equitable title—a title good against all men—a right *in rem*—a
title good against a *bona fide* purchaser for value without notice?
No, certainly not, equity never gave any such right. The Court
of Appeal reversed the judgment. Lindley L.J. put the matter
succinctly. 'Reliance was placed upon the provisions of the
Judicature Acts, and it was contended that the effect of them was
to abolish the distinction between law and equity. Certainly that
is not the effect of these statutes: otherwise they would abolish
the distinction between trustee and *cestui que trust*.' A desperate
effort was made to say that the pawnbroker had constructive
notice of the bill of sale; the Lords Justices rejected this contention in words that I have already read.[1] We see then that
merely equitable rights keep their peculiar character still—there
is here no conflict between law and equity.

When considering the case of *Joseph* v. *Lyons* it is worth
noticing that 'declarations of trust without transfer' may be
bills of sale within section 4 of the Bills of Sale Act 1878;[2] and
also that under the Bills of Sale Act 1882, s. 5, a bill of sale
given by way of security for money will be void, except as
against the grantor, as regards any chattels of which the grantor
was not the true owner at the time of the making of the bill of
sale.

Another very interesting case is *Britain* v. *Rossiter* (1879)
11 Q.B.D. 123. For our present purpose we may state it thus.
The plaintiff agreed to serve the defendant for longer than a
year. After some months he was dismissed and then brought
this action for wrongful dismissal. The defendant relied on the
4th section of the Statute of Frauds, on the fact that there was
no note or memorandum in writing of the agreement. In answer
to this the plaintiff urged that the agreement had been in part
performed, and that the rule of equity was that 'part performance takes a case out of the statute'. True that before 1875 this

---

[1] P. 146 above.
[2] Notice also that any agreement 'by which a right in equity to any personal chattels, or to any charge or security thereon, shall be conferred' is a
bill of sale within that section.

contract could never have come before a court of equity at all, because equity had no jurisdiction to compel the specific performance of contracts of hire and service; but now the Judicature Acts provide that when there is a conflict between law and equity the rules of equity must prevail, and the rule of equity is that part performance takes the contract out of the statute. The answer to this given by the Court of Appeal was in effect this: that to read the Judicature Acts in the way suggested would be to alter not merely procedural rules but substantive rights. Before 1875 in breach of this agreement no right to sue for damages would have accrued to the plaintiff—specific performance was out of the question—breach of the agreement even though part performed would not have enabled him to call on equity for assistance. Before the Judicature Acts he would have had no remedy either in law or in equity, and he has none now. Brett, the Master of the Rolls, added, what is very true, that the cases in the Court of Chancery as to the part performance of contracts relating to land 'were bold decisions on the words of the statute'. Cotton L.J. pointed out that they had a peculiar origin and a limited scope. When the contract is for the sale of land, payment of a part or even the whole of the purchase money would not serve to dispense with the written evidence required by the statute: it was only the purchaser's possession of the land, a fact hardly explicable save by the supposition of some contract for its sale or lease that would have this effect.

These cases then will serve to show that the 11th sub-section can have but a very limited operation.

THE PRESENT RELATIONS OF EQUITY
AND THE COMMON LAW

THE Judicature Act 1873, s. 25, sub-s. 11, speaks, we have seen, of cases in which there is a conflict or variance between the rules of the common law and the rules of equity. We have seen, however, that normally the relation between equity and law has not been one of conflict. How could it have been otherwise? After all, for centuries past this country has been decently governed and reasonably peaceful, and this would not have been so if we had really had two conflicting systems of law in full operation. 'The courts of common law said that the trustee was the owner, but the Court of Chancery said that the *cestui que trust* was the owner'—if we take this crude statement literally it is an invitation to civil war. No, we ought to think of the relation between common law and equity not as that between two conflicting systems, but as that between code and supplement, that between text and gloss. And we should further remember this, that equity was not a self-sufficient system—it was hardly a system at all—but rather a collection of additional rules. Common law was, we may say, a complete system—if the equitable jurisdiction of the Chancery had been destroyed, there still would have been law for every case, somewhat rude law it may be, and law imperfectly adapted to the needs of our time, but still law for every case. On the other hand, if the common law had been abolished equity must have disappeared also, for at every point it presupposed a great body of common law.

It is a little difficult therefore to say what this sub-section means when it speaks of conflict and variance, and it is very much easier to find cases in which a despairing appeal has been made to these words than to find cases in which such appeals have been successful. I think we must say that in some few cases the joint operation of law and equity produced a result so capricious that they might be regarded as at conflict or at variance. Such cases were rare; we have for instance seen in *Joseph* v. *Lyons*[1] that there was no conflict between them as to the effect of an assignment of chattels hereafter to be acquired; we have seen in *Britain* v. *Rossiter*[2] that there was no conflict between them as to the effect of the part performance of an agreement of which there is no note in writing, though one is required by the Statute of Frauds. Was there a conflict about (so-called) equitable waste? Perhaps there was. If a tenant for life, made unimpeachable for waste, cut down ornamental timber, he could not be made to pay damages in an action at law, but equity would prevent him from so doing by injunction, or if he did it would compel him to account. So we might here say that equity did consider that he must pay for his act, while law held that he need not. But it is needless to speculate about this matter, for the Act specially provided for it. By section 25, sub-section 3, an estate for life is not to confer any legal right to commit waste of the description known as equitable waste, unless a contrary intention has been expressed. And so again as to stipulations being of the essence of a contract, the 7th sub-section provided that stipulations which would not have been deemed to be or have become of the essence of a contract in a court of equity should receive in all courts the same construction and effect as they would have heretofore received in equity. Before the Act we might certainly have had results which could be called capricious and inelegant. A contract had ceased to be enforceable in a court of law by action for damages because the party who might have wished to enforce it had himself broken it, while in equity the contract (being one belonging to the genus enforceable by specific performance) might still be enforceable, the broken stipulation being treated as one which was not of the essence of the matter. What would have happened had this point not been specially dealt with by the Act, had it been left to the general words of the 11th sub-section, we need not speculate. I doubt it could be said that there was any conflict here, any self-contradiction, in the statement that a decree for

[1] 15 Q.B.D. 280.
[2] 11 Q.B.D. 123.

the specific performance of this contract will be made, but no damages can be given for its breach.[1]

The best example that I have found of the operation of sub-section 11 is *Job* v. *Job*, 6 Ch. D. 562. The assets of a testator come to the hands of his executor, and are afterwards lost to the estate without any wilful default on the part of the executor; can the executor be made liable for their value? It is probable, though perhaps not quite certain, that the common law said 'Yes, if they have once come to his hands he can be made liable, default or no default.' Equity however had come to a different rule, namely, that to make the executor liable one must prove wilful default. Now, supposing these rules to be so, there was something that might reasonably be called a conflict, for the question might have come before a court of law in an action for devastavit, or before a court of equity in an administration suit, and in each case the question would have really been the same, viz. is the executor bound to restore the value of these goods. And so in *Job* v. *Job*, Jessel M.R. treated the case as one of conflict or variance, and held that the rule at law as well as in equity now is that an executor or administrator is in the position of a gratuitous bailee, who can not be charged with the loss of his testator's assets without wilful default. That is one example.

Another illustration is to be found in the case of *Lowe* v. *Dixon*, 16 Q.B.D. 455. Several persons, A, B, C, D, enter into a joint adventure, *e.g.* buying and selling corn, a loss ensues; one of them, A, is compelled by the creditor, X, to pay the whole loss, say £1000. Of course he has some right to call upon his fellows to contribute, and there being no agreement to the contrary they ought to contribute in equal shares—this is law and equity—B, C and D, each of them ought to pay A £250. But suppose that one of them can not pay, *e.g.* D has not a farthing in the world, how much can A get from B and from C? The view taken by courts of law was that each adventurer agreed with his fellows to contribute one quarter of the loss and no more. In this case A, having paid away £1000 to X, could at

---

[1] Not any more conflict than in the converse statement (which is still good law in countless cases): Damages will be given for the breach of this contract but specific performance of it will not be decreed.

law obtain a quarter of that sum from B, and another quarter from C, but no more; thus he himself would lose £500, while B lost but £250, and C but £250. Equity had taken a different, and to us it must seem a more sensible view; the whole loss should be borne equally. The whole loss is £1000, therefore, since D has nothing, A can get £333. 6s. 8d. from B, and a like sum from C. The consequence of course would have been that before the Judicature Act A would not have brought an action at law against B and C, but would have brought a suit in equity. Thus the legal rule had become a *caput mortuum* before the Act. The case of *Lowe* v. *Dixon* merely shows that this *caput mortuum* has disappeared altogether. We are no longer obliged to say that A can recover two-thirds of the loss, but that this is a result of equity since at law he can recover but half the loss; we can simply say that A can get two-thirds in whatever division of the High Court he may bring his action. I do not think that in this matter there has been any real change in the substantive law.

One other illustration, *Walsh* v. *Lonsdale*, 21 Ch. D. 9, a somewhat difficult and dangerous case, *i.e.* one which may lead us to suppose that the 11th sub-section has done more than really it has done.

By a written agreement L agreed to let to W a cotton mill for seven years at a rent which was to be payable in advance if demanded. This was not a lease, for it was not made by deed, it was merely an agreement for a lease. W entered and occupied the mill, and for some time paid the rent, but not in advance. Then L demanded a year's rent in advance, and this demand not being complied with he distrained. W then brought an action against L claiming damages for an unlawful distress.

Now before the Judicature Act the position of affairs would have been this. The agreement for a lease did not in the view of a court of law operate as a lease. The only facts that a court of law could have considered were these: W has entered on land of L, and has paid rent periodically, this shows that W is holding the land of L as tenant from year to year at a rent. Now if I have a tenant from year to year holding of me at a rent, that does give me a power to distrain for rent in arrear, but it does not give me power to distrain for rent in advance: therefore in this case L has done wrong. On the other hand a court of equity would have granted specific performance of the agreement for a lease. If W had come to it with a bill for specific performance it would have decreed that L should perform his contract by accepting a lease in accordance with the agreement. What is more, had L distrained for rent in advance he would have been doing an unlawful act—an act unlawful in the narrow sense—and at law W would have had an action for damages against him: but I think that L might have applied to a court of equity to enjoin W from bringing that action, on the ground that W had agreed to pay rent in advance, and was occupying the land under that agreement. Now if this be so, then the Court of Appeal in deciding that under the Judicature Act L could distrain for rent in advance, did but give effect to the net result of the previously existing rules of law and equity. Jessel M.R. however put the matter thus, at p. 14 of the report in 21 Ch. D.:

'There is an agreement for a lease under which possession has been given. Now since the Judicature Act the possession is held under the agreement. There are not two estates as there were formerly, one estate at common law by reason of the payment of the rent from year to year, and an estate in equity under the agreement. There is only one court, and the equity rules prevail in it. The tenant holds under an agreement for a lease. He holds, therefore, under the same terms in equity as if a lease had been granted, it being a case in which both parties admit that relief is capable of being given by specific performance. That being so he can not complain of the exercise by the landlord of the same rights as the landlord would have had if a lease had been granted. On the other hand he is protected in the same way as if a lease had been granted; he can not be turned out by six months notice as a tenant from year to year. He has a right to say "I have a lease in equity, and you can only re-enter if I have committed such a breach of covenant as would if a lease had been granted have entitled you to re-enter according to the terms of a proper proviso for re-entry." That being so, it appears to me that being a lessee in equity he can not complain of the exercise of the right of distress merely because the actual parchment has not been signed and sealed.'

Now I am not sure that these words are not a little misleading, and I have heard remarks upon *Walsh* v. *Lonsdale*
which seemed to imply that since the Judicature Act an agreement for a lease is in all respects as good as a lease. Now Jessel
certainly did not say this, and to say it would certainly be
untrue. An agreement for a lease is not equal to a lease. An
equitable right is not equivalent to a legal right; between the
contracting parties an agreement for a lease may be as good as
a lease; just so between the contracting parties an agreement for
the sale of land may serve as well as a completed sale and conveyance. But introduce the third party and then you will see the
difference. I take a lease; my lessor then sells the land to X;
notice or no notice my lease is good against X. I take a mere
agreement for a lease, and the person who has agreed to grant
the lease then sells and conveys to Y, who has no notice of my
merely equitable right. Y is not bound to grant me a lease.[1]

The later case of *Swain* v. *Ayres*, 21 Q.B.D. 289, has made it
clear that the Judicature Act has not abolished the difference
between a lease and an agreement for a lease. An agreement for
a lease is not a lease within section 14 of the Conveyancing Act
1881, which says that the right of re-entry or forfeiture under
any proviso or stipulation in a lease for breach of any covenant
or condition in the lease shall not be enforceable unless a certain
notice has been served by the lessor on the lessee. Note that the
law was extended by section 5 of the Conveyancing Act of 1892,
and 'lease' and 'under-lease' are made to include for this
purpose any agreement for a lease or for an under-lease where
the lessee has become entitled to have his lease (or under-lease)
granted.

The case of *Lowther* v. *Heaver*, 41 Ch. D. 248, is also worth
consulting; as is also the case of *Manchester Brewery* v. *Coombes*
[1901] 2 Ch. 608. There Farwell J. at p. 617 said: 'Although it
has been suggested that the decision in *Walsh* v. *Lonsdale* takes
away all differences between the legal and equitable estate, it, of
course, does nothing of the sort, and the limits of its appli-
cability are really somewhat narrow. It applies only to cases

---

[1] But if at the time that he buys I am in possession of the land under the
agreement Y will have constructive notice of all my equitable rights.

where there is a contract to transfer a legal title, and an act has
to be justified or an action maintained by force of the legal title
to which such contract relates'...and at p. 618: 'It is not
necessary to call in aid this doctrine in matters that are purely
equitable; its existence is due entirely to the divergence of legal
and equitable rights between the same parties, nor does it affect
the rights of third parties.'

In the case of *Foster* v. *Reeves* [1892] 2 Q.B. 255, the defendant
entered on premises of greater value than £500 under an executory agreement for a lease. He subsequently gave six months
notice and left. An action was brought against him for rent
accruing due after he had given up possession. It was held by
the Court of Appeal that the equitable doctrine that a person who
enters under an executory agreement for a lease is to be treated
as in under the terms of the agreement, can only be applied if
the Court in which the action is brought has power to give
judgment for specific performance, and the action was therefore
dismissed, but solely on the ground that it had been brought in
a County Court which in cases above the value of £500 had not
such power.

I have now mentioned the main cases in which some effect
has been attributed to the 11th sub-section of section 25 of the
Judicature Act. The other cases in which an operation has been
found for this sub-section hardly rise above the region of procedure. Doubtless the full force of this provision has not yet
been spent, and those who live longest will know most about its
meaning; but it has been law these thirty years, and has produced very little fruit. And one thing it certainly has not done,
it has not discharged us from the necessity of learning the true
nature of equitable estates and interests.[1]

I pass to a final illustration of our theme. We all know some-

---

[1] The following cases may also be noticed: *Performing Rights Society* v.
London Theatre of Varieties [1924] A.C. 1 (means by which an equitable
owner of copyright can enforce his rights against an infringer); *Mathews* v.
Usher [1900] 2 Q.B. 535 (rights of a mortgagor against a lessee, but cf.
Turner v. *Walsh* [1909] 2 K.B. 484); *Gentle* v. *Faulkner* [1900] 2 Q.B. 267
(a declaration of trust is not an assignment within the meaning of a covenant
not to assign); *Steeds* v. *Steeds* 22 Q.B.D. 537 and *Vibart* v. *Coles* 24 Q.B.D.
364 (further examples of a conflict or variance between the rules of law and
the rules of equity).

thing of the common law doctrine of covenants running with the land, and probably we have heard about covenants which run with the land in equity though they do not run with the land at law. Now our point will be to contrast common law rules with equitable rules and to understand that the term 'a covenant running with the land in equity though not at law', though it may be a useful term, is one that might easily lead to mistakes.

First as regards the common law rules: I do not propose to go into them very deeply—there is an excellent tabular statement of them in Pollock, *Contracts*, 9th edition, pp. 251 *et seq.*—but still a few words must be said about them.

I. In the first place we must mark off from all other cases those in which the covenant in question is *contained in a lease*; and about such covenants there are some elaborate rules. There seem to be four cases for consideration—for we have to consider the burden and the benefit of the lessor's and the lessee's covenants respectively. We have also to note that some of our rules are ancient common law while others are due to a statute of 1540, 32 Hen. VIII, c. 34.

(1) *The Burden of the lessee's covenants.* As to this the common law made provision. The assignee of a lease is bound by the lessee's covenants (i) as to an existing thing parcel of the land demised, whether assignees be expressly mentioned in the covenant or no, (ii) as to something to be newly made upon the premises, if, but only if, assignees be mentioned.[1]

The classical authority is *Spencer's Case*, 5 Co. Rep. 16a (1 Smith's L.C. 51, 13th edition).

You should read also the case of *White* v. *Southend Hotel Co.* [1897] 1 Ch. 767, where it was held by the Court of Appeal that a covenant not to sell any wines in the demised house except those purchased from the lessor runs with the land at law without mention of assigns.

(2) *The Burden of the lessor's covenants.* Whatever may have been the case before 1540 (and perhaps this matter is not free

---

[1] As regards covenants made after 1925 the distinction between existing things and things 'in posse' is abolished and the convenantor is in all cases deemed to enter into the covenant on behalf of himself and his successors in title. See Law of Property Act 1925, s. 79.

from doubt) the assignee of the reversion is bound by the lessor's covenants under section 2 of the Statute of Henry VIII.[1]

(3) *The Benefit of the lessee's covenants.* It seems certain that at common law, *i.e.* before the statute, the assignee of the reversion could not sue upon the lessee's covenants—the statute says as much, 'by the common law of this realm no stranger to any covenant shall take any advantage or benefit of the same by any means or ways in the law, but only such as be parties or privies thereunto' (cf. the rule that a chose in action is not assignable). The statute proceeds to give the assignee of a reversion the benefit of the lessee's covenants.[2]

(4) *The Benefit of the lessor's covenants.* This runs with the tenancy at common law. (See *Spencer's Case.*)[3]

These provisions of the common law and of the statute of Henry VIII have been in some respects amplified by sections 10 and 11 of the Conveyancing Act of 1881, but into their details we must not examine at present; the changes are not of very great importance.

Let us notice in passing that when a lessee assigns his lease there is no transfer of the liability on his covenants from him to the assignee. The original lessee remains liable on his covenants throughout the term. But the assignee also becomes liable and remains so while he has the term, but his liability ceases when he assigns the term, *i.e.* he is not liable for what happens after that. Also the assignee is liable to indemnify the lessee in respect of any breaches of covenant which take place after assignment.

Notice also that 'assignment' does not include 'under-lease'. The under-lease is not liable on the lessee's covenants, and this is the reason why when leaseholds are mortgaged they are usually mortgaged by way of sub-demise, in order that the mortgagee may not become liable on the lessee's covenants.

Note the case of *Bryant* v. *Hancock* in the Court of Appeal [1898] 1 Q.B. 716.[4] I covenant that I, my executors, administrators or assigns, will not use in a certain way a house which

---

[1] Now Law of Property Act 1925, s. 142.
[2] Now Law of Property Act 1925, s. 141.
[3] See also Law of Property Act 1925, s. 78.
[4] Affirmed on another point [1899] A.C. 442. See also *Wilson* v. *Twamley* [1904] 2 K.B. 99.

you demise to me. I make an under-lease. My under-lessee uses the house in the prohibited way. You can not sue me (for he is not an 'assign'), nor can you sue him, for the same reason.[1]

II. As to other cases of covenants relating to land—*i.e.* cases other than those between landlord and tenant—these fall into two classes:

(*a*) Covenants of this kind entered into with a landowner for the benefit of the land; the benefit runs with the estate, if the covenant touches and concerns the land of the covenantee, *e.g.* vendor's covenants for title.

(*b*) Covenants of this kind entered into by a landowner—it seems that the burden never runs with the land even though assigns be mentioned.

Now all these rules are rules of law—and the liability of the assignee is quite independent of his having or not having notice of the covenant. On the one hand in an action for damages against the assignee of a lease, it would be no defence for the assignee to urge that he never had notice of the covenant—that his assignor had by some clever fraud contrived that he should not have notice. On the other hand the lessor could not bring an action against the under-lessee on the lessee's covenants, even though the under-lessee when he took his under-lease had notice—as would usually be the case—of the covenants in the lease. Notice and absence of notice are quite immaterial. It will neither give nor take away rights. Further, no distinction is drawn at law between positive and negative covenants.

Then comes the equitable gloss developed by a long line of cases of which *Tulk* v. *Moxhay* (1848) 2 Phil. 774 is the leading case. Until lately it would have been expressed thus: Anyone coming to the possession of land with notice actual or constructive of a covenant entered into by someone through or under whom he claims, restricting the use to be made of that land, will be prohibited from doing anything in breach of the covenant. Now, since the case of *In re Nisbet and Potts' Contract*

---

[1] The point of the decision simply is that, since the covenant referred only to "assigns", use in the prohibited manner by an under-lessee was no breach of covenant. Yet, even if the covenant had been expressed to cover under-lessees, the lessor could not have sued the under-lessee at common law since there was neither privity of contract nor privity of estate between them.

[1906] 1 Ch. 386 (with which I will deal presently) we must perhaps say merely that anyone coming to the land with notice actual or constructive of a covenant entered into by some previous owner of the land, restricting the use to be made of that land, will be prohibited from doing anything in breach of that covenant.

Let us see the foundation of this doctrine. Why should equity interfere at all, and first, why should it interfere between the original covenantor and covenantee? Because the remedy which the common law gives in such covenants is an inadequate one. I have covenanted with you that I will not build on a certain piece of land, or that a certain house shall not be used as a public house. Now practically the common law would render it possible for me to force you to sell the right given you by the contract, to oblige you to accept in lieu thereof a sum of money assessed by a jury as damages. Equity then begins interfering between covenantor and covenantee, restraining by injunction the covenantor from using the land in defiance of his contract. Once started on this task—it could hardly stop here—by a very little conveyancing machinery, a collusive conveyance, the covenantor might practically set himself free from the covenant. So equity began restraining grantees, assignees, under-lessees of the land from doing anything in breach of the restrictive covenant, if they came to the land with notice of it, and this regardless of the question whether the covenant ran with the land at law. And so the conception was formed of covenants running with the land, not at law, but in equity. The phrase however is not a very happy one. The injunction does not go against the grantee or assignee or sub-lessee on the ground that he has come to the land, it goes against him on the ground that he has come to the land with notice—express notice or constructive—of this restrictive obligation. The covenant must be a restrictive one, a negative one. This point was decided in *Haywood* v. *Brunswick Building Society*, 8 Q.B.D. 403. A covenant not to build falls within the doctrine—as regards a covenant to build equity would have nothing to say, the parties are left to the rights, if any, which the common law gives them.

The Judicature Acts have not made any confusion of these

different principles. Let us examine an instructive case, *Hall* v. *Ewin* (1887), 37 Ch. D. 74. Hall demised a house to Tarlington for 80 years, and the lessee covenanted that he, his executors, administrators and assigns would not use the premises or permit or suffer them to be used by any person for any noisome or offensive business. Tarlington sub-demised the premises by way of mortgage to Ruddach for the term of 80 years less three days. Under the power of sale in this mortgage, Ruddach's executors sold and assigned the premises to Ewin for the residue of the 80 years term less the three days. Ewin then sub-let to McNeff for 21 years, and McNeff covenanted not to carry on any noisome or offensive trade or business, but proceeded to open a wild beast show. Hall then sued McNeff and Ewin. We may take it (1) that the wild beast show was an offensive business, and (2) that both Ewin and McNeff had notice of the covenant contained in the original lease. This being established it could not be disputed that an injunction ought to go against McNeff. But how about Ewin—could he be enjoined from suffering the nuisance to continue? Kekewich J. granted an injunction against him on the ground that 'he was equitably bound by the covenant and that as he had power to enforce the covenants contained in the sub-lease to McNeff and to stop the nuisance, he had broken the covenant against suffering the premises to be used for the purpose of a noisome occupation'. The Court of Appeal dissolved the injunction against Ewin. The first point that we have to notice is that Ewin was not at law liable on the covenant; he was not an assignee of the original lease, but had a derivative term created by the mortgage deed. Then as to equity, Cotton L.J. put the matter thus: 'There is no doubt that under the principle of *Tulk* v. *Moxhay*[1] if a man had actually done anything in contravention of the covenants of which he had notice the Court would grant an injunction. As I understand *Tulk* v. *Moxhay* the principle there laid down was that if a man bought an under-lease, although he was not bound in law by the restrictive covenants of the original lease, yet if he purchased with notice of those covenants the Court of Chancery could not allow him to use the land in contravention of the covenants.

[1] 2 Phil. 774.

That is a sound principle. If a man buys land subject to a restrictive covenant he regulates the price accordingly, and it would be contrary to equity to allow him to use the land in contravention of the restriction. But here the Plaintiff does not seek to restrain Ewin from using the house in a particular way, or from doing something which will enable the tenant so to use it, but to compel him to bring an action against his tenant who is in possession of the house'....The Court of Appeal in '*Haywood* v. *Brunswick Permanent Benefit Building Society*[1]...laid down that the principle in *Tulk* v. *Moxhay* was not to be applied so as to compel a man to do that which will involve him in expense'.

And Lord Justice Lindley said (at p. 81) 'It is important to bear in mind that Ewin is not an assignee of the original lease, and is not bound at law by the covenants. It is true that the distinction between an assignee and an under-lessee of the term, less a few days, is a very nice and technical one, but we can not help that; we can not hold that Ewin is bound at law by any covenant, nor can he be made liable for damages in any action at law. Therefore the Plaintiff is driven to bring him within the principle of *Tulk* v. *Moxhay*. I do not think that he has succeeded in doing so. This is an attempt to extend the principle of that case beyond its proper limits, and I think that such attempts ought not to be encouraged.'

The position of a person who has come to land with notice of a covenant but without becoming legally liable on that covenant is thus a peculiar one; it would be unconscientious of him to do anything by way of active breach of a negative covenant; but this is all that equity can expect of him, at law he is not bound by the covenants and equity expects no more than that he will not actively break down. But note that an injunction may go against a mere managing occupier, *Mander* v. *Falcke* [1891] 2 Ch. 554. It is not at all necessary that the person enjoined should be standing in the legal shoes of the covenantor.

An argument which might at first sight seem plausible would bring us to a different result. Law says that an under-lessee is not bound by covenants in the original lease; Equity says that

[1] 8 Q.B.D. 403.

he is bound; the Judicature Act says that when there is any conflict between the rules of Law and Equity the rules of Equity are to prevail, therefore, he is bound. But we have seen the danger of this very rough reasoning. There was no conflict— equity was but supplementing the law, adding a liability founded on notice to the liabilities created by the legal doctrines about covenants running with the land. It has been, and still is, so hard for a purchaser of land to buy without constructive notice of all covenants affecting the land; it has been, and still is, so next to impossible for an under-lessee to have no notice of the covenants contained in the original lease—that we may easily come to the notion of an equitable obligation running with land in the same way that the burden of a covenant may run with land. But every now and then, owing perhaps to some ingenious fraud, arises the case of a *bona fide* purchaser or lessee getting the legal estate for value and without notice, and then we may see that the land or the purchaser's interest in the land is not bound by the covenant, that the covenant does not really run with the land. The very difficulty that there is of purchasing without notice makes it all the more necessary for us to insist on the abiding difference that there is between a legal and an equitable right in land.

A turning point in this doctrine is Sir George Jessel's judgment in *London and South Western Railway Company* v. *Gomm*, 20 Ch. D. 562. He there suggested (at p. 583) that the doctrine of *Tulk* v. *Moxhay* might be treated as an extension in equity of *Spencer's Case* or of the doctrine of (legal) negative easements. In the latter case an equitable estate would be subject to it.

The last extension of the doctrine is to be found in the case of *In re Nisbet and Potts' Contract* [1905] 1 Ch. 391, Farwell J., affirmed in the Court of Appeal [1906] 1 Ch. 386.

In 1872 X conveys a farm to A in fee. A covenants not to build within 30 feet of a certain road.

Sometime or another B enters as a squatter (disseisor or abator[1]), remains in possession, and in 1890 sells and conveys to C. At this time neither B nor C knows of the covenant. In

---

[1] For this distinction see Challis, *Law of Real Property*, 2nd edition, p. 207.

1903 C sells to D, and by the conditions of sale the title was to commence with the deed of 1890. Someone on behalf of X (or of those who stand in the shoes of X) gives warning to D of the covenants. D declines to fulfil the contract of sale. Is he bound to fulfil it?

Remember how the Statute of Limitations operates (3 & 4 Will. IV, c. 27, amended by the Real Property Limitation Act 1874). The action to recover the land is lost and then the former owner's right is extinguished, not conveyed to the now possessor.

Can this negative covenant be enforced against B the disseisor before time has run in his favour? Yes. And after? Yes. He is not a *bona fide* purchaser for value. He is held bound because the rule is being stated thus, 'all occupiers are bound except the man who has purchased for value in good faith and without notice actual or constructive'. Thus the negative covenant is put on a level with an easement—though one subject to a peculiar exception, viz. that it is destroyable by a *bona fide* purchase for value with the legal estate.

But was not C a *bona fide* purchaser without notice? C had no actual notice. What of constructive notice? Yes, it is there said, he had constructive notice. If he had bought on an open contract he would have had the right to a 40 years title, and a title under the Statute of Limitations would not have been forced upon him. He 'must take the consequences'.

As to the burden of proof see Farwell J. in the court below, at p. 402. 'The plea of purchaser for value without notice is a single plea, to be proved by the person pleading it. It is not to be regarded as a plea of purchaser for value, to be met by a reply of notice. . . . It is therefore for the vendor (Nisbet) to prove that he had no notice from the prior deeds, and he can only do this by producing such deeds.'

The burden of proof is thus thrown upon the person who asserts that he has no notice. Equity in its dealing with restrictive covenants began at the opposite end to this.

Note, too, that this equity is enforced against one who is not a party to the transaction creating the equity, and who does not claim through or under any party. A curious class of negative easement is here created.

NOTE ON RESTRICTIVE COVENANTS

MAITLAND is mainly concerned to discuss the question against whom covenants can be enforced. His conclusions on this point may be summarized as follows:

(a) Covenants between lessor and lessee stand upon a peculiar footing; the law as regards them is stated on p. 160 above.

(b) Other covenants can at common law be enforced only against the original covenantor and, of course, his estate after his death.

(c) In equity, however, a covenant can be enforced by injunction against subsequent owners or occupiers of the land of the covenantor if

    (i) The covenant is a restrictive and not a positive covenant.

    (ii) It is a covenant intended to bind the land of the covenantor, *i.e.* not merely a personal covenant.

    (iii) The person against whom it is to be enforced is not a purchaser for value without notice of the covenant.

There are some further points in connexion with covenants, not discussed by Maitland, which should be noticed. They are dealt with in this note under three headings:

    I. Who can enforce the covenant.

    II. Obsolete covenants.

    III. Restrictions binding chattels.

I. WHO CAN ENFORCE THE COVENANT

In an action upon a covenant, whether at law or in equity, the plaintiff must show not only that the defendant is bound by the covenant but also that he, the plaintiff, is a person entitled to enforce the covenant. It is this second requisite that we shall now discuss. In this discussion we shall consider the position both at common law and in equity and shall leave out of account covenants in leases, since the position of these is in some ways peculiar.

Take first the position at common law. A person wishing to enforce a covenant of any sort at common law, unless he is himself the original covenantee or the personal representative of the original covenantee, must show that the benefit of the covenant has become vested in him. This he can do in two ways, namely:

(a) By proving that the benefit of the covenant has been expressly assigned to him, in a case where the covenant is of such a nature to be assignable; or

(b) By proving that the benefit of the covenant has passed to him as an incident of land which he has acquired.

The case of express assignment needs no further comment, but the case of a covenant which passes as an incident of land is more interesting. Where A covenanted with B to do something which related to land owned by B, the Common Law Courts regarded the benefit of the covenant as becoming in a sense annexed to the land, so that on a sale of the land it would pass as an incident of the land to subsequent owners and could be enforced by them. For this to happen it was necessary that the covenant should relate to the land; it is not quite clear whether or not it was also necessary to find in the instrument containing the covenant an intention that the benefit of the covenant should pass as an incident of the land. Probably any covenant relating to the land would become annexed to the land unless a contrary intention appeared. This appears at any rate to be the law in regard to covenants entered into after 1925, since under section 78 of the Law of Property Act 1925 a covenant relating to any land of the covenantee is deemed to be made with the covenantee and his successors in title and therefore, one would suppose, passes to the successors in title as an incident of the land.

These accordingly are the two modes by which the benefit of a covenant can pass at common law. Before considering the position in equity two further points should be noted:

(*a*) For the benefit of a covenant to pass at common law as an incident of the land of the covenantee it is not necessary for the covenant in any way to relate to the land of the covenantor. Thus if A, a prior, covenants with B that A and his convent will every week sing in a chapel belonging to B the benefit of this covenant passes as an incident annexed to the chapel.[1]

(*b*) In using the words 'the covenantee' one normally has in mind an instrument made between two parties A and B in which A covenants with B to do something for B's benefit. It is however possible for A to covenant to do something for the benefit of C, a third person not a party to the instrument, and under a rather obscure statutory rule now contained in section 56 of the Law of Property Act 1925 (replacing with amendments section 45 of the Real Property Act 1845) it may then be possible for C to enforce the covenant although he is not a party to the instrument (see as an example *Dyson* v. *Forster* [1909] A.C. 98). The effect of this section is by no means clear and is not worth investigating here, but it should be noted that 'the covenantee', though he will usually be a party to the instrument containing the covenant, is not necessarily such. He may sometimes be a third person.

We may now consider who can enforce restrictive covenants in equity under the rule in *Tulk* v. *Moxhay*. We shall assume in every case that the person against whom the covenant is to be enforced is a

---

[1] See *The Prior's Case*, Co. Litt. 385 (*a*) stated in Smith's Leading Cases, 13th edition, vol. I, p. 55.

purchaser of the land of the covenantor bound by the covenant who bought with notice of the covenant. Against such a person the covenant will not be enforceable at law but will be enforceable in equity if the plaintiff is a person who is entitled to enforce it.

The first rule to be noted is that the covenant will only be enforced under the rule in *Tulk* v. *Moxhay* for the protection of land. The plaintiff, even if he be the original covenantee himself, must show that the covenant was entered into for the protection of land of the covenantee and that the plaintiff has an interest in some at least of the land intended to be protected. Thus if A the owner of Blackacre covenants with B not to build on Blackacre, B can only enforce the covenant against a purchaser from A of Blackacre if he B had, at the date of the covenant, land in the neighbourhood of Blackacre intended to be protected by the covenant and still retains some of that land. If B never had any neighbouring land or has parted with all the land which he had, he can no longer enforce the covenant against a purchaser from A (*L.C.C.* v. *Allen* [1914] 3 K.B. 642, *Kelly* v. *Barrett* [1924] 2 Ch. 379 and *In re Union of London and Smith's Bank Conveyance* [1933] 1 Ch. 611; and see too *Formby* v. *Barker* [1903] 2 Ch. 539).

As regards the original covenantee himself this would seem to be the only requirement. So long as he retains some of the land intended to be protected he can enforce the covenant.

As regards persons other than the original covenantee it must also be shown that the plaintiff has acquired the benefit of the covenant. It is not enough that he has acquired some of the land intended to be protected, though this is of course necessary. A person can show that he has acquired the benefit of the covenant in one of three ways, namely:

(1) By showing that the benefit of the covenant was assigned to him; or

(2) By showing that the benefit of the covenant was annexed to land which he has purchased and accordingly has passed to him as an incident of the land; or

(3) By showing that there was a building scheme.

The first two of these ways are similar to the ways whereby, as we have already seen, the benefit of a covenant can pass at common law. The third is peculiar and will be discussed later.

The difficulty in determining whether the benefit of a covenant has passed either by assignment or as an incident of land arises mainly from two facts: first, that the original covenantee will often be intending to sell in separate lots the land which he intended to be protected and may well wish to keep the power of enforcing the covenants in his own hands and not wish the purchasers of all the lots to have this power, since that would prevent him from later releasing the covenants if he wished to do so, and secondly that the instrument containing the covenant may well not state what land is intended to be protected. The working out of the principles is best seen by examining some of the decided cases.

In *Renals* v. *Cowlishaw* (9 Ch. D. 125, 11 Ch. D. 866)[1] A, who owned a house and adjoining lands, sold part of the adjoining lands to B and took a covenant from B restricting the user of the lands sold. A retained the house and the remainder of the adjoining lands. There were no express words in the conveyance to annex the benefit of the covenant to the house or any other of the lands retained by A, nor did the conveyance state which of the lands retained were intended to be protected. Later A sold the house to C, but C did not buy that part of the adjoining lands which A had originally retained, some of which lands had in fact already been sold to D. In the conveyance from A to C there was no mention of the covenant. Held that C could not enforce the covenant against a purchaser from B, since the benefit of the covenant was not expressly assigned to him and there was nothing to annex the benefit of the covenant to the house which he bought, so as to make it pass as an incident attached to the house.

In *Rogers* v. *Hosegood* [1900] 2 Ch. 388 four partners who owned building land sold a plot to A, who entered into a restrictive covenant. The covenant was expressed to be entered into to the intent that it should enure for the benefit of the partners their heirs and assigns and others claiming under them all or any of their lands adjoining or near to the premises sold to A. Later the partners sold to B another plot, near to A's plot. B, at the time of the purchase, did not know of the existence of A's covenant and there was no mention of it in the conveyance to B. Held nevertheless that the persons claiming under B could enforce the covenant against the defendants, who were purchasers of A's plot with notice of the covenant, since the benefit of the covenant had been expressly annexed to B's plot and passed as an incident of the land though it was not mentioned in the conveyance to B.

In *Ives* v. *Brown* [1919] 2 Ch. 314 the facts were rather complicated. Somewhat simplified they were as follows. A and B owned a building estate which they held upon trust for A for life with remainder to such persons as A should appoint. In 1876 they sold a piece of the estate to C, who entered into a restrictive covenant expressed to be made with A and B 'their heirs or assigns or the persons deriving title under them or either of them'. B died in 1885. Between 1876 and 1917 a considerable portion of the building estate was sold but there remained scattered pieces which had not been sold. In 1917 A died, having, in exercise of his power of appointment, appointed the unsold parts of the building estate to D and having appointed D and E to be his executors. In 1918 D and E sued the persons deriving title under C for an injunction to restrain breach of the covenant. Held that the

---

[1] See too *Reid* v. *Bickerstaff* [1909] 2 Ch. 305.

benefit of the covenant had not been annexed to the parts of the estate retained by A which had passed to D so that D could not sue simply as owner of the land; but held also that D and E together could sue, for the benefit of the covenant had passed to them as executors of A and they satisfied the requirement of having land intended to be protected, since D had such land. They were in fact in the same position as purchasers from the covenantee who have bought part of the land intended to be protected and at the same time have taken an express assignment of the covenant.

With this case one should compare *Chambers* v. *Randall* [1923] 1 Ch. 149, in which the facts were briefly as follows. A sold land to B, who entered into a restrictive covenant, but the benefit of the covenant was not annexed to any particular land. Later A conveyed to C and D part of the land intended to be protected, without assigning to C and D the benefit of the covenant. Before A died he had disposed of the remainder of the land intended to be protected. A then died having appointed C and D his executors. It might be thought that on the principle of *Ives* v. *Brown* C and D could have enforced the covenant, for by purchase from A they had acquired part of the land intended to be protected and as executors of A the benefit of the covenant would vest in them on A's death. Nevertheless, it was held that C and D could not enforce the covenant. The case is distinguished from *Ives* v. *Brown* on the ground that, on A parting with all the land intended to be protected, the covenant ceased to be enforceable and the fact that on A's death the benefit of it would again vest in persons who owned part of the land intended to be protected did not revive it.

Finally, one should read *In re Union of London and Smith's Bank Conveyance* [1933] Ch. 611, where the principles of law are fully discussed in a judgment of the Court of Appeal. In that case the benefit of the covenant was not annexed to any particular land and the claim to enforce the covenant was based upon the grounds:

(a) That the claimant had purchased from the original covenantee part of the land intended to be protected; and

(b) That the benefit of the covenant had been expressly assigned to him.

His claim failed because he could not show that the land which he had purchased was part of the land intended to be protected; the original covenantee had retained much land in the neighbourhood and there was nothing to show which of it he intended to be protected. The claim might perhaps also have failed on the further ground that the assignment of the benefit of the covenant was executed some years after the conveyance to the claimant of his land and might therefore have been ineffective on the principle of *Chambers* v. *Randall*, but it was not necessary fully to explore this point.

A few observations may be helpful upon the question how the

benefit of a covenant can be annexed to particular land. Supposing the covenant is entered into with 'A and his assigns'—do these words annex the covenant to the land of A in the neighbourhood? Probably not. One is apt to read the word 'assigns' as meaning assigns of the neighbouring land, but it is equally capable of meaning and usually does mean 'assigns of the benefit of the covenant'. In short the word 'assigns' has not the effect of annexing the benefit of the covenant to land. Suppose next that the covenant is 'with A and his successors in title to the X estate'. Here we have annexation to the X estate as a whole, but even here it does not necessarily follow that the benefit is annexed to each part of the X estate so as to pass to the purchaser of a part. A form of words which clearly annexes the benefit to each part of the estate is that used in *Rogers v. Hosegood*.[1] Finally, we should note section 78 of the Law of Property Act 1925, whereby, in an instrument made after 1925, a covenant relating to land of the covenantee is to be deemed to be made with the covenantee and his successors in title, which phrase is to include in regard to restrictive covenants the owners and occupiers for the time being of the land of the covenantee intended to be benefited. The effect of the section is not quite clear. It would certainly seem to annex the benefit of the covenants to the land to be benefited as a whole, but it probably does not annex the benefit to each part of such land.

It remains to consider the enforcement of restrictive covenants under a building scheme. A building scheme is, as it were, a private scheme of town planning. The essence of it is a scheme of restrictive covenants imposed over an area with the intention that the scheme should be a local law for the whole area. It usually occurs when a large estate is sold in lots for building and the scheme is imposed to maintain the character of the neighbourhood, but one may also have a building scheme where property is leased in lots (*Spicer* v. *Martin*, 14 App. Cas. 12). There probably cannot be a building scheme unless all the property in the area affected is derived, by purchase or lease, from a common vendor or lessor. When a building scheme has been shown to exist the following results ensue:

(a) The owner of any one lot can enforce the covenants in equity against the owner of any other lot.

(b) The vendor himself is bound by the scheme and, if he still retains lots unsold, the covenants which, under the scheme, ought to be imposed on the unsold lots can be enforced against him and he can be restrained from selling these lots subsequently without taking the proper covenants (*McKenzie* v. *Childers*, 43 Ch. D. 265, *In re Birmingham and District Land Co.* [1893] 1 Ch. 342 and *Spicer* v. *Martin*, 14 App. Cas. 12). Equally it

[1] See above, p. 171.

would seem that if he then sells one of the unsold lots and omits to take the proper covenants the purchaser will nevertheless be bound in equity by the covenants, if he bought with notice that the lot was affected by the scheme.

The covenants are of course enforceable only in equity, except as between the vendor and the original purchasers, and a purchaser of a lot without notice of the covenants will not be bound by them.

In practice it is difficult to prove that a building scheme exists, for it is not enough that a vendor has sold his estate in lots and has taken restrictive covenants from each purchaser. Parker J. in *Elliston* v. *Reacher* [1908] 2 Ch. 374, 665, formulated the propositions which (in the case a building scheme on a sale) one must establish. They are as follows:

(a) That the Plaintiff and Defendant derive title under a common vendor.

(b) That before selling the lands to which the Plaintiff and Defendant are entitled, the vendor laid out his estate (or a defined part of it which included the Plaintiff's and Defendant's lands) for sale in lots subject to restrictions intended to be imposed on all the lots and which, though varying in details as to particular lots, are consistent and consistent only with some general scheme of development.

(c) That the covenants were intended by the vendor to be and were for the benefit of all the lots intended to be sold, whether or not they were also intended to be and were for the benefit of other land retained by the vendor.

(d) That both the Plaintiff and Defendant, or their predecessors in title, purchased their lots from the common vendor on the footing that the restrictions subject to which the purchases were made were to enure for the benefit of the other lots included in the general scheme, whether or not they were also to enure for the benefit of other lands retained by the vendor.

II. Obsolete Covenants

In course of time restrictive covenants may become obsolete. Nevertheless, each time that the land is sold they will be set out or referred to in the conveyance and the land will be sold subject to them. Thus the title will carry an incubus of antique covenants of which every purchaser will necessarily have notice. Sometimes there will in fact be no one who is still able to enforce them; sometimes, though perhaps enforceable, they will through a change in the character of the neighbourhood have lost their purpose, so that to enforce them would be merely capricious. Nevertheless, so long as they remain upon the title, they will clog the user of the land. Suppose for example that a man wishes to build a shop which will cost him £200,000 to build and has found a suitable site, but on investigating the title discovers that it is subject to a covenant that it shall not be used otherwise than for a private dwelling house. The covenant may no longer be enforceable but the man will probably refuse to buy the site, since there is always the chance that someone can still enforce the covenant and he cannot risk an injunction after he has started to build. Covenants which appear upon the title, even if they are in fact quite dead, will still operate 'in terrorem'.

The equitable doctrine of acquiescence did something to meet this position. When a covenantee by allowing the covenant to be broken a number of times without protest had led the covenantor to believe that the covenant had been waived and on that belief to act in breach of the covenant, the covenantee might be debarred by his acquiescence from obtaining an injunction to restrain the further breach (*Sayers* v. *Collyer*, 28 Ch. D. 103, *Roper* v. *Williams*, 1 T. and R. 18). This principle was however of limited application and, in general, acquiescence in one breach of covenant was not regarded as a waiver of the right to enforce the covenant in the future (see for example *Western* v. *MacDermott* (1866) L.R. 2 Ch. 72 and *Gaskin* v. *Balls* (1879) 13 Ch. D. 324).

Where, as in the case of a building scheme, covenants had been imposed for the protection of a whole neighbourhood the Courts went rather further. In such a case, through breaches of covenant being permitted and from other circumstances, the character of the neighbourhood might so change that the covenants no longer served any useful purpose and the Courts would then refuse an injunction. An area might be demarcated under a building scheme as a residential area and appropriate covenants against setting up shops—especially beershops—be imposed. In time however shops were built and the area ceased to be residential. It became maybe 'studded with beershops'. When this had happened it would be merely capricious for the covenantee to restrain a particular person from setting up a beershop and in cases of this type the Courts would not grant an injunction (see *Duke of Bedford* v. *Trustees of the British Museum* (1882) 2 Myl. and K. 552, *Knight* v. *Simmonds* [1896] 2 Ch. 294, *Sobey* v. *Sainsbury* [1913] 2 Ch. 513 and *Chatsworth Estates* v. *Fewell* [1931] 1 Ch. 224).

These principles of equity however did not go far enough to meet the difficulty arising from outworn covenants and special provisions to meet the difficulty were enacted by section 84 of the Law of Property Act 1925, which should be read. It provides (briefly) for the discharge or modification of restrictive covenants in the following cases:

(a) Where the covenant is obsolete through change in the character of the property or the neighbourhood. This deals with the cases such as *Duke of Bedford* v. *Trustees of the British Museum* referred to above.

(b) Where all parties have agreed whether expressly or by implication by their acts or omissions to the discharge or modification of the covenant. Presumably the type of acts which a Court of Equity would have regarded as acquiescence amounting to a waiver of the covenant would here be treated as assent to its discharge.

(c) Where the discharge or modification will not injure the persons entitled to the benefit of the restriction.

In any of these cases the application to modify or discharge the covenant is to be made to a special Authority which consists of arbitrators appointed in accordance with sub-section 9 of the section, although in some cases the Court has probably concurrent jurisdiction (but see *Feilden* v. *Byrne* [1926] Ch. 620).

In addition the section gives the Court power to declare whether a restriction affects particular land, what is the extent of the restriction and whether it is enforceable and by whom. These questions are mainly questions of law which the Court is the proper tribunal to decide. The questions which the Authority is to decide are chiefly questions of fact and it is presumably thought that for these arbitrators, who can visit the neighbourhood and act less formally than the Court, will be a cheaper and better tribunal. *In re Sunnyfield* [1932] 1 Ch. 79, an application to the Court under the section, in which covenants were declared to be unenforceable, shows the advantages of the section. Briefly the advantages are that a person claiming the right to enforce the covenants, who apart from the section would be able after announcing his claim to sit by until a breach was committed, can be brought before the Court and made to produce his documents and prove his claim, and that if for some reason some person who might claim escapes notice he will nevertheless be bound by the order. In short, if the covenants are in fact unenforceable, they can be cleaned off the title before a purchaser has spent money in buying the land or starting to build upon it.

III. Restrictions Binding Chattels

It has at times been thought that the principle of *Tulk* v. *Moxhay* applied only to land and not to chattels, *i.e.* that it was not possible to impose a covenant restrictive of the user of a chattel so that purchasers of the chattel with notice of the covenant would be bound by it. For this proposition reliance was placed upon *Taddy* v. *Sterious* [1904] 1 Ch. 354 and *McGruther* v. *Pitcher* [1904] 2 Ch. 306,[1] in both of which cases an attempt was made, as part of a price maintenance agreement,

---

[1] See also *Dunlop* v. *Selfridge* [1915] A.C. 847 and *National Phonograph Co.* v. *Menck* [1911] A.C. 336 at p. 347.

to attach to a chattel a condition that it should not be sold at less than a certain price. In both cases the Court held the condition unenforceable against a subsequent purchaser of the chattel, even though he bought with notice of the condition. Recently, however, in *Lord Strathcona S.S. Co.* v. *Dominion Coal Co.* [1926] A.C. 108 the Privy Council applied the principle of *Tulk* v. *Moxhay* to a ship. In that case the A. Co. chartered a ship for a long term from the B. Co. who owned it. The B. Co. subsequently sold the ship and after a number of intermediate sales it was finally bought by the C. Co., who, as well as all intermediate purchasers, were treated as having bought with notice of the charterparty. The A. Co. did not by the charterparty acquire a legal interest in the ship; they were not in the same position as lessees of land and had not at law any right against the C. Co., who were not parties to the charterparty, to have the terms of the charterparty carried out. Nevertheless, the Privy Council held that there was implied in the charterparty a term that the ship should not be used otherwise than in accordance with the charterparty and that, under principles similar to those of *Tulk* v. *Moxhay*, this negative term bound the C. Co. since they purchased with notice of it. Accordingly an injunction was granted against the C. Co. from using the ship otherwise than in accordance with the charterparty. The practical effect of the injunction would be to enforce the charterparty against the C. Co., for their only alternative would be to lay up the ship.

There are two grounds upon which this case might be distinguished from the earlier cases of *Taddy* v. *Sterious* and *McGruther* v. *Pitcher*, namely

(a) That a ship stands in a position different from that of other chattels; or

(b) That the restriction in *Taddy* v. *Sterious* and *McGruther* v. *Pitcher* was a restriction upon alienation and not upon user. Even in the case of land it is conceived that the law would not recognize a restriction upon alienation as binding the land under the rule in *Tulk* v. *Moxhay*.

Unfortunately neither of these was the ground upon which the cases were decided and, indeed, if one looks only at the *ratio decidendi* of each case there appears to be a conflict which cannot be reconciled. The student who wishes to pursue the point should refer to an article by Mr E. C. S. Wade in vol. XLIV of the *Law Quarterly Review* at p. 51.

An undoubted qualification upon the rule, if such there be, that a restriction cannot be made to run with chattels exists in the case of patented articles (*National Phonograph Co.* v. *Menck* [1911] A.C. 336). A patentee has under his patent a monopoly of the manufacture, sale and use of the patented article. Other persons who sell or use it do so only under licence express or implied from the patentee. If indeed the patentee sells the article without restriction, the purchaser obtains, by implication, the right freely to use and sell that article and subsequent purchasers from him will equally obtain such right. If however the patentee on selling imposes a restriction on user or sale and the purchasers have notice of it, their implied licence to use and sell is subject to the restriction and, if they offend against the restriction, they are guilty of infringing the patent. Thus the patentee can effectively impose a restriction—which may even be a restriction upon alienation—so as to make it run with the patented article and can enforce such restriction by an action for infringement of the patent against purchasers who have notice of the restriction. It should however be noticed in this connexion that section 38 of the Patent and Designs Act 1907 prohibits the attaching of certain types of condition on the sale of patented articles.

LECTURE XIII

MORTGAGES[1]

You will have read how Equity came to interest itself in mortgages. In consequence of its doctrine that a mortgage is merely a security for money, a security which can be redeemed although, according to the plain wording of the mortgage deed, the mortgagee has become the absolute owner of the land, it drew almost every dispute about mortgages into the sphere of its jurisdiction and had the last word to say about them.

I think that I may best serve you by speaking of the structure of mortgage deeds. We shall have to consider what they say and what they do. You will know that the Conveyancing Act of 1881 has very much shortened the forms hitherto in use. It has done this by saying that in the absence of any expression of a contrary intention a mortgage deed is to be deemed to contain certain clauses. These clauses are like, though not exactly like, certain clauses which used to be expressly inserted in the deed— set out in full. But it will be expedient that for a while we should go behind the Act and we will consider a mortgage of the most simple and elementary kind. Doe is tenant in fee simple of Blackacre, in which he has an unencumbered estate; Nokes is going to lend him £1000 upon the security of Blackacre and the debt is to bear interest at the rate of £4 per cent. per annum. Let us begin.

'This Indenture made the 1st day of January 1880 between Doe of the one part and Nokes of the other part Witnesseth that in consideration of the sum of £1000 upon the execution of these presents paid by the said Nokes to the said Doe (the receipt of which said sum the said Doe doth hereby acknowledge) He the said Doe doth hereby for himself his heirs, executors and administrators covenant with the said Nokes his executors and administrators that the said Doe his heirs executors or adminis-

---

[1] The law has been considerably altered by the Law of Property Act 1925. See note on p. 206 below. In the original edition of the book this lecture was lecture XXI.

trators will on the 1st day of July next pay to the said Nokes his executors, administrators or assigns the sum of £1000 with interest for the same in the meantime at the rate of 4 per cent. per annum And that if the said sum of £1000 or any part thereof shall remain unpaid after the said 1st day of July the said Doe his heirs executors or administrators will pay to the said Nokes his executors administrators or assigns interest for the said sum of £1000 or for so much thereof as shall for the time being remain unpaid at the rate of 4 per cent. per annum by equal half-yearly payments on the 1st day of January and the 1st day of July.'

Here ends one section of the deed and as yet we have come upon nothing that affects Blackacre, nothing that can be called a mortgage. We have a mere covenant, creating of course a specialty debt, that Doe will repay the loan with interest six months hence, and that in case of non-payment on a certain day Doe will go on paying interest half-yearly. Then opens a second section of the deed.

'And this Indenture also witnesseth that for the consideration aforesaid the said Doe doth hereby grant unto the said Nokes his heirs and assigns All that piece of land called Blackacre [Here you describe the property—"the parcels"—and you used to insert the "general words" and the "estate clause"][1] To have and to hold unto the said Nokes his heirs and assigns to the use of the said Nokes his heirs and assigns subject to the proviso for redemption hereinafter contained.'

You see you make an absolute conveyance of the fee simple to Nokes, just mentioning at the end of it that it is subject to a proviso for redemption which is coming. This proviso for redemption—in strictness it were better called a proviso for reconveyance—comes immediately.

'Provided always and it is hereby agreed and declared that if the said Doe his heirs, executors, administrators or assigns shall on the 1st of July next pay to the said Nokes his executors administrators or assigns the said sum of £1000 with interest for the same in the meantime at the rate of 4 per cent. per annum, then the said Nokes his heirs or assigns shall at any time there-

---

[1] See now Law of Property Act 1925, ss. 62 and 63.

after upon the request and at the cost of the said Doe his heirs, executors, administrators, or assigns reconvey the said premises to the use of the said Doe his heirs and assigns or as he or they shall direct.'

Now there is a mortgage. It is a very imperfect deed, it does not give to Nokes, the mortgagee, nearly all the rights that should be given to him. Still here is all that is essential to make a mortgage—a loan of money, in consideration thereof a conveyance of land, subject to a proviso that if on a given day the debt be paid off with interest the mortgagee shall reconvey that land to the mortgagor. Now here let us pause for a while and consider the effect of this short instrument, for thereby we shall come to the reasons why mortgages were not as a rule such short affairs as this. What are the rights and duties of Doe the mortgagor, and Nokes the mortgagee?

Well, in the first place we note that Doe has bound himself by covenant to pay Nokes a certain sum with interest on a certain day. So soon as that day, the 1st of July, 1880, is passed without payment of the money, Nokes will have an action on the covenant against Doe, will be able to obtain a judgment for what is due, will then have a judgment debt owing to him, will be able to obtain execution against all Doe's chattels and all Doe's land by *fieri facias*, *elegit* or the like. Of course this is a somewhat small thing, every creditor who has a specialty debt owing to him has as much as this, and now-a-days every simple contract creditor is almost as well off as a specialty creditor. A man advancing money upon mortgage wants something better than this, he wants some *jus in rem*, some right in certain specific things as well as the mere *jus in personam* that the mortgagor's covenant will give him. Still note that the mortgagee has this *jus in personam*, for in easily imaginable circumstances it will be of use to him. He has advanced £1000 upon the security of Blackacre and we may suppose that like a prudent man he has observed the wholesome rule which the court enforces upon trustees, and has not lent more than two-thirds of the value of Blackacre. Still in these days of agricultural depression it is by no means impossible that he may hereafter find that Blackacre is not worth £1000. Then his personal remedy against Doe, the mortgagor, who may be a solvent, wealthy person, will be of great value to him. He may sell Blackacre for £800 and get £200 more by suing Doe upon the covenant, and even if Doe be insolvent, be bankrupt, he will have his choice between realizing his insufficient security and taking a dividend proportioned to the sum still due, or abandoning his security and taking a dividend proportioned to the whole debt. You should understand that it is by no means of the essence of a mortgage that the mortgagee should look to the mortgaged property alone for the repayment of the loan, on the contrary he always or almost always can also look to the personal liability of the mortgagor. He is not the less a creditor because he is a secured creditor.

But of course it is more important to him that he should have rights in Blackacre. And on the face of the mortgage deed it seems plain enough that if the 1st of July passes without his debt being paid to him with interest, he will be the absolute owner of Blackacre—or, to be more accurate, unqualified tenant in fee simple of Blackacre. Of course if on that day he be paid or tendered his principal and interest then under the express words of the proviso for reconveyance, he will be bound to reconvey. But then it is an extremely rare, an almost unheard of, event, that there should be this punctual payment or tender—indeed Nokes, who thinks that he has found a permanent investment for his £1000, would probably be much annoyed if on the 1st of July Doe appeared with his 1020 sovereigns in hand. That is the worst of our mortgage deed—owing to the action of equity, it is one long *suppressio veri* and *suggestio falsi*.[1] It does not in the least explain the rights of the parties; it suggests that they are other than really they are.

Though the 1st of July has passed, yet at any time before foreclosure or sale Doe will be able to redeem the mortgage, will be able to demand from Nokes a reconveyance if he tenders to him his principal, his interest, and his costs. I say 'until foreclosure or sale'—how there comes to be any talk of a sale I shall explain hereafter. But what is a foreclosure? Well, equity in

---

[1] Cf. Lord Bramwell's remarks in *Salt* v. *Marquess of Northampton* [1892] A.C. pp. 18 and 19.

effect said this: A mortgagee shall not become the absolute owner of the mortgaged thing until he has come into my court, until the mortgagor has had an opportunity of saying anything that he has to say, and also a last opportunity definitely limited to him by my order of paying what is due and redeeming the land. Only after a judicial proceeding can the mortgagee become the owner of the land. Let us understand a little about this judicial proceeding.

For some reason or another Nokes wishes to foreclose this mortgage. After due notice he begins an action against Doe, the mortgagor, claiming by his writ[1] that the mortgage may be foreclosed. Of course it may happen that there is some defence to this action—Doe, it is possible, may dispute the existence of the mortgage, or say that it was obtained by fraud—but if Doe has no such defence, if he is merely unable or unwilling to pay the debt then he has no valid defence at all. Very probably he will not appear in the action, for he would gain nothing by appearance. At any rate judgment is given against him. The judgment is in this form:

Let an account be taken of what is due to the plaintiff for principal and interest on his mortgage in the pleadings mentioned and for his costs of this cause, such costs to be taxed. And upon the defendant paying to the plaintiff what shall be certified to be due to him for principal, interest and costs as aforesaid within six calendar months after the date of the Master's certificate at such time and place as shall be thereby appointed, let the plaintiff reconvey the hereditaments comprised in the said mortgage and deliver up on oath all deeds and writings in his custody or power relating thereto to the defendant or to whom he shall appoint. But in default of the defendant paying what shall be so certified to be due to him for such principal, interest and costs as aforesaid by the time aforesaid, the defendant is from thenceforth to stand absolutely debarred and foreclosed of and from all right, title, interest and equity of redemption of, in and to the said mortgaged hereditaments.[2]

---

[1] Foreclosure can now be obtained on an originating summons.

[2] For forms of foreclosure orders see Seton on Judgments and Orders, pp. 1825 *et seq.* (7th edition).

Then in the judge's chambers Nokes the mortgagee will prove what is due to him. The Master will then draw up a certificate stating that this is the sum due and naming some place and hour on the day six months from the date of the certificate—I think that it was usual to name the Rolls Chapel[1]—at which the money is to be paid. If matters have gone so far as this we may be pretty certain that the money will not be paid—it is only in novels, and in novels written by ladies, that the mortgagee's hand is stayed at the last moment by some god out of the machine. Yet another order from the Court is still necessary before the foreclosure is complete. We have as yet but an order *nisi* for foreclosure—the defendant is to be foreclosed *unless* he pays—an order for foreclosure absolute is necessary before the plaintiff mortgagee will be safe. So he, or his solicitor on his behalf, attends on the appointed day, and waits an hour (the certificate generally gives the defendant an hour, *e.g.* 12 to 1, for his appearance) on the outlook for the mortgagor. An affidavit is sworn in proof of this default, and a motion of course (a mere form) is then made before the Court for foreclosure absolute.[2] Thereupon 'this Court doth order that the defendant Doe do from henceforth stand absolutely debarred and foreclosed of and from all right, title, interest and equity of redemption of, in and to the said mortgaged hereditaments'. There are cases in which the mortgagee can get an absolute foreclosure at once—in particular if the mortgagor appears and consents to this; but here I can only follow up the ordinary course of practice.[3]

Just by the way I must mention an improvement introduced by the Judicature Act—for it is typical of many other improvements. Before 1875 a proceeding for foreclosure was of course a proceeding in equity. In the eye of a Court of Common Law the mortgagee was already owner of the land: nothing that such a court could do would make him more of an owner than he was.

---

[1] Now a room at the Royal Courts of Justice.

[2] The application for foreclosure absolute is now made by summons and not by motion whether the proceedings commenced by originating summons or writ.

[3] Notwithstanding the changes made in 1925 Maitland's summary of the procedure on foreclosure still substantially represents the present practice.

On the other hand there was one thing that a Court of Equity could not do for him—it could not give a judgment on the mortgagor's covenant for the payment of the money. An action on a covenant was given by Courts of Law, and if he wanted such a judgment (as well he might) he would have had to go to a Court of Law. But now, though the redemption and fore-closure of mortgages are among the matters specially assigned to the Chancery Division, that Division can since the Judicature Act give all relief, whether equitable or legal, that the plaintiff is entitled to. Now-a-days therefore in his foreclosure action the mortgagee can obtain not only foreclosure, but a judgment on the mortgagor's covenant.[1]

But to return from this bye-point. Now you might well think that Nokes the mortgagee having taken these judicial proceedings, having obtained a judgment for foreclosure—first an order *nisi*, then an order absolute—would at last be able to look upon Blackacre as his very own and to treat Doe as having no interest in it. It is not so. A Court of Equity will as the phrase goes 'reopen a foreclosure' and permit the mortgagor to redeem, and it has refused to lay down any precise rules as to the circum-stances in which it will do this. I need say nothing of fraud, but fraud apart, it will sometimes permit a foreclosed mortgagor to redeem. I think that the last important case about this matter is *Campbell* v. *Holyland*, 7 Ch. D. 166, in which Jessel M.R. dis-cussed the circumstances in which a foreclosure would be reopened. If the mortgaged property was far more valuable than the mortgage debt, if it had for the mortgagor a *pretium affectionis* being an old family estate, if the mortgagor was prevented from redeeming by some accident, if he has come speedily—these all are circumstances in favour of permitting him to redeem, though an absolute order for foreclosure has been made against him. The Court's power to open the fore-closure is a highly discretionary power—all the circumstances of the particular case may be considered. What is more that power may be exercised not only as against the mortgagee but

---

[1] *Poulett* v. *Hill* [1893] 1 Ch. 277, and see *Williams* v. *Hunt* [1905] 1 K.B. 512. If judgment on the covenant is wanted the action must be started by writ and not by originating summons.

as against one who after foreclosure has purchased the estate from the mortgagee. One is not very safe in purchasing a foreclosed estate, and owing to this meddlesome equity foreclosure is not a procedure upon which prudent mortgagees will place much of their reliance.

Well, we have considered two cases open to the mortgagee—he can sue upon the covenant, he can foreclose. But is there not another course open to him? Why should he not enter and take possession of the land that has been conveyed to him? Suppose the mortgagor in possession, why should not the mortgagee turn him out, cultivate the land and take its profits? Suppose that the land when it was mortgaged was occupied by tenants for years, why should not the mortgagee—since he cannot turn them out—demand their rents from them? In short, why should not Nokes enter into the possession or the receipt of the rents and profits of Blackacre. Certainly he can do this. If Doe the mortgagor resisted him, refused to quit possession, a Court of Law would give Nokes its assistance. Nokes would bring an ejectment action against Doe. To this action under the old law Doe would have had no defence even had he been willing and able to pay to Nokes his principal, interest and costs—for in the eye of a Court of Law the time for payment had passed. True a Court of Equity would have prohibited Nokes by injunction from going on with his action, if, but only if, Doe commenced a suit to redeem the mortgage and offered to pay all that was due. What is more, by a statute passed as early as the reign of George II—7 Geo. II, c. 20 (1743)[1]—this mock equity had been introduced into the procedure of the common law courts, that in an action for ejectment by mortgagee against mortgagor (no suit for foreclosure or redemption being then pending), the mortgagor might bring into court the sum due upon the mortgage, and thereupon the Court was to compel the mortgagee to make a reconveyance. But neither by legal nor by equitable procedure could the mortgagee be prevented from ejecting the mortgagor unless the latter was ready and willing to pay what was due. And so it is now. If Doe can not or will not pay what is due Nokes may, without foreclosing, enter into possession of

---

[1] And see the Common Law Procedure Act 1852, ss. 219 and 220.

the mortgaged land. If need be the Court will aid him to obtain possession of it.

Well, here we seem to have a third course open to Nokes the mortgagee—without foreclosing the mortgage he can enter upon the mortgaged lands. But, owing again to the interference of equity, this means of availing himself of his mortgage is not nearly so pleasant as it may look at first sight. 'The situation of a mortgagee in possession is far from an eligible one' (Davidson).[1] On the principle that a mortgagee must make no advantage out of his mortgage beyond the payment of principal, interest and costs, he is bound to account upon terms of great strictness. The common decree is for an account of what he has received or what but for his wilful default he might have received. He is chargeable with an occupation rent in respect of property in hand (*i.e.* property not let to tenants), and is liable for voluntary waste, as in pulling down houses or opening mines. He may charge his actual expenses, but can not stipulate for an allowance or commission to himself for the trouble of collecting the rents. If he recovers rents or profits in excess of the sum due for interest, the Court will often direct an account with half-yearly rests—that is to say, it will direct that in taking the past accounts a balance shall be struck at the end of each half-year, and that any sum in excess of interest that the mortgagee shall have received during that period shall be struck off from the principal sum. On the whole it is not a pleasant thing to be a mortgagee in possession. In general a mortgagee is very loath to take possession, and only does so when he is forced into doing it. The right upon which a mortgagee most frequently places his main reliance is given him by a power of sale, an extra-judicial power of sale. I say an extra-judicial power because I wish to distinguish this from the power of sale under the Conveyancing Act of 1881. Under section 25 of that Act[2]—which in this respect superseded and enlarged the provisions of an earlier Act of 1852 (15 & 16 Vic., c. 86, s. 48)—the Court has now a very wide power of ordering a sale of the mortgaged property in any action for the redemption or the

---

[1] Davidson's *Precedents*, 4th edition, vol. II, part II, p. 90.
[2] Now replaced by the Law of Property Act 1925, s. 91.

foreclosure of a mortgage. That is a very useful power. Often it is to the interest of both parties that instead of a redemption on the one hand or a foreclosure on the other, there should be a sale, a payment to the mortgagee of what is due to him, and a payment of the residue of the price (if any) to the mortgagor. Still the mortgagee does not want to go to court in order to obtain payment of what is due to him. He wants to have a power of sale which he can exercise without applying to the Court.

Now I want you to observe, for this is not unimportant, that a mortgagee with the legal estate had always in a certain sense a power of sale. We take up the brief mortgage which we have supposed to be given by Doe to Nokes in the year 1880. As soon as the 1st of July is passed without any payment of the debt then Nokes is, at law, the absolute owner of the land. The proviso for reconveyance has failed to take effect because Doe has failed to pay his debt on the appointed day. Well of course at law—*i.e.* so far as a court of common law can see—Nokes is able to sell the land and make a good title to it. It has not been *said* that he can sell, but there is no good in saying that an absolute owner can sell; of course he may. Nevertheless, Nokes so long as the mortgage is unforeclosed is under an equitable obligation not to sell. If he attempts to sell, equity will stop him by injunction. Put the case that he does sell and does convey to a purchaser, the mortgagor will in all probability be able to get back that land from the purchaser, to redeem it out of the purchaser's hand. But mark these words 'in all probability'. It is not very likely that this land will come to the hands of a *bona fide* purchaser for value who has obtained the legal estate without notice of the mortgagor's right to redeem—still this is conceivable, for occasionally men are hardy enough to forge title deeds—well in that case we shall find out that the sale and conveyance by the mortgagee who had been given no power of sale is not a nullity—the purchaser, perhaps a sub-purchaser, will be able to laugh at the merely equitable rights of the mortgagor.[1] Indeed in no case will the sale and conveyance be a nullity; it

---

[1] Since 1925 the mortgagor has a legal interest in the land. See note on p. 206 below.

will at least be a transfer of the mortgage, a transfer of such rights as the mortgagee had at law and in equity, and it will be from the purchaser that the mortgagor will have to redeem the land. Still of course this merely legal power of sale, this power which is involved in the legal estate, a power the exercise of which equity will restrain, is not what the mortgagee wants. He wants a power of sale exercisable in equity as well as at law, a power which he can exercise without doing anything condemnable by a Court of Equity.

Before Lord Cranworth's Act 1860 (23 & 24 Vic. c. 145), if he was to have such a power, such a power had to be given him expressly, and a great deal of ingenuity had been spent by conveyancers in devising a thoroughly convenient power. The statute just mentioned gave a somewhat similar power—but it was not in all respects quite so beneficial to mortgagees as that which was commonly in use amongst conveyancers, and very little reliance was placed upon this statutory power. A far more successful attempt to abbreviate mortgages was made by the Conveyancing Act 1881.[1] It took the wise course of giving to mortgagees—unless an intention to the contrary was expressed —a somewhat more beneficial power of sale than that which it has been usual to give them. It follows the old forms in this respect that a really good form would begin by declaring not that in certain events, *e.g.* if the interest was in arrears for so many months, the mortgagee might sell, but that so soon as ever the mortgage debt should become payable the mortgagee might sell—then however it would go on to say that this power was not to be exercisable except on the happening of certain events— and then lastly it would absolve the purchaser from inquiring whether those events had happened. This form had been devised in order to give the mortgagee the utmost freedom in dealing with purchasers, and a purchaser the utmost freedom in dealing with mortgagees. Thus to return to the mortgage on Blackacre which Doe has been giving to Nokes. After the proviso for reconveyance we should find something of this kind —I shall abbreviate the full form very much:

'And it is hereby agreed and declared that it shall be lawful

---

[1] See now Law of Property Act 1925, ss. 101 and 103.

for the said Nokes at any time after the 1st of July next without any further consent on the part of the said Doe to sell the said premises or any part thereof. Provided always that the said Nokes shall not execute the power of sale hereinbefore declared until default shall have been made in the payment of some principal money or interest hereby secured at the time appointed for payment thereof and he shall have given a notice in writing to the said Doe to pay off the monies due upon the security of these presents and default shall have been made for six calendar months from the time of such notice, or until the whole or some half-yearly payment of interest shall have become in arrear for three calendar months.

'Provided also that upon any sale purporting to have been made in pursuance of the power in that behalf, the purchaser shall not be bound to see or inquire whether either of the cases mentioned in the last preceding clause has happened or whether any default has been made in the payment of any principal money or interest intended to be hereby secured at the time appointed for payment thereof or whether any money remains due upon the security of these presents or otherwise as to the propriety or regularity of any such sale and notwithstanding any impropriety or irregularity whatsoever in any such sale the same shall so far as regards the safety and protection of the purchaser be deemed to be within the aforesaid power in that behalf and be valid and effectual accordingly, and the remedy of the mortgagor in respect of any breach of the last preceding clause or provision or of any impropriety or irregularity in any such sale shall be in damages only.'

Thus you see the person who purchases from the mortgagee who is professedly exercising a power of sale given in this form is absolved from making inquiry as to whether a proper case has arisen for the exercise of the power. Suppose *e.g.* that the mortgagee sells when no interest is in arrear, still the purchaser will be safe against the mortgagor, and the mortgagor's only remedy will be an action for damages against the mortgagee, founded on his wrongful use of the power.

Then after this in the old mortgage—I mean the mortgage as drawn before the Act of 1881—came a clause declaring what was to be done with the money arising from any sale under the power. The mortgagee shall in the first place reimburse himself and pay or discharge all the costs and expenses incurred in or about the sale, and in the second place apply the monies in or towards satisfaction of the mortgage debt and then pay the surplus if any to the mortgagor, his heirs or assigns.

You will understand that a sale under the power of sale put a complete end to the right to redeem—the equity of redemption was extinguished—the purchaser became owner at law and in equity and the mortgagor if he had a right to anything, had a right only to be paid by the mortgagee any surplus that there might be when the amount due upon the mortgage for principal, interest and costs had been deducted from the price paid by the purchaser.[1]

Now the Conveyancing Act[2] has given to every mortgagee, where the mortgage is made by deed, a power of sale which closely follows that given by the forms in use among conveyancers. The mortgagee so soon as the debt has become due may sell; but he is not to exercise this power unless (*a*) notice has been given to pay off the debt and default has been made in so doing for *three* months after the notice, or (*b*) some interest is in arrear for *two* months, or (*c*) there has been a breach of some provision contained in the mortgage deed on the part of the mortgagor other than a covenant for the payment of money. Then however the purchaser is protected in the usual way; he is absolved from inquiring whether any of these three cases has arisen. This statutory power of sale is a little more beneficial to the mortgagee than that which was formerly in use—it can be exercised if any interest be in arrear for two months (three months was usual) or if after notice to pay off the debt default in so doing is made for three months (six months was usual).

Then in the old forms came the covenants for title, and the rule was that a mortgagor had to give absolute covenants for

---

[1] If there is a second mortgage of which the first mortgagee has notice he must of course pay the proper part of the balance to the second mortgagee and not to the mortgagor; *West London Commercial Bank* v. *Reliance Building Society*, 29 Ch. D. 954.

[2] The power of sale under the Law of Property Act 1925 is substantially the same.

title. Without any limitation of his liability he covenanted that he had good right to convey, that the mortgagee after default should quietly enjoy the land free from incumbrances, and that the mortgagor would do all things (if any) necessary for his further assurance. These covenants will now be imported into the mortgage deed by force of the Conveyancing Act if the mortgagor is therein said to convey 'as beneficial owner'.[1]

I believe that now-a-days in the preparation of mortgage deeds great reliance is placed upon this Act, and that it has become usual to omit a power of sale and covenants for title. However of course in each particular case the mortgagee or his adviser should see that the powers given by the Act are really the powers that he wants.

You will well understand that a mortgage deed may contain many other clauses. But taking the simple elementary case of a plain mortgage in fee we may say that down to 1881 it contained five parts: (1) the covenant to pay principal and interest, (2) the conveyance, (3) the proviso for redemption or reconveyance, (4) the power of sale with its attendant clauses, (5) the covenants for title. In general the Conveyancing Act will enable you to omit the 4th and 5th parts. The Act attempted to do somewhat more. By a different section (26) from that to which I have been referring (19) it declared that certain very short forms given in a schedule were to be deemed to contain all sorts of things that they do not contain. These are the forms of 'statutory mortgage'.[2] I do not think that much use has been made of them or that they are likely to be employed save in very simple cases where very small sums are lent and every shilling is of importance. A deed may be too short.

The form which I have been describing was the form of a legal mortgage in fee simple. This we may take as the typical form of mortgage, but of course many variations were necessary in order to adapt it to other estates, interests and forms of property. Thus it is common to find a tenant for life mortgaging

---

[1] See now Law of Property Act 1925, s. 76 (1) (C) and (D), and Schedule II, Parts III and IV.

[2] See now the forms in the 3rd, 4th and 5th Schedules to the Law of Property Act 1925.

his life estate in the settled land. But a life estate of course is but a poor security, for it is constantly disappearing. Therefore if a man borrows money on a life estate he has generally to effect a policy of insurance upon his life and then to mortgage that policy also to the person who advances the money. In such a case you will have three 'witnessing parts' in your deed: (1) the covenant to pay principal and interest, (2) the conveyance of the life estate subject to a proviso for redemption, (3) the assignment of the policies subject to a proviso for redemption.[1] Then leaseholds you mortgage by way of sub-demise;[2] this you do in order that there may be no privity between the mortgagee and the lessor, in order that the mortgagee may not become liable on the covenants contained in the lease. Here by the mortgage deed the mortgagor will demise the land to the mortgagee for the residue of the term less the last day thereof, subject to a proviso for redemption; and then the mortgagor will go on to declare that he holds the original term upon trust for the mortgagee, but subject to the proviso for redemption.

Copyholds one mortgages by conditional surrender. A surrender is made conditioned to be void on payment of the mortgage debt and interest at a specified time, so that on payment of the money at that time the mortgagor would remain tenant as of his old estate. This condition corresponds to the proviso for the reconveyance of freeholds. The surrender is accompanied by a deed which contains the usual covenants for the payment of the mortgage debt and interest.

Personalty also can be mortgaged. Corporeal personalty, if I may use that phrase; physical goods and chattels one mortgaged very much in the same way that one mortgaged lands. One assigned them by deed to the mortgagee subject to a proviso that they should be reassigned if the debt was paid off on the day fixed for its payment. But you know that mortgages of such things are bills of sale and are subject to the provisions of certain statutes of which I am not going to speak, since they have

---

[1] Note that since 1925 the life estate will be an equitable and not a legal interest and that notice of the mortgage must be given to the trustees of the settlement since the rule in *Dearle* v. *Hall* will apply; see p. 209 below.

[2] This still remains after 1925 the method of mortgaging leaseholds.

nothing to do with the doctrines of equity. Then you can mortgage your share, your reversionary share it may be, in a personal trust fund, *e.g.* a share which belongs to you under your parent's marriage settlement, but which will not be paid to you until after their deaths. So you can mortgage a debt— you can mortgage a mortgage debt—that is a sub-mortgage. In all these cases it is usual to follow as closely as may be the type set by the ordinary mortgage of land. There is the covenant to pay the debt on a certain day with interest, then the conveyance or assignment of whatever is to be mortgaged—then the proviso for reconveyance or reassignment in case the debt be duly paid on the specified day. The ordinary equitable doctrines about redemption and foreclosure apply to these things. Before 1881 you would have given to the mortgagee of them a power of sale. You will now find that the sections of the Conveyancing Act giving the power of sale apply as well to mortgages of personal as to mortgages of real property.

I want however to say a little more than I have yet said about the nature of the mortgagor's rights—and let us keep before our minds the simple and typical case of a legal mortgage in fee simple. Doe, who is tenant in fee simple, mortgages to Nokes. We often say that subject to the mortgage Doe is still tenant in fee simple. But remember what this means. So soon as the day appointed for payment of the money has gone by, Doe's rights are purely equitable rights—in many respects they are like the rights of a *cestui que trust*—that is to say, they will not hold good against a purchaser who gets the legal estate *bona fide* for value, and without notice.[1] Still it is true that subject to this limitation Doe is treated as a tenant in fee simple. He has a heritable estate, he has real estate. If by his will he devises all his real estate to one man and bequeaths all his personalty to another man, the former, not the latter, will take this equity of redemption. If he dies intestate the equity of redemption descends to his heir; if the land be gavelkind land this equity of redemption descends to his heirs according to the custom of gavelkind. There could

---

[1] And see as showing the purely equitable nature of the mortgagor's estate before 1926 *Copestake* v. *Hoper* [1908] 2 Ch. 10. Since 1926 the mortgagor has a legal estate.

be courtesy of an equity of redemption, and since the Dower
Act of 1833 there can be dower of an equity of redemption.[1]
Then Doe can convey this to another, or he can settle it—create
life estates and estates tail in it (nothing is commoner than to
find that a settled estate is subject to a mortgage, to many
mortgages, so that the whole settlement is overridden by the
mortgage, and so that all the limitations in the settlement give
but equitable estates), or again he can make another mortgage;
but since he himself has only equitable rights he can only confer
equitable rights on others.[2]

Now any person who thus becomes entitled to any interest in
the equity of redemption may redeem—thus the heir or the
devisee may redeem, the tenant by the courtesy or the doweress
may redeem, a tenant for life in the equity of redemption may
redeem, a second mortgagee may redeem, even a judgment
creditor who by issuing execution has obtained an interest in the
land may redeem.[3] It follows that if the mortgagee desires to
foreclose he has in general to bring before the Court every
person who has any interest in the equity of redemption, so that
each and all of them may have an opportunity of redeeming
before they lose the land. A decree for foreclosure is sometimes
a very elaborate affair. I have before me one in which a first
mortgagee is suing a second, third, fourth, fifth mortgagee and
the mortgagor. If we compress it, it takes this form: if second
mortgagee pays on such a day let first mortgagee reconvey to
him, but in default let second mortgagee be foreclosed, in that
case give third mortgagee six months from thence in which to
pay; if he pays let first mortgagee reconvey to him, if not let
him be foreclosed; in that case give a day six months thence to
fourth mortgagee, and so forth. The rule is that where there are
more incumbrancers than one, the mesne incumbrancers must
successively redeem all prior to them or be foreclosed and must

---

[1] Since 1925 of course personalty and realty descend to the same persons
on intestacy and custom of gavelkind, courtesy and dower are, save for some
trivial exceptions, abolished.

[2] For the position after 1925 see p. 206 below.

[3] See *e.g. Tarn* v. *Turner*, 39 Ch. D. 456, where a lessee for years under
a lease made by the mortgagor after the mortgage was held entitled to
redeem.

be redeemed by or will be entitled to foreclose all subsequent to them.[1]

Seeing then that there are many mortgages which are merely equitable, which confer upon the mortgagee no legal rights whatever in the land, we are led to examine these equitable mortgages a little more closely.[2] Doe, tenant in fee simple, has mortgaged Blackacre to Nokes, and the mortgage is a legal one. He now goes on to mortgage it to Styles. The mortgage deed will probably take almost precisely the form of a first mortgage —except that probably there will be a recital of or some reference to Nokes's first mortgage and that the land will be conveyed to Styles expressly 'subject to' the previous mortgage. Now at law this deed will have but little effect. It will contain a covenant for the payment with interest of the money lent by Styles, and the right to sue on this covenant will of course be a legal right, Styles will become a creditor by specialty. Here is one reason for having a deed. But at law Doe can not convey Blackacre to Styles: he has already conveyed it to Nokes, and Nokes's estate has become at law an absolute estate since Doe did not pay him his debt on the appointed day. Therefore Styles can get no legal rights in the land, and there can be no talk of Styles being tenant at law while Doe is tenant in equity. Nevertheless, courts of equity construed equitable mortgages in much the same fashion as that in which they construed legal mortgages. Subject to the first mortgage the land is conveyed to Styles, but until fore-closure or sale, or even in certain cases after foreclosure, Doe will be entitled to redeem it from him. And so it was usual to give a second mortgagee a power of sale closely resembling that given to a first mortgagee. But what could the second mortgagee sell—what could such a power enable him to sell? He could sell the land subject to the first mortgage—he could sell the equity of redemption. You will find that the Conveyancing Act 1881 enables a second or yet later mortgagee if his mortgage is made by deed (and here is a second reason why a second mortgage should be made by deed) to sell subject to the prior mortgages.

[1] See Seton on Judgments and Orders, pp. 1907 *et seq.* (7th edition).
[2] The discussion which follows represents the law before 1926. See note on p. 206 below.

Indeed that Act gives a second or later mortgagee a certain power of selling the estate free from incumbrances if he makes a provision for the satisfaction of the incumbrances that are prior to his own—into the details of this process I can not go.[1] Now we have seen more than one reason why as a matter of prudence a second mortgage should be made by deed—still a deed is not essential to an equitable mortgage. Of course it is essential to a legal mortgage, for a legal estate is not to be transferred without deed. But signed writing is all that is required for the equitable mortgage. Suppose X lends me money and in return I write on a piece of paper 'In consideration of £1000 lent to me by X I agree to execute a proper mortgage of all my freehold estates in the County of Middlesex to secure the repayment of the said sum with interest at 4 per cent.' This already is an equitable mortgage, and X can go to the Court and ask for foreclosure or sale. In form it is an agreement to give a mortgage, an agreement which satisfies the 4th section of the Statute of Frauds since I have signed it. It is an agreement of which specific performance can be compelled.[2] That being so X is already in equity a mortgagee. Mark the words 'in equity' and think of the rights of a *bona fide* purchaser who gets the legal estate without notice of this memorandum. That X is already in equity a mortgagee means this, that he can go to the Court and obtain an order for foreclosure or for sale. It would be requiring a round-about process were it necessary for X to ask for specific performance of the agreement to grant a mortgage, and then, the mortgage having been granted, to ask for foreclosure. X can ask for foreclosure at once. An opportunity will be given me to redeem, and if I do not pay on the appointed day I shall be foreclosed and compelled to convey the land to X. Such a conveyance will be necessary if I have the legal estate— a judgment declaring me foreclosed would not pass the legal

[1] The reference would appear to be to section 5 of the Conveyancing Act 1881, now section 50 of the Law of Property Act 1925, which in certain circumstances allows of a sale free from prior incumbrances upon payment into Court of a sum to meet the incumbrances. The ordinary power of sale of a mortgagee is now contained in section 104 of the Law of Property Act 1925.

[2] A mere agreement to lend on mortgage, when the money has not been advanced, is not specifically enforceable, see p. 304 below.

estate from me to X; but the Court will compel me to convey the land to him free from all equity of redemption. What can be done by a signed writing stating an agreement to grant a mortgage can be done also by a signed writing declaring that the land is charged with the repayment of the loan. It is best not to trust to informal papers; they would not give one the covenant for repayment which may be useful, they would not give the convenient extra-judicial power of sale—the Conveyancing Act would not interpolate such a power into them; one would get no covenants for title. Still an equitable mortgage can be created by very informal writings. If you can find a written agreement for a mortgage such that equity would enforce specific performance of it, then you have already the equitable mortgage.

But the Court of Chancery went further than this: it enabled people to make equitable mortgages without any writing at all. An equitable mortgage (enforceable by an order for foreclosure or for sale) can be made by a deposit of title deeds if they were deposited with intent that the land which they concern shall be security for the payment of a debt. You may well say that this doctrine is hardly to be reconciled with the 4th section of the Statute of Frauds. The foundation of the equitable doctrine is an agreement, an agreement of which the specific performance will be compelled. The depositor has agreed to mortgage his land. But then the Statute says that 'no action shall be brought upon any contract or sale of any lands, tenements or hereditaments or any interest in or concerning them, unless the agreement upon which such action shall be brought or some note or memorandum thereof shall be in writing and signed by the party to be charged therewith or some other person by him lawfully authorized'. Well certainly it is not very easy to reconcile the mortgage by deposit of title deeds with the words of this clause. Let us just notice this—that the mortgage by deposit is an outcome or offshoot of the equitable doctrine of part performance. A lets B take possession of land of which A is owner. Here according to the Court of Chancery is cogent evidence of the existence of some agreement between A and B. What agreement? We will allow either of the parties to prove that it was an agreement for a sale, although he has no note or memorandum of that agreement. And so it is here. A has handed over the title deeds of a certain estate to B. Why on earth should he have done this? Here is cogent evidence of some agreement between them. Something we must do. To say that B has no charge upon the land and yet to allow him to keep as his own, or to destroy the title deeds of another man's property, this would be absurd. On the other hand it would be hard to force B to give back the title deeds when it is plain that they were put into his hand for some purpose about which there was an agreement between him and A. So we allow B to prove, though he has no note or memorandum in writing, what this agreement really was, we allow him to prove that there was an agreement for a mortgage.[1] I think that we ought to regret this doctrine of equity; it has done a good deal of harm; but there it is.[2] It does harm in this way—an intending purchaser or an intending mortgagee may somewhat easily get constructive notice of a mortgage by deposit, and thus costs are accumulated and titles are rendered insecure. If you are purposing to buy land or to take a mortgage, you must be careful to see that you get all the title deeds, otherwise you may find yourself, even though you have the legal estate, postponed to some banker who is holding a few deeds. If A's deeds are in B's hands and there be no written agreement B may prove by oral evidence that they were deposited with him by way of security; but if there be a written agreement then (according to the ordinary rule) oral evidence is not admissible to contradict that writing or vary its terms.

Equitable mortgages are not very safe things. I have before now referred to the doctrine of tacking.[3] Let me once more recall the two main rules. (*a*) A first mortgagee having the legal

---

[1] See *Russel* v. *Russel*, 1 Bro. C. C. 269; White and Tudor L.C. vol. II, p. 69 (9th edition).

[2] Maitland's regrets would probably not be universally shared, since the mortgage by deposit is an exceptionally convenient form of security for short term loans and for that reason has flourished. It is noteworthy that charges by deposit are common practice with types of property other than land—*e.g.* a charge by deposit of share certificates—and that the Land Registration Act 1925 makes special provision for informal mortgages of registered land by deposit of the 'land certificate'.

[3] See pp. 129 to 136 above and p. 207 below.

estate makes a further advance to the mortgagor without having
notice of a second mortgage; he may tack his further advance
to the original debt and hold the land until he has been paid both
the debts. For this reason it is that on taking a second mortgage
one should always give notice of it to the first mortgagee, for
this will prevent his having a right to tack to his original debt
any advances that he may make after he has received that notice.
(*b*) A third or subsequent mortgagee who when he lent his money
had no notice of the second mortgage becomes entitled by paying
off the first mortgage and getting a conveyance of the legal
estate, to tack his own debt to the first mortgagee's so that the
second mortgagee's right will be postponed to both these debts.
This doctrine of tacking was abolished by the Vendor and
Purchaser Act 1874, s. 7, but in the next year it was restored, for
that section was repealed as from its commencement by the
Land Transfer Act of 1875.[1]

Another danger was created by the doctrine of the consolidation of mortgages. The Conveyancing Act 1881, s. 17,[2]
has robbed this doctrine of some but not all of its importance.
That section says that 'A mortgagor seeking to redeem any one
mortgage shall be entitled to do so, without paying any money
due under any separate mortgage made by him or any person
through whom he claims on property other than that comprised
in the mortgage which he seeks to redeem.' But then it adds
'This section applies only if and so far as a contrary intention is
not expressed in the mortgage deeds or one of them.' So in a
mortgage one can still stipulate for the benefit of the old doctrine, and I believe that this is not infrequently done. So let us
see what the old doctrine was and, we may say, still is. Where
distinct estates are separately mortgaged as securities for distinct
debts by the same mortgagor to the same mortgagee, the latter
had the right to consolidate, *i.e.* to hold all the estates as a
security for the aggregate of all the debts and to require that the
mortgagor should not redeem one without redeeming all. The
doctrine was useful to a mortgagee when one of the estates was

---

[1] Tacking is now abolished; see p. 207 below.
[2] Reproduced substantially unaltered by the Law of Property Act 1925,
s. 93.

insufficient, while the other was more than sufficient to provide the sum charged upon it. He could say 'You shall not redeem this overcharged estate unless you will pay all that you owe me upon both the mortgages.' The rule has been extended to cases in which the same person makes two mortgages of different estates to two different persons, and afterwards by assignment these two mortgages have become vested in one person—that person can say 'You must redeem both or you can redeem neither.' However it is not probable that this doctrine will be extended.[1] In a modern case the House of Lords had to decide on these facts (*Jennings* v. *Jordan*, 6 App. Cas. 698)—A mortgages Blackacre to X; then conveys the equity of redemption in Blackacre to M; then mortgages Whiteacre to X. M can redeem Blackacre without redeeming Whiteacre. But it would be otherwise if both these mortgages to X were made before the conveyance of the equity of redemption.[2]

Some other alterations have been made in the law of mortgages by the Conveyancing Act which may be noticed here as they may serve to illustrate the way in which mortgages have been regarded by courts of common law and courts of equity. When land is mortgaged the creditor gets rights of two distinct kinds —the right to be paid a debt, certain rights in land. Let us first suppose, for this is the simplest case for our present purpose, that what is mortgaged is a house held by the mortgagor for a term of years—he mortgages it either by assigning the term to the mortgagee, or by sub-demising it for a shorter term to the mortgagee. Either way the mortgagee becomes entitled to the chattel real known as a term of years. He is also entitled to a chose in action, a debt, the benefit of a covenant for the payment of money. One sees that the two are distinct if one looks at the transfer of a mortgage—for a mortgagee can transfer his rights, and this without the concurrence of the mortgagor. What does he transfer? You will find that he transfers, he assigns 'All that

---

[1] See *Pledge* v. *White* [1896] A.C. 187.

[2] If A had first mortgaged Blackacre to X, then Whiteacre to Y, and then assigned for value the equity of redemption in Blackacre to Z, and subsequently B had taken a transfer to himself of both mortgages, he, B, could not consolidate against Z. *Harter* v. *Colman*, 19 Ch. D. 630; *Minter* v. *Carr* [1894] 3 Ch. 498.

the sum of £1000 due upon a certain Indenture of Mortgage and all interest due or to become due in respect of the same.' This he assigns absolutely. Then he goes on to assign 'All that house et cetera, to hold to the transferee, his executors, administrators, and assigns during the residue of the said term'—the term for which the transferor has been holding them 'subject to the proviso for redemption contained in the Indenture of Mortgage.'[1] I said that this was the simplest case, for in it all the rights of the mortgagee bear the character of personalty. If he dies both the debt and the leasehold interest in the land will go the same way; they will go to his executors or (as the case may be) his administrators. The mortgagor will have only one person or only one set of persons (two or three executors) to deal with —they can give him a valid receipt for the debt and they also can reassign or surrender the leasehold house to him. And so if a transfer is to be made the executors or the administrator can do all that has to be done and the transferee will be safe in dealing with them—one is very safe in dealing with personal representatives who are disposing of the personal property of the testator or intestate. And so again they can exercise the power of sale contained in the mortgage deed or given by statute. But it was far otherwise when what was mortgaged was an estate in fee simple. The mortgagee's rights were some of them personalty, while others of them were realty. There was the debt which passed to the personal representatives, there was the estate which descended to the heir at law, unless it had been given by will to some devisee. For the mortgagee like any other tenant in fee simple, like the trustee in fee simple, could devise the estate. The usual course was to insert in every will a clause saying that the testator devised all freehold estates vested in him upon trust or by way of mortgage unto the same persons whom he appointed his executors; this kept the estate in the same hands as the right to the money. Unless this were done there would like enough be a difficult question as to whether a general devise of 'all my real estates' comprised estates vested in the testator

---

[1] The transfer need not now distinguish between the land and the rights under the covenant. See Law of Property Act 1925, s. 114, and the statutory form of transfer in the third Schedule to that Act.

by way of mortgage. Often enough the estate would descend as undisposed of to the heir at law. Now the Court of Chancery held that in substantial essence the right of the mortgagee in fee simple was personalty, a right to a sum of money. Thus for example if he gave all his real estate to X and all his personal estate to Y, the latter phrase and not the former would carry the real benefit of the mortgage. The heir or the devisee would be treated as a trustee for the personal representative, bound to dispose of the estate in fee that had vested in him in such manner as the personal representative should direct. Thus the personal representative could foreclose. The power of sale was always so drawn that it should be exercisable by him—'and it shall be lawful for the mortgagee, his executors, administrators or assigns [not his heirs] to sell'. When I say that the power was always so drawn, I mean that to have given the power to the mortgagee 'and his heirs' would have been a bad mistake, inducing confusion. But for all this in almost every transaction concerning the mortgage the presence and concurrence of the heir or devisee was necessary. If the mortgagor wanted to pay off the mortgage, he had to pay the money to the personal representatives, but he had a right to a conveyance of the estate, and the estate was vested in the heir or the devisee. So if the personal representatives desired to transfer the mortgage they were obliged to obtain the concurrence of the heir or the devisee, for otherwise there could be no transfer of the estate, though there might be a transfer of the debt. The transfer would have to consist of two parts. In the first the personal representatives would assign 'All that sum of £1000 due upon such and such an Indenture of Mortgage' to the transferee, his executors, administrators and assigns. By the second the heir or devisee would grant 'All that piece of land called Blackacre' to the transferee, his heirs and assigns, 'subject to the proviso for redemption contained in the said Indenture of Mortgage'. Then again if the personal representatives employed the power of sale, the concurrence of the heir or devisee was necessary in order that the estate might be conveyed to the purchaser. The heir or devisee could in these cases be compelled to do what the personal representatives desired him to do: he was a trustee for them.

But often enough it might be difficult to obtain his concurrence —he might be an infant, a lunatic, beyond the sea; if he made any difficulties an application to the Court was necessary. Some of these cases were dealt with by the Trustee Act of 1850 (13 & 14 Vic. c. 60)—thus if the mortgage estate had come to a lunatic or an infant the Court could by what was called a Vesting order take it out of him and vest it in some other person—still this of course necessitated an application to the Court. Another partial tentative step was taken by the Vendor and Purchaser Act 1874, s. 4. The legal personal representative of a mortgagee of a freehold estate was enabled on payment of all the sums secured by the mortgage, to convey the mortgaged estate. The mortgaged estate was not under this section to pass, on the mortgagee's death, to his personal representative; it was to pass as of old to his heir or devisee, but in a certain event the personal representative was to have power to convey it. This rather clumsy device had but a limited application. For example it was held that this section did not apply to the transfer of a mortgage (*In re Spradbery's Mortgage*, 14 Ch. D. 514). But now the Conveyancing Act 1881, s. 30, has repealed this section and given us a different rule. Where an estate of inheritance is vested in any person solely upon trust or by way of mortgage that estate shall notwithstanding any testamentary disposition devolve to and become vested in his personal representatives or representative from time to time in like manner as if the same were a chattel real. Therefore for the future it must at least be very rare for us to find the right to the mortgage debt vested in one person while the mortgage estate is vested in another person.[1]

It is, I think, in connexion with this section that we ought to read section 51 of the same Act. That section says that in a deed it shall be sufficient in the limitation of an estate in fee simple to use the words 'in fee simple' without the word heirs. That section may have struck you as a very odd and unnecessary one. It says that one sacramental phrase shall be as good as another sacramental phrase—for mark that it only does this: it only

[1] Since both land and personalty now vest in the personal representatives the difficulty discussed by Maitland no longer exists.

gives you the choice between two phrases and does not give you liberty to invent other phrases which you may choose to think are just as good as these—and the one phrase is no shorter than the other. 'In fee simple' contains precisely the same number of letters as 'and his heirs'. The explanation, I take it, is to be found in the 30th section. It seems rather silly to convey land to a man and his heirs when one does not intend that in any event his heir shall have anything whatever to do with the land. This is now the case when one is conveying to a trustee or a mortgagee, and I think that it is a little prettier in such a case to say 'in fee simple' than to say 'and his heirs'—a little less misleading.[1] But the day I hope is coming when we shall see that two systems of intestate succession are one system too many.[2]

---

[1] No sacramental phrase is now necessary. A conveyance of freehold land without words of limitation passes the fee simple unless the contrary intention appears; Law of Property Act 1925, s. 60. Thus a conveyance 'to A' will now pass the fee simple whereas before 1926 it would have passed only a life estate. In practice the phrase 'to A in fee simple' is still generally used.

[2] The student should remember that in this lecture Maitland attempts to give a general view of the mortgage as a legal and equitable institution. Important points, such as the doctrines of consolidation and tacking, are only glanced at and some startling consequences of the intervention of Equity in the contract that the parties have made for themselves pass unnoticed. The student should note, for instance, the maxim 'once a mortgage always a mortgage', and the doctrine forbidding any 'clog on the equity of redemption'. See *Noakes* v. *Rice* [1902] A.C. 24; *Bradley* v. *Carritt* [1903] A.C. 253; *Samuel* v. *Jarrah etc. Co.* [1904] A.C. 323 and *Kreglinger* v. *New Patagonia Meat Co.* [1914] A.C. 25.

NOTE ON THE LAW OF PROPERTY
SINCE 1925

U pon the topics dealt with in the last four lectures, the law has been radically changed by the Property Acts of 1925. While the details of the new law are beyond the scope of this book it is proposed to point out certain specific alterations in matters dealt with in these lectures and to discuss the general effect of the new Acts on the relation of legal and equitable estates. The matters discussed in this note are:

I. Mortgages

(a) Form of Mortgage

We have seen in Lecture XIII that under the old law the legal owner in fee simple of land would create a legal mortgage by conveying the land outright to the mortgagee subject to a proviso that if the mortgage money was repaid in six months the land was to be reconveyed to the mortgagor. After the six months had expired the mortgagor would no longer have any legal interest in the land but he would retain an equitable right to have the land reconveyed if he paid off the mortgage. Thus (after the six months had expired) the right of the mortgagor who had granted a legal mortgage was purely equitable. The mortgagor could create a second mortgage by conveying his equity of redemption to a second mortgagee subject as before to a proviso for redemption. Since the thing conveyed to the second mortgagee was the equity of redemption under the first mortgage—a purely equitable interest in land—the second mortgagee had only an equitable interest in the land. So under the old system there could only be one legal mortgage of land; all subsequent mortgages were bound to be equitable mortgages.

Under the new law this is no longer so. The owner of the land now creates the mortgage by granting to the mortgagee, not the whole legal fee simple, but a legal term of 3000 years, subject as before to a proviso that if the mortgage money should be paid off in six months the term is to be surrendered to the mortgagor. After the six months has expired the mortgagor still retains an equity of redemption—namely a purely equitable right to have the term surrendered if he pays off the mortgage —but besides this equitable right he retains also a legal estate in the land, namely the reversion after the expiry of the 3000-year term. Thus since 1925 the mortgagor retains a legal estate in the land. To create a second mortgage the mortgagor grants to the second mortgagee a term of 3000 years plus one day, subject to the first mortgagee's term of 3000 years and subject also to the usual proviso for redemption. The term granted to the second mortgagee is a legal term and accordingly the second mortgagee has a legal estate in the land. So too with third and subsequent mortgagees. In short since 1925 any number of successive mortgages can be created and yet the mortgagor and all the mortgagees will have legal estates in the land.

This change in the form of mortgages is often treated as an important alteration in the law and in theory perhaps it is. In practice it has probably made no substantial difference. Questions of priority, where it might have made a difference, are now for the most part governed by statutory rules which apply equally whether the mortgage is legal or equitable. Questions of foreclosure, redemption, sale by the mortgagee and the like are all substantially unaltered by the change. It is of course still possible to create an equitable mortgage, for example by deposit of title deeds. In this case the mortgagee will only acquire an equitable interest and the mortgagor if he already had a legal interest will retain it.

The Law of Property Act 1925 has also created a new form of charge called a 'charge by way of legal mortgage'. The rights of the chargee and chargor under such a charge are the same as the rights of a mortgagee and mortgagor under a legal mortgage by sub-demise.[1] Such a charge allows a rather simpler form to be used when freeholds and leaseholds are to be mortgaged together, since a sub-demise for 3000 years, which would be suitable for the freeholds, would clearly be inapplicable to a leasehold having a term of (say) 300 years only. Apart from this the advantages of such a charge over a mortgage by sub-demise have not yet become apparent and in the absence of any advantage conveyancers generally prefer to use the mortgage by sub-demise, which they know, rather than the new charge which may involve unsuspected dangers.

(b) Tacking

The doctrine of tacking is abolished by section 94 of the Law of Property Act 1925. To make it possible for a mortgagor to obtain further advances from a mortgagee, provision is made whereby the mortgagee can in some circumstances tack the further advances to the original mortgage, but the tacking in such cases depends on the form of the mortgage and not upon any superiority attributed to the legal estate.

[1] Law of Property Act 1925, s. 87.

(c) *Priorities*

The rules regarding the priority of competing mortgagees have been radically altered by the introduction of registration. This point is discussed later.

(d) *Trusts affecting mortgage debts*

The student should notice the provisions of the Law of Property Act 1925, which are designed to keep off the title any trusts affecting the mortgage debt. The following example will illustrate the type of difficulty which arose before 1926. Blackacre was mortgaged to A and B who were trustees holding the mortgage debt as part of the trust funds. A died. A new trustee C was appointed and B transferred the mortgage debt to himself and C. Finally the trust came to an end and one of the beneficiaries D became absolutely entitled to the mortgage debt, which was accordingly transferred to him by B and C. Suppose now that D and the mortgagor combined to sell Blackacre. The purchaser would be obliged to see that D was the person actually entitled to the mortgage. If in his investigations he obtained notice of the trust affecting the mortgage, he would be bound to see that the transfers from B to B and C and from B and C to D were not made in breach of trust, that is to say that C was properly appointed trustee and that D was in fact entitled to have the mortgage debt transferred to him, which would involve an inquiry into the equitable rights under the trust. To avoid this complication efforts were made before 1926 to prevent the purchaser acquiring notice of the trusts. The original mortgage to A and B would be a mortgage to them jointly and would not refer to the trusts. But a difficulty at once arose, for the purchaser, seeing that A and B were apparently beneficially entitled to the mortgage money, would assume that, although the mortgage was made to them jointly, they were in equity entitled to the money as tenants in common and on the death of A would require to be satisfied that A's personal representatives were not interested in the mortgage. To avoid this difficulty a clause (known as the joint account clause) would be introduced into the original mortgage to the effect that the mortgagors A and B were entitled to the mortgage money jointly (*i.e.* not as tenants in common) in equity as well as at law. This clause was of course a lie, but the purchaser was entitled to assume that it was true. In 1881 the Conveyancing Act[1] made this clause unnecessary by expressly providing that when a mortgage was made to more than one person the mortgagees should be deemed to be entitled jointly unless the contrary was stated in the mortgage. Even then the difficulties were not at an

---

[1] Section 61; now Law of Property Act 1925, s. 111.

end, for if the purchaser did in fact get notice of the trust he might still be bound to investigate the validity of the transfers (see *In re Blaiberg and Abrahams' Contract* [1899] 2 Ch. 340) and there were several circumstances which might give him notice of the trust. For example, in the illustration given above, he would find that the transfer to B and C was stamped with a 10*s.* stamp, the proper stamp for a transfer to new trustees but (if the mortgage was for a large sum) not the proper stamp for transfer on a sale or gift. The Conveyancing Act 1881[1] provided that the mere fact that the stamp was for 10*s.* only did not give him notice of the trust, but he would wish to be satisfied that the deed was properly stamped and his inquiries might elicit the fact that the trust existed. Again he might wish to know whether death duties were paid on A's death and might be given the explanation that none were payable because A was a trustee.

The Law of Property Act 1925 has met these difficulties by providing, in section 113, that even if the purchaser does get notice of the trusts he shall not be concerned with them. Thus the interests of beneficiaries under a trust affecting mortgage money, like interests under a settlement or trust for sale, are placed behind a curtain, which hides them from the purchaser, and even if the curtain is accidentally raised the purchaser will not be affected by notice of what he has seen.

II. Constructive Notice

The Law of Property Act 1925 contains provisions restricting the inquiries which a purchaser under an open contract may make into the title of the vendor. In particular under section 44 of the Act the period for which the vendor must show title is reduced from forty to thirty years. The section also provides that the purchaser shall not be deemed to have notice of anything which he might have discovered if he had made inquiries beyond those which under an open contract he would be entitled to make, unless he does in fact make such inquiries. This provision overrules the decision in *Patman* v. *Harland*,[2] where a lessee was held to have constructive notice of defects in his lessor's title although by statute he was debarred from investigating the lessor's title.

III. Assignment of Choses in Action

Section 137 of the Law of Property Act 1925 contains important provisions in regard to the rule in *Dearle* v. *Hall*, namely the rule that the priority of competing assignees of a chose in action is to be determined by the order in which they gave notice of assignment to the

[1] Section 13; now Law of Property Act 1925, s. 112.
[2] 17 Ch. D. 353.

debtor or trustee. The section extends the rule, which formerly applied only to personalty, to cover also dealings with equitable interests in land. Thus, for example, it will now apply to assignments of equitable interests under a strict settlement of land. The section also provides that the notices must be in writing and makes provision for cases in which for some reason—*e.g.* because there are no trustees—it is impossible to give notice. Further, section 138 provides that a settlor in creating the settlement may nominate a trust corporation to receive the notices. It is clear that Parliament has aimed at making the rule into what is almost a system of private registration.

IV. Relation of Legal and Equitable Estates

The basic distinction between legal and equitable interests is of course left untouched by the Acts of 1925 and the Acts cannot be appreciated or understood unless that distinction is borne in mind. It is however possible for the law to be fundamentally altered in practice without any formal change in its basic principles and in regard to the land law the Acts of 1925 have done this. It will be many years before the new system becomes fully effective and so long as interests created before 1926 remain outstanding the old principles will still have to be applied, but for a proper understanding of the Acts it is instructive to consider what the law will be when the pre-1926 interests have disappeared. It will be found that the distinction between legal and equitable interests is of less practical significance under the new system than under the old.

For a proper understanding of the new system one must look not only at the substantive law but also at the manner in which a purchase of land is in practice carried out. The land may be subject to both legal and equitable interests. Now it is not enough for the law to provide that the owner of a legal interest has an indefeasible right and that the owner of an equitable interest has a right enforceable against a purchaser only if he has notice. The law must also secure, so far as possible, that a purchaser who takes the proper precautions shall not find himself subject to legal interests of which he was not aware and that the owner of an equitable interest who takes proper precautions will not lose his rights by the occurrence of a purchase without notice. The purchaser must be protected against prior legal interests and the owner of an equitable interest must be protected against subsequent purchasers. The system prevailing before 1926 depended entirely upon title deeds. The purchaser was protected to this extent, that if he investigated the title in the ordinary way he probably would discover the existence of any existing legal interests. To make the protection more perfect it would have been necessary for the law to have put upon the owner of a legal interest a duty to take reasonable steps to ensure that the purchaser would acquire notice of his interest, but, except in regard to the custody of the title deeds, the owner of a legal interest was under no such duty. The owner of an equitable interest was protected by the law of constructive notice; the law put upon the purchaser a duty to investigate title for a period of forty years and the owner of an equitable interest could protect himself either by securing that notice of his interest appeared upon the face of the title deeds, as would generally be the case with a restrictive covenant, or by actually retaining the title deeds in his own possession, as would be the case with an equitable mortgage.

The old system had the following defects:

(1) It involved a lengthy and expensive investigation of title.

(2) When the title had been investigated and the various legal and equitable interests in the land discovered the actual conveyance to the purchaser might still be a lengthy business. The purchaser would require that every person who had an outstanding interest in the land, whether legal or equitable, should join in the conveyance. If the land was settled or had become divided among tenants in common or was charged by will with legacies and annuities, there might be many persons who would have to join in the conveyance.

(3) Certain equitable interests were inadequately protected. A second mortgagee, for example, would not hold the title deeds in his custody and his mortgage might not appear on the face of the deeds; his interest therefore might easily escape the notice of a purchaser and be overridden.

(4) The purchaser was not adequately protected against prior legal interests. The law did not impose on the owner of a legal interest any duty to see that notice of his interest appeared on the title deeds so that a purchaser could by reasonable inquiries discover its existence. The only protection to the purchaser was the fact that in practice such interests did commonly appear on the title and that the owner of a legal interest did owe a certain duty to take care of the actual title deeds.

The first and second of these defects were the most serious. They are overcome under the new Acts by the creation of what in practice, though not in form, is almost a new class of interest, namely an interest which so long as the land is unsold is an interest in land, but which on a sale ceases to attach to the land and attaches instead to the purchase money.[1] The third and fourth defects are to a large extent met by the system of registration introduced by the Land Charges Act 1925.

The first change introduced by the new Acts is the restriction of the possible types of legal interests.[2] Most interests which complicated

---

[1] This change was not entirely new in 1925 since it was begun by the earlier Settled Land Acts, but for simplicity only the completed system as established in 1925 will be considered.

[2] See Law of Property Act 1925, s. 1.

conveyancing, such as life interests and other interests under settlements and wills, tenancies in common, and estates vested in infants, are transformed into equitable interests and can no longer subsist as legal interests.

This change by itself is not of much practical importance, for an equitable interest which appears on the face of the title deeds is as inconvenient to conveyancers and is almost as well protected as a legal interest. The substantial change is effected by other provisions of the Acts, which secure that interests of the sorts mentioned above can only subsist under either a trust for sale or a settlement and that a sale by the trustees for sale or the tenant for life under the settlement will override all interests under the trust for sale or settlement. The scheme of the Acts is so worked out that the documents shown to the purchaser will only disclose the fact that a settlement or trust for sale exists and that certain named persons are the tenant for life and trustees of the settlement or the trustees for sale. The purchaser will not be concerned to go behind these documents and, even if he does happen to acquire information about the equitable interest under the trust for sale or the settlement, will not be affected by such information. If, in the case of a settlement, the sale is by the person appearing on the documents as tenant for life and the purchase money is paid to two persons appearing on the documents as trustees of the settlement, or, in the case of a trust for sale, the sale is by two trustees for sale and the money is paid to them, the purchaser will get a title free from the equitable interests under the settlement or trust for sale. Thus we have a new class of equitable interests which are less well protected than equitable interests of the sort that existed before 1926. The latter, provided that they appeared on the face of the title deeds, were substantially as well secured as legal interests and would in practice attach to the land until released by their owner. Interests of the new class attach to the land only to a limited extent; they can always be overreached by a sale properly made and their real protection lies in the fact that on a sale the money must be paid to trustees who will be responsible to the owners of the equitable interests.

There is a further class of interests which cannot be treated in this way. A restrictive covenant for example is destroyed altogether if it ceases to attach to the land. Moreover an ordinary mortgage would become rather insecure if the land was always liable to be sold and the mortgagee had to rely on trustees who would receive the purchase money. For interests of this class a system of registration is introduced by the Land Charges Act 1925. The interests which require registration include amongst others the following:

    (*a*) Puisne Mortgages, *i.e.* all legal mortgages not protected by deposit of title deeds.

    (*b*) A number of charges which can arise under various statutes as for example a charge for Death Duties.

(c) Other equitable charges. These include annuities, limited owner's charges and a group known as 'general equitable charges', which includes all other equitable charges not arising under a trust for sale or settlement and not protected by deposit of title deeds.

(d) Restrictive covenants.

(e) Equitable easements.

(f) Estate contracts, *i.e.* contracts to grant a legal estate or interest, such as the agreement for a lease in *Walsh* v. *Lonsdale*.

It will be noticed that, while most of these interests are equitable interests, mortgages, unless protected by deposit of title deeds, are registrable whether they are legal or equitable—if legal as puisne mortgages, if equitable either as estate contracts or general equitable charges.

An interest which can be registered is void against a purchaser if it has not been registered, even if the purchaser has notice of it,[1] and, on the other hand, a purchaser is (subject to an exception mentioned below) deemed to have actual notice of all interests which are in fact registered whether or not he inspected the registry.[2] Accordingly the enforcement of such interests depends no longer upon notice in the real sense but on the fact of registration.

The effect of this Act on mortgages should be observed. In an ordinary case the first mortgagee will get the title deeds. Whether his mortgage is legal or equitable he will be well secured, for, if the mortgagor sells, the purchaser will require the title deeds and the mortgage will be disclosed. A second mortgagee will not get the title deeds but he will be protected by registration, whether his interest is legal or equitable. Moreover a purchaser is protected against prior legal mortgages, for these will be protected either by registration or by deposit of the title deeds and in either case they will come to the purchaser's notice. As we have seen the law before 1925 was open to two objections. It did not sufficiently protect a second mortgagee and it did not sufficiently protect a purchaser against prior legal interests. In the case of mortgages the new system meets both of these objections.

In one respect the old law in regard to priorities (as discussed on pp. 117 to 138 above) will apparently still be applicable. A mortgage or charge, whether legal or equitable, does not require to be registered under the Land Charges Act 1925 if it is secured by deposit of title deeds. The Acts do not say what is the priority of an interest so secured and presumably the old law still applies. A purchaser will usually acquire notice of any prior interest secured by deposit of title deeds and in that case he will presumably take subject to such interest, but

---

[1] Land Charges Act 1925, s. 13, and Law of Property Act 1925, s. 199 (1).

[2] Law of Property Act 1925, s. 198.

there may be cases where owing to negligence of one party or the other no notice is acquired and to such cases the principles laid down in *Oliver* v. *Hinton* [1899] 2 Ch. 264, *Walker* v. *Linom* [1907] 2 Ch. 104 and like decisions will still be applicable. If such case should arise, the fact that since 1925 there can be more than one legal mortgage on the same land will have to be borne in mind.

Attention should be paid to section 94 (2) of the Law of Property Act 1925, which provides that where a prior mortgage is expressly made for the purpose of securing a current account or further advances the mere fact of registration of a subsequent mortgage is not to be deemed to be notice to the prior mortgagee. The provision is no doubt intended to protect banks, who commonly take an equitable charge by deposit of title deeds to secure an overdraft on current account. Without the provision the bank would be obliged to inspect the register every time it cashed a cheque, since each cheque cashed would increase the overdraft and operate as a further loan and the bank's security for such further loan would be subject to any other charge of which the bank had notice at the time of cashing the cheque; and, but for section 94 of the Act, the bank would be deemed to have actual notice of any charge that might then be registered. Unfortunately, the section is badly drafted since it only provides that the registration of mortgages shall not be notice to the bank and does not in terms include registrable charges other than mortgages, for example estate contracts. This seems to be a flaw in the Act and unless put right by Parliament may well give rise to some difficult cases on priorities.

We may now summarize the position when the new Acts have come into full effect. There will then be three classes of interests, namely:

(*a*) Legal interests other than mortgages. In regard to these the new system does not alter the position. The purchaser will still have to search the title to discover legal interests.

(*b*) Equitable interests under settlements and trusts for sale. With these the purchaser is concerned only to the extent of seeing that there is a settlement or trust for sale and that the purchase money is paid to the proper persons. The rules about constructive notice will presumably still be applicable if a vendor attempts to conceal the fact that there is a settlement or trust for sale, but once the existence of the settlement or trust for sale appears the purchaser is no longer concerned with the equitable interests.

(*c*) Mortgages and other registrable interests. These will be protected either by deposit of title deeds or by registration and there is little scope left for the doctrine of constructive notice.

The purchaser will be obliged to investigate title deeds for three purposes only, namely:

(*a*) To satisfy himself that the vendor is the legal owner of the land

and that there are no outstanding legal interests. This he must do for his own protection.

(b) To discover whether the land is subject to a trust for sale or settlement and, if it is so subject, to see (to the limited extent to which he will be entitled to inquire) that the proper persons are selling and receiving the purchase money.

(c) To ensure that the title deeds are in the proper custody and not in the hands of a mortgagee whose mortgage is not registered.

Except to this extent he will be able to disregard equitable interests, since (subject to any imperfections that may be found in the Acts) these will either be registered or be overreached by the conveyance.

Maitland rightly lays great stress on the difference between legal and equitable interests and it is a difference which will always be of great importance for understanding the law. As a practical matter, however, it is important to remember that an equitable interest, if it can be properly protected, is very nearly as secure as a legal interest. It should be the object of the law to provide means whereby equitable interests can be properly protected, except where of deliberate policy it allows them to be overreached. When this object has been secured— and as regards land the Property Acts of 1925 should in time secure it— the distinction of practical importance will be between interests which can be protected and interests which can be overreached. Although the statutes which achieve this object may formally retain the distinction between legal and equitable interests they will have forced the old law into a new mould and the old distinction will lose most of its practical importance. When we have legal interests which are void unless registered or (as was the case under the old Settled Land Acts) legal interests which can be overreached on a sale, we have arrived at a stage where the old distinction between legal and equitable interests begins to lose its practical significance. There will, it is true, always be a residuum of advantage in holding a legal interest, for whatever system the law provides may be defeated by some elaborate fraud, such as forgery of a register, and in that event the owner of an equitable interest may find that he has lost his rights through a *bona fide* purchase for value. Such elaborate frauds however are much less frequent in practice than would appear from the law reports and do not as a rule enter into the calculation of persons who wish to buy or sell.

LECTURE XIV

THE REMEDIES FOR BREACH OF TRUST

In considering the nature of equitable estates and interests we have partially answered a question to which we ought now to turn; namely, what are the remedies for a breach of trust?

Now if a trustee in breach of trust has alienated the trust property, in general the best remedy that the *cestui que trust* can wish for is that he should be able to recover that property from the person who is holding it. Fraudulent people are apt to be impecunious people and a merely personal remedy against the trustee who has been guilty of a fraud is apt to be of little value. Therefore the *cestui que trust* will be anxious to recover the trust property, let us say the land from its present possessor. But can he do so? Already we have an answer. He can recover it from one to whom the trustee has given it without valuable consideration, he can recover it from one who purchased it with notice of his equitable rights unless indeed it had already passed through the hands of one who had obtained the legal estate *bona fide*, for value and without notice; again his equitable right will, as a general rule, prevail against any merely equitable right which is posterior to it in order of time. On the other hand if once the land has passed to a person who obtained the legal estate *bona fide*, for value and without notice, *cestui que trust* will not be able to get back that land again, unless indeed by some chance it should come into the hands of the guilty trustee.

Failing this remedy the *cestui que trust* can proceed personally against the guilty trustee. For every breach of trust there is this personal remedy against the trustee—the trustee is bound to restore the trust fund or trust property that has been alienated, or has perished, or has been deteriorated owing to a breach of trust, and the courts are severe—I must not go into details—in taking accounts against trustees who have misconducted themselves; in charging them with interest, in holding them liable not merely for what they have received, but also for what they might have received, but for their wilful default. But it will sometimes happen that a *cestui que trust* will have a somewhat better remedy than this merely personal remedy against the trustee.

To this remedy we ought to give a moment's attention—it is known as following the trust fund. Suppose that T holds a fund upon trust for A, and in breach of trust invests this fund, or rather the money produced by selling this fund, in the purchase of land, of which he obtains a conveyance in his own name. A can now say that the trust fund is represented by that land— he can obtain that land from T. Even if T be bankrupt A can, if I may so speak, pull this piece of land out of T's estate, and say 'No this is not part of the fund divisible among T's creditors, it is mine, bought with my money.' If T sells that land or gives it away, then A's power to obtain that land depends on considerations of which we have already spoken at some length. A is treated as having an equitable estate in that land; the question whether he can enforce that estate against X, the person now holding the land, raises the questions with which we are familiar: Has X got the legal estate? Did he obtain it *bona fide*, for value, without notice? Does he claim under one who obtained it *bona fide*, for value, without notice, and so forth?

But—and this may be a newer point to you—a *cestui que trust* is also allowed to follow money into investments or into the hands of the trustee's banker. T is a trustee for A of a plot of land, or of a sum of Consols. Wrongfully, and let us suppose it, with dishonest intent, he sells that land or that fund of Consols for £1000—this sum is paid to him in cash or in bank notes. Now of course in one sense A will not be able to follow the coins or the notes. A third person will be perfectly safe in receiving those sovereigns or those bank notes, unless indeed he is a participator in the trustee's fraud. But suppose that the trustee on having received the money or the notes at once goes and buys with them a number of shares in the Great Northern Railway Company—can A lay hold of those shares, and say 'They are mine'? Can he do so if the trustee is bankrupt, or will those shares form part of the trustee's estate and be divisible among all his creditors? We may complicate the question by sup-

posing that T sells the Great Northern shares and buys a Great
Eastern debenture, and then sells the Great Eastern debenture
and buys shares in the Cambridge Water Works. Can A, when
T is bankrupt, point to those Water Works shares and say,
'They are mine, bought with my money—I trace my fund from
investment to investment and I find it here.' There is no doubt
that in all these cases the *cestui que trust* is allowed to pursue the
fund from investment to investment and to claim it in whatever
shape he finds it.

We get the idea of a trust fund as a thing, an incorporeal
thing, which can be invested, that is dressed up in one costume
or another, but which remains the same beneath all these changes
of apparel: and that idea suffices us in many cases.[1]

But I have been putting simple cases and the courts have gone
much further than this in enabling a *cestui que trust* to follow
the trust fund. In the cases that we have put we have supposed
that the trustee does not mix up the proceeds of the trust fund
with his own money. But very often this may happen. He sells,
let us say, a trust estate or trust fund for £1000 and then we find
him investing a sum of £2000 in the purchase of railway shares
or the like. Or perhaps we find that he pays in the £1000 to his
own account at his bankers, where already he has a credit, and
he then proceeds to draw various cheques on that account and
to pay them to various tradesmen as the price of articles that he
has bought. Even in such cases as these the *cestui que trust* has
been allowed to follow the trust fund. Take the former, the
trustee sells the trust fund for £1000 and with £2000 he purchases land, or he purchases shares in a company; it is considered that as against the trustee and the creditors of the
trustee the *cestui que trust* has a charge, a specific charge, on the
land or the shares for the sum of £1000. Take the second case,
the trustee pays the £1000, the proceeds of the trust fund, to his
own account at his bankers—in other words he lends the £1000
to his bankers—and then he pays in other money to the same

---

[1] See *Sinclair* v. *Brougham* [1914] A.C. 398, which shows the extent to
which a fund can be traced and illustrates the different principle applied
when funds have been mixed accidentally and not through fraud or breach
of trust.

account, and then he begins drawing out sums of money from this account and paying them to tradesmen and the like. It has been contended that in such a case, a rule known as the rule in *Clayton's Case*, a rule which is certainly applicable for certain other purposes, ought to be applied, and that the items on the two sides of the account should be set against each other in the order in which they occur. Let me explain—T had an account with his bankers which showed a credit to the amount of £500. He then paid in £1000 which was trust money, and then £250 which was not trust money. Then he drew several cheques amounting in all to £750—the result is that he has now a credit of £1000. The *cestui que trust* now begins his action; if we suppose that the trustee draws out first the moneys which he pays in first, then £250 of the *cestui que trust's* money (if such we may call it) is gone. But this is not the rule. The rule as laid down by Jessel M.R. in the case of *In re Hallett's Estate*, 13 Ch. D. 696, is that neither the trustee nor his creditors, who stand in his place, can be heard to say that he acted dishonestly, that he drew out and spent upon his own purposes the trust monies which were standing to his account. It must be taken that his cheques were drawn against his own money, and the *cestui que trust* will have the first claim to any balance that the account may show.

The rule in *Clayton's Case*, 1 Mer. 572, is a rule which was evolved for the purpose of settling the liabilities of partners in banking firms. X banks with a firm of A, B and C (not being a corporate body); his account shows a credit of £1000; at this moment C dies: A and B continue the business and X banks with them; X pays in £500; then draws out £500; then the bank breaks and A and B are insolvent; C's estate is solvent; X wants to know how much he can claim from C's estate. When C died A, B and C owed X £1000. We consider that C (or his estate) incurs no new liability. In such a case we follow the chronologic order of the payments, for the purpose of settling the liability of the continuing and the departed partners. By the rule in *Clayton's Case* the items drawn out are attributed to the earliest items paid in and not to the last items nor merely to items paid in to the surviving partners. Consequently the £500 drawn out goes to reduce the £1000 for which alone C's estate was liable. X can recover from C's estate only £500. But between a *cestui que trust* and the creditors of his trustee or trustees we do not apply this rule: we suppose that the trustee takes for his own purposes his own money and not the money of the *cestui que trust*.

However as between various trusts the rule in *Clayton's Case* is applied. I hold £1000 upon trust for A, £1000 upon trust for B; I pay to an account at my bank, first A's £1000, then B's £1000; I begin drawing out for my own purposes; as between A and B, I am drawing against A's £1000 until all of it is gone. See *In re Hallett*, 13 Ch. D. 696, at p. 726 *et seq.* and *Hancock* v. *Smith*, 41 Ch. D. 456.

Just let us consider the application of the rule in *Clayton's Case* as between two *cestui que trusts* of one trustee.

T, a trustee, has an account at his bank which shows a balance of £500. He pays in £500 of trust money held for A. Afterwards he pays in £500 of trust money held for B, and then £500 of his own, and then be begins drawing out. It is held that he first exhausts all of the £1000 that is his own—then he begins to exhaust A's.

I have great doubts of the convenience of all this. It may be hard that a *cestui que trust* should not have 'his' property, but it is also hard that creditors should go unpaid. Courts of Equity, which in this matter have had the upper hand, have thought a great deal of the *cestui que trust*, much less of creditors. This result has been obtained under cover of the metaphor of investment—the idea of a 'fund' preserving its identity during any change of investment. Equity has been always striving to prevent the *cestui que trust* from falling to the level of an unsecured creditor. T sells for 100 sovereigns some land which he holds upon trust. He has the sovereigns in his purse, he spends them upon a banquet, the fund is gone, the *cestui que trust* is merely an unsecured creditor. Or with those sovereigns the trustee buys a horse which dies, the fund is represented by the carcase. But if he changes those sovereigns for some chose in action the *cestui que trust* has a charge on this for the amount of 100 sovereigns or he may elect to take this chose in action itself as being in equity his—an investment by his trustee of the trust funds which he, the *cestui que trust*, may adopt, although it was unauthorized or wrongful.

It is not for the trustee to dictate to the *cestui que trust* in what shape he shall make his claim.

So far as regards following the proceeds of a rightful or wrongful disposal of the property there is no difference between the cases of an express trustee, or an agent, or a bailee, or a collector of rents or anybody else in a fiduciary position.[1] As was said by Sir George Jessel in *Hallett's Case*, at p. 710, 'the moment you get into a Court of Equity, where a principal can sue an agent as well as a *cestui que trust* can sue a trustee, no such distinction was ever suggested'—and 'the moment you establish the fiduciary relation the modern rules of Equity as regards following trust money apply'.

Thus you see that the *cestui que trust* is no mere creditor of the trustee who has committed a breach of trust. I lend you £100; you buy a horse with it; if you go bankrupt I can not claim that horse, I must take my dividend (perhaps 2*d*. in the pound) along with your other creditors. But if you are a trustee for me I may be able to trace the trust fund from investment to investment, and this even although you have mixed it up with your own money.

We have next to notice that it is possible for a *cestui que trust* to lose all or some of his remedies by lapse of time.[2] This is a subject about which unfortunately there is now a great deal of confused and complicated statute law. To explain it fully would take several lectures; but just a little may be said. In the first place we must distinguish between two cases—(1) the *cestui que trust* is seeking a remedy against one who has been expressly made a trustee for him, or against the representative of one who has been expressly made a trustee for him—(2) the *cestui que trust* is seeking a remedy against one who is but constructively a trustee for him.

(1) Now the old rule was that in the case of an express trust and as between the *cestui que trust* and the trustee lapse of time was no bar. Suppose that T has undertaken to hold land upon trust for A. T is in possession of the land, but instead of paying

---

[1] See p. 230 below.   [2] On this topic see p. 229 below.

over the profits to A, he put those profits in his own pocket. He may do this for 10, 20, 60 years, and yet he will never get rid of his obligation to hold the land in trust for A. In other words, a trustee could not acquire a title to the property by lapse of time. You will observe that in such a case there would be nothing that could be called an adverse possession. The trustee's possession could not be adverse to his *cestui que trust*. You could not say that the trustee was wrongfully in possession, for by law he was entitled to be in possession. Of course it was a quite different question whether you could make the trustee refund all the profits that he had wrongfully appropriated to his own use. The rule might have been that though the trustee could never acquire the land by adverse possession against his *cestui que trust* still he could only be made to refund the profits which he had wrongfully pocketed during the last 10 years or the last 20 years. Such however was not the rule. The rule was that in this case also time would not be a bar to an action by *cestui que trust* against the express trustee. Thus if for the last 40 years I had been holding land upon trust for you, owing (let us say) to some mistake I had been appropriating the profits to my own use and paying nothing to you, not only would you have been able to claim the land from me, but you would have been able to make me account for all the monies that I had misappropriated ever since the misappropriation began.[1]

Then in 1873 this rule was laid down in very positive terms by section 25 sub-section 2 of the Judicature Act of that year. 'No claim of a *cestui que trust* against his trustee for any property held on an express trust, or in respect of any breach of such trust, shall be held to be barred by any Statute of Limitation.' I very much doubt whether this altered the law. I suppose that the legislature thought well to declare the rule expressly at a moment when a new court which was to administer both common law and equity concurrently was being created.

In 1888, however, the current of legislation turned in favour

---

[1] Although in such a case no Statute of Limitations is applicable the *cestui que trust*, if he has delayed bringing his suit, may be prevented by his 'laches' from recovering the arrears in full. See for example *Thomson* v. *Eastwood*, 2 App. Cas. 215.

of the trustee. A section of the Trustee Act of that year (51 & 52 Vic. c. 59, s. 8) dealt with the matter.[1] It is a complicated section —but put very roughly its result is I think this:

(*a*) If the *cestui que trust* is attempting to recover property that the trustee is holding upon an express trust, no Statute of Limitations bars his action. Thus say that for 40 years I have been holding land and under the terms of some settlement I ought to have been holding it upon trust for you, but all the while I have been pocketing the profits instead of paying them to you, you can still recover the land from me, in other words, you can compel me to do my duty for the future, my duty being to hold that land upon trust for you.

But (*b*) unless there has been fraud a *cestui que trust* can not recover from his trustee income which the trustee has mis-applied more than six years ago, or, under certain circumstances, if the trust was created by deed more than 20 years ago. For the purposes of the Statutes of Limitation a breach of trust is for the future—if there be no fraud—to be treated as though it merely created a debt due from the trustee to the *cestui que trust* —and, as you know, the general rule is that one can not sue for a simple contract debt after six years or for a specialty debt after 20 years. These periods are now introduced in favour of a trustee who has been guilty of a breach of trust. His breach of trust is for this purpose to be treated as creating a debt, a specialty debt if he has executed a trust deed, a simple contract debt if no trust deed has been executed by him; and this debt (if in the meanwhile there be no written acknowledgement of it) will be barred in the one case after 20 years and in the other after six years.[2]

---

[1] This section is still in force.

[2] This paragraph is perhaps misleading. The Trustee Act 1888 does not protect a trustee who has converted property to his own use and accordingly if the trustee has put the income into his own pocket neither the Act nor any other Statute of Limitations will protect him against the *cestui que trust*. If however the trustee has honestly but wrongfully paid the profits to other beneficiaries the *cestui que trust* properly entitled will only be able to recover six years arrears of income in a suit for breach of trust. The fact that the trust was created by deed probably does not increase the amount of arrears which the *cestui que trust* can recover in an action for breach of trust. He may however be a party to the deed whereby the trust was created and be able to

But (2) we have to consider the case as it stands between the *cestui que trust* and one who has purchased the property from the trustee—one that is who is only bound by the trust because when purchasing the property he had notice of the trust. This case was met by the Real Property Limitation Act of 1833 (3 & 4 Will. IV, c. 27, s. 25). This in effect said that as between *cestui que trust* and the purchaser of trust property, the ordinary statutory rules as to limitation were to apply, and that the statutory period was to run as from the time of the conveyance to the purchaser. The ordinary statutory period introduced by that Act was 20 years. The Real Property Limitation Act of 1874 curtailed this period, substituting 12 years for 20. The rule therefore is that in favour of a purchaser from a trustee time begins to run against *cestui que trust* as from the date of the conveyance—and in the normal case the limiting period is now 12 years.

One curious result is produced by these statutes.

You will remember what we have said before, that an executor while acting merely as executor is not a trustee—but that the will often makes the same persons executors and trustees, and that it is often difficult in a given case to say whether an action is that of a legatee for his legacy or that of a *cestui que trust* against his trustee. Under the Act of 1888 the *cestui que trust* has often less time (six years) for his action against his trustee based on a breach of trust than a legatee has against an executor (12 years—under section 8 of the Act of 1874).

Read *In re Timmis* [1902] 1 Ch. 176.[1] There the defendant was concerned to say I am trustee, not executor. It is a curious reversal of the old position. Our Statutes of Limitation are indeed in a great mess.

The term 'express trust' used in this context is by no means so plain as it might be. There are interesting judgments on this

bring a common law action for breach of covenant. In such an action he could recover 20 years' arrears. If the only suit he can bring is a suit for breach of trust the fact that the trust is created by deed is probably immaterial. The point is however possibly open to doubt and depends upon the construction of a badly drafted clause of the Trustee Act. On the effect of the Trustee Act generally see note on p. 229 below.

[1] See also *In re Richardson* [1920] 1 Ch. 423.

point in the case of *Soar* v. *Ashwell* [1893] 2 Q.B. 390, to which I have already referred you.[1]

Let me remind you once more of the Judicial Trustees Act 1896. Under section 3 of that Act the Court may relieve from personal liability for breach of trust a trustee who has acted honestly and reasonably if in the opinion of the Court he ought fairly to be excused from such liability. This section seems destined in time to produce a large crop of cases.

There is much more to be said about this matter; but I think that we have more profitable matters before us than these Statutes of Limitation which are very complicated and, in some points, very obscure.

Before we leave this subject we should just consider for a moment first the possibility of criminal proceedings against the trustee and secondly the possibility of his imprisonment in civil proceedings.

1. As to criminal proceedings. For a trustee (properly so called) to convert to his own use the trust property was no crime at all until the year 1857. The Act passed in that year was replaced by several sections of the Larceny Act of 1861. See Stephen's *History of the Criminal Law*, vol. III, pp. 156 etc.

Section 80 of the Larceny Act of 1861[2] hits the 'trustee' who misappropriates the property of the trust, but, by the definition given in section 1, 'trustee' is limited to 'trustee on some express trust created by some deed, will or instrument in writing' and to the representatives of such a trustee or persons upon whom the duty of such a trust may have devolved. Section 80 therefore won't work unless the trust has been created by writing.

Sections 75 and 76 of the Act of 1861 hit some classes of agents misappropriating property entrusted to their care. For these sections the Larceny Act of 1901[3] substitutes more general clauses dealing with the criminal liability of agents and persons entrusted with property, but the trustee on an express trust is still (by express reservation in section 1 sub-section 2) left to

---

[1] The reference is to p. 74 above. See also the note on p. 227 below.

[2] Now replaced by the Larceny Act 1916, s. 21.

[3] Repealed by the Larceny Act 1916. The corresponding provisions are contained in s. 20 of the 1916 Act.

section 80 of the old Act of 1861. Probably, however, most other trustees are hit by the extremely wide and general terms of the new sections in the Act of 1901.

2. As to imprisonment in civil proceedings. The Debtors Act of 1869 abolished imprisonment for debt except in certain cases. One of the cases excepted is that of default by a trustee or person acting in a fiduciary capacity and ordered to pay by a Court of Equity any sum in his possession or under his control.

NOTE ON TRUSTS

In this note it is proposed to refer to a number of cases upon trusts, which illustrate certain important distinctions between trusts and other equitable relationships and give a fuller understanding of the conception of a trust.

A trustee is subject as such to certain special rules, of which the most important for the present purpose are as follows:

(1) The trustee cannot make a profit out of the trust.

(2) Trust property may be followed in the hands of the trustee and claimed by the *cestui que trust* as against the creditors of the trustee in the event of the trustee going bankrupt.

(3) The trustee cannot (apart from the Trustee Act 1888) plead the Statute of Limitations against his *cestui que trust*.

(4) Under the Debtors Act 1869 a trustee who is ordered to pay money into Court and does not do so can be imprisoned, whereas an ordinary debtor is not liable to imprisonment.

Interesting cases have arisen in connexion with all, and more especially the first three, of these rules, but it is in connexion with the Statutes of Limitations that the points here to be discussed have been most completely elaborated. Unfortunately, the law upon the Statutes of Limitations has become rather confused and it will be helpful, before going farther with the subject of trusts, to examine in rather more detail than Maitland has done the question how far the Statutes of Limitations apply to trusts.

The principal Statutes of Limitations in force at the present day are the Limitation Act 1623, which still governs most personal actions and formerly governed also actions to recover land, the Real Property Limitation Acts of 1833 and 1874, which have superseded the Act of 1623 so far as concerns actions to recover land and are the statutes now applicable on all questions concerning land or money charged on land, the Civil Procedure Act 1833, which bars actions to recover specialty debts, and lastly the Trustee Act 1888, which is the first statute that expressly protects trustees. The law has developed out of the Act of 1623, which was the first important Statute of Limitations. This Act applied in terms only to certain forms of action at common law and did not include any suits in equity. The Courts of Equity, however, in accordance with their usual practice of following the law, adopted the statute whenever a suit in equity was analogous to an action at common law to which the statute would apply, unless there was some good equitable reason, such as fraud, why the Statute should not be applied. From the first they took the view that the Statute would not be applied in a suit by a *cestui que trust* against a trustee. It seems, however, that the word trust was in early times rather loosely used and might connote almost any equitable relation. Thus in 1821 Lord Eldon said, with his habitual caution :[1]

'There is a vast difference between things to which we give the same denomination, I mean trusts. You have a trust expressed: you have a trust implied: you have relations formed between individuals in the matters in which they deal with each other in which you can hardly say that one of them is a trustee and the other a *cestui que trust*; and yet you cannot deny that to some intents and for some purposes one is a *cestui que trust* and the other a trustee.'

Thus it became necessary to define more closely the trusts to which the Statutes of Limitations did not apply and for this purpose two distinctions had to be made. First, the trust proper had to be distinguished from relations, such as that between a mortgagor and mortgagee, which might loosely be called trusts but which were in fact relations of a different type. Secondly, certain types of constructive trust had to be distinguished from the main body of trusts. In almost every instance where one man is under an equitable obligation to transfer property to another there can be said to be an implied or constructive trust, but in many of such instances, which involved no real fiduciary relation, it would have been wrong not to have allowed the constructive trustee to plead the Statute of Limitations. Unfortunately the criterion first conceived for effecting this second distinction was a bad one. It came to be thought that if you could find a trust expressly created that trust would be outside the Statute, but that if the defendant was apparently the owner of the estate and the trust could only be established by entering into controverted facts the Statute would apply.[2] Thus the distinction was based upon the form in which the trust was created and the manner in which its existence would be established rather than upon any substantial difference in the nature of trusts.

In 1833 the Real Property Limitation Act was passed, which provided and (as altered by the Real Property Limitation Act 1874) still provides the law of limitation in regard to all actions relating to land. This Act expressly applied to suits in equity as well as to actions at law, but section 25 of the Act excluded suits by a *cestui que trust* against a trustee holding land upon an 'express trust'. In the light of the distinction previously made by the Courts it seems probable that the phrase 'express trust' was meant to be confined to trusts created by express words and in regard to land this is the view originally taken by the Courts, although it is not easy to say whether it still represents the law. As a result of the Act, however, the phrase 'express trust' came to

[1] *Cholmondely* v. *Clinton*, 4 Bligh 1, at p. 96.
[2] See *Beckford* v. *Wade* (1810) 17 Ves. 87.

be a term of art used to signify any trust, whether of land or personalty, which is excluded from the Statutes of Limitations. It is, for example, in this wide sense that the term is used in section 25 of the Judicature Act 1873.[1] Now as regards personalty at least many trusts are outside the Statutes of Limitations which would normally be classified as implied or constructive trusts. It must be remembered therefore that in regard to these Statutes the phrase 'express trust' is an ambiguous phrase and in its widest sense includes many trusts not properly termed express.

Putting the matter broadly the result of cases upon the Statutes of Limitations appears to be as follows: that the Statutes will not apply where there is a trust which implies a real fiduciary relationship, but that where the word 'trust' is used to describe a relationship which is not really a trust at all or where there is an implied or constructive trust which is a mere equitable obligation having no real fiduciary character, then the Statutes of Limitations will apply notwithstanding the so-called trust. This is of course only an approximate statement of the law and in particular would need qualification in regard to land, where the matter is one of construing the words 'express trust' in the Real Property Limitation Act 1833, and also in regard to certain constructive trusts which arise through improper dealing with property already subject to a trust; as regards the latter the law, which is not easy, will be found stated in *Soar* v. *Ashwell*.[2]

Locking v. *Parker*[3] illustrates how one may have a relationship which is called a trust but which is in fact a relationship of a different kind, to which the Statutes of Limitations will apply. In that case by a curiously framed deed property was conveyed on trusts which were designed to put the parties in the same position as if there had been a mortgage. The 'mortgagee' went into possession and remained in possession for 36 years. The 'mortgagor' then sued for administration of the trusts and an account. The Court held however that the transaction, though in form a trust, was in substance a mortgage and that the suit was barred by the Real Property Limitation Act 1833, under which a suit for redemption by a mortgagor against a mortgagee in possession is barred in 20 (since reduced to 12) years.

The rule that a trustee cannot plead the Statutes of Limitations was to a large extent reversed by section 8 of the Trustee Act 1888, of which sub-section 1 reads as follows:

' 1. In any action or other proceeding against a trustee or any person claiming through him, except where the claim is founded upon any fraud or fraudulent breach of trust to which the trustee was party or

---

[1] Sub-section 2 of this section reads: 'No claim of a *cestui que trust* against his trustee for any property held on any express trust or in respect of any breach of such trust shall be held to be barred by any Statute of Limitations.'

[2] [1893] 2 Q.B. 390.   [3] L.R. 8 Ch. 30.

privy, or is to recover trust property or the proceeds thereof still retained by the trustee, or previously received by the trustee and converted to his use, the following provisions shall apply:

'(*a*) All rights and privileges conferred by any Statute of Limitations shall be enjoyed in the like manner and to the like extent as they would have been enjoyed in such action or other proceeding if the trustee or person claiming through him had not been a trustee or person claiming through him.

'(*b*) If the action or other proceeding is brought to recover money or other property, and is one to which no existing Statute of Limitations applies, the trustee or person claiming through him shall be entitled to the benefit of and be at liberty to plead the lapse of time as a bar to such action or other proceeding in the like manner and to the like extent as if the claim had been against him in an action of debt for money had and received, but so nevertheless that the statute shall run against a married woman entitled in possession for her separate use, whether with or without a restraint upon anticipation, but shall not begin to run against any beneficiary unless and until the interest of such beneficiary shall be an interest in possession.'

The exceptions set out at the beginning of the sub-section are important and should be remembered. Where the action falls within one of these exceptions one is thrown back upon the earlier law and must consider whether apart from the Trustee Act the trust is outside the Statutes of Limitations. Apart from the exceptions, the Act extends to all trustees including fiduciary agents and, so far as they are not already protected, personal representatives. The period of limitation applicable under the Act will depend upon whether the case falls within Clause (*a*) or Clause (*b*). It is however by no means easy to find cases which fall directly within Clause (*a*) and the meaning of that Clause has not yet been made clear.[1]

We are now in a position to discuss general questions concerning trusts and will deal first with an important class of persons, known as 'fiduciary agents' who, though not trustees in the fullest sense, are for many purposes regarded as trustees. A fiduciary agent is an agent who has been entrusted with the management of the property of his principal. Like a trustee he is debarred from pleading the Statute of Limitations, he is not permitted to make a secret profit at the expense of his principal and he is liable to imprisonment under the Debtors Act 1869 if being ordered to do so by the Court he does not pay over to his principal money which belongs to the principal. Moreover, as

---

[1] See *In re Bowden* 45 Ch. D. 444, *How* v. *Earl Winterton* [1896] 2 Ch. 626, *In re Allsop* [1914] 1 Ch. 1, *In re Richardson* [1920] 1 Ch. 423.

with a trustee, the principal can follow his property into the hands of the agent so long as it can be traced. Unlike a trustee in the full sense of the word, the agent may himself have no estate at all in the property of his principal and will not be bound by the conservative rules in regard to investment and like matters which apply to trustees; in such matters the duty of the agent is to carry out his agency and this may involve most hazardous dealings with the property.

A good example of a fiduciary agent may be found in *Burdick* v. *Garrick*.[1] A solicitor in London was entrusted by power of attorney with wide powers of dealing with the land belonging to his principal, an American. He sold some of the land and put the money he received into the general account of his firm. Many years later the personal representatives of the principal sued him for the money. Held that he was a fiduciary agent, that he had received the money as trustee for the principal and that he could not set up the Statute of Limitations.

A particularly important class of fiduciary agents who should be noticed are the directors of a company. In their dealings with the company's property they are for many purposes regarded as trustees for the company.[2] They cannot plead the Statutes of Limitations against the company and they are not allowed to make a profit at the company's expense. They are not of course obliged to invest the company's money in trust securities, for that would defeat the object for which the company exists. Nor are they, as are the trustees of a marriage settlement, the owners of the property of which they are trustees; the property remains both at law and in equity the property of the company; the directors merely manage the property as agents for the company, but as such agents they are treated as being in a sense trustees.

It is convenient here to notice the distinction between a trustee and a debtor. Take the example of a banker. In a popular sense the banker cares for other people's money but from a legal point of view the position is different. When a person deposits money with a banker the money thereupon ceases to be the property of the depositor and becomes the property of the banker; the banker can deal with it as he wishes, he can mix it with his own, he can use it to make a profit for himself, he can lose it in a hazardous speculation, and the depositor will have no ground to object; the only right of the depositor is the legal right of a creditor to have the debt which arose on the deposit repaid; if the banker goes bankrupt the depositor has no claim to follow his money but must claim as a creditor in the bankruptcy. Very different is the position of a fiduciary agent. He receives the property of his principal as trustee, he must not use it to make a profit for himself

---

[1] L.R. 5 Ch. 233.
[2] See *e.g. In re Sharpe* [1892] 1 Ch. 154, *Great Eastern Railway* v. *Turner*, L.R. 8 Ch. 149.

and he must not mix it with his own. In equity the property remains the property of the principal and on the agent's bankruptcy the principal can follow his property and, so far as it can be traced, recover it as against all the other creditors. There is thus a great distinction between an agent, such as a banker, who becomes only a debtor of the property he receives and a fiduciary agent who becomes a trustee of the property.[1] The distinction is of the utmost importance in the law of bankruptcy and has often arisen in relation to the Statute of Limitations.[2] No general rule for making the distinction can be laid down, for each case depends upon the particular circumstances of the agency and especially upon the usage of the trade in which the agent is engaged.

Next we should notice a further class of trustees who are called 'trustees de son tort', but who may better be described as 'de facto' trustees. If a person, without being appointed a trustee, gets possession of trust property and assumes the position of trustee and acts as such, he will be held liable as if he were in fact a trustee. In particular he will not be able to plead the Statutes of Limitations against the *cestui trust*. The point is not one which needs elaborating but reference should be made to three interesting cases: *Lyell* v. *Kennedy*,[3] *Life Association of Scotland* v. *Siddal*[4] and *Barnes* v. *Addy*.[5]

Next we may notice certain cases where persons who have covenanted to settle property upon trusts have been held to be trustees upon a principle similar to that applied in *Walsh* v. *Lonsdale*.[6] In *Pullan* v. *Koe*[7] a husband and wife covenanted in a marriage settlement to transfer to the trustees, to be held on the trusts of the settlement, any property worth £100 or more which the wife might acquire in the future. In 1879 the wife received a gift of £285 from her mother. This money, which should have been transferred to the trustees, was put into the husband's banking account and shortly afterwards invested in two bonds. About 30 years later the trustees of the marriage settlement, on behalf of the wife and the children of the marriage, sued the husband's representatives to have the two bonds, which were still in existence, assigned to them. The husband's representatives pleaded that the only claim the trustees could put forward was for breach of the covenant to transfer the money and that this was barred by the Statute of Limitations. Swinfen Eady J. however held that the husband became a trustee of the money as soon as it came into his possession, that on investing it in the bonds he became a trustee of the bonds and that, the

---

[1] The distinction is discussed at length in *Foley* v. *Hill* 2 H.L.C. 28.
[2] See for example *Friend* v. *Young* [1897] 2 Ch. 421 and *Henry* v. *Hammond* [1913] 2 K.B. 515.
[3] 14 App. Cas. 437.
[4] 3 De G. F. and J. 58.
[5] L.R. 9 Ch. 244.
[6] 21 Ch. D. 9; see above, p. 156.
[7] [1913] 1 Ch. 9.

bonds being still intact, his representatives were prevented by the trust from pleading the Statute of Limitations. Compare *In re Plumptre's Settlement*[1] where the facts were very similar but the claimants were the next of kin of the wife, who were the beneficiaries ultimately entitled under the marriage settlement in default of issue of the marriage. Here it was held that the next of kin could not compel the husband to transfer to the trustees a fund which he ought to have, but had not, settled. Compare also *Stone* v. *Stone.*[2] There the husband covenanted to pay £1000 to the trustees within twelve months after the date of the settlement to be held upon the trusts of the settlement. The £1000 was never paid and more than 20 years later the children of the marriage sued the estate of the husband for payment of the £1000. Held that they were barred by the Statute of Limitations.

These three cases are an excellent illustration of the rule that equity treats as done what ought to be done and the limitations on that rule. When a covenant is such as equity would enforce by specific performance, equity will not allow the covenantor to benefit by not doing what he could have been compelled to do. When however the covenant is not one which would have been specifically enforced the doctrine no longer applies. Moreover equity will not enforce a covenant in favour of a volunteer and, although the wife and children are deemed to be purchasers under a marriage settlement and not volunteers, the next of kin of the husband or wife, even if beneficiaries under the settlement, are mere volunteers. So if the husband covenants to settle specific property, as for example property to be acquired in the future, the wife and children (or the trustees on their behalf) will be entitled to have the covenant specifically enforced as soon as the property comes into the hands of the husband and, on the principle that equity treats as done what ought to be done, the husband as soon as he receives the property is regarded, so far as the wife and children are concerned, as a trustee of it. This is *Pullan* v. *Koe.* The next of kin however being volunteers could not get specific performance and so far as they are concerned the husband is not regarded as a trustee of the property. This is *In re Plumptre's Settlement.* Finally if the covenant is merely to pay a sum of money it is not such as equity will specifically enforce even in favour of purchasers. The trustees could enforce it at law but any action at law will be subject to the Statute of Limitations. This is *Stone* v. *Stone.*

Finally, we shall discuss the distinction between trustees and personal representatives. As stated by Maitland the distinction is a matter of history.[3] In essence a personal representative is very like a trustee and most of the ordinary rules applicable to a trustee—as for example that the trustee cannot make a profit from his trust and that

---

[1] [1910] 1 Ch. 609.   [2] (1869) L.R. 5 Ch. 74.
[3] See above, p. 48.

9

the *cestui que trusts* can follow the trust property—apply equally to a personal representative. There are however certain distinctions between trustees and personal representatives, of which the most important are as follows:

(1) One of several personal representatives can sell and give the purchaser a good title to personalty, whereas no one trustee can dispose of the trust property without the concurrence of the others.[1]

(2) A sole personal representative (but not one of several personal representatives) can sell land belonging to the estate, whereas since 1925 there must be at least two trustees (or a trust corporation) to sell land belonging to a trust.

(3) There are Statutes of Limitations which a personal representative can, but a trustee can not, plead.

The distinction between a trustee and a personal representative has been elaborated principally in connexion with the Statutes of Limitations. The position under these is as follows: The Real Property Limitation Act 1874[2] bars a suit by a legatee to recover a legacy in 12 years and this (apart from the Trustee Act 1888) is the only Statute of importance in connexion with personal representatives at the present day. Until 1926 a suit by the next of kin against the administrator of an intestate's estate was barred in 20 years.[3] In certain cases a creditor could bring a common law action for devastavit against an executor who had misapplied the assets of the estate and such action was barred in six years by the Limitation Act 1623.[4] None of these periods of limitation were available to trustees. In addition to these Statutes of Limitations there is the Trustee Act 1888, which applies both to personal representatives and trustees.

There are three cases in which it may be hard to tell whether a person is a personal representative or a trustee: first, when for some purpose a statute calls a personal representative a trustee, secondly, when a testator by his will gives property to his executors to be held by them as trustees, and thirdly, when personal representatives who are not constituted trustees by a will nevertheless continue, after having performed their duties as personal representatives, to administer the estate for the benefit of the beneficiaries.

On the effect of a statute which refers to personal representatives as trustees one should read and compare *In re Lacy*[5] and *Toates* v. *Toates*.[6] *In re Lacy* arose under the Executors Act 1830, which was

---

[1] See *Attenborough* v. *Solomon* [1913] A.C. 76.

[2] Section 8, replacing section 40 of the Real Property Limitation Act 1833 under which the period of limitation was 20 years.

[3] Law of Property Amendment Act 1860; now repealed.

[4] See *In re Hyatt* 38 Ch. D. 609, *Lacons* v. *Warmoll* [1907] 2 K.B. 350 and *In re Blow* [1914] 1 Ch. 233.

[5] [1899] 2 Ch. 149.   [6] [1926] 2 K.B. 30.

passed in the following circumstances. The appointment of an executor automatically vested in the executor the personal estate of the deceased testator. If the property was disposed of by the will the executors were obliged, after paying the testator's debts, to transfer the property to the legatees, but if there was personal property not disposed of by the will the executors were entitled until 1830 to keep it for themselves unless a contrary intention appeared in the will. The Executors Act 1830 provided that the executors should hold the undisposed-of personalty on trust for the next of kin unless it appeared from the will that they were intended to take it for themselves. Thus the Act reversed the presumption that had previously been made. In *In re Lacy*[1] the question arose whether the next of kin were barred by the Statute of Limitations in suing the executors for undisposed-of personalty. The argument of the next of kin was that the Act of 1830 by its terms made the executors trustees and as trustees they could not rely on the Statute of Limitations. It was held however that the Statute of Limitations applied. The real ground for this decision, which can be better understood after reading *Toates* v. *Toates*,[2] seems to be that the Act of 1830 merely changed the presumption that previously existed and that the relation between the executors and the next of kin (as presumed legátees), although for want of a better word it was called by the Act a trust, was in fact an executor-legatee relation and not a trust. In *Toates* v. *Toates* a similar question arose on the Land Transfer Act 1897. By that Act freehold land, which previously had vested directly in the heir or devisee, was made to vest in the personal representatives and the Act provided that the personal representatives should hold the land as trustees for the persons beneficially entitled to it. Here the Court held that the personal representatives could not plead the Statute of Limitations against the heir or devisees. The land had never before vested in the personal representatives; there was no existing relation which the word 'trustees' in the Act might be intended to describe; the Act said they were to be trustees and trustees they were.

Although the principle of these decisions is no doubt still valid, the actual law has been changed by the Administration of Estates Act 1925. The administrators of an intestate and the executor in case of partial intestacy are expressly made trustees for the persons beneficially entitled on the intestacy,[3] and since the Law of Property Amendment Act 1860 has been repealed there is now no Statute of Limitations on which the personal representatives can rely in an action by the next of kin on an intestacy. The Land Transfer Act 1897 is repealed and, except in the case of settled land or where there is an intestacy, the personal representatives are no longer made trustees of the land which devolves

[1] [1899] 2 Ch. 149. [2] [1926] 2 K.B. 30.
[3] Administration of Estates Act 1925, ss. 33, 46, 47 and 49 (b).

upon them.[1] Accordingly where there is no intestacy they can, it would seem, plead the Statute of Limitations (the Real Property Limitation Act 1874) against the devisees of land. As against legatees of personalty the personal representatives can still, as they could before 1926, rely on the Real Property Limitation Act 1874, which bars an action by the legatees after 12 years.

When a testator, by his will, gives property to his executors to be held upon a trust, the rule is that the property vests in them as executors and they continue to be executors until they have assented to the gift. After they have assented they become trustees. It will often be difficult to say whether they have assented. It is a question of fact to be decided from all the circumstances of the case.[2]

Even if there is no trust created by the will it is no doubt possible for a personal representative to constitute himself a trustee if instead of paying over the property to the beneficiaries he continues to administer it for them. In such a case, however, there must be some conduct which amounts to a declaration of trust and the Courts have been chary of holding that in such circumstances an executor has made himself a trustee.[3]

---

[1] Administration of Estates Act, ss. 1 and 2 and Settled Land Act 1925, ss. 6 (2) and 7 (1).

[2] The most instructive case is *Attenborough* v. *Solomon* [1913] A.C. 76. See also *Dix* v. *Burford* 19 Beav. 409, *Phillipo* v. *Munnings* 2 Myl. and Cr. 309, *In re Swain* [1891] 3 Ch. 233, *In re Timmis* [1902] 1 Ch. 176 and *In re Oliver* [1927] 2 Ch. 323.

[3] See *In re Davis* [1891] 3 Ch. 119, *In re Barker* [1892] 2 Ch. 491, *In re Mackay* [1906] 1 Ch. 25 and *In re Rowe* 58 L.J. Ch. 703.

LECTURE XV

SATISFACTION AND ADEMPTION

MANY of the rules which equity has added to our legal system are rules establishing presumptions, rebuttable presumptions. They take this form—in this or that class of transactions it is presumed that the parties, or the settlor, or testator have or has this or that intention, and it is for those who contend for a different intention to prove their case. They are presumptions as to the intention of a person in cases in which the primary rule is that the intention of that person is to take effect. Indeed they are occasionally treated by text-writers rather as rules of evidence than as rules of substantive law.

It is to one group of these rules that I ask your attention this morning. And the first matter that we have to consider is the legacy given to a creditor. The case is this: A person A owes a debt to another person X, and this debt is not a portion debt. That phrase 'a portion debt' I shall explain by and by; suffice it for the present that the debt that is owing to X is a debt of an ordinary kind, incurred, let us suppose, in the course of trade. Then A makes a will and by it he gives some benefit to X, and then A dies, the debt being still unpaid. Is X to have the benefit that is given to him by the will, and is he also to be able to exact his debt? Or, on the other hand, are we to say that the provision made for him by the will is intended as a satisfaction of the debt and that if he insists, as of course he may insist, on being paid his debt he can not claim the benefit given him by the will, or can only claim a certain part of it.

Now the rule to which our Courts have come in this matter is that if the legacy be equal to the debt or greater than the debt then the legacy is intended to be a satisfaction of the debt, and the creditor if he insists on his debt can not claim any part of this equal or greater legacy. On the other hand if the legacy be less than the debt the presumption is the other way—the testator does not intend the legacy to be a partial satisfaction of the debt. Of course it stands to reason that a debt can not be fully satisfied by a legacy of smaller amount; the only question can be as to whether the legacy is to be deemed a partial satisfaction, or satisfaction *pro tanto*; and the rule is that it is not a satisfaction *pro tanto*; the creditor may exact his debt and also claim the whole legacy. Indeed the Courts have not of late much favoured the doctrine of the satisfaction of debts by legacies, and though the first part of our rule holds good in a general way, and a legacy of an amount equal to or greater than that of the debt is in general deemed to be given in satisfaction of the debt, still the scope of this rule has been narrowed, that is to say, the Courts have been very ready to find in the will an indication that the debt is not to be satisfied by the legacy. For example, if the testator says in his will—and very often he does—'I direct that my debts shall be paid', that excludes this presumption of satisfaction. Or again he gives to the creditor not a certain sum of money, not a pecuniary legacy, but the residue, or a share of the residue of his personal estate; in this case it is held that the gift of an uncertain sum, even though in the event that sum proves to be larger than the debt, is not be be deemed a satisfaction of the debt. And small differences between the debt and the testamentary benefit have been thought sufficient to exclude the presumption. Long ago Sir Thomas Clarke M.R. said 'I remember a case before the Lord Chancellor where an old lady, indebted to a servant for wages, by will gave ten times as much as she owed or was likely to owe; yet because it was payable in a month after her own death, so that the servant might not outlive the month, although great odds the other way, the Court laid hold of that.'[1] On the whole it is not very often that a debt, not being a portion debt, is satisfied by a legacy.[2]

Observe that the presumption of satisfaction, if it arises at all, arises only where the debt is incurred before the will is made. There is no presumption whatever that by my will I intend to satisfy debts that I have not yet incurred, and though for very many purposes a will is considered to speak at the moment of

[1] (1755) *Mathews* v. *Mathews*, 2 Ves. Sen. at p. 636.
[2] For a recent instance see *Fitzgerald* v. *National Bank Ltd* [1929] 1 K.B. 394.

the testator's death, is treated as being the words that he uttered just as he was leaving the world, still this is one of the purposes for which we must look to the date of the will, and there can be no presumption that he intended a legacy to be a satisfaction of a debt that did not exist at the time when he executed the will.

For my own part I think that it would be well if our Courts had stopped here. Unfortunately, however—at least I think it unfortunate—they have evolved a different doctrine about one class of debts, namely, portion debts, a class that is not very easily defined. I use the term 'portion debts' but in your books you will find that the doctrine of which I am about to speak is spoken of as the doctrine concerning the satisfaction of portions by legacies. There is no great harm in this phrase, only you must not allow it to mislead you. We are to deal with a case in which a father has incurred a debt of a particular kind and then gives a legacy. You must, of course, distinguish this from a case in which a father has made a completed gift *inter vivos* and then gives a legacy. The doctrine of satisfaction presupposes that there is some obligation to be satisfied; but a completed gift is a completed gift, and can not require satisfaction. Thus if I establish my son in trade, buy a business for him for £5000 and pay the money, or if when my daughter marries I transfer £5000 worth of shares to the trustees of her settlement, here is a completed gift; if afterwards I bequeath £5000 or any other sum to my son or daughter, there can in this case be no talk of satisfaction, for there is nothing to be satisfied. Otherwise is it if when my son starts in business I enter into a bond conditioned for the payment of £5000, or if when my daughter marries I covenant with the trustees of her settlement that I will pay a sum of money or transfer a sum of stock to them. Here I become a debtor, I am under an obligation, an obligation that ought in some way or another to be satisfied, and the question may arise whether a provision that I make by my will is meant to be a satisfaction of this obligation. Therefore it is that I prefer to speak not of the satisfaction of portions by legacies, but of the satisfaction of portion debts by legacies.

Mark what our case is: the existence of a debt of a particular kind, a portion debt, followed by a provision made in the debtor's will—this raises the question of satisfaction. Afterwards I shall treat of the converse case where the execution of the will is followed by an action constituting a portion—this raises the question of 'ademption', is the legacy adeemed by the portion?

Well, in our case of satisfaction a portion debt exists and then a will is made. What do we mean by a portion debt? Seemingly this, a debt incurred by a father or mother[1] by way of making provision for a child of his or hers, or a debt incurred by some person who stands *in loco parentis* to another in favour of that other. The doctrine of satisfaction of portion debts does not apply in other cases. In other cases you would have to turn to those rules about the satisfaction of ordinary debts which have already come before us, rules which make the satisfaction of a debt by a legacy a pretty rare occurrence. But a debt incurred by a father by way of provision for his child stands on a quite different footing. Here there is a strong presumption that if afterwards the father gives by his will some benefit to or in favour of that child, he is intending to satisfy the debt thus incurred, either totally or partially. This special doctrine does not apply to a debt incurred by a husband by way of provision for a wife, or by a brother by way of provision for a sister. It holds only where there is the parental relation or what is called a quasi parental relation. In all cases other than that of parent and child you have in the very first place to consider whether the testator had placed himself *in loco parentis* to the beneficiary. For this purpose a putative father is not necessarily *in loco parentis* to his illegitimate child. Lord Eldon once remarked that this rule was hard on legitimate children, the Court presuming that a man does not intend to make two provisions for a legitimate child while it has no such rule against the bastard. What is meant by placing oneself *in loco parentis*? The only answer that we can get in general terms is that I place myself *in loco parentis* to a child if I come under a moral obligation to make a provision for that child. Nothing that could in a

[1] But query whether a mother is not for this purpose in the same position as a stranger, so that the doctrine only applies to her if she has made herself morally bound to provide for the child. See *In re Ashton* [1897] 2 Ch. 574 (reversed on appeal on another point [1898] 1 Ch. 142) and *In re Eardley's Will* [1920] 1 Ch. 397, 408.

popular sense be called adoption of the child is necessary—I say
in a popular sense, for adoption has no legal meaning in England.[1] The child to whom I place myself *in loco parentis* need
be no orphan, he or she may be living with his or her parents,
and may be maintained by them. It is not necessary that I
should assume or attempt to assume all those moral duties
which a father owes to his child. In short it seems enough that
I should do or say such things as would give rise to the belief
that I held myself morally (of course not legally), but morally
bound to make some pecuniary provision for that child such as
fathers make for their children. Of course it is easier to establish
such a relationship where there is some bond of consanguinity
or affinity between the two persons. It might easily be shown
that a wealthy grandfather had placed himself *in loco parentis* to
the children of a dead son. Still no such bond is essential, I may
have placed myself *in loco parentis* to the child of one who was
a perfect stranger to me. I think that if you will look at the cases
you will agree with me that the Court of Chancery entered on a
very difficult task when it adopted this phrase '*in loco parentis*'.

Then the parental relation being established, there is a strong
presumption that a benefit given by the will is meant to be a
satisfaction of what I have called the portion debt. The Court,
it is said, leans strongly against double portions. We are dealing,
you will remember, with cases in which the testator has incurred
a debt before he has made his will. The creditor of course has
the ordinary right of a creditor; nothing that the testator can
do by his will can deprive him of this right. The only question
will be whether besides insisting on this right the child can also
claim the benefit given by the will. If the benefit given by the
will be equal to or greater than the amount of the portion debt,
then, as in the ordinary case where it is not a portion debt, there
is a presumption of satisfaction; if the benefit given by the will
be less than the portion debt, then there is here—what there is
not in the case of an ordinary debt—a presumption of satisfaction
pro tanto; which means in effect, that the child can not claim the
legacy. But further it is well settled that small differences
between the provision promised by the testator in his lifetime

---

[1] But see now Adoption of Children Act 1926.

and that made by him in his will are not sufficient to exclude the presumption. It is indeed necessary that the two provisions should be of somewhat the same character: a covenant to pay £1000 would not be satisfied by a devise of Blackacre, even though Blackacre was worth more than £1000;[1] a covenant to pay £1000 in any event would not be satisfied in whole or in part by a legacy of £1000 contingent on the happening of a particular event; a covenant to pay £1000 would not be satisfied by a testamentary gift of an aliquot share of the testator's personalty if the testator had by his will directed that his debts should be paid.[2] But I can best show you how far the doctrine has been carried by reference to a modern case which is instructive because great judges disagreed about it. The case is *In re Tussaud*, 9 Ch. D. 363. The facts were these: In 1867 T, on the marriage of his daughter, covenanted with the trustees of the marriage settlement that his executors or administrators would within twelve months after his death transfer £2000 Consols to be held upon the trusts of the settlement, which were for such persons as the wife with the consent of the trustees or trustee for the time being should appoint, and in default of appointment in trust for the wife for life for her separate use, then for the husband for life, then for such children of the marriage as being sons should attain 21 years, or being daughters should attain that age or marry, and in default of children for the husband absolutely. In 1871 T satisfied one half of the covenant by paying over a sum to the trustees, so that thenceforth he was only bound to transfer to them a sum of £1000 Consols. In 1873 he made his will, and thereby bequeathed £2800 to certain trustees in trust for his daughter for life for her separate use without power of anticipation, and after her death for such of her childen as should attain 21 in equal shares.

This case came before Sir George Jessel M.R. There were, you will see, very considerable differences between the two settlements. Under the marriage settlement £1000 Consols was due. By the will £2800 was given. Under the marriage settlement the wife had a power of appointing the whole fund with the

---

[1] Cf. *In re Jaques* [1903] 1 Ch. 267.
[2] *Chichester* v. *Coventry*, L.R. 2 H.L. 71.

consent of the trustees to any person whom she chose. Under the will she had no such power. Under the marriage settlement the husband had a life interest, under the will he had none. Under the marriage settlement the wife was not restrained from anticipating her income, under the will she was restrained. The Master of the Rolls admitted that there were differences, he even called them important differences. Further he said 'I strongly suspect that what I am about to say will not carry out the intention of the testator'—but he felt himself bound by the decided cases to hold that those differences were not substantial enough to remove the presumption of satisfaction. His decision was that the wife and children must elect between the £1000 due on the covenant contained in the marriage settlement and the £2800 settled upon them by the will, the latter having been meant (according to this interpretation which equity put upon the transaction) to be a satisfaction of the former. The husband of course was put to no election; nothing was given to him by the will; he had simply to rely on the settlement.

However, the Court of Appeal came to a different opinion. It said that the differences between the two provisions were not slight, but substantial. No new principle was laid down; in every case a judge has to decide whether or no in his opinion the differences are sufficiently substantial to exclude the presumption. I have mentioned this case because we may well say that when the Court of Appeal overruled Jessel M.R. the case was very near the border line.

In this case it was allowed in both Courts that differences sufficient to exclude the presumption of satisfaction might well be insufficient to exclude the converse presumption of ademption. Let us turn to the doctrine of the ademption of legacies by portions.

First let us notice that the term ademption often occurs in another context. We often hear of the ademption of specific legacies by the alienation or the destruction of the subject-matter of the legacy. I give you in my will my black horse Dobbin or my copy of Coke upon Littleton, I sell the horse or the book, the horse dies or I lose the book. In such a case the legacy is adeemed; you can not call upon my executors to pay you the value of the horse or of the book—you will get nothing at all.[1] Well it is in a somewhat similar sense that we talk of a legacy being adeemed by a portion. By my will I give my son Thomas a legacy of £1000, then on his marriage I pay or I covenant to pay a certain sum to him or to the trustees of his marriage settlement, or I buy him a business, or without buying him a business I make him a present of money. Here the question of ademption is raised, just as it is raised if I bequeath you a particular horse and then sell that horse to another. It is the question whether that legacy to my son is or is not to take effect, is or is not to be struck out of my will.

Now in this case the so-called leaning against double portions has been allowed a great scope. Notice first that it only takes effect where the person making the two provisions is the parent of or stands *in loco parentis* to the beneficiary. In the second place it is not every gift, every provision made by a parent for the benefit of his child, that is a portion. I think that a portion implies something that having regard to the circumstances of the parties may be called a substantial provision. If I had left my son a £10,000 legacy, he would not be called to account for every five pound note that I gave him on his birthday. On the other hand the term portion does not imply that there is a solemn marriage settlement, or the purchase of a business or an estate—any considerable gift of money might be regarded as a portion (see *Leighton* v. *Leighton*, L.R. 18 Eq. 458). Then again you will observe that in this case we have not to distinguish between completed gifts and obligations. By my will I bequeath £1000 to my daughter. On her marriage I actually pay over £10,000 to the trustees of her marriage settlement, or I covenant that I will pay them £10,000. In either case the presumption of ademption will arise. This marks off ademption from satisfaction, two things which are somewhat easily confused. Satisfaction, as I have already said, presupposes an obligation—there

---

[1] For an instance of the application of this doctrine even to an appointment under a special power, see *In re Dowsett* [1901] 1 Ch. 398. There a testator, having a special power of appointment, by his will appointed Blackacre to an object of the power. Later Blackacre was bought by a company under statutory powers of compulsory purchase. The appointment by the testator was held to fail. And see *In re Slater* [1907] 1 Ch. 665.

must be something to be satisfied, and a completed gift leaves
nothing to be satisfied. But a legacy may be adeemed either by
a completed gift or by the acceptance of an obligation—by a
settlement or by a covenant to settle. You should notice this
distinction, for many of the rules which apply to satisfaction
apply also to ademption. We must, however, say that the presumption in favour of ademption is somewhat stronger even
than the presumption in favour of satisfaction. A legacy can be
adeemed by a gift or a covenant to give an equal or a greater
sum, it can be adeemed *pro tanto* by a less sum. Indeed some
time ago the rule was held to be that a legacy might be totally
adeemed by a less sum. Observe this, for it brings out once
more a difference between satisfaction and ademption. Of
course I can not wholly satisfy a debt of £100 by a legacy of £50.
But by my will I have bequeathed to my son £1000; I then give
him £500. Here it is, or rather was, quite possible to contend
that by giving £500 I had shown an intention that that should
be my son's portion, and that he should take it in lieu of the
provision made for him by my will. That contention, after
having been considered sound, was overruled by the case of
Pym v. *Lockyer*, 5 My. and Cr. 29, which decides that a smaller
portion will be deemed an ademption of a larger legacy *pro tanto*,
but *pro tanto* only. You understand me? In the case just put I
bequeath £1000 to my son and then give him £500 by way of
portion, he will on my death be able to demand another £500.
I have adeemed half of the legacy but not the whole.

The two provisions even in the case of ademption must have
somewhat of the same character. A bequest of £10,000 was not
adeemed by a subsequent settlement of a beneficial lease. But
very considerable differences—at least I should have called
them very considerable—between the two provisions will not
exclude the presumption. You will remember the case of *In re
Tussaud*. The Court of Appeal seems to have thought that had
that case been one not of satisfaction but of ademption, the
result would have been different. A legacy to a daughter may well
be adeemed by a settlement which gives her only a life interest
with a subsequent life interest for her husband, and settles the
corpus on the children of the marriage. 'In a case of ademption'

said Cotton L.J. (9 Ch. D. at p. 380) 'where the will is first, that is a revocable instrument, and the testator has an absolute power of revoking or altering any gift thereby made. But where the obligation is earlier in date than the will, the testator when he makes his will, is under a liability which he cannot revoke or avoid. He can only put an end to it by payment, or by making a gift with the condition, expressed or implied, that the legatees shall take the gift made by the will in satisfaction of their claim under the previous obligation. It is therefore easier to assume an intention to adeem than an intention to give a legacy in lieu or in satisfaction of an existing obligation.'[1]

In re Furness [1901] 2 Ch. 346, a testator by his will made in 1885 gives £20,000 to his daughter directing that £15,000 shall be settled on certain trusts for her and her children. On her marriage in 1893 he settles £7300 Consols upon her and her children, but the trusts are not the same. It is indisputable that as regards her interest there is ademption *pro tanto*, the question is whether it is to be treated as in ademption of the settled £15,000 or of the unsettled £5000. Joyce J. holds that it is in partial ademption of the former. The case shows the strength of this presumption.

In re Smythies [1903] 1 Ch. 259 is a good case to illustrate the doctrines of ademption. It was the case of a legacy of £500 upon trust for a great niece of the testator and a subsequent voluntary settlement of exactly the same sum. It was decided that there was no ademption because there was no parental relationship.

Lastly note that these presumptions of satisfaction or ademption are but presumptions, and can be rebutted by parol evidence of the settlor's or testator's intention. Seeing two provisions made by a father for one of his children, Equity, in accordance with the rules that we have tried to state, presumes that he did not mean to give that child two portions; but then you may

---

[1] A bequest of a share of residue, if made to a child, will be presumed to be adeemed *pro tanto* by a subsequent portion given, with the result that the sum given by way of portion must be brought into hotchpot. Note that the rule that a legacy is adeemed by a subsequent portion is only applied so as to produce equality between children and 'quasi-children'. It will not be applied so as to benefit a stranger at the expense of a child; *In re Heather* [1906] 2 Ch. 230, *In re Dawson* [1919] 1 Ch. 102.

produce evidence to show that, on the contrary, he did mean to give two portions. This point also is illustrated by the case of *In re Tussaud*.[1] An affidavit was there tendered to prove that the testator had used expressions indicating that he did not intend that the legacy in his will should be a satisfaction of the obligation to which he was subjected by his daughter's marriage settlement, and that affidavit was received in evidence. Then of course if evidence be thus let in to rebut the presumption, evidence will be received to support the presumption, to show that a decision in conformity with the presumption will really carry out the intention of the testator. On the other hand you can not produce external evidence, evidence outside the documents, in the first instance in order to raise the presumption. If for example a man covenanted to settle £1000 upon his daughter, and then by his will devised Blackacre to her, here the presumption of satisfaction would not arise, and you could not produce external evidence to show that the testator had intended his daughter to take Blackacre in lieu of the £1000.

[1] 9 Ch. D. 363.

LECTURE XVI

ADMINISTRATION OF ASSETS[1] (I)

AMONG the departments over which equity is said to have exercised an exclusive jurisdiction it was usual to mention the administration of the estates of dead persons, and by the Judicature Act of 1873, s. 34, the administration of the estates of deceased persons is one of the matters which is assigned to the Chancery Division of the High Court of Justice. But it will strike you at once that the exclusive jurisdiction of equity in this matter must have been of a somewhat different kind to its exclusive jurisdiction in matters of trust. For of the trust a Court of Common Law would take no notice at all; on the other hand the Court of Chancery in administering the estate of a dead man was, at least to a very large extent, giving effect to rights which were perfectly well known to other Courts. The creditor's right to sue the executor or administrator of his dead debtor was a right known to and protected by the Courts of Common Law; it would be enforced by an action of debt or of assumpsit and judgment would be given that the defendant should pay the sum due to the plaintiff out of the assets of the testator or intestate.[2] In some cases too, as you know, the creditor would be able to sue the heir, and under the Statutes 3 and 4 W. and M. c. 14 he might sue the devisee of his debtor. As to the legatee he, it is true, had no action in a Court of Common Law. From of old the enforcement of the last will of the dead man had been a matter for the ecclesiastical court; still

[1] The law on the administration of assets has been completely altered by the Administration of Estates Act 1925. The present lecture represents only the law before 1926. The law since 1926 is summarized in the note on p. 270 below.

[2] Notice the decisions that such a judgment *de bonis testatoris* operates as a conclusive admission of assets, with the result that unless at the time of that action he has pleaded either *plene administravit* or *plene administravit praeter* the executor will have to pay the debt as well as the costs even out of his own assets. See *e.g. In re Marvin* [1905] 2 Ch. 490, and Williams on Executors, 12th edition, p. 1240. Even if he fails to prove either plea he, by the plea, limits his liability to the assets. Here is a solemn jugglery.

in the ecclesiastical court the legatee would find a tribunal which would compel the executor to pay the legacy. It may seem then that there was little reason why the Court of Chancery should interfere in this matter.

But interfere it did. Already in Elizabeth's day a legatee instead of going to the ecclesiastical court will sometimes file a bill in Chancery; by this time the ecclesiastical courts have grown too feeble to protect themselves. It may be that the cases in which the Chancery first interfered were cases in which the legatee was not a mere legatee but was also a *cestui que trust*. But at any rate the Court of Chancery soon became the regular court for actions by legatees. Then again the creditor had often an occasion to go thither. He had no specialty, or no specialty that bound the testator's heir, and the testator's personal estate was inadequate for the payment of his debts; on the other hand the testator, being an honest man, had devised his real estate to X and Y upon trust to pay his debts. Here the creditor wanted the aid of a Court of Equity because he wanted to enforce a trust. Thus in one way and another the Court obtained a footing in this field and gradually it subdued the whole province of administration. It had a machinery for taking accounts; it could call upon all the creditors of the deceased to come in and prove their debts and then by its injunctions it could prevent the creditors from suing in any other Court. At the instance of a creditor, or of a legatee, or of the personal representative of the dead man it would decree that the estate should be administered by the Court; it took upon itself the duty imposed upon the personal representative, and called upon all creditors to come in and distributed the estate in accordance with the rules of law and equity. Of law, I say, and equity—for some of the rules that it had to apply were old legal rules, while others were new rules of its own invention to which it came gradually in the course of its business as an administrator of estates.

Now of these rules I intend to speak briefly; and first we must consider the various kinds of debts. Of course the main distinction that meets us directly we think of the debts of a dead man is this, that some of them may be secured debts while others of them may be unsecured. By a secured debt we mean this, that the creditor, besides having a personal right against the debtor, has some mortgage or charge upon a specific portion of the debtor's property. For instance he has a mortgage on Blackacre, a bill of sale of certain chattels, a charge upon a certain trust fund. Then of course he has some means of availing himself of this security. Thus in the case of a mortgage of Blackacre he probably has several different remedies open to him; he can enter on Blackacre and take the rents and profits, he can sell Blackacre, he can foreclose the mortgage—to use a common phrase, he can realize his security.

Now the chief thing that we have to notice in this region is an old rule of equity about the rights of a creditor who has a security, but an insufficient security for his debt. A dies owing X £2000 and this debt is secured by a mortgage of Blackacre. X realizes his security; he sells Blackacre, but the sale produces only £1000. Well of course X is still entitled to be paid another £1000 and if A's estate is sufficient for the payment of all his debts then X will get that other £1000. But suppose that A's estate is insolvent, X will certainly be entitled to something besides the £1000 that he got out of Blackacre. It would I think be natural to say that X's right is to prove against the testator's estate a debt of £1000, and take a dividend, whatever it may be, say five shillings in the pound, proportional to that debt of £1000, for £1000 is what is due to him after Blackacre has been sold. Now that was the rule to which the Court of Bankruptcy came in the administration of the insolvent estates of living persons. Its rule was this, the creditor with an insufficient security may do one of two things; he may abandon his security (abandon Blackacre) and prove for his whole debt (prove for £2000), or he may realize his security and prove for what still remains due to him after such realization—thus in the case I have put he may pocket £1000, the price of Blackacre, and then claim a dividend on the other £1000 which still remains due to him. But the Court of Chancery in its administration of the estates of dead persons came to another rule, usually known as the rule in *Mason* v. *Bogg*.[1] The mortgagee may realize his security and may also prove against the general estate for the

[1] (1837) 2 My. and Cr. 443.

whole of his debt, provided always that he is not to get more than twenty shillings in the pound. Thus in our case X might keep the £1000 that he gets from the sale of Blackacre, and then he may also prove against the general estate of the dead man for the whole £2000; but of course he is not to get in all more than the whole debt, the whole £2000 that is due to him. This rule may seem to you unjust, and it has seemed unjust to Parliament; it seems to favour the secured creditor unduly at the expense of unsecured creditors. However you can see that there was a certain logic in it. The mortgagee has two distinct rights, the right *in personam*, the personal right against the debtor, and the real right, the right in Blackacre. Why should he not use both of these? Why should the fact that he has used one of them, hamper him when he desires to make good the other. He sells Blackacre, well and good; but the dead man owed him £2000, why should he not prove against the dead man's estate for the whole of this debt? However it is needless now to consider whether or no there was much justice in this reasoning, for a section of the Judicature Act of 1875—section 10—declared in effect that in the administration of the estates of dead persons the bankruptcy rule was to prevail as between the secured and the unsecured creditors. To this section I shall have to return hereafter; meanwhile (for this will save us trouble and I have a complicated story to tell) I will ask you to remember the rule in *Mason v. Bogg.*

We can now leave the treatment of securities out of account, and looking at debts merely as debts we have to notice that the debts of a dead man are not all of equal rank. In the administration of his estate out of Court and by his personal representatives the debts may, I believe, be ranked according to the following order.[1]

1. Debts due to the Crown by record or specialty.

2. Debts to which a priority has been given by certain particular statutes, *e.g.* debts due to a friendly society by its officers, and regimental debts.

[1] In strictness this order applied only in the administration of legal assets. Until an order was made for administration in the Chancery Division or in Bankruptcy under section 125 of the Bankruptcy Act of 1883 the executor was obliged to follow these rules. See per Lindley L.J. in *In re Hargreaves*, 44 Ch. D. 236, at p. 242.

3. Debts due upon judgments obtained in courts of record against the dead person. These are to be paid rateably *inter se.*

4. Recognizances, and (could these ever occur now-a-days) statutes staple and statutes merchant—that is to say debts acknowledged with certain formalities prescribed by ancient statutes which have long become obsolete.

5. Debts due upon judgments recovered against the executor or administrator, whether registered or not, and whether recovered in respect of specialty or of simple contract. These are payable according to priority of date.[1]

6. Debts due upon specialty or simple contract.

You will remember that until the year 1870 specialty debts had a preference over simple contract debts. Hinde Palmer's Act (32 & 33 Vic. c. 46) threw them together. What is the exact position of a simple contract debt due to the Crown is somewhat doubtful. The old order used to be, specialty debts, debts due to the Crown upon simple contract, other simple contract debts. The Act of 1869 says nothing about the Crown—is the result of it that simple contract debts due to the Crown now rank in the very high place assigned to specialty debts due to the Crown? This seems doubtful, and is not very important. However in 1897 it was decided that a simple contract debt due to the Crown has preference over ordinary simple contract debts but not over specialties.[2]

7. Voluntary covenants and bonds. These are usually placed last. But at law they were of equal validity and ranked with other specialties. But Equity in its administration postponed them to all obligations incurred for valuable consideration.[3]

Now we ought to observe the character of these rules. At least in the main, they are legal, they are common law rules, though modified by statute. They mean this, that an executor or administrator ought to pay the testator's debts in a certain order, and that if he pays them out of this order he is answerable, personally answerable, for any loss that he may thereby inflict

---

[1] *In re Williams's Estates*, L.R. 15 Eq. 270.

[2] *Bentinck v. Bentinck* [1897] 1 Ch. 673. But see *In re Samson* [1906] 2 Ch. 584, at p. 592.

[3] *Payne v. Mortimer*, 4 De G. and J. 447, and *In re Whitaker*, 42 Ch. D. 119, at p. 124.

upon any creditor. Suppose, for example, that an executor pays
away the whole of the testator's assets in satisfying simple
contract debts, and then a creditor with a bond makes his
appearance; under the law as it stood before 1869 the executor
was himself liable to pay that bond debt; and even now the case
is the same if the creditor who thus makes his appearance
instead of having a bond debt has a judgment debt. In paying a
debt of a lower order while a debt of a higher order is outstanding an executor commits the legal wrong known as a
devastavit, he has been guilty of wasting the estate of his
testator. Now-a-days under a statute of 1859 (22 & 23 Vic. c. 35,
s. 29)[1] an executor or administrator has power to protect himself
by issuing advertisements calling upon the creditors of the dead
person to send in their claims; but still you should understand
that an executor or administrator does wrong in paying a debt
of a lower order while a debt of a higher order is yet outstanding,
and should he do this without issuing the proper advertisements,
and should the estate of the dead man prove insufficient for the
satisfaction of all his debts, then the executor will have made
himself liable, liable in a common law action, to the privileged
debtor whose privilege he has ignored. Here of course we may
find one strong reason which drove executors and administrators to seek the protection of the Court of Chancery and as
the phrase went to 'throw the estate into Chancery' and thereby
shuffle off their risky duties.

Then within each of these classes of debts that I have mentioned there was in general no priority whatever—thus among
the specialty creditors of the dead man the executor might single
out one of them and pay him in full, though this payment would
exhaust the assets and thereby deprive the other specialty
creditors of their remedy. And at the present day the executor
or administrator may still do this, he may prefer one creditor to
another, he may do so at any time before the Court has given
judgment for the administration of the estate, even though an
action for administration has been commenced.[2] Here was

---

[1] Now replaced (with alterations) by the Trustee Act 1925, s. 27, as
amended by the Law of Property (Amendment) Act 1926, Schedule.

[2] For a statement of the reasons for this rule see *In re Samson* [1906] 2 Ch.
584, at p. 594.

another strong motive for administration suits in the Court of Chancery. A creditor who feared that the executor was going to prefer some other creditor to him would make haste to obtain a decree that the estate should be administered by the Court.

A corollary of this doctrine that an executor or administrator may prefer one debt to another of equal degree is his right to retain for his own debt. If he may prefer a creditor and he himself is a creditor, he will very naturally prefer himself. He might prefer his own debt to any debt of equal degree, but he could not prefer it to a debt of a higher degree. Of this right of retainer or self-preference he was not deprived even by a decree declaring that the estate was to be administered by the Court. At any time before the distribution of the estate he might claim payment of his debt in preference to debts of equal degree.

Now the rules which instituted what we may call a hierarchy of debts, rules developed in Courts of Law, were from time to time taken over by the Court of Chancery when it had begun to concern itself with the administration of estates. It would do what a personal representative ought to do, it would respect the legal order of debts. Within each class it would pay creditors rateably—that is to say, if there was not enough for the whole class it would pay each member of it a dividend proportional to his debt; but the hierarchy of debts it would respect. However in course of time the Court found that it sometimes had property to distribute among the creditors to the distribution of which these legal rules had never been applied. Thus a testator devised all his real estate upon trust for the payment of debts— here was property available for distribution and yet it was property which either was not vested in the personal representative of the dead man, or if it was vested in his executor was vested in him not *qua* executor but *qua* devisee. Here equity could neglect the old rules—it could say, and did say, that an equal or rather a proportional distribution among all the creditors was the fairest mode of distribution. It had come by certain property which could be called equitable assets as opposed to legal assets; it could say that these equitable assets should be distributed without regard to the legal rank of debts, it could even forbid the executor to give himself an advantage by retaining his own debt out of these equitable assets.

What are equitable assets? The accepted definition seems to be: Equitable assets are property which is applicable for the payment of the dead person's debts but which is not vested in his personal representative, his executor or administrator, *virtute officii*. It is necessary to be somewhat careful about this matter, for one plausible definition might lead us astray. We can not say that equitable assets include all assets that can not be made available without the aid of a court of equity. Put this case, T holds a term of years upon trust for A; A dies having appointed M his executor; that term of years, that interest in the land is legal assets, though it is but an equitable interest in the land. It becomes vested in M, because he is executor of A, that is enough to decide that it is legal assets. On the other hand if A be legal tenant in fee simple and devises his realty to M, upon trust to pay debts, and appoints M his executor; then although M's estate in the land is a legal estate it is equitable assets, for M does not take this freehold estate *virtute officii*, he does not take it as executor, he takes it because it has been devised to him.[1]

At the present day we seem to have two or perhaps three kinds of equitable assets, all other assets being legal. In the first place there is the oldest kind of equitable asset—it consists of freehold and copyhold estates which the testator has by his will either devised for the payment of his debts or charged with the payment of his debts. And here I may remark that in old days the Court was extremely anxious to find in a will a charge of debts upon the real estate and that to this day a charge of debts upon the real estate will be very easily found. For example, if a testator says 'In the first place I direct that all my debts be paid and then I give my real estate to A and my personal estate to B', this is quite enough to charge the real estate with the payment of debts. The reason for this anxiety will be apparent to you if you will remember that until the year 1833 freehold and copy-

---

[1] See the judgment of Kindersley V.C. in *Cook* v. *Gregson*, 3 Drew. 547. For a recent discussion of the distinction between legal and equitable assets see *O'Grady* v. *Wilmot* [1916] 2 A.C. 231.

hold estates were not assets for the payment of simple contract debts or even of specialty debts unless the heir was mentioned in the specialty—therefore unless a charge of debts could be found in his will a testator might die leaving large estates and yet his creditors would go unpaid. The rule of construction which easily finds a charge of debts was begotten by these circumstances, but it still holds good though since 1833 the dead man's freeholds and copyholds have been assets for the payment of all debts. Well, if there be a charge of debts on the realty, then the realty is equitable assets. Secondly we come to the Act of 1833 (3 & 4 Will. IV, c. 104) which made realty assets for the payment of all debts, made, as I understand it, all realty which was not devised for the payment of debts or subjected to a charge for the payment of debts, equitable assets, but subject to this rule that out of such realty a creditor with a specialty binding on heirs, was to be preferred to creditors with specialties not binding on heirs and simple contract creditors. Then the Act of 1869 abolished this preference—and so, as I understand it, the result is reached that freeholds and copyholds are equitable assets whether or no they be charged by the testator with the payment of his debts (see *Walters* v. *Walters*, 18 Ch. D. 182). Then under the old law, I mean the law as it stood before the Married Women's Property Act of 1882, the separate estate which a married woman left behind her was equitable assets for the payment of her debts—the separate estate, and the debt payable out of separate estate, were purely equitable institutions. I am not aware that under the Statute which enables a married woman to have separate property at law as well as in equity there has been any decision as to the character of the assets that she leaves behind her; but that ill-drawn Act is full of traps.[1]

It will strike you that if the dead person's estate consists partially of legal and partially of equitable assets, there must be considerable difficulty in adjusting the claims of the two systems. Out of the legal assets the debts are to be paid in order of their rank, out of the equitable assets they are to be paid rateably

---

[1] In the MS. of the lecture there is a marginal note at this place as follows: 'Query as to the effect of the Land Transfer Act of 1897? Apparently its effect is to increase the legal assets.' The question was raised but not decided in the case of *In re Williams* [1904] 1 Ch. 52.

without regard to their rank. The adjustment has been effected by one branch of the doctrine—other branches of it will come before us hereafter—which is known as marshalling. The rule may be stated thus: a creditor who has obtained part payment of his debt out of the legal assets is not to be paid anything out of the equitable assets unless he will bring what he has received back into hotchpot. Thus to put a case, a testator leaves £1000 of legal assets and £2000 of equitable assets; he owes a judgment debt of £1200 and simple contract debts to the amount of £3000. The judgment creditor has a right to carry off in this case all the legal assets; these will satisfy £1000 out of the £1200 that is owing to him; £200 will remain due, but he can have no more unless he will throw the £1000 into hotchpot with the £2000 and permit the whole £3000 to be divided rateably among all the creditors. Were he to do this, instead of getting £1000 he would get something less than £860, so of course he will not do it. I might easily however have chosen figures which would make it worth his while to abandon his preferential claim on a small sum of legal assets in order that he might share rateably with the other creditors in a division of a large sum made up of legal and equitable assets.

Since the Act of 1869, Hinde Palmer's Act, the rank of debts, the distinction between legal and equitable assets, and this doctrine of marshalling have been far less important than they used to be—for specialties and simple contracts have been placed on the same level; but still judgment debts have a priority and therefore the principles with which we have been dealing are existing law. As we shall see next time the Judicature Acts by their so-called fusion of law and equity did not abolish the distinction between legal and equitable assets.

ADMINISTRATION OF ASSETS[1] (II)

IN my last lecture I was speaking of the mode in which legal and equitable assets respectively are applied for the payment of debts. I ended with the remark that the section of the Judicature Act which provides for the prevalence of the rules of equity over the rules of the common law made no change in this matter. There was no conflict, no variance between the two sets of rules. Each held good within its own sphere. And so it is now. Within the common law sphere, *i.e.* in the distribution of legal assets, the rules of the common law still prevail, while the rules of equity are applicable only within the equitable sphere, that is to say, in the distribution of equitable assets.

But the Judicature Acts contained another provision that touched our theme. The Act of 1873 had in it a certain clause, section 25, sub-section 1, which dealt with the administration of assets; but this never came into force, for it was repealed and replaced by section 10 of the Act of 1875, which said that in the administration by the Court of the assets of any person who should die after the commencement of this Act and whose estate might prove to be insufficient for the payment in full of any of his debts or liabilities, the same rules should prevail and be observed as to the respective rights of secured and unsecured creditors and as to debts and liabilities provable and as to the valuation of securities and future and contingent liabilities respectively as might be in force for the time being under the law of bankruptcy.

Now this section caused a great deal of difficulty and gave rise to many decisions. I must try to explain the general nature of the difficulty. You will remember that as regards the rights of a secured creditor the Court of Chancery in its administration of the estates of dead persons had come to one rule, while the Court of Bankruptcy in its administration of bankrupts' estates had

---

[1] This lecture gives the law before 1926. The present law under the Administration of Estates Act 1925 is summarized in the note on p. 270 below.

come to another rule. The Chancery rule—it is convenient to speak of it as the rule in *Mason* v. *Bogg*—was that the secured creditor with an insufficient security might realize that security and also prove against the general estate for the whole of the debt, but of course he was not to get more than was due to him, more than 20*s.* in the pound. The Bankruptcy rule was less favourable to him, therefore more favourable to the unsecured creditors. He was put to his choice, either he might abandon his security and prove for the whole debt, or he might realize his security and prove for such part of his debt as remained unpaid after the security had been realized. Now there was no doubt at all that section 10 of the Act of 1875 had in this respect introduced the bankruptcy rule into the administration of the estates of dead persons, and, now-a-days, when the Court is administering the estate of a dead person this bankruptcy rule as to the relative position of secured and unsecured creditors prevails. But the question was whether that section had not done far more than this, whether it had not swept away the old rules of administration in mass and replaced them by the rules observed in bankruptcy.

In order to explain this I must remind you that from the very first our bankruptcy law has been statute law, law to be found in successive Acts of Parliament, and, if I may so speak, it has gone its own way unaffected by those rules which courts of law and of equity applied to the payment of the debts of dead persons not made bankrupt in their lifetime. Thus the Bankruptcy Acts have ignored that legal hierarchy of debts of which I have been speaking; consequently they would ignore the distinction between legal and equitable assets. As a general rule all the bankrupt's debts were to be paid rateably, *pari passu.* On the other hand certain debts to which no preference would have been given in the administration of a dead man's estate have been expressly preferred. Section 40 of the Bankruptcy Act of 1883 set out three classes of preferential payments. This part of section 40 is repealed and is now represented by section 1 of the Preferential Payments in Bankruptcy Act 1888, which is in very similar terms. We find there a preference given for (*a*) certain taxes and parochial and local rates, (*b*) the wages or salary of a clerk or servant in respect of services rendered during the last four months and not exceeding £50, (c) the wages of any labourer or workman in respect of services rendered during the last four months not exceeding £25 (under the Act of 1883 this was £50). These preferential debts are to rank *pari passu* among themselves; and then it is said that all other debts proved in the bankruptcy shall be paid *pari passu*. Then again divers Acts of Parliament have provided that in case of bankruptcy divers past transactions may be wholly or partially avoided in favour of the creditors, and have thus increased the assets of the bankrupt divisible among his creditors. The Bills of Sales Acts have done this, and you will find that the Married Women's Property Act 1882, by section 3, did this also. If a married woman lends money to her husband for the purpose of any trade or business carried on by him, that money is to be treated as assets in the case of her husband's bankruptcy, and the wife's claim to repayment is to be postponed to the claims of all other creditors.

Now the question occurred in a great variety of forms whether the 10th section of the Judicature Act 1875 had merely swept away the rule in *Mason* v. *Bogg*, or whether it·had introduced into the administration of the estates of dead persons all these bankruptcy rules. On the words of the section the question was a very open one, and for a while there were contradictory decisions. Until comparatively lately the tendency of the Courts was to set a very narrow limit to the operation of the section. In the case of *In re May*, 45 Ch. D. 499, you will find North J. deciding that a widow, the administratrix of her late husband, whose estate was insolvent, might retain out of his assets a sum of money which she had lent him to be used in his business. Had he been made bankrupt in his lifetime the widow would have been postponed to all other creditors. As it was, she was allowed to prefer herself to all other creditors.

But in the case of *In re Heywood* [1897] 2 Ch. 593, it was decided that the bankruptcy preferences for rates and wages, set out in the Preferential Payments in Bankruptcy Act of 1888, were introduced by the operation of section 10 of the Judicature Act of 1875.

Then such cases as *In re Maggi*, 20 Ch. D. 545, and *Smith* v.

Morgan, 5 C.P.D. 337, to the effect that judgments still have priority, are disapproved and are apparently overruled by *In re Whitaker* [1901] 1 Ch. 9, where the Court of Appeal decided that the effect of section 10 of the Judicature Act 1875 is to introduce into the administration of the estates of deceased insolvents the bankruptcy rule that voluntary creditors are to be paid *pari passu* with creditors for value.

Thus the inclination to a narrow construction has given way to an inclination to a wide construction. All the recent judgments of the appellate courts point this way. The bankruptcy rules are introduced except those which go to augment the bankrupt's assets as against third persons. It is well settled that those rules apply only in actual bankruptcy. After *In re Whitaker*, *semble* judgment debts have lost their priority and *semble* also the bankruptcy preferences are admitted.

Query whether the prerogative of the Crown is not touched. You have to know the new law and the old law too.

But I have not yet finished the story. The Bankruptcy Act of 1883, by section 125,[1] introduced certain quite new provisions. A man cannot be made bankrupt after his death, but for the first time this Act authorized the administration by courts having bankruptcy jurisdiction of the estates of persons who have not been made bankrupt in their lifetime. If within three months before my death I commit an act of bankruptcy then after my death a creditor may take bankruptcy proceedings against my estate—he may obtain an order for the administration of my estate in bankruptcy, and if he does this then (with considerable modifications)[2] the bankruptcy rules come into play. Thus the executor's right to retain debts due to himself still

[1] Now Bankruptcy Act 1914, s. 130.

[2] That which is administered is the dead man's estate, that only which passes to his personal representatives, and subject to all liens, charges and rights of other persons. It has been held that an order under section 125 of the Bankruptcy Act 1883, which divested the interest of the personal representatives, did not increase the assets to be administered or affect the rights of third persons therein. Thus the rights of execution creditors were not affected, *Hasluck* v. *Clark* [1899] 1 Q.B. 699 (C.A.), nor did the executor who was a creditor lose his right of retainer, *In re Rhoades* [1899] 2 Q.B. 347. And see also *In re Mellison* [1906] 2 K.B. 68. The position under section 130 of the Bankruptcy Act 1914 would appear to be the same as that under the 1883 Act.

exists after an order made under section 125 of the Bankruptcy Act; and the existence of the executor's right of retainer still necessitates a knowledge of the hierarchy of debts and preserves the distinction between legal and equitable assets. For you will remember that the executor can not retain against a debt of higher rank than his own, nor is his right of retainer available against equitable assets. The result of this is I think very unfortunate and very capricious. The whole law as to the administration of the estates of dead persons sadly needs a thorough reform.

I turn to another part of our subject. We have considered the order in which debts should be paid. We have now to consider the order in which assets should be applied in the payment of debts. First let us note a great difference between these two sets of rules. Over the one a testator has no control; over the other he has complete control. Before the Act of 1869 it would have been no good for a testator to say 'I declare that my executors are to pay my simple contract debts in preference to my specialty debts', and now it would be of no avail for him to say that a simple contract debt was to be preferred to a debt of record due to the Crown. On the other hand it is perfectly competent for me to say, and to say with effect, in my will 'My real estate is to be the primary fund for the payment of my debts, if that be insufficient then let my plate be sold, and if that be insufficient my library', and so forth—for in saying all this I am not attempting to affect the rights of my creditors, I am merely deciding as between my various legatees and devisees, what they respectively are to have, and none of them have any rights save such rights as I choose to give them.

The following rules therefore as to the order in which the assets are to be consumed in the payment of debts are rules which hold good only in so far as the dead man has not by his will (if any) declared a contrary intention.

The executor or administrator must apply to the satisfaction of the debts of a dead man the property which may be available, but in the following order:

1. Personalty not specifically bequeathed, retaining a fund sufficient to meet any pecuniary legacies.

2. Realty specifically appropriated for, or devised in trust for (and not merely charged with) payment of debts.

3. Realty that descends to the heir.

4. Realty charged with the payment of debts.

5. Fund (if any) retained to pay general pecuniary legacies.

6. Realty devised whether specifically or by general description and personalty specifically bequeathed *pro rata* and *pari passu*.

7. Property which did not belong to the dead man, but which is appointed by his will in exercise of any general power of appointment.

Doubt was occasioned by the case of *In re Bate*, 43 Ch. D. 600, as to which ought to go first, realty charged with the payment of debts or a pecuniary legacy. Kay J. held that the pecuniary legacy must go first, but, *semble* wrongly, and in the later cases of *In re Salt* [1895] 2 Ch. 203, and *In re Roberts* [1902] 2 Ch. 834, it was decided that where a will contains a general direction for payment of debts the pecuniary legatees are entitled to have the assets marshalled as against specific devisees of the real estate.

Then note that a lapsed share of residue is not applicable before other shares. I give all my personalty to A, B and C in equal shares. (A, B and C are not descendants of mine—those of you who have read the Wills Act[1] will know why I make this remark.) A dies during my lifetime, so his share lapses to my next of kin. The three shares must contribute equally to the payment of my debts. You are not to throw the debts on to the lapsed share for the benefit of the other shares. (*Trethewy* v. *Helyar*, 4 Ch. D. 53.)

Next observe that specific and residuary devises and specific bequests all rank together. I devise Blackacre to A, the rest of my real estate to B, my black horse Dobbin to C and the rest of my personalty to D. First you exhaust my residuary personalty, *i.e.* all my personalty except the horse. Then the rest of my property contributes rateably, A, B and C contribute rateably. True that the devise to B is a residuary devise, and you might well think that whatever is comprised in this should be exhausted before we turn to Blackacre or to Dobbin—but that is not so.

---

[1] Wills Act 1837, s. 33.

A residuary devise is for this purpose put exactly on the same footing as a specific devise.

Lastly note than when a dead man's own property has been exhausted you may turn to certain property which in strictness was not his own. If he had a general power of appointment and exercised this power by his will then he thereby made the appointed property part of his assets for the payment of his debts, but a part that is only to be absorbed in the last resort, when all else has failed. This doctrine you must remark only applies where the power is a general power. If under my marriage settlement I have power to appoint a fund among my children, and I exercise that power, I do not make the appointed fund assets for the payment of my debts. But to make the fund assets I must actually exercise the power. If I have a general power of appointment and leave it unexercised, my creditors will not be able to touch the fund.

I think that you will hardly be able to understand the import of these rules unless you will attempt to work out a few imaginary cases. I will suggest one or two.

A man dies intestate leaving realty and personalty. In what order are the assets applicable for the payment of his debts?

A testator made his will in these words—'I give my freehold estate called Dale to A, my leasehold house in Brook Street to B, my gold snuff box to C, £1000 to D, the rest of my realty to E and the rest of my personalty to F'. [The order will be this: F loses all, then D loses all, then A, B, C and E contribute rateably.]

A testator, tenant in fee simple of Blackacre, Whiteacre, Greenacre, and entitled to a leasehold house in Brook Street and other personalty, makes his will as follows—'I give Blackacre to A. I declare that my debts shall be a charge on the rest of my real estate. I give Whiteacre to B, and my house in Brook Street to C. I give £1000 to D, all my books to E, and the residue of my personalty to my cousins F and G in equal shares.' G dies before the testator; the testator dies leaving H his heir at law and K his sole next of kin. Greenacre is undisposed of, there being no residuary devise. In what order are his assets to be applied for the payment of his debts? [The answer is this: Exhaust the personalty bequeathed not specifically, but as residue, to F and G (that is the whole personalty except the books and £1000 deducted for D's legacy), showing no preference to F the legatee over K who, as the testator's next of kin, takes the lapsed share. Next turn to Greenacre as real estate descended to the heir, next to Whiteacre as being realty charged with debts, next to the £1000 set apart to pay D's legacy. Lastly, when those are exhausted, the books, the house in Brook Street and Blackacre must contribute *pari passu*.]

But now let me repeat once more that a testator can upset this order if he pleases. He can direct that as between the various persons entitled under his will this or that part of his property shall be the first fund for meeting debts—he can make the last first, or the first last. For example he may say, and effect will be given to his saying, that all his real estate is to be absorbed before his personal estate is touched. But if he wishes that this shall be so, he must say it clearly—a mere charge of debts on real estate will, as we have seen, have some effect in altering the order in which the assets are to be consumed, but it will not put the real estate thus charged before the general or residuary personalty, and if only part of the realty is thus charged with the payment of debts this will not even put that part before other realty which is not disposed of by the will and descends to the heir as heir. There is a strong presumption that the general or residuary personalty is to be the very first fund for the payment of debts, and if a testator wants to put his realty before his personalty he ought to say, not merely 'I charge my debts upon my real estate', but 'I charge my debts on my real estate to the exoneration of my personalty'. For this purpose you want, it is said, not merely words onerating the realty, but words exonerating the personalty.

Then again it is quite possible that the order of assets in administration may be disturbed—assets may be applied out of their proper order in the payment of debts. I want you to perceive that the order of assets is nothing to creditors. Before the Land Transfer Act a specialty[1] creditor might, as the phrase

---

[1] Until that Act the specialty creditor had a direct remedy against the land; he could sue the heir or devisee directly; the simple contract creditor had to take administration proceedings in order to make the land liable for his debt.

went, upset the order of assets. Take this case as occurring before the Act of 1897. I had a debtor owing me a sum of money under a deed, he died and we will suppose that he died intestate. His real estate descended to A, his heir at law, his personal estate vested in an administrator B who, when debts are paid, must distribute it among the next of kin. Well, as between heir and next of kin the personalty was the first fund for the payment of my debt; but that was nothing to me. I could sue the administrator or the heir. I chose to sue the heir, and the heir was liable to pay me to the extent of the assets that had descended upon him. But then, as between the persons claiming under my debtor, comes in a principle of marshalling. It is put thus: 'Where the order in which assets are liable to pay debts is disturbed by creditors it will be put right by marshalling.' If in the case just put the heir paid me my debt he had a right to claim repayment out of the personal estate.

The Act of 1897 has lessened the chances of any disturbance in the established order of liability of assets through the action of a creditor. Real estate, you remember, now passes in the first instance to the executor or administrator and it would seem clear that until he (as and when required to do by the Act) assents or conveys, in the case of land devised, or conveys in the case of land descended, a creditor could bring no action against the devisee or heir. Still cases in which marshalling is required may occur. To take simple examples, the executor or administrator may perhaps fail at first to discover some part of the personalty and may thus apply real estate in paying debts before all the personalty which comes under a prior liability has been exhausted; or he may fail to discover that the deceased was entitled to some realty which will descend to his heir and, in ignorance of that realty, the executor or administrator may have sold articles specifically bequeathed, which should come after, not before, realty descended to the heir; or it may happen that after either assent or conveyance under the Act of 1897 the devisee or heir may find a creditor making a claim against him which should be discharged by the personal estate. The exact effect of the Land Transfer Act upon the legal liability of the heir or devisee must however be said to be very doubtful.

But there remains a point that we have hitherto avoided. In discussing the order of assets we have spoken as though all the debts were unsecured; but what of secured debts? Among the debts owed by the dead man there was one debt which was secured by a mortgage of Blackacre. Does the fact that this debt was thus secured make any difference when we are discussing the question what fund is the primary fund for its payment? The old answer to this question was (as a general rule) none at all. Here is a debt and it must be paid like other debts. If the dead man has not made a will and therein given some direction to the contrary the first fund for the payment of his debts, including this debt, consists of his general or residuary personalty. Put the simplest case. He owed £1000 upon mortgage of Blackacre, of which, subject to the mortgage, he was tenant in fee simple. He dies intestate. His real estate, including Blackacre, descends to his heir at law, while his personalty will be distributed among his next of kin. But first debts must be paid, including the mortgage debt on Blackacre, and all his personalty must be swallowed up in paying debts before any part of his realty, including Blackacre, could be touched. This seemed unfair, and by three Acts, the first of which is always spoken of as Locke King's Act, Parliament has tried to set this matter straight. The three Acts are 17 & 18 Vic. c. 113 (1854), 30 & 31 Vic. c. 69 (1867), and 40 & 41 Vic. c. 34 (1877). The last of these Acts says in effect that in the administration of the estate of any testator or intestate dying after the 31st of December, 1877, seised or possessed of any land or other hereditaments of whatever tenure which shall at the time of his death be charged with the payment of any sum by way of mortgage or any other equitable charge, including a lien for unpaid purchase money, the devisee or heir at law shall not be entitled to have such sum satisfied out of any other estate of the testator or intestate unless (in the case of a testator) he shall have signified a contrary intention, and that a contrary intention shall not be deemed to be signified by a charge of or direction for payment of debts out of residuary real and personal estate or residuary real estate.

That, at least for the time being, is the last word in the history of a muddle. Of the earlier acts it seems only necessary to say that it was discovered that owing to defective workmanship the first Act (1854) would not apply to an equitable mortgage by deposit of title deeds, nor to a vendor's lien for unpaid purchase money, nor to leaseholds for years—though the specific legatee of a leasehold was entitled to have it exonerated at the expense of the general personalty. The second Act declared that the word mortgage was to include a lien for unpaid purchase money upon any lands purchased by the testator—it corrected one omission but made another blunder, for after testator it should have added 'or intestate', and so a third Act was necessary. Even this third Act is giving rise to some difficulties, and may, I think, give rise to more. However most loopholes are by this time stopped and we may say in pretty general terms that as between the various persons claiming under a dead debtor real property which forms the security for any debt is the primary fund for the payment of that debt. A contrary intention expressed in the dead man's will will prevail; but we may say that such an intention has to be clearly expressed. But these Acts, the Real Estates Charges Acts, to give them their statutory title, have nothing to do with mortgages or charges upon chattels or upon choses in action or upon anything but realty passing to an heir or devisee.

Instructive cases as to what amounts to the expression of a contrary intention are *In re Smith*, 33 Ch. D. 195; *In re Fleck*, 37 Ch. D. 677.

Let us take an illustration of the working of the rules that we have been considering.

A is entitled as tenant in fee simple to Blackacre, of the value of £1000, but mortgaged for £500. He is entitled also to Whiteacre, now of the value of £800 only, but mortgaged for £1000; also to personalty of the value of £1500. He owes unsecured debts to the amount of £1200. He makes his will: he devises Blackacre to B, gives a legacy of £500 to C, and bequeaths the residue of his personalty to D. He says nothing of Whiteacre. E is his heir at law. What, if any, part of his legacy will C obtain?

The debts are £500 secured by Blackacre + £1000 secured by Whiteacre + £1200 unsecured. Total £2700.

Assets £1500 + £1000 + £800 = £3300. The estate is not insolvent. There is a surplus of £600.

The mortgagee of Blackacre can get his whole £500, and for this Blackacre is the first fund.

The mortgagee of Whiteacre can certainly get £800 by realizing his security on Whiteacre, thus leaving a balance of £200 due to him.

The debts now remaining unpaid are £1200 + £200 = £1400.

You must begin by applying the personalty not specifically bequeathed, £1500, after retaining out of that £1500 £500 for C's legacy. That gives you £1000 towards the £1400, but it still leaves £400 due.

What is now left of A's estate? £500 of his personalty, which you have retained for the pecuniary legacy, and £500, the surplus value of Blackacre; £400 of debts are still unpaid.

The competition is between B who is devisee of Blackacre and C who has been given a pecuniary legacy. The liability of the pecuniary legacy comes first and C can only get £100 out of the £500 that has been left to him. B gets his £500, the whole balance left of the value of Blackacre. It would have been otherwise if Blackacre had been charged with the payment of debts. B would then have had to lose the £400 and C would have got his pecuniary legacy in full. D, the residuary legatee, and E, the heir at law, of course get nothing.

NOTE ON ADMINISTRATION OF ASSETS

THE Administration of Estates Act 1925 has completely altered the law on the administration of assets. In this note the present law will be summarized under the three headings:

    I. The order of payment of debts.
    II. The personal representative's right of retainer and the distinction between legal and equitable assets.
    III. The order in which the assets of a solvent estate are applicable in payment of debts.

I. THE ORDER OF PAYMENT OF DEBTS

The assets of a deceased person available for payment of debts include all real and personal property belonging to him and all real and personal property over which he has a general power of appointment, provided that he has exercised the power.[1] Since a tenant in tail now has statutory power to dispose by will of the entailed property[2] such property will now be assets for payment of debts if the statutory power has been exercised. When the estate is insolvent the assets must be applied as provided by the first Schedule to the Administration of Estates Act 1925, which reads as follows:

'1. The funeral, testamentary and administration expenses have priority.

'2. Subject as aforesaid, the same rules shall prevail and be observed as to the respective rights of secured and unsecured creditors and as to debts and liabilities provable and as to the priorities of debts and liabilities as may be in force for the time being under the law of bankruptcy with respect to the assets of persons adjudged bankrupt.'

The priority of debts in bankruptcy, which by this Schedule is applicable in the administration of an insolvent estate, is at present regulated by section 33 of the Bankruptcy Act 1914 and is briefly as follows:

    1. Certain debts due to a Friendly Society or a Trustee Savings Bank from an officer of the Society or Bank rank first.[4]
    2. Next rank the following debts which among themselves are payable 'pari passu':
        (a) Arrears of rates and taxes subject to certain limits of time.

---

[1] Administration of Estates Act 1925, s. 32.
[2] Law of Property Act 1925, s. 176.
[3] See Administration of Estates Act 1925, s. 34 (1).
[4] Bankruptcy Act 1914, s. 33 (9).

(*b*) Wages or salary of clerks or servants and wages of labourers and workmen subject to certain limits of time and amount.

(*c*) Amounts due in respect of compensation under the Workman's Compensation Act.

(*d*) Contributions payable under the National Insurance Act subject to certain limits.

3. Next rank all other debts including Crown debts (except so far as they are included in the preferred debts already mentioned), specialty debts, judgment debts and simple contract debts, but excluding the deferred debts mentioned below. All these debts are payable *pari passu* among themselves.

4. Finally there are certain deferred debts not payable until all other creditors are satisfied. These are

(*a*) Loans to a partnership or trader bearing interest which varies with profits.[1]

(*b*) Claims by a wife or husband for property lent to the husband or wife for the purposes of his or her trade or business.[2]

Let us see how far the Administration of Estates Act 1925 has changed the law.

In the first place it has abolished the difference that previously existed between an administration by an executor out of Court and an administration by the Court. Section 10 of the Judicature Act 1875 only applied to an administration by the Court and the executor administering out of Court was bound to apply a different set of rules, as stated on p. 251 above. Under the 1925 Act there is one uniform set of rules as regards priorities, secured creditors, etc., equally applicable whether the administration is by the executor out of Court or by the Chancery Division or by the Court of Bankruptcy.

In the second place the 1925 Act has made clear, what had given rise to difficulty under the old Act, that the bankruptcy rules as to priority of debts as well as the rules as to secured creditors are to be in force in the administration of the estate of a deceased person.

Thirdly, the 1925 Act has not introduced any more than did section 10 of the Judicature Act the bankruptcy rules which go to swell the assets available, as distinct from the rules as to how the assets are to be distributed. The rule, for example, whereby a payment to a creditor can be set aside in bankruptcy as a fraudulent preference will not, it would seem, be applicable in an administration whether in bankruptcy or by the Chancery Division or by the executor out of Court.

---

[1] Partnership Act 1890, s. 3, and Bankruptcy Act 1914, s. 33 (9).

[2] Bankruptcy Act 1914, s. 36.

II. The Personal Representative's right of retainer and the distinction between legal and equitable assets

The personal representative's right of retainer and his right to prefer creditors are expressly saved by section 34 (2) of the Administration of Estates Act 1925. Moreover, while previously these rights could be exercised in respect of legal assets only they may now be exercised in respect of all assets, whether legal or equitable. The right of retainer is now limited to debts owing to the personal representative in his own right (whether solely or jointly with another person) and does not, for example, apply when the debt is owing to the personal representative as a trustee.

Now before the Judicature Act 1875 the executor could exercise his right of retainer only as against a debt of priority equal to or lower than his own. Section 10 of the Judicature Act 1875 and subsequent legislation introduced a new order of priority for debts and the question accordingly arose whether the executor could exercise his right of retainer as against a debt which under the Judicature Act and subsequent legislation had priority over the executor's own debt. The question was one of some difficulty but has now been settled by the decision of the House of Lords in *A.-G.* v. *Jackson*.[1] There an executrix was a creditor of the testator for a sum of money lent to him. The estate was insolvent and large sums were due to the Crown for arrears of taxes, part of which sums were a preferred debt under the Bankruptcy Act 1914. The executrix attempted to exercise her power of retainer as against the Crown. The House of Lords held that she could not do so. It would seem therefore that since 1925 the power of retainer can be exercised only as against debts which under the bankruptcy rules for the time being rank in priority equal to or lower than the executor's debt.

It remains to be seen whether the old distinction between legal and equitable assets is any longer of importance. Before 1926 the distinction could arise in two cases, namely on an attempt by the executor to exercise his power of retainer and in the administration of an insolvent estate out of Court (for the priorities of the debts were different according as the assets were legal or equitable). As we have seen the power of retainer is now exercisable in respect of both legal and equitable assets and the priority of debts in an administration out of Court is now governed by the bankruptcy rules and is the same for all assets. It would seem therefore that the distinction between legal and equitable assets has ceased to be of any significance. It should however be mentioned that an almost identical distinction still arises under the

[1] [1932] A.C. 365.

Finance Act 1894 in regard to estate duty, for whereas estate duty on personal property which passes to the executor as such is payable primarily out of the testator's general estate, the estate duty on personal property which does not pass to the executor as such is payable out of the property itself.[1]

III. THE ORDER IN WHICH THE ASSETS OF A SOLVENT ESTATE ARE APPLICABLE IN PAYMENT OF DEBTS

The question here discussed arises as between the various beneficiaries under a will when the estate is solvent. The question is out of whose interest under the will are the testator's debts and the funeral and other expenses to be paid. The present law is contained in Part II of the First Schedule of the Administration of Estates Act 1925. Subject to any contrary intention expressed in the will the assets are applicable in payment of debts in the following order:

1. Property not disposed of by the will (including a lapsed share of residue[2]) subject to retention of a fund to meet pecuniary legacies.
2. Property included in a residuary gift subject to retention of a legacy fund.
3. Property specifically appropriated for the payment of debts.
4. Property charged with the payment of debts.
5. The fund retained to meet pecuniary legacies.
6. Property specifically devised or bequeathed, rateably according to value.
7. Property appointed by will under a general power (including the statutory power to dispose of entailed interests) rateably according to value.

This order should be compared with the order under the old law set out on p. 262 above. The main difference is that under the new order land and personalty stand on exactly the same footing. It will be noticed also that, whereas under the old order undisposed of personalty (which goes to the next of kin) stood on the same footing as residuary personalty (which goes to the residuary legatee), under the new order the undisposed of personalty is applicable before the residuary personalty. It may be helpful to consider the effect of the new order on the two examples given by Maitland on p. 264 above.

A testator makes his will in the following words: ' I give my freehold estate called Dale to A, my leasehold house in Brook Street to B, my gold snuff box to C, £1000 to D, the rest of my realty to E and the rest of my personalty to F.' The order since 1926 will be this: E and F lose

[1] See for example *O'Grady* v. *Wilmot* [1916] 2 A.C. 231.
[2] *In re Tong* [1931] 1 Ch. 202.

all (or if there is sufficient without their losing all, contribute rateably), then D loses all, then A, B and C contribute rateably according to the value of the property specifically devised or bequeathed to them.

A testator, tenant in fee simple of Blackacre, Whiteacre and Green-acre and entitled to a leasehold house in Brook Street and other personalty makes his will as follows: 'I give Blackacre to A. I declare that my debts shall be a charge on the rest of my real estate. I give White-acre to B, and my house in Brook Street to C. I give £1000 to D, all my books to E, and the residue of my personalty to my cousins F and G in equal shares.' G dies before the testator. The testator dies leaving H his heir at law and sole next of kin. (N.B. since 1926 the undisposed of land and personalty will in any case devolve upon the same person.) Greenacre is undisposed of, there being no residuary devise. In what order are his assets to be applied for the payment of his debts? The answer would appear to be as follows: First exhaust Greenacre and the lapsed share of personalty given to G (to both of which H is entitled); then F loses all; then B loses all (for Whiteacre is specifically charged with the payment of debts); then D loses all; finally A, C and E contribute rateably.

The solution of the second problem is given with some diffidence for certain of the decisions since 1926 have made it hard to see what the law is. The difficulty arises from the fact that undisposed of property and residuary property are under the statute applicable to pay debts before property specifically appropriated or charged with the payment of debts. Now a testator who has specifically appropriated property to the payment of debts probably intended that such property was to be the first to be applied towards paying debts and the statutory order, in requiring the undisposed of and residuary property to be applied before specifically appropriated property, would seem to be disregarding the testator's expressed intention. Nevertheless the Act expressly states that the testator can vary the order by his will. If therefore it be the case that the statutory order necessarily involves disregard of the testator's intention the question may well arise whether a particular will displaces the statutory order or merely expresses an intention which the Statute requires the Court to disregard. There is room here for some nice difficulties.

See *In re Atkinson.*[1] There a testator devised all his land to A and bequeathed all his personalty to trustees on trust to pay thereout his debts and other expenses and to hold the balance on trust for B, C and D in equal shares. A died before the testator so that the residuary devise to him lapsed and the testator's land passed as on intestacy. The question arose whether the debts and expenses were payable primarily out of the land or the personalty. Looking at the Act one would I

[1] [1930] 1 Ch. 47.

think say that the land, being property undisposed of by will, should have borne the debts, but Clauson J. held that the testator clearly showed his intention that the debts should be paid out of the personalty and that this intention was sufficient to vary the statutory order. Accordingly the personalty bore the debts.

Now see *In re Kempthorne.*[1] A testator gave all his personal property, subject to and after payment of his funeral and testamentary expenses and debts, as to one-seventh each to A, B and C and as to two-sevenths each to D and E. A, B and D died before the testator and accordingly the residuary bequest of personalty lapsed as to four-sevenths, which passed as on intestacy. Should the debts be paid primarily out of the lapsed shares of residue or in equal proportions out of the lapsed shares and the shares which had not lapsed. Held by Maugham J. that the lapsed shares should bear the debts, for a contrary intention was shown only by the fact that the whole residue had been appropriated in payment of debts and paragraph 3 of the Schedule to the Act expressly put property undisposed of by will before property specifically appropriated to pay debts. But held unanimously by the Court of Appeal, reversing Maugham J., that the debts were payable out of the whole personalty, including the shares which had not lapsed, for the testator had said that the debts should be paid out of the personalty before it was divided into shares and until the debts had been paid there were no shares and nothing given to any of the residuary legatees.

These decisions are not easy to understand and one may be led to think that the Courts have boldly discarded paragraphs 3 and 4 of the Schedule to the Administration of Estates Act 1925. This however is probably an incorrect view.[2] The Court of Appeal in *In re Kempthorne* gave a construction of the Schedule which explains their decision. On their construction paragraphs 3 and 4 of the Schedule do not begin to apply until the undisposed of and residuary property mentioned in paragraphs 1 and 2 have been used up. Accordingly an appropriation of residue towards payment of debts does not fall within paragraph 3 at all. When the question is between residue and undisposed of property or between different blocks of residue paragraphs 3 and 4 are out of the picture and an appropriation of a particular fund of residue to pay debts can be treated at its face value as indicating an intention of the testator that the debts should be paid in the first instance out of that fund. This is a rather subtle construction of the Schedule but certainly gives results more in keeping with the intention of testators than would the more straightforward and obvious construction.

Finally there remains the question who is to bear the cost of paying

[1] [1930] 1 Ch. 268.
[2] See however *In re Littlewood* [1931] 1 Ch. 431, which if correctly decided does seem to reduce the statutory provisions to a nullity—at least where the will is one made before 1926.

a debt which is charged upon property devised or bequeathed by the will. We have seen that before 1926, as a result of the Real Estates Charges Acts, when land subject to a charge was devised by the will the charge was payable primarily out of the land charged and not out of the general estate of the testator, but that this rule did not extend to personalty. Section 35 of the Administration of Estates Act 1925 reproduces this rule and extends it to personalty bequeathed subject to a charge, to which it did not previously apply.

CONVERSION

THE equitable doctrine of conversion is the outcome of the fact that we have two systems of intestate succession, the one for realty the other for personalty: but for that unfortunate fact there would have been no need of this doctrine.[1]

The Land Transfer Act of 1897 makes hardly any difference; the land vests in the personal representatives, but the beneficial interests are unaffected.

The equitable doctrine of conversion has its root in this simple principle that when property has been given to a trustee it must not be in the power of that trustee to alter the devolution of the beneficial interests by committing a breach of trust.

A testator devises land to a trustee upon trust that he shall sell it, invest the proceeds of the sale, pay the dividends of the invested fund to the testator's wife during her life and hold the capital in trust for his son. The trustee in breach of trust neglects to sell the land; meanwhile during the wife's life, the son dies and, let us say, dies intestate. Now who is to be entitled to what was destined for the son? On the one hand the son's heir makes a claim, saying that what was destined for the son was land, and that an equitable estate of fee simple in the land has descended to him. On the other hand the administrator claims on behalf of the next of kin, urging that what was intended for the son was not land but an invested fund of personalty. The Court decides in favour of the administrator. If the trustee had done his duty there would have been no land, there would have been a fund of personalty, which would have gone to the administrator. The fact that the trustee has not done his duty must make no difference; the land is held upon trust for the administrator.

Take the converse case. A testator leaves £10,000 to a trustee upon trust to purchase land and settle it to the use of the

---

[1] There is now only one system of intestate succession, but the question of conversion can still arise. See *In re Kempthorne* [1930] 1 Ch. 268.

testator's wife for life, with the remainder to the use of his son. The trustee omits to buy any land. Meanwhile during the wife's life the son dies, and dies, let us say, intestate; his heir at law shall have the money.

The root of the doctrine then is this, that a breach of trust is not to affect the devolution of equitable interests. Had it remained in this, its first form, the doctrine could never have been called into operation save when there had really been a breach of trust—save when some trustee had been guilty of not effecting a conversion which he was bound to effect.

But the doctrine was found a convenient one and was extended beyond the simple principle in which it had its origin. It was discovered that settlors and testators might give their trustees a certain discretion as to the external form which the property should take, *i.e.* whether it should be land or money, and at the same time make the devolution of the equitable interests independent of any exercise by the trustees of their discretion. For example it often happens that a testator wishes the whole of his property to devolve in one way; he has some freehold land, but he does not wish 'to make an eldest son'; he wishes his wife to enjoy during her life the whole income of his fortune, and he wishes that fortune, subject to her life interest, to be divided equally among his children, and if a child dies during the wife's life he does not wish that one part of that child's share should be treated as realty, another as personalty; so far as is possible he wishes to treat his fortune as a single whole. By an extension of the principle that we have been considering he is enabled to effect this object to a very considerable extent. He devises and bequeaths all his realty and personalty to trustees upon trust to convert it into money, and to invest that money, and then he declares how the invested fund shall be held, on trust for his wife for life and so forth. But he does not mean that the trustees should be bound to make an immediate sale of the land—such a sale might be very improvident—so he goes on to give his trustees the widest discretion as to the time at which they shall sell; they may postpone the sale so long as they shall think fit.

Now in this case if the trustees do postpone the sale they are committing no breach of trust. Nevertheless it is held that as between the real and personal representatives of the beneficiaries the land is to be considered in equity as though it were a sum of money; it is according to a common phrase impressed with a trust for conversion, albeit that trust is accompanied by a discretionary power of postponement. It will be needless to state a converse case in which money is to be turned into land. Occasionally, though less frequently, a testator making what we may call a primogenitary settlement of his land, desires that his personalty shall be expended in the purchase of yet more land to be settled in similar fashion. Here of course it will be very expedient that the trustees should have power to postpone the purchase of land, it may be long ere they will find in the market what would be a suitable addition to the family estate. By means of a trust for conversion and a discretionary power of postponement, the testator can at once give the trustees all the time requisite for finding suitable lands and at the same time provide that the delay thus occasioned shall have no effect on the devolution of the equitable interests in his personal estate.[1]

The working out of this principle is of course not free from difficulties. In the first place wherever it is alleged that there has been an equitable conversion of land into money or money into land we must first make certain that there is a trust for conversion. On the one hand a trust for conversion accompanied by a power of retention will be effectual, on the other hand a mere power to convert will not be enough. Of course in a badly drawn instrument it may be difficult to say which of these has been created, and thus questions of construction arise. Good conveyancers are careful in the first instance to make an absolute trust for conversion, declaring that the trustees are to sell the land, or to lay out the money in the purchase of land, and then, generally by some later and independent clause, they give such a discretionary power of postponing the sale or pur-

---

[1] Before 1926 it was impossible to create an entailed interest in personalty and for that as well as other minor reasons a trust for conversion into land was necessary if personalty were to be settled so as to follow the devolution of land subject to a strict settlement. By the 1925 Acts the law of personalty and the law of realty have been assimilated and the need for conversion will much less often arise in the future.

chase of land as is desirable, and add that in the meanwhile the land is to be impressed with the character of personalty, or the personal fund with the character of realty. But the great principle is that to effect an equitable conversion there must be a trust for conversion, and not a mere power to convert.

This doctrine of a notional conversion of realty into personalty, or personalty into realty, has been worked out with logical consistency. If once a fund of personalty has been subjected to a trust for the purchase of freehold land, then until something happens which has the effect of reconverting it into personalty, it is treated as realty for all purposes of succession and devolution. Thus there may be dower and courtesy of such a fund, and again one may have an estate tail in such a fund.[1] In order that such an estate tail may be barred a deed enrolled under the Fines and Recoveries Act is required. Section 71 of that Act (3 & 4 Will. IV, c. 74) deals specially with this matter: for the purposes of this Act money subject to be invested in the purchase of lands to be settled so that any person would have an estate tail therein is in effect treated as though it were land purchased and settled. Great use has been made of this idea by the modern Acts of Parliament which enable railway and other companies to compel a sale of settled land, and also by the Settled Land Act of 1882. Under this last Act the money arising from the sale of settled land and any securities upon which such money is invested shall 'for all purposes of disposition, transmission and devolution be considered as land and shall be held for and go to the same persons successively in the same manner and for and on the same estates, interests and trusts as the land wherefrom the money arises would, if not disposed of, have gone under the settlement'. (45 & 46 Vic. c. 38, s. 22 (5).)[2]

Further, this idea has been introduced into the interpretation of wills and other documents. If, for example, a trustee is holding money upon trust to purchase land and convey it to A in fee simple, and A dies having devised all his realty to X and

---

[1] Subject to unimportant exceptions dower and courtesy are now abolished. An entailed interest can now be created in personalty without conversion; Law of Property Act 1925, s. 130.

[2] Now Settled Land Act 1925, s. 75 (5).

bequeathed all his personalty to Y, it is X, not Y, who will be
entitled to the money—it will pass by a general devise of all
lands, tenements and hereditaments; it will not pass by a general
bequest of personal estate.[1]

The cases which have occasioned most difficulty have been
those in which the object which was to be gained by the conversion of the property has wholly or partially failed. Let us
begin with a simple case. A by his will leaves land to trustees
upon trust to sell and to pay the proceeds to B; B dies in the
lifetime of A and (not being a descendant of the testator—see
the Wills Act, s. 33) the disposition of the proceeds of sale fails
utterly. The sale then is not required for any purpose whatever,
and as between the testator's heir at law and his next of kin, we
shall I think have little difficulty in deciding in favour of the
heir. But A by his will leaves land to trustees upon trust to sell
and divide the proceeds between B and C; B survives the
testator, C does not. Now a sale is required by the will, it is
required in order that B may have what the testator has intended to give him, namely money and not land. But this will
exhaust but half of the fund (B and C were not made joint
tenants but tenants in common). What is to become of the
residue? The testator's heir at law and his next of kin seem both
to have plausible claims. The land must be turned into money
in order that B may get his share, will not the other moiety also
be personalty, and is it not the rule that a dead person's undisposed of personalty goes to his next of kin? In the famous
case of *Ackroyd* v. *Smithson* (1 Bro. C. C. 503) this reasoning
was overruled. The land, it is true, must be sold, but that is
merely in order that B may get that moiety of the price which A
has given to him. As between his real and his personal representatives the testator has made no choice. The property comes
to them not because the testator has said that it shall come to
them, but because he has not effectually given it to anyone else;
they are not entitled under the will, they claim in consequence
of a partial intestacy—and our law is that if a tenant in fee simple
dies intestate his land descends to his heir. So here the testator's
heir takes the moiety of the property that was destined for C.

---

[1] Cf. *In re Kempthorne* [1930] 1 Ch. 268, which is the converse case.

In this case the gift to C lapses in consequence of C's death in the testator's lifetime. The result would be the same if the gift to him had failed for any other reason, for instance, as being contrary to law.

Thus suppose the case last put to have occurred before the Mortmain Act of 1891, and suppose C to have been a charitable institution, the testator at that time could not give the proceeds of the sale of his land to a charity. (I mention this because one might have thought that the doctrine of conversion might have enabled him to do this, but this is not so. Under the Act of 1736 (9 Geo. II, c. 36), a charity could not take either money impressed with a trust for conversion into land or land to be converted into money, and I take it that the consolidating Act of 1888 (51 & 52 Vic. 42) did not alter the law in this respect.[1]) So, the gift to the charity failing, the testator's heir at law would have become entitled. The same is the case if the testator directs the sale of land, and forgets to dispose of some share of the fund to arise from such sale, the testator's heir at law (not his next of kin) becomes entitled to that share.

A further point is well established, namely that in all these cases where the heir at law becomes entitled to an undisposed of share of money to arise from the sale of land he takes it not as realty but as personalty. A devises land upon trust for sale, and the proceeds are to be divided between B and C, C dies in A's lifetime, A's heir at law becomes entitled to half the property; but before the sale is made he dies—perhaps he dies intestate and the question is between his heir and his next of kin—or perhaps he has left a will devising his realty to X, and bequeathing his personalty to Y—any way, his real and his personal representatives both claim the share, and the question is decided in favour of his personal representatives (*Smith* v. *Claxton*, 4 Madd. 484). The heir has become entitled—to what? To land that is subject to a trust for conversion into money—a trust which B can enforce—he has become entitled to personalty. *In re Richerson* [1892] 1 Ch. 379.

---

[1] Under the Mortmain and Charitable Uses Act 1891, 'land' is defined so as to exclude personal estate arising from or connected with land and accordingly since 1891 the doctrine of conversion will apply.

In re Wood [1896] 2 Ch. 596 is a very pretty case. In 1893 the testatrix dies without an heir, having devised a house of which she was legally seised in fee simple to her executors upon trust for sale, and out of the proceeds to pay her debts, funeral expenses and legacies. There was no gift of residue. Her house is sold, and the proceeds are more than sufficient to pay all her debts, funeral expenses and legacies. Who is entitled to the surplus? But for the Intestates Estates Act 1884, the executors would be entitled for their own use. Till then there had been no escheat of an equitable interest. But under section 4 of the Act of 1884 the Crown successfully claimed the fund. Admittedly if there had been an heir he would have taken the surplus proceeds of this land.

We turn to the other side of the picture and we find the same principles prevailing. The testator bequeaths personalty to trustees upon trust to purchase land and convey it to B and C. Of course if both B and C die before the testator there is an utter end of the trust; the testator's next of kin will become entitled to the personal estate and will become entitled to it as personalty—for there is no trust for turning it into realty. But suppose a partial failure—C dies before the testator but B outlives him—or the gift fails in whole or in part owing to some rule of law, *e.g.* the rule against perpetuities, or the testator has forgotten to declare trusts of some share of the land that is to be bought. Whatever he has not effectually disposed of his next of kin will take, not his heir at law, he has shown no preference for his heir at law, whichever party is to succeed must claim under the law of intestate succession, which gives personalty to the next of kin (*Cogan* v. *Stephens*, 5 L. J. Ch. (N. S.) 17). But again the question arises on the death of one of these next of kin who dies before any land is purchased—who will become entitled, his real or his personal representative? His real representative—his heir at law or perhaps a devisee of 'all my realty'; for what he becomes entitled to is realty, for it is a share in a fund of money that is subject to an existing trust for the purchase of land (*Curteis* v. *Wormald*, 10 Ch. D. 172).

The doctrine of conversion is not confined to cases where there is a trust for sale created by a settlement or a will. It is applied also where there is a contract to sell. As soon as I have bindingly contracted to sell freehold land I have, as between those who can claim my property at my death, rather personalty than realty. Similarly if I contract to buy freehold, I have rather realty than personalty. See the case of *In re Isaacs* [1894] 3 Ch. 506.

The doctrine is set going by an option to purchase in a lease. A demised to B on lease with the option to purchase within six months of A's decease. A died intestate. B exercised the option. Here at A's death there is freehold land, his heir is entitled to it until the option is exercised, and so he gets the profits, but when the option is exercised the price is part of A's personalty and goes to his next of kin.[1]

The ideal or 'notional' conversion of realty into personalty or personalty into realty continues until either an actual conversion takes place or until some person competent to elect does elect to take the land as land or the money as money, until he elects, that is, to put an end to the trust for conversion. A person may well be in a position to make such election. Suppose the very simple situation that a trustee holds land upon trust to sell and pay the proceeds to me, or holds money upon trust to buy land and convey it to me in fee simple—in the former case I would rather have land, in the latter case I would rather have money. Of course it would be ridiculous that land should be sold in order that I might buy land with the proceeds, or that land should be purchased when next day I should advertise it for sale. I am entitled to say to the trustee I will take the land as it is, or I will take the money as it is, and he is bound to obey my expressed wishes. If then I have openly expressed my wish then at my death there will be no question. I have taken the land as land and it will pass at my death as realty, or I have taken the money as money and it will pass at my death as personalty. But it often happens that no plain declaration can be produced or has been made—then the Court, looking at my behaviour, will have to say whether I have manifested an intention to put an end to the trust for conversion. Among the acts which have been relied on

---

[1] On the effect of an option to purchase see generally White and Tudor, L.C. vol. I, pp. 312 *et seq.* (9th edition).

as showing this intention are the granting of leases not authorized by the trust; such leases granted by my concurrence would show that I did not intend to have the land sold under the trust. In one case a fact much relied on was that a bill was introduced into Parliament authorizing a railway company to make a line through the land, and the *cestui que trust* presented a petition against the bill as owner of the land stating that he desired to lay out the estate for building. That case is *In re Davidson*, 11 Ch. D. 341. Another case which will serve to show how such questions are dealt with is *In re Gordon*, 6 Ch. D. 531.

Where there is a single *cestui que trust* absolutely entitled the principle is simple even though it may be difficult of application because his conduct has been very ambiguous. He has an absolute right to effect a reconversion and the only question will be whether he has shown an intention of taking the subject of the trust in its unconverted state. But when there are several persons entitled to share the subject-matter of the trust between them, then another principle comes into play, and it has been held to make a distinction between land which is to be turned into money, and money which is to be turned into land. The principle is just this that one of several *cestui que trusts* can not put an end to the trust, even so far as his own share is concerned, if thereby he would be damaging his fellows. Land is held upon trust for sale and the proceeds are to be divided between A, B and C: A by himself of course can not put an end to the trust; but he can not even say (without the concurrence of B and C) 'I for my part shall keep my undivided one-third of the land, while you if you like can have your undivided two-thirds sold according to the trust.' The reason given for this is simple, namely that the price of two undivided shares of the land will probably be far less than two-thirds of the price of the whole land. On the other hand it has been held that similar reasoning does not apply to what we may call the converse case. Money is held on trust for the purchase of land to be conveyed to A, B and C as tenants in common in fee; any one of them may insist on taking his share as money; for it is said that in so doing he will not affect the interests of his fellows. Whether this distinction shows a deep insight into the theory of value I must leave you to consider; but it seems well established.[1]

Can a mere remainder-man elect? The question is not free of difficulty. A testator devises land at Dale to trustees upon trust to sell, to invest the proceeds, pay the income to his wife for life, and hold the capital upon trust for his son. The son dies during the widow's life, and while the land is yet unsold, having declared explicitly to the trustees that should the land not be sold in his mother's lifetime, he will take it as land and not have it sold. We will suppose him to die intestate, and the question to arise between his heir and his next of kin. The case of *Meek* v. *Devenish*, 6 Ch. D. 566 (1877), makes it a probable opinion that his election to take the land as land is effectual to settle the course of devolution of his interest, is effectual to decide that his heir becomes entitled in consequence of this prospective election. But how far this can be carried seems rather doubtful, for the remainder-man's so-called election can not prevent the tenant for life from insisting on a sale of the land, and if between the act of prospective election and the death of the remainder-man a sale is made, then is his heir to take money which is subject to no trust for conversion into land? May it not be said that if this be allowed we practically enable the remainder-man to make a will in favour of his heir by a mere declaration of intention, without any of those formalities required by the Wills Act? We may yet see some cases on this point.[2]

---

[1] See *e.g. Holloway* v. *Radcliffe*, 23 Beav. 163, *Seeley* v. *Jago*, 1 P.W. 389.

[2] The whole question of conversion is fully discussed in the notes to *Fletcher* v. *Ashburner* and *Ackroyd* v. *Smithson* in White and Tudor, L.C. vol. I, pp. 293–340 (9th edition), to which the student is referred for further details.

LECTURE XIX

ELECTION

THE doctrine of Election may be thus stated: That he who accepts a benefit under a deed or will or other instrument must adopt the whole contents of that instrument, must conform to all its provisions and renounce all rights that are inconsistent with it. If therefore—this is the simplest application of the rule —a testator has affected to dispose of property which is not his own and has also given some benefit to the person, X, to whom that property belongs, that person, X, if he accepts the benefit thus destined for him by the testator, must make good the testator's attempted disposition of the property that belonged to him, X. If on the other hand X insists on his proprietary rights, will not give up that property of his which the testator has endeavoured to give away, then equity will sequester the benefit that the testator has given to X for the purpose of making satisfaction to the persons whom he disappoints by insisting on his proprietary rights—X it is said must elect to take under the will or against the will; he can not it is said 'blow hot and cold', or to use a phrase that our Courts have borrowed from Scotland, he can not both 'approbate and reprobate' the will.[1]

Let us put a simple instance: X is tenant in fee simple of Blackacre; a testator says 'I devise Blackacre to Y and I bequeath to X a legacy of £1000.' Now X can not be allowed both to keep Blackacre and to take the legacy of £1000. He may do one of two things. He may elect to take the legacy that has been given to him and abandon Blackacre to Y. Or he may elect to stand upon those proprietary rights that he has outside the will, may say 'Blackacre is mine and I am not going to abandon it.'

---

[1] Cf. *Douglas-Menzies* v. *Umphelby* [1908] A.C. 224, where a man had made two separate wills, one for his Scottish and one for his Australian estate. His widow having claimed her 'tierce' and *jus relictae* against the Scotch will was held to have made her election, and was ordered to make compensation out of her interest under the Australian will. For a discussion of the principle of the doctrine of election and an extended application of it, see *In re Macartney* [1918] 1 Ch. 300.

In this latter case there has in times past been a controversy as to what ought to happen. The debated question was sometimes stated thus: Is the principle that we are to enforce against X the principle of forfeiture, or the principle of compensation? Are we to say to him: Very well, you insist on your rights outside the will, therefore you can take nothing under the will, or are we to say to him merely, You insist on rights outside the will, therefore you can take nothing under the will unless you make compensation to the person whom you will disappoint by your election to stand on your rights? To return to our case; X says Blackacre is mine and I am not going to give it up. Are we to say to him: Very well, then you must abandon all claim to the £1000, or are we to say to him merely: You must abandon so much of the £1000 as will serve to compensate Y for the loss of that benefit, namely, Blackacre, which the testator designated for him? Of course if the value of Blackacre is equal to or greater than £1000 these two principles will lead to one and the same result: if X insists on retaining Blackacre then he loses all claim to the £1000. But suppose that Blackacre is worth but £500, then the question becomes important. Shall we say: If you keep Blackacre you can claim no part of the legacy—or shall we say: If you keep Blackacre you must compensate Y by giving him the value of Blackacre? In the one case, you see, X will merely keep Blackacre and take nothing under the will, in the other he will be able to keep Blackacre and also to claim one half of the legacy—since the legacy of £1000 minus £500, the value of Blackacre, leaves £500.

It is now well settled that the principle of compensation is the true one.[1] We do not say to X: By insisting on rights outside the will you forfeit all rights under the will. We say to him: If you insist upon rights outside the will you can take no benefit under the will until you have compensated those who are disappointed by your refusal to give effect to the whole will as it stands.

Such is the principle. It is immaterial whether the testator

---

[1] There was a long conflict of judicial opinion before the principle of compensation was definitely accepted; see the earlier authorities collected in 1 Swanston n. (*a*), p. 433.

knew or did not know that he was attempting to give away another person's property. It may seem to you at first sight that the rule should only be applied where the testator has been acting under a mistake, where he has given, *e.g.* Blackacre, believing that Blackacre is his. But our Courts have refused to go into the question—it would often be a very difficult one—as to the testator's ignorance of his want of title. Thus, though I know well that Blackacre belongs to you and not to me, I can put you to your election by taking upon myself to devise Blackacre to a third person if at the same time I devise to you another estate or bequeath to you some legacy.

In order that a case of election may be raised it must be clear that the testator has affected to dispose of something that does not belong to him and you may not have recourse to external evidence to prove that by some general phrase he intended to give away what is not his own. Thus suppose that the testator devises 'All my real estate' to Y, you may not prove by oral evidence that he was in the habit of treating as part of his real estate a field that belonged to X. You must find in the will itself that the testator has attempted to dispose of a certain thing that belongs to X. As already said, you need not find that the testator knew that that thing belonged to X, but you must find in the words of the will itself an attempted disposition of that thing, and therefore a general devise of my real estate, or general bequest of my personal estate will be insufficient. A good illustration of this may be found in cases relating to wills made before 1838. Under the old law, you will remember, a testator could devise only such real estate as he was entitled to at the time when he made his will—in other words, real estate acquired between the date of the will and the date of his death would not pass under his will. Very well—a testator having no real estate said 'I give all my real estate to X.' Here there was ground for a fair argument that the testator must have meant something by these words, must therefore have intended to give away some real estate that did not belong to him. That argument however was rejected.

Difficult cases sometimes arise in which a testator who is entitled to but a partial interest in certain property uses a phrase which may be sufficient to describe the whole property. Thus he gives 'my freehold house called Dale Hall', and he is but one of several tenants in common of Dale Hall. Or again he gives 'my freehold house called Dale Hall', and he is not tenant in possession of Dale Hall but merely tenant in remainder, there being perhaps several life estates preceding his estate in fee. Is he attempting to give away more than his own interest? This is a question of construction and may be one of great difficulty. No general rule can be laid down save this, and it is a natural one, namely that you must have clear words to induce the conclusion that a man has attempted to give away more than belonged to him. Still of course, here as elsewhere, you may look at the will as a whole, and you may find that the testator has dealt with the property in some manner that shows that he was not disposing of a partial interest in it. Again if a testator having an estate which is subject to an incumbrance gives this estate to Y and gives a legacy to the incumbrancer X, this will not put X to his election between his incumbrance and the legacy. In order that such a case of election may be raised you must find that the testator has given or attempted to give to Y the estate freed from the mortgage, and the rule is that if I simply give Blackacre to Y, without saying more, I mean that he shall take it subject to any incumbrances that affect it.

Under the old law of dower a great crop of cases arose as to whether a widow was by her husband's will put to her election between her dower and those benefits that were destined for her by the will. You will remember that under the old law when dower had once attached to the land, the husband could not get rid of it by act *inter vivos* or by will—a fine levied by husband and wife was necessary. If then a husband affected to devise land that was subject to his wife's right of dower to Y and gave other benefits to his wife, a question often arose as to whether the doweress was put to her election. Many rules had been elaborated. Thus, for example, it was settled that a devise in general terms, 'all my land', would not oblige her to elect. But we need not go into this matter, for under the new law of dower, I mean the law introduced in 1833, even a general devise is sufficient to bar the widow of her dower and so no case of election can arise. The widow under the new law can only be endowed of land which her husband has not disposed of during his lifetime or by his will.[1]

The doctrine of election is applicable to cases of appointments under powers. Suppose that a person has a limited power of appointment in favour of a certain class of persons and he proposes to make an appointment in favour of one who is not an object of that power, and by the same instrument gives a benefit to some one of the persons who are entitled to the property in default of appointment, that person will be put to his election. Thus, for example, I have a power to appoint by will or deed a fund of £1000 in favour of all or any of my brother's sons and in default of appointment that fund is to be divided among all my brother's sons equally. By my will I profess to appoint this £1000 to my brother's daughter, and I bequeath £500 to one of my brother's sons; that son will be unable to dispute the appointment unless he is willing to compensate his sister. But on the other hand it seems that an object of the power will not be put to his election unless he also is (he usually will be) the person or one of the persons entitled in default of appointment. Put this case. I have power to appoint a fund of £1000 among my brother's sons, but if I make no appointment the fund will go to the Charing Cross Hospital. My brother has but one son. By my will I affect to appoint that the £1000 shall be divided between himself and his sister, and I further devise Blackacre to him. Here the appointment to the sister is of course a void appointment. One half of the fund is unappointed and the Hospital will get it. But it seems that my brother's son will not be put to his election, he will be able to keep the £500 and also to keep Blackacre, for I have not attempted to give to his sister *what belonged to him.* He had no right to any part of the £1000 until an appointment was made, and if no appointment was made the money was to go not to him but to the Hospital.

But again we must distinguish between cases in which a person attempts to make an appointment to some person who is not an object of the power from cases in which he makes an

[1] As regards persons dying after 1925 dower is now abolished; see Administration of Estates Act 1925, s. 46.

appointment to one who is an object of the power, but superadds some proviso or condition in favour of some one who is not an object of the power. Put the case that I have a power to appoint £1000 among my children. I appoint the whole sum in favour of my eldest son, but I add that he is to settle it upon his wife and children, who are not objects of the power, and then I proceed to devise Blackacre to my said son. Here there is no case of election.[1] I have made a valid appointment in favour of a person who was a proper object of the power. I have followed this up by a direction that he is to do this or that with it. This is a void clause and may simply be neglected. The result is that I have made a good appointment in favour of my son and have also made a valid devise to him; he is not put to his election, for I have not attempted to give to any other person what belonged to him. However if you will look at the case of *White* v. *White*, 22 Ch. D. 555, you will find that this distinction is a somewhat fine one. In that case a testator having power to appoint certain lands among the children of his first marriage, appointed them (describing them as his own property) in favour of a son of his first marriage subject to a charge in favour of his other children, including the children of his second marriage (who were not objects of the power), and he devised property of his own to the same son subject to the same charges in favour of his other children, 'so as to equalize the shares of all my children in all my property'. Fry J. held that in this case there was enough to put the son to his election.

We must, it seems, distinguish between an appointment to a person not an object of the power and an appointment which is bad for remoteness, as infringing the rules against perpetuities.

The validity of that distinction was denied by Kekewich J. in the case of *In re Bradshaw* [1902] 1 Ch. 436. A by will gives property upon trust for B for life and after his death upon trust for such of his children and other issue (such other issue to be born within the limits allowed by law) as B shall by will appoint, and in default of appointment for B's children equally.

B, by his will, purports to appoint in favour of his son C for

[1] See *e.g. Carver* v. *Bowles*, 2 R. and M. 301; *Churchill* v. *Churchill*, L.R. 5 Eq. 44.

life, and after the death of C for such of C's children as are then living. The latter part of this appointment is void. (Read back the appointment into A's will. Then there would be a gift to those great-grandchildren of the testator who shall be living at the death of a grandchild.)

But B gives his own property in the same way. Is there here a case of election? Kekewich J. (but with the current of authority against him) says yes. The objection is that a sort of indirect validity is thus given to a disposition which the law, on grounds of policy, pronounces void. The testator says: You must treat my void disposition as valid, otherwise you will be losers. But Kekewich J. assimilates this to an appointment in favour of a non-object, a person not within the power.[1]

Turning to another question, in *In re Wheatley*, 27 Ch. D. 606, Chitty J. adopted the general rule laid down by Lord St Leonards in his treatise on powers. 'Where a man having power to appoint a fund, which in default of appointment is given to B, exercises the power in favour of C and gives other benefits to B, although the execution is merely void, yet if B will accept the gifts to him, he must convey the estate to C according to the appointment.'

I refer you to this case of *In re Wheatley* chiefly because it raises a question which has more than once troubled the Courts of late years, and seems to have been now set at rest. Can a married woman, by reason of this doctrine of election, be compelled to make compensation out of a fund that is settled to her separate use without power of anticipation? Put a simple case. Blackacre belongs to Mary, the wife of John. By my will I devise Blackacre to Peter and bequeath £10,000 to trustees upon trust to pay the income thereof to Mary for her separate use without power of anticipation. Can Mary retain Blackacre and at the same time insist that she ought to have the income of the £10,000, or must she make compensation out of this income to the disappointed Peter? There have been contradictory decisions about this matter. In the case that I have mentioned Chitty J. decided that the married woman was not bound to elect, but

---

[1] *In re Bradshaw* was overruled in *In re Nash* [1910] 1 Ch. 1. See too *In re Oliver* [1905] 1 Ch. 191.

could take both benefits. Shortly afterwards *In re Vardon's Trusts*, Kay J. came to an opposite conclusion, but the Court of Appeal reversed his judgment, 31 Ch. D. 275.

In that case Miss Vardon, who was an infant, married Mr Walker. A settlement was made. The lady's father settled £5000 upon trusts which gave the wife a life interest for her separate use without power of anticipation. By the same deed she covenanted that any property that she might afterwards acquire should be settled upon certain trusts in favour of herself, her husband, and the children of her marriage. Then her brother died having by his will given her a sum of £8000 for her separate use. Now the covenant as a covenant was invalid, for as I have said when she entered into it she was an infant. But the trustees of the settlement raised the question whether she was not put to her election. Could she say this covenant is invalid and I will take the £8000 and yet go on receiving the income of the £5000 that was provided for her by the settlement? Would not this be both approbating and reprobating the deed? The Court of Appeal held that she was not put to her election. Had it not been for the restraint on anticipation she would have been put to her election, for even an infant can not say I will take the benefits provided for me by this settlement, and yet reject the covenants by which I professed to bind myself. But the Court of Appeal treated the matter thus. The doctrine of election rests upon the general presumption that the authors of an instrument intend that effect shall be given to every part of it. But this intention can be rebutted by an express declaration that the doctrine of election is not to be applied. Thus for example if I give Blackacre (which belongs to Peter) to John, and also give Peter £1000, the doctrine will apply, but it will not apply if I go on to say 'Nevertheless I hereby declare that Peter shall not be bound to elect between Blackacre and the £1000.' So here if this settlement had contained an express declaration excluding the doctrine of election, there would have been no difficulty. But does it not contain something that really is equivalent to such a declaration? 'What,' asked Fry L.J., 'is the force and effect of this restraint on anticipation? It provides that nothing done or omitted to be done by Mrs Walker shall deprive her of

the right to receive from the trustees the next and every suc-
ceeding payment of the income of the fund as it becomes due.
But if she be put to her election and if she deprives herself of
the right to receive subsequent payment of the income until her
husband and children are compensated, it follows that she has
by the act of election, or by the default in performing her
covenant, deprived herself of the benefit of the income in the
way of anticipation, which is the very thing that the settlement
declares that she can not do. This settlement, therefore, in our
judgment contains a declaration of a particular intention, inconsistent with the doctrine of election and therefore excludes
it.'[1]

This well brings out the point that the doctrine depends upon
a presumed intention. It can be excluded by words definitely
stating that it is to be excluded, it can be excluded also by words
which show a contrary intention, and by giving property to a
married woman 'without power of anticipation' one in effect
says that as regards that property she is not to be put to her
election.

That it is matter of intention is well illustrated by *Haynes* v.
Foster [1901] 1 Ch. 361. A testator owns lands in Turkey, he
devises them upon trust to sell them and the proceeds are to
form one fund with his residuary estate. He disposes of his
residuary estate in such wise that interests in it are given to a
son, X, and to two daughters, Y and Z, who are subjected to
restraint against anticipation. By Turkish law his disposition of
the proceeds of the sale of his land is invalid. They go, as to
two-fourths to the son, while each daughter takes one-fourth
share. This is a clear case of election against the son. But at the
time when the question rises one of the daughters, Y, is a
married woman, but the other, Z, is a widow. Following the
case of *In re Vardon's Trusts* it was held that Y is not bound to
elect. But what of Z—the widow—since for the time the
restraint on anticipation is inoperative? But it was held to be
a matter of intention. The testator has shown an intention that
Z shall not be put to her election by saying that her share is to
be inalienable. Kekewich J. thinks that the result would be the

[1] 31 Ch. D. at p. 280.

same if the testator had attempted to deprive a man of the power of alienation, notwithstanding that such an attempt must be futile. What is important is not the validity of the restraint but the attempt to render inalienable which is in effect a declaration that the doctrine of election is excluded.[1]

Then (to turn to another point) as regards the power to make an election, there never was a doubt that a married woman could make an election if the property was given to her separate use, and there was no restraint on anticipation in the case. An infant can not make a binding election: but on behalf of infants the Court will elect. It will direct an inquiry as to which of the two alternatives is the more beneficial to the infant, and adopt that one on his behalf.

An election may be inferred from conduct—it need not be made by any formal instrument. You may discover as a matter of fact that a person has elected to take under the instrument, or that he has elected to take against the instrument, and in this latter case he will be liable to make compensation to those persons whom he has disappointed by his election.

You will have noticed from what has already been said that an infant may be bound to elect—also that an infant may be bound to elect by reason of his or her own act. This is a point that has often to be considered in relation to marriage settlements executed by infants. A covenant in a marriage settlement made by an infant is not void but is voidable at the infant's option (*Smith* v. *Lucas*, 18 Ch. D. 531 at p. 543). The Infants Settlement Act 1855 validates such settlements (by a boy if over 20, or by a girl if over 17 years) if made with the sanction of the Court. But apart from this an infant, when of full age, may be put to an election.

This case leads us to consider a second application of the general principle of election. We have hitherto been speaking as though that principle only came into play in a case in which a person attempts to dispose of property that does not belong to him since it belongs to some other person. But the same or a very similar principle may be applied to cases in which a person

---

[1] This is not now good law. See *In re Tongue* [1915] 1 Ch. 390 and *In re Hargrove* [1915] 1 Ch. 398.

affects to dispose of property that really is his own, but of which, owing to some personal disability such as coverture or infancy, he or she can not effectually dispose. Here again there can be no case of election unless in the same transaction the person in question acquires some benefit from another. An infant on the occasion of his or her marriage affects to make a settlement of his or her property in favour of his or her future wife or husband and the children of the marriage. Now if this be all—if there is no benefit provided by some one else for this infant settlor— there can be no talk of election. But suppose that such a benefit is provided, then the infant, when he is of full age, may be bound to make his choice, repudiating the settlement as a whole or adopting the settlement as a whole. Thus, suppose a female infant, on the occasion of her marriage, covenants to settle all her property, present and after acquired, in a manner that benefits her husband and the children of the marriage, and by the same deed the husband brings property into the settlement for the benefit of the wife and children. Here we have a question of election. Can this woman be allowed to say I repudiate my covenant, but I intend to receive the benefits provided for me on the part of my husband? No. That is not to be suffered.

Either you must fulfil your covenant or out of the benefits that you receive under the settlement you must make compensation to those whom you disappoint by not fulfilling your covenant.

Of late years there has been a considerable number of cases illustrating this principle—that you must accept the settlement as a whole or reject it as a whole. One of them is *Greenhill* v. *North British Insurance Co.* [1893] 3 Ch. 474.[1] On her marriage a woman (of full age) agreed to settle *inter alia* a reversionary interest in a policy of insurance, a memorandum of this agreement was signed before the marriage by the husband alone, and he after the marriage executed the settlement. It was held that

---

[1] As to this case note (*a*) that the property agreed to be settled included real estate and that the agreement was one made in consideration of marriage, hence the question as to the Statute of Frauds, (*b*) that the woman's title to the policy of insurance accrued before Malins' Act 1857 came into operation and hence was not assignable by her during coverture, and an assignment which she had in fact made was invalid.

if the wife took the benefits given her by the settlement she was bound thereby to fulfil her own side of the agreement. Further it was held that her conduct amounted to an election—that by taking benefits under the settlement she had adopted it and was bound to fulfil her side of the bargain. Here the difficulty was occasioned not by her infancy but by the Statute of Frauds and her incapacity arising from coverture—but the principle is the same—you are not to approbate and reprobate.

NOTE ON ELECTION

THE application of the doctrine of election to settlements made by a person under a disability, which are void or voidable by reason of the disability, is rather more difficult than appears from Maitland's text. Some confusion arises from the fact that the word 'election' has two meanings. Whenever a transaction is voidable at the instance of one party, by reason of infancy or fraud or for any other reason, that party must choose whether to ratify or to avoid the transaction and such choice is sometimes called election, but in such a case the word is used in a rather different sense from that which it bears in the lecture. It will be convenient in this note if we use the word only in the sense which it has borne earlier in the lecture.

Suppose then that a person under a disability, as for example infancy or coverture, has attempted to settle property, but that by reason of the disability the settlement is void or voidable. How far can the doctrine of election apply?

Take first the case of a marriage settlement entered into by an infant. Such settlement is not void, but is voidable by the infant on coming of age. The infant will then have to choose whether to ratify or to avoid the settlement and whichever choice he makes he must treat the settlement as a whole and cannot ratify the parts which are beneficial to him while avoiding the parts which are not beneficial. So far no question of election in the strict sense arises; the question is merely one of applying the ordinary principles of the law of contract. A difficulty arises however if the settlement is part of a transaction which cannot be set aside *in toto*. Suppose for example that before a marriage the husband and wife join in a settlement under which they both settle their property upon each other and the children of the marriage and suppose that the wife was an infant at the date of the settlement. It would seem that the wife could on coming of age avoid her part of the settlement, but nevertheless the husband's settlement must stand since the unborn children are interested under it. Can the wife, while avoiding her settlement, continue to receive benefits under the husband's settlement? Probably not (see *Hamilton* v. *Hamilton* [1892] 1 Ch. 396). If she avoids her settlement any interest she takes under the husband's settlement will, it would seem, be used to compensate the husband and the children for what they would have received under her settlement had it not been avoided. Here we have an application of election in the strict sense.

Now take the case where the disability renders the transaction void and not merely voidable. *Harle* v. *Jarman* [1895] 2 Ch. 419 is a case of this sort. There a husband and wife entered into a separation deed under which (*inter alia*) the husband covenanted to pay the wife an annuity during her life and the wife covenanted that on the death of the husband she would assign to his executors a reversionary interest to which she was entitled under a settlement. By reason of her coverture the covenant to assign the reversionary interest was void. Nevertheless she received the annuity during the husband's life but on his death she refused to assign the reversionary interest. It was argued that by accepting the annuity she had elected to stand by the settlement and that she could not on his death go back on it. North J. however held that she was not bound by the covenant to transfer the reversionary interest. The covenant was void initially and during coverture she was disabled from entering into such a covenant. To hold that by accepting the annuity during her husband's life she had bound herself to perform the covenant would be to hold that a person who by reason of disability was incapable of binding herself to such a covenant had effectively bound herself by receiving money—a result which would plainly be bad law. It is probable that after the coverture had ceased (*i.e.* after the husband's death) she could then have been made to elect whether to give up the annuity or to continue to receive the annuity and assign her reversionary interest, but this point was not raised in the case. In *Codrington* v. *Codrington* L.R. 7 H.L. 854, in very similar circumstances, a lady was required to elect after the coverture had come to an end. It would seem therefore that so long as the disability continues the person under disability cannot be made to elect and will not by accepting benefits during the continuance of the disability become bound to perform an obligation to which by reason of the disability she is incapable of binding herself, but that after the disability has ceased she may be made to elect whether to stand by the whole transaction and accept benefits under it or to reject both the obligations and the benefits.

Greenhill v. *North British Insurance Co.*, which is cited in the text, is a peculiar case. The agreement by the woman to settle her reversionary interest was a valid agreement (since she was not at the time either married or an infant) but was unenforceable against her by reason that there was no memorandum in writing signed by her. It was held that by accepting benefits under the agreement she had made it enforceable against her although at the time she accepted the benefits she was a married woman and could not have then entered into and bound herself to a similar agreement. Although the case was treated as one of election it seems to be more nearly akin to the doctrine of part performance, since the only question really arising was whether the Statute of Frauds prevented the agreement from being sued upon.

Since the Married Women's Property Act cases in which the transaction is void are not likely to arise.

LECTURE XX

SPECIFIC PERFORMANCE

In the past we have seen Equity inventing certain new rights
and obligations, rights and obligations of a substantive kind.
We have seen it inventing the trust, conferring on *cestui que
trust* a right where he had none at law, imposing an obligation
on the trustee, though at law he was under no such obligation.
We have seen it inventing the equity of redemption, giving a
right to the mortgagor after he had lost his rights at law and
putting a new duty upon the mortgagee. We have also seen it
enforcing its peculiar theories as to the way in which assets
should be administered. We have now to observe it inventing
not, at least in the first instance, new substantive rights, but new
remedies. Two great remedies it invented, remedies peculiar to
itself—the decree for the specific performance of a contract, and
the injunction.

In granting a decree of specific performance—or a judgment
for specific performance—the Court in effect says to the defendant, You must perform specifically the contract into which
you entered—that is to say you must do the very thing that you
promised to do on pain of going to prison as a contemner of this
Court. For instance, if you have sold land, you must convey it
to the purchaser, he being ready to pay you the agreed price.
If you have bought land you must pay the price to the vendor,
he being ready to convey the land to you.

The original foundation of this jurisdiction no doubt is this.
There are many cases in which if a contract be broken no amount
of damages that a jury will give will be a sufficient remedy to
him who suffers by the breach. A man for example agrees to buy
land, and he agrees perhaps to give for it more than any one else
would have given. The seller refuses to perform his part of the
agreement, it may be that no damages that could be given to the
buyer would be a just compensation to him for his loss. What
damages can you give? Even if land can be said to have a

market value, still a man may well have consented to pay more than its market value and yet be very anxious that the agreement should be performed; to him the land has a fancy value. Our courts of common law, too, held that on a contract for the sale of land the purchaser was not entitled to any damages for the loss of his bargain if the sale went off by reason of the vendor being unable to make a good title to the land; that the buyer could only recover the expenses to which he has been put in relation to the attempted purchase. This rule laid down in *Flureau* v. *Thornhill*, 2 W. Bl. 1078, was confirmed by the House of Lords in 1874 in the case of *Bain* v. *Fothergill*, L.R. 7 H.L. 158. But too wide a scope must not be attributed to these decisions. They only protect a vendor who without fraud and without his default is unable to make a good title, not a vendor who wantonly refuses to complete the purchase or wilfully abstains from doing what is necessary to make a good title.[1] But if the purchaser chooses to accept such title as the vendor has he may have his decree of specific performance. Starting then with the principle that when the legal remedy was inadequate it would grant its own remedy of specific performance, the Court of Chancery acquired a large jurisdiction.

Let us first ask—To what contracts has it been applied?

It has been applied to contracts for the sale of land and for the lease of land. It has been applied at the suit of a vendor as well as at the suit of a purchaser, at the suit of one who has contracted to grant a lease as well as at the suit of one who has contracted to take a lease. This may seem a little strange. A vendor has a mere pecuniary demand against the purchaser who refuses to complete, a demand which may be enforced by a common law action. If the conveyance has been executed, he may in such an action recover the whole purchase money; if no conveyance has been executed then he has the land, and may recover the difference between the price agreed on and the estimated price on a resale. His case, therefore, is not one in which the common law remedy is inadequate. But the Chancery came to the doctrine, convenient for the spread of its jurisdiction,

---

[1] See *Day* v. *Singleton* [1899] 2 Ch. 320, *In re Daniel* [1917] 2 Ch. 405, *Braybrooks* v. *Whaley* [1919] 1 K.B. 435 and *Keen* v. *Mear* [1920] 2 Ch. 574.

that 'remedies should be mutual', that if the contract was of such a kind that Equity would decree specific performance of it at the suit of the one party, it would also decree specific performance of it at the suit of the other party. In this way the vendor of land acquired the remedy of specific performance.

Now these are the common cases. We generally see the remedy given when the contract is for the sale or for a lease of land. Still these are not the only cases. As a general rule a contract for the sale of goods will not thus be enforced—the legal remedies are adequate; but specific performance may be decreed of a contract for the sale of unique chattels, rare china or the like.[1] So again an agreement will not as a general rule be specifically enforced if it be for the sale of stock, *e.g.* Consols, such as may always be had in the market; still it has been granted of a contract for the sale of railway shares such as were not always to be had in the market. Then as a general rule you can not compel the specific performance of a contract to do work, to erect buildings or to make other things—still sometimes when the agreement to build or to repair is a mere subsidiary term in an agreement for the sale of land or for a lease of land a judgment for specific performance can be obtained. I have a decree before me which says (Seton on Decrees (1901), vol. III, p. 2281)[2] 'And it appearing that a plan of the house to be erected in pursuance of such agreement has been approved of between the parties, let the defendant S forthwith proceed to construct and erect a house on the ground comprised in the agreement in accordance with such plan.'[3] So a decree for the specific performance of an agreement for the sale of the good will of a business has been denied, but such a decree has been granted where the good will was sold as an adjunct to a house.[4] An agreement to execute a mortgage will be specifically enforced when the money has been advanced—a large part of the

---

[1] The Sale of Goods Act 1893, s. 52, authorizes judgment for specific performance, if the Court thinks fit, in any action for breach of contract to deliver specific or ascertained goods.

[2] See Seton's Judgments and Orders, 7th edition, p. 2211.

[3] *Cubitt* v. *Smith* (1864) 11 L.T. 298, and see *Wolverhampton Corporation* v. *Emmons* [1901] 1 K.B. 515.

[4] See *Darbey* v. *Whitaker*, 4 Drew. 134 at p. 139.

doctrine of equitable mortgages depends on this, but an agreement to lend money will not be thus enforced. The reason usually given is that to enforce it would be nugatory, since at the next moment the lender might demand his money back again. But the rule is now general and extends to cases where the lender could not at once demand his money back again.[1] An agreement to serve can not be specifically enforced, otherwise men might in effect sell themselves into slavery. See *Ryan* v. *Mutual Tontine Association* [1893] 1 Ch. 116.

On the whole I think that we may say that specific performance applies to agreements for the sale or the lease of lands as a matter of course; its application outside these limits is somewhat exceptional and discretionary.

Having convinced ourselves that the agreement before us is one of a kind of which equity will decree specific performance, we have next of course to be sure that this particular agreement is a valid, enforceable contract. And we may take as a main rule this—that equity will only enforce specific performance of a contract that is valid at law and provable in courts of law. In particular, since we are mainly concerned with contracts which come within the 4th section of the Statute of Frauds,[2] contracts for the sale of some interest in lands, or for the lease of lands— we must say that the note or memorandum in writing is as necessary in a court of equity as in a court of law—the doctrine as to what it must contain and how it must be executed was not peculiar to a court of law, or to a court of equity.

To this however there was, and is, one large exception or apparent exception in the purely equitable doctrine of part performance. Equity would sometimes enforce an agreement which, owing to the absence of any written note of it, could not be relied on in a court of law. A bold step certainly was here made: but yet perhaps a necessary one. A agrees to sell land to B—there is no writing—he lets B take possession of the land. What is one to do? Leave B in possession though he has not

[1] See *South African Territories* v. *Wallington* [1898] A.C. 309, but this particular form of agreement to lend money—viz. on debentures to a company—was excepted from this rule by the Companies Act, 1907, s. 16, now s. 76 of the Companies Act 1929.
[2] Now Law of Property Act 1925, s. 40.

paid the price? Allow A to treat B as a trespasser? Under the 17th section of the Statute such a problem as this did not arise, for if the goods have changed hands, if even a part of the goods has changed hands—there is no need for the written note. It is a pity that the 4th section did not contain similar words. A Court of Equity in effect set itself to supply them.

In order to give rise to this equitable doctrine it is, as I understand, necessary that the Court should find the parties unequivocally in a different position from that in which according to their legal rights they would be were there no contract. You find A letting B into possession and you say that this is cogent evidence of the existence of some agreement between them, and of some agreement relating to this land. Thus we get the rule that delivery of possession is a sufficient part performance on the part of the vendor to sustain his suit against the purchaser, and that acceptance of possession is a sufficient part performance on the part of the purchaser to sustain his suit against the vendor.

But you must find some cogent evidence in the situation of the parties before you can receive oral evidence of the agreement. Thus put the case that B has paid A a sum of money, £1000, and that he is ready to swear and bring plenty of witnesses to swear that he paid it as part or even as the whole of the purchase money of Blackacre which A had sold to him. You can not admit this evidence; there may have been any one of a thousand causes for this payment; it is in no way connected with Blackacre. So part payment, or even full payment of the price can not be relied upon as an act of part performance so as (such is the phrase) 'to take the case out of the Statute'.[1] Again take marriage— A in consideration that B will marry his daughter promises to settle Blackacre upon him. B marries A's daughter. This is not enough.[2] The fact that B has married A's daughter in no way points to Blackacre as being involved in any bargain. Again, A induces B to serve him as his housekeeper without wages by promising to leave her certain lands by his will; he does not

---

[1] *Hughes* v. *Morris*, 2 De G. M. and G. at p. 356; *Britain* v. *Rossiter*, 11 Q.B.D. at p. 130.

[2] *Lassence* v. *Tierney*, 1 Mac. and G. 551.

leave her the lands, and there is no signed memorandum of the promise. Here the fact that B has gone on serving A without wages is not unequivocal; indeed it does not in any way point to the lands in question; and it can not be relied on as a part performance to take this case out of the Statute. This was decided by the House of Lords in 1883 in the case of *Maddison* v. *Alderson*, 8 App. Cas. 467.

I believe, indeed, that the only things that can be relied on as acts of part performance for the purpose of our doctrine, are delivery and acceptance of possession of land, and in some cases retention of possession of land. Of the change of possession from A to B I have already spoken—this will be enough to let in oral evidence of an agreement. I mentioned a retention of possession because there are cases in which this when coupled with other acts may be enough. A has let land to B; the lease expires, but B continues in possession. If this be all, then B can not produce oral evidence of an agreement for a sale or for another lease and thus disturb the relation which the law implies between a landlord and a tenant who is holding over after the determination of his lease. But it is said that the retention of possession may, in special circumstances, be treated as part performance of an agreement for the sale of the land or for another lease—it is said to be thus if the tenant in possession lays out money upon the land upon the faith of an agreement. But the cases seem to show that some quite unequivocal act is required of the tenant.[1] So much as to the doctrine of part performance.

I think we may say that subject to this doctrine the plaintiff who goes to equity for a decree of specific performance must prove an agreement which in a court of law was a valid contract. At one time certain judges in the Court of Chancery had almost succeeded in inventing a doctrine that equity would compel a person to 'make good his representations'—I am not speaking of representations of existing facts, but of representations of intentions—and would thus go beyond the law of contract. But

---

[1] As to payment of an increased rent see *Nunn* v. *Fabian*, L.R. 1 Ch. 35, and *Miller and Aldworth Ltd.* v. *Sharp* [1899] 1 Ch. 622. Compare *Chapronière* v. *Lambert* [1917] 2 Ch. 356.

the wholesome influence of the Judicature Act and the decision in *Maddison* v. *Alderson*,[1] seem to have given the death blow to this loose doctrine. If you go to equity for specific performance there must have been a valid contract. But I say 'must have been', not 'must be'. Let us take this distinction, though now-a-days it belongs to the past.

It not unfrequently happened that one of two contractors could go to equity for specific performance, though he could not go, though he had lost his right to go, to law for damages. Note this case, a contractor could sometimes go to equity though he could not go to law, just as he could sometimes go to law though he could not go to equity. As a general rule a man can not sue upon a contract at law if he himself has broken that contract, though of course, as you know, there are many exceptions to this statement. Now in contracts for the sale of land it very frequently happens that a breach of the terms of the contract has been committed by the person who wishes to enforce it. Such a contract will be full of stipulations that certain acts are to be done within certain times. Within 14 days, for example, after the seller has delivered his abstract of title to the purchaser, the purchaser is to make all his requisitions and objections. On a certain day the sale is to be completed by a conveyance of the land and payment of the price—and so forth. Well you know that equity held that as a general rule these stipulations as to time were not of the essence of the contract—that for example a purchaser might sue for specific performance although he had not in all respects kept the days assigned to him by the contract of sale for his various acts. This was the general rule—these stipulations as to time were not essential unless the parties declared them to be so.[2] There were exceptions—the court looked at the whole contract to see whether time was or was not essential. Thus it is said that time is of the essence of the contract on the sale of a public house as a going concern,[3] on the

---

[1] (1883) 8 App. Cas. 467; and see this doctrine discussed, Pollock, *Contract*, 9th edition, Note I, p. 757.

[2] *Seton* v. *Slade*, 7 Ves. 265; 6 R.R. 124. See generally on the question when time is of the essence of the contract, Fry on Specific Performance, 6th edition, chap. xxv.

[3] *Cowles* v. *Gale*, L.R. 7 Ch. 12.

sale of a reversion, on the sale of a life estate, or life annuity, on the sale of a leasehold held for a short term, and generally when the property is of a fluctuating value or of a determinable character.[1] Thus it would often come about that a man could enforce a contract in equity though he could no longer enforce it at law. But, as you know, the Judicature Act of 1873, by section 25, sub-section 7, has removed this anomaly, 'Stipulations in contracts as to time or otherwise which would not before the passing of this Act have been deemed to be or to have become of the essence of such contracts in a Court of Equity, shall receive in all Courts the same construction and effect as they would heretofore have received in equity.'

So I think that we may say now that any one who goes to equity for specific performance must (subject to the doctrine of part performance) show a contract that is binding in law. Suppose now the contract to be one of a kind of which specific performance is usually granted, for instance a contract for the sale of land, can we go on to say that in the particular case before us specific performance will be decreed? I believe that as a general rule we may. It used to be said, and from time to time this sort of thing is still repeated, that specific performance is a discretionary remedy, but I think that of late years this talk has lost its old meaning, and that the right to specific performance may now be regarded as a right which normally accrues to every contractor when a contract falling within certain recognized classes has been broken. The exceptions have been brought under heads.

For the more part these exceptions are best treated now-a-days as part of our law of Contract, and you will find them discussed in your books on Contract. Thus of course there is much to be said about Fraud, Misrepresentation, and Mistake. You will, however, remember that in this region we can not, even under the new regime, argue from a refusal of the remedy by specific performance to the invalidity of the contract, though one may, at least in general, argue in the reverse direction. Thus

---

[1] See *Hipwell* v. *Knight*, 1 Y. and C. 401 at p. 416; *Newman* v. *Rogers*, 4 Bro. C.C. 391.

[2] Now Law of Property Act 1925, s. 41.

under the head of Mistake one may mention a case *Malins* v. *Freeman* (1837) 2 Keen, 25, in which the Court refused to grant specific performance against a purchaser who at a sale by auction bid for and bought a lot different from that which he intended to buy; he had acted with considerable negligence, and the question was left open whether there was not a valid contract on which damages might be recovered at law.[1]

Very often indeed the Court in an action for specific performance has to consider the effect of some misdescription of the land, either as regards its character, its quantity, or its title contained in the particulars or conditions of sale. Often when the misdescription is not of a very serious character it is able to say to the plaintiff vendor, 'Yes we will decree specific performance, but only if you will make compensation for this misdescription by accepting a somewhat lower price than that which was agreed on.' We have indeed three cases:[2]

(1) If the misdescription be but slight equity will enforce the contract at the instance of either party, but only with compensation. If the purchaser will get substantially what he bargained for he can be obliged to take it with a compensation for deficiency—that is, at an abated price.[3]

(2) Then we have the case of more serious misdescription in which the purchaser has the option of fulfilling the contract with compensation or avoiding the contract altogether. He has his choice—he can say I will not take this, or I will take this with compensation.[4]

(3) The misdescription may be so material that the Court will not enforce the contract at all, even with compensation. A sells Blackacre to B as freehold land; when the title is examined it turns out to be copyhold. The Court will not compel A to convey and make compensation.[5] One can not in such a case

---

[1] But cf. *Tamplin* v. *James*, 15 Ch. D. 215; and see these cases discussed in *Van Praagh* v. *Everidge* [1902] 2 Ch. 266 (reversed on appeal on another point [1903] 1 Ch. 434); and see Williams, *Vendors and Purchasers*, 3rd edition, pp. 751-2 and 763-5.

[2] See Pollock, *Contract*, 9th edition, pp. 581 *et seq.*

[3] See *e.g. Esdaile* v. *Stephenson*, 1 S. and S. 122 and *Powell* v. *Elliott*, L.R. 10 Ch. 424.

[4] See note 2, paragraph (*a*), on following page.

[5] See *Rudd* v. *Lascelles* [1900] 1 Ch. 815.

calculate the proper compensation. Of course if B will take the copyhold land without compensation he is entitled to have it, but the Court will not compel A to convey the land with compensation. It will leave B to his common law remedy, the action for damages, and that, as we have seen, will give him nothing for the loss of his bargain.[1]

But the cases on this subject are complicated by conditions of sale. There are two conditions in common use which have contrary effects. The one says that if any mistake or omission be discovered in the description of the property this shall not annul the sale, but the vendor or the purchaser is to allow compensation, and the amount of the compensation is to be settled by two referees or their umpire. It is well settled, however, that such a condition will not prevent a really serious misdescription from making the sale voidable at the option of the purchaser. Another condition, less frequently used, says that any error shall not annul the sale, nor is the vendor or the purchaser to claim any compensation in respect thereof. This again will not prevent the purchaser from resisting an action for specific performance if the misdescription goes to the root of the matter.[2]

Mistake, misdescription and fraud are topics with which both law and equity have had to deal. But to the action for specific performance there may be other defences which the common law would not recognize. It is, I think, a little doubtful whether

---

[1] Above, p. 302.

[2] The effect of these two conditions appears to be as follows:

(a) Notwithstanding a condition that an error shall not annul the sale the purchaser is entitled to rescind if the misdescription goes to the root of the matter. See *Flight* v. *Booth*, 1 Bing. N.C. 370, *In re Arnold*, 14 Ch. D. 270, *In re Puckett and Smith's Contract* [1902] 2 Ch. 258, *Lee* v. *Rayson* [1917] 1 Ch. 613.

(b) If the condition provides that an error shall not give a right to compensation the purchaser cannot get specific performance with compensation for the error, whether or not he would be entitled to rescind. *In re Terry and White's Contract*, 32 Ch. D. 14, *Curtis* v. *French* [1929] 1 Ch. 253.

(c) Where the misdescription is slight either party can get specific performance with or without compensation (according as to whether the condition allows compensation). *In re Courcier and Harrold's Contract* [1923] 1 Ch. 565.

(d) A misdescription is more likely to be regarded as not going to the root of the matter when the condition allows compensation than when it does not. Compare *Jacobs* v. *Revell* [1900] 2 Ch. 858 and *In re Fawcett and Holmes Contract*, 42 Ch. D. 150.

we ought not here to mention a gross inadequacy of price. It is not impossible that there are cases in which the Court, while holding that there was a contract enforceable by action for damages, would yet hold that owing to the gross inadequacy of the price that contract could not be enforced specifically. But I am not very certain that this class of cases really exists, or that now-a-days the Court would on the ground of inadequacy refuse to order specific performance, unless it was treating that inadequacy as evidence of fraud or of undue influence which rendered the contract voidable.

Among the defences to the action of specific performance one will sometimes find mention of 'want of mutuality'. But this seems to disappear on examination.[1] It was at one time thought that if the purchaser had signed an agreement to purchase, but the vendor had not signed an agreement to sell, the vendor could not obtain specific performance. That 4th section of the Statute of Frauds requires, you will remember, only the signature of the party to be charged; but it was argued that a Court of Equity would not enforce a contract against one party while the other was free. However, this argument was overruled on the ground that the vendor by filing a bill asking for specific performance became bound by the contract, so that from that moment there was the desired 'mutuality'.[2] So it has been said sometimes that if a man agrees to sell what is not his he can not enforce specific performance of the contract. Observe that a man may agree to sell what is not his and yet be able to fulfil his agreement. I agree to sell Blackacre to you; Blackacre belongs to X; but having made this agreement I buy Blackacre and am ready to convey it to you. It was said that in such a case you could not obtain specific performance of the contract against me, since at the time when it was made I could not have obtained specific performance against you—for the Court of course could not compel you to buy Blackacre since it could not compel X, to whom it then belonged, to sell it. But on the whole the cases seem to show that this supposed 'want of mutuality' is no

---

[1] See the question discussed in Ashburner on Equity, pp. 404–5 (2nd edition) and Fry on Specific Performance, chap. VIII (6th edition).

[2] See *Martin* v. *Mitchell*, 2 J. and W. at p. 426.

defence if when the time comes for completing the contract I show a good title to Blackacre; you can not resist my action on the ground that I acquired that title after the date of the contract.[1]

Other defences there are. The Court will not by a judgment for specific performance order a man to do what he can not do, or can not do lawfully. I thought that Blackacre was mine; I agreed to sell it to you; upon examination it turns out that Blackacre belongs not to me, but to X; the Court will not order me to convey to you an estate that belongs to X. I am a trustee of Blackacre; in breach of my trust I agree to sell Blackacre to you; the Court will not compel me to convey it to you. I am owner of Blackacre; I agree to sell it to A, and then I agree to sell it to B; the Court will not compel me to convey it to B. It will not compel me to do a wrong. You will notice that we are not here trenching on the subject of contracts tainted by illegality. But the case—it may very easily happen—that I offer a great mass of lands for sale, and that when my title deeds are examined it is discovered that I have agreed to sell a piece of land that is not mine; here is a contract for breach of which damages may be recovered; it is in no way tainted by illegality—but I can not be compelled to perform it specifically.

Lastly it used to be said that the Court would not thrust a doubtful title upon a purchaser. If the purchaser could show that there was some doubtful point of law involved in the vendor's title, then the Court would not compel the purchaser to take it. The Court would not decide the question; it would say 'Here is a seriously arguable question—that is a sufficient obstacle to specific performance at the suit of the vendor.' But of late years the Courts have grown much bolder in this matter. Of course you will understand that a judgment of specific performance is in no sense a judgment *in rem*. A purchaser may well be compelled to take what afterwards proves to be a bad title. For example a purchaser may bind himself to demand no more

---

[1] *Hoggart* v. *Scott*, 1 R. and M. 293; *Salisbury* v. *Hatcher*, 2 Y. and C. C. C. 54. But note that until the seller has acquired the land the buyer may repudiate the contract; and see the whole matter discussed in *Halkett* v. *Lord Dudley* [1907] 1 Ch. 590. See also *Brickles* v. *Snell* [1916] 2 A.C. 599.

than a five years' title, or to demand no title at all. He is held to his contract, and afterwards it may turn out that he got a bad title. But even when the purchaser has not thus contracted away his right to require a good title it may happen that a bad title will be thrust upon him. A sells to B; B objects to A's title; urges that according to the deeds the estate belongs to X not to A; A brings his action against B; the Court decides the point in A's favour; compels B to complete the purchase. Some years afterwards X appears upon the scene; he sues B for the land. The judgment which compelled B to accept the title is not a defence for him, it is no estoppel against X; X can say 'This judgment is *res inter alios acta*—I have not as yet been heard.' Therefore it was natural that the Courts should be somewhat reluctant to force dubious titles upon unwilling purchasers. However, the modern cases oblige us to say that the doubt which is to serve as the purchaser's defence must be a very serious doubt. A purchaser has even been compelled to accept a title under an obscure will when the judge—it was Sir George Jessel—before whom the case came had to dissent from another judgment pronounced on the very same will before he could hold that the title was a good one (*Baker* v. *White*, L.R. 20 Eq. 166); and a purchaser has often been compelled to accept a title where no one could have said that there was not a very arguable question to be decided.[1]

Our dealings with specific performance should induce us to say a little more about agreements for the sale of land and their effect. Normally in this country a considerable time elapses between the agreement for sale and the conveyance, during which time the purchaser is engaged in investigating the vendor's title. Of course it is just possible that there never should be any agreement, or any binding agreement, for sale distinct from the conveyance. In conversation you make me an offer of £1000 for Blackacre, and I at once sit down and make a deed of conveyance, and you at once pay the price. However this is not the way in which business is done. Usually there are

---

[1] See *In re Carter and Kenderdine's Contract* [1897] 1 Ch. 776. The cases are discussed in Fry on Specific Performance, 6th edition, chap. XVIII, and Williams on Vendors and Purchasers, 3rd edition, p. 1069.

two distinct acts in the law; the agreement on the one hand, the conveyance on the other; and weeks or months elapse between the two.

Now we have on a previous occasion seen the error of Austin's dictum that the mere agreement for sale transfers the *dominium*, the *jus in re*. In the sale of specific goods in a deliverable state that is so, but in the sale of land the agreement does nothing of the kind. The most that it does is that it gives to the purchaser an equitable estate in the land, a right good against those who claim under the vendor by gratuitous title, or who have or ought to have notice of it. In this sense the purchaser acquires an estate in the land—suppose that he has agreed to buy the fee simple, there is something to descend to his heir, there is something that will pass by a devise of all my real estate. But for the Acts of Parliament which it is convenient to refer to collectively as Locke King's Acts,[1] the heir or devisee would even have a right to call upon the executor or administrator to pay for this estate out of the purchaser's personal estate. As it is, though he can no longer claim this exoneration from the vendor's lien, yet the estate comes to him as part of the purchaser's realty. And so when the contract is signed the purchaser has rights that he can convey to another; they are not treated as a mere chose in action; for the purpose of conveyance he has already an equitable estate in the land, though one which is subject to the vendor's lien for the unpaid purchase money. But the vendor has as yet the legal estate in the land, and any one who purchases from the purchaser must purchase subject to those legal rights. Unless in the case of some very peculiar agreement the vendor may keep the legal estate, and may keep possession of the land until he is paid his price. If you say that the contract passes ownership, be careful to say that it does so only in equity.

So again it is common enough to say that the vendor becomes a trustee for the purchaser. And for certain purposes this is true enough. For example a man contracted to sell land, the title was accepted, but before conveyance he died, having by his will devised his real estate to X, and all real estate held by him upon any trust to Y; it was held by Jessel M.R. that the legal estate in the

---

[1] See p. 267 above.

land sold passed under the latter devise and not under the former (*Lysaght* v. *Edwards*, 2 Ch. D. 499).[1] He had become a trustee of the land that he had contracted to sell. Still the trusteeship of the unpaid vendor is a very peculiar trusteeship; one that stands by itself. In some respects he is rather in the position of the mortgagee than of the trustee. He can say I will not part with this land, I will not give up the legal estate, I will not deliver possession until I am paid. Then if the purchaser will not pay he has a right resembling that of foreclosure. He can go to the Court; the Court will order the purchaser to pay within a reasonable time, and in default of payment the purchaser will lose his right to the land under the contract, and the vendor will be in the same position as that in which he was before the contract was made, he will be owner at law and in equity.

Then again we may say that in another respect the purchaser, so soon as the contract is made, is treated as though he were the owner, provided that the contract is enforceable specifically. In the absence of agreement to the contrary the risk of loss is with him. The house that is sold is burnt down by accident; the purchaser must bear the loss.[2] So on the other hand if trees be blown down these windfalls belong in equity to him.[3] And so again if the vendor wilfully damages the land that he has sold he must pay for it; nay more, he is expected to take reasonable care of what he has sold, so long as it is in his possession.[4] In all these respects, it may be said, equity treats the purchaser as owner, the vendor as one who is in possession of another person's property. But then remember that there is a sphere into which equity can not enter; suppose that this vendor sells and conveys to one who has no notice of this previous contract for sale, then you will see soon enough what ownership 'in equity' means.[5] That contract passed no *jus in rem*.

[1] Cf. *In re Thomas*, 34 Ch. D. 166. This point cannot now arise; see p. 85 above.   [2] *Paine* v. *Meller*, 6 Ves. 349.

[3] *Magennis* v. *Fallon*, 2 Molloy, 561, 591, and *Poole* v. *Shergold*, 1 Cox, 273.

[4] *Royal Bristol Society* v. *Bomash*, 35 Ch. D. 390, *Clarke* v. *Ramuz* [1891] 2 Q.B. 456 and *Golden Bread Co.* v. *Hemmings* [1922] 1 Ch. 162.

[5] And remember that since 1925 the contract will not be enforceable by the first purchaser against the second purchaser unless it has been registered under the Land Charges Act 1925.

And then observe the effect of conveyance. We will suppose that the vendor makes a conveyance without receiving the price, or without receiving the whole price. He is still said to have a lien for the unpaid purchase money. This term 'vendor's lien' is often applied indifferently to the rights of a vendor who has not yet been paid and has not yet conveyed, and to the rights of a vendor who has not yet been paid but who has conveyed. But really these rights are of different orders. In the first case the vendor is legal owner of the land, and he can refuse to part with the land until he is paid—unless indeed he has expressly contracted to do so: he relies on this legal right. In the latter case he has parted with his land; the only right that the common law gives him is a purely personal right, a right to sue for the purchase money. Equity does something more for him: it gives him what is (with no great accuracy) called a lien on the land—with no great accuracy, for in general a lien signifies a right to retain what you have already in your possession, and here our vendor has parted with possession. It is a handy equitable right. It comes to this, that against the purchaser and those persons—but only those persons—against whom an equity will prevail, the unpaid vendor after conveyance has a charge upon the land, which charge he can enforce by demanding that the estate be sold and that he be paid what is due to him out of the proceeds of the sale. Against whom is such an equity good? Against whom are equitable estates in general good? This equity can be enforced against the purchaser, his representatives, those claiming under him as volunteers, against any later equity (unless there is some ground, such as negligence, for postponing the older to the younger equity), even against those who have legal rights in the land, unless there has been a *bona fide* purchase for value without notice of this vendor's lien. But the acquisition of the legal estate *bona fide* for value and without notice puts an end to the lien.[1] You see then that the rights of the unpaid vendor are radically altered by the conveyance.

You must not think that an unpaid vendor always has this right, this lien for unpaid purchase money. He may expressly waive it, and often a question may arise whether he has not by

---

[1] See *Harris* v. *Tubb*, 42 Ch. D. 79. Since 1925 the vendor's lien will require to be registered as a land charge.

implication waived it by taking some other security for his money. The general rule seems to be that if he takes another security, or if for example he takes a charge on a sum of stock, or a mortgage on another estate, or if he takes a mortgage on a part only of the estate that he has sold, this is presumably an abandonment of his lien; but taking a promissory note, a bill of exchange, or a bond is not sufficient. It must be remembered that the burden of proving the waiver is upon those denying the existence of the lien.[1]

The vendor is not precluded from insisting on this equitable right by a statement either in the conveyance or on the back of the conveyance that he has received the purchase money. Equity was inclined to treat the receipt clause in the body of the deed and also the endorsed receipt as forms.[2] At law the receipt clause in the body of the deed being under the vendor's seal would estop him from denying that he had received all that he said that he had received. But in equity as against the purchaser the vendor was allowed to prove that despite these receipt clauses he had not really received his money. As against persons claiming for value under the purchaser—sub-purchasers let us call them—the rule I believe was that if there was a proper receipt on the back of the deed, then, at all events if there was also a receipt in the body of the deed, this sub-purchaser would not have notice of the vendor's lien; but the absence of a receipt on the back of the deed was sufficient to give him implied notice of a vendor's lien, even though there was a receipt in the body of the deed. Therefore in perusing titles one was always careful to see that there was a proper endorsed receipt. The law has been altered in some respects by the 54th and 55th sections of the Conveyancing Act 1881.[3] A receipt in the body of the deed comes now to serve all the purposes that were served by the two receipts which were formerly usual; and in favour of a subsequent purchaser a receipt either in the body of the deed or endorsed therein is to be sufficient evidence that the money was really paid unless that purchaser has some other notice that it was not paid.

[1] See *Mackreth* v. *Symons*, 15 Ves. 329, White and Tudor, L.C. vol. II, p. 848 (9th edition).

[2] See *Kennedy* v. *Green*, 3 M. and K. 699, 716.

[3] Now Law of Property Act 1925, ss. 67 and 68.

LECTURE XXI

INJUNCTIONS

By means of its decrees for specific performance the Court of Chancery obtained command of one great province of law, namely of contracts for the sale of land. It fashioned another weapon, namely the injunction, which was far more flexible, far more generally applicable, and thereby it obtained not merely certain particular fields of justice, but a power of making its own doctrines prevail at the expense of the doctrines of the common law.

Let us see what an injunction is. It is an order made by the Court forbidding a person or class of persons from doing a certain act, or acts of a certain class, upon pain of going to prison for an indefinite time as contemners of the Court. This penalty will not be mentioned in the injunction, but if knowing of an injunction you break it, then the Court has a large discretionary power of sending you to prison and keeping you there.

I will give you an example or two of the form that an injunction takes. 'Let an injunction be awarded against the defendants the Mayor, Aldermen and Burgesses of Leeds to restrain the said defendants, their servants, agents and workmen from causing or permitting the sewage of the borough of Leeds or any part thereof to flow or pass through the main sewer or any other outfall into the river Aire unless and until the same shall be sufficiently purified and deodorized so as not to be or create a nuisance or become injurious to the public health.'

'Let the defendant E be restrained from infringing the plaintiff's trade marks registered under the Trade Marks Registration Act 1875, or either of them, and from selling or offering for sale any tea in, or from otherwise using, wrappers having imprinted thereon any imitation or colourable imitation of the plaintiff's trade marks or either of them.'

'Let an injunction be awarded to restrain the defendant from using or permitting to be used the premises called X or any part thereof for the purpose of balloon ascents, fireworks, dancing, music, or other sports or entertainments, whereby a nuisance may be occasioned to the annoyance or injury of any inmates of the asylum in the pleadings mentioned.'

There are certain technical terms the meaning of which you should understand if you are to read about injunctions. Very often a plaintiff wants an injunction at once; he wants to have it the moment he has begun his action and long before that action can be tried. Put the case that my neighbour is building a wall close to my land and is thereby beginning to block out the light from ancient windows of mine. I want an injunction at once, and I shall prejudice my case for an injunction if I allow him to go on building until the action can be tried—very possibly though I proceed with the utmost despatch the action will not be tried for many months to come. So soon as I have begun my action, so soon as I have served a writ of summons upon my adversary, I shall make an application, a motion to the Court for an injunction.[1] This will be an 'interlocutory application', and the injunction if granted will be an interlocutory injunction. Proceedings which take place in an action before the trial are said to be interlocutory. I shall serve my adversary with a notice telling him that on the next motion day (in the Chancery Division one day a week is usually given for the hearing of motions) my counsel will apply to the Court[2] for an injunction. Then if by the affidavit that I produce I make what the judge considers a sufficient case, he will grant an injunction. This however will not be a perpetual injunction; it will be an interlocutory injunction to hold good until the trial of the action. And I shall be obliged if I obtain it to give 'an undertaking in damages'—that is to say by the mouth of my counsel I shall have to undertake to pay any damages which the Court may hereafter award to the defendant in consequence of my having obtained an injunction

---

[1] Commonly leave is obtained to serve notice of this motion with the writ.

[2] In the King's Bench Division applications for interlocutory or 'interim' injunctions are made to the judge in Chambers either *ex parte* or on a summons, and not by motion in Court.

when I ought not to have had one. The order will be in some such form as this.

'Upon motion by counsel for the plaintiff and upon hearing counsel for the defendant and upon reading such and such affidavits, and the plaintiff by his counsel undertaking to abide by any order that this Court may make as to damages in case this Court shall hereafter be of opinion that the defendant shall have sustained any by reason of this order which the plaintiff ought to pay, this Court doth order that the defendant, his servants, workmen and agents, be restrained by injunction from &c. until judgment in this action, or until further order.'

But further there is sometimes so much need for speedy procedure, that the plaintiff can not even wait to serve upon the defendant a notice of motion, but having obtained his writ and filed an affidavit about the facts applies to the Court *ex parte*, and obtains from the Court an *ex parte* injunction—these words *ex parte* signifying that the defendant has not had an opportunity of being heard. In general such an injunction will be limited to a few days, *e.g.* until the next motion day, and then the defendant will have an opportunity of appearing and saying what he has to say against a continuance of the injunction until the trial. In such cases the Court is acting upon *prima facie* evidence—in the case of the *ex parte* injunction it acts upon the evidence produced by the plaintiff without hearing the defendant's version of the story. Then comes the trial, and the plaintiff either establishes his right to a perpetual injunction, or fails to do so. In the former case an injunction is granted without any limit of time which forbids the defendant to do the acts in question. In the other case the action is dismissed and an inquiry is ordered as to the damages which the defendant has suffered by reason of the interlocutory injunction, and the plaintiff will be ordered to pay these damages.

In general an injunction forbids a defendant to do certain acts, but sometimes it forbids him to permit the continuance of a wrongful state of things that already exists at the time when the injunction is issued. The Court does not merely say 'Do not build any wall to the injury of the plaintiff's right of light'; it can say 'Do not permit the continuance of any wall to the injury of the plaintiff's right of light.' If such a wall already exists then the defendant is, in effect, told to pull it down. An injunction which takes this latter form, an injunction forbidding the defendant to permit the continuance of an existing state of things is called a mandatory injunction.[1] A mandatory injunction is less easily to be had than a merely prohibitive injunction; in general it will not be granted until the plaintiff has fully proved that the existing state of things is wrongful.

Now this weapon was fashioned by the Court of Chancery and was used by it for all manner of purposes. One of these purposes is of great historical importance. It was the injunction which in the last resort enabled that Court to enforce its equitable doctrines, for it would grant an injunction to prevent a man suing in a court of law, or taking advantage of a judgment obtained in a court of law. I have already told you how this right of the Chancery was established in the reign of James I after the great quarrel between Coke and Ellesmere.[2] It gave the Chancery the upper hand. The Chancellor could say to a person 'You must not go to a court of law,' and the court of law had no power to say 'You must not go to a court of equity.' Well, when the Judicature Acts came into force in 1875 all this came to an end. It was expressly enacted by the Act of 1873, s. 24 (5), that no cause or proceeding at any time pending in the High Court should be restrained by prohibition or injunction. If in an action in the King's Bench Division—one of the old common law actions—the defendant has some equitable defence, he can plead it, and the court must listen to it and administer the rules of equity as well as the rules of law. However our Court still has power, and occasionally exercises it, to prohibit persons from suing in Colonial or foreign courts. I say this because I wish to remind you that the Chancery never claimed any superiority over the Courts of Common Law. It could not send orders to them; but it could prohibit a person from going to them. And just so now our High Court of Justice has no

---

[1] A mandatory injunction is now usually put in the form of a direct order to do the act required by the Court.

[2] P. 9 above; and see the notes to the *Earl of Oxford's Case*, White and Tudor, L.C., vol. I, p. 615 (9th edition).

superiority over a Colonial court, and of course it has no superiority over a French or German court, nevertheless, in a proper case it will prohibit a person from suing there. Equity acts *in personam*—this has been an important maxim. Equity did not presume to interfere with or to control the action of the common law courts. It acted upon the person who was inequitably suing in those courts.[1]

In this way the Judicature Act curtailed the field of injunctions; in another way it extended that field. But first I ought to remark that the Common Law Procedure Act of 1854, s. 79 (now repealed), gave to the Courts of Common Law what in terms was a very large power of granting injunctions, but that those courts being unaccustomed to the exercise of such a power made very little use of it.

Then came the Judicature Act of 1873 (s. 25, sub-s. 8).[2] 'A mandamus or an injunction may be granted or a receiver appointed by an interlocutory order of the Court in all cases in which it shall appear to the Court to be just or convenient that such order should be made; and any such order may be made either unconditionally or upon such terms and conditions as the Court shall think just; and if an injunction is asked either before or at or after the hearing of any cause or matter, to prevent any threatened or apprehended waste or trespass, such injunction may be granted, if the Court shall think fit, whether the person against whom such injunction is sought is or is not in possession under any claim of title or otherwise, or (if out of possession) does or does not claim a right to do the act sought to be restrained under any colour of title; and whether the estates claimed by both or by either of the parties are legal or equitable.'

Now this is the statute law of the land, and you will observe how wide are the terms employed, how large a power of granting injunctions it gave to the Court. That power now certainly goes

---

[1] Although the Court will not now grant an injunction to restrain proceedings pending in the High Court it will, in proper cases, achieve the same result by an order staying such proceedings. See Supreme Court of Judicature (Consolidation) Act 1925, s. 41, and the notes on that section in the Annual Practice. For an example of an injunction restraining a person from enforcing a foreign judgment, see *Ellerman Lines* v. *Read* [1928] 2 K.B. 144.

[2] Now replaced by Supreme Court of Judicature (Consolidation) Act 1925, s. 45, which is to the same effect.

beyond the power that was formerly possessed by the Court of Chancery. The concluding phrases of the section show that this —at least in certain definite respects—was the intended effect of the section. One of the few definite restrictions—and after all this was not very definite—which the Court of Chancery had set to its own power of granting injunctions was to be found in an unwillingness to interfere in disputes about legal rights in land when no equitable rights were involved. X was in possession of land, A was asserting title to that land, a purely legal title; he was bringing an action of ejectment against X. Meanwhile X was cutting down timber, pulling down houses, or committing other acts which would be waste if committed by a tenant for life. Equity was in such a case unwilling to interfere —for the question at stake was a purely legal question, namely whether X or A was owner of the land. It would only interfere against flagrant acts of spoliation which would immediately damage the disputed land. And so again if X was in possession and A without claiming title entered on the land and committed acts of trespass, equity was not very willing to interfere against A. The whole matter might well be left to a court of law—still if A was doing irreparable damage to the land the Court of Chancery would interfere. Well, the last phrases of the section that I have read are aimed against this restriction. Before or at or after the hearing the Court may grant an injunction to prevent threatened or apprehended waste or trespass, if the Court shall think fit, whether the person against whom such injunction is sought is or is not in possession under any claim of title or if out of possession does or does not claim a right to do the act sought to be restrained under any colour of title; and whether the estates claimed by both or either of the parties are legal or equitable.

But further the High Court now has got not only the old power of the Court of Chancery, it has also the powers granted by the section of the Act of 1873 that I have read. The consequence is that since 1875 injunctions have been granted in cases in which they were not granted before that Act. I have already spoken of matters of waste and trespass; the Court of Chancery's unwillingness to meddle with questions of pure common law title to land no longer stands in the way. But in the second place it had been settled that the Court of Chancery would not grant an injunction to restrain, either before trial or after trial, the publication or continued publication of a libel. The reason was this. The publication of a libel is usually a crime, and the Chancery having no jurisdiction in criminal matters steered very clear of the field of crime—there was to be no criminal equity. Besides, as we are often told, the question of libel or no libel is pre-eminently one for a jury, and the Court of Chancery knew no trial by jury. However, since 1875 it has been decided that the Courts of Common Law, though they had not exercised this power, had under the Common Law Procedure Act of 1854 obtained power to grant an injunction against the publication of a libel, and that the High Court now has this power, and can grant the injunction at the trial (a perpetual injunction) or before the trial (an interlocutory injunction). Its power is only limited by what is just and convenient. However, a good many cases are now tending toward establishing the rule that an interlocutory injunction against a libel is hardly ever to be had. An action for libel is one of the actions in which a defendant has a right to trial by jury. When the jury has found him guilty of publishing a libel there is no difficulty about granting an injunction to prevent a continuance of the publication as an additional remedy beside the judgment for damages. But before trial an injunction is hardly to be had. The defendant may allege that the libel is true; in this case he does no civil wrong in publishing it, and we ought not to assume against him before the trial that he will not be able to set up this defence and make it good. This was the effect of the decision of the Court of Appeal in the case of *Bonnard* v. *Perryman* [1891] 2 Ch. 269. But the Court has clear jurisdiction to grant an interlocutory injunction, even in an action for libel, if a proper case for it be made out. See *Monson* v. *Tussauds* [1894] 1 Q.B. 671, a case that you will find both amusing and instructive.[1]

Well, our written, our statute law now says that an injunction, even an interlocutory injunction, may be granted whenever it is

[1] On injunctions to restrain libel, see Kerr on Injunctions, chap. XII (6th edition).

just or convenient. Of course, however, as I have just shown by reference to the case of libel, judges must follow the stream of decisions in adjudging that the issue of an injunction will or will not be just or convenient.

I think that we shall best divide the work of injunctions by taking as our two heads Tort and Contract.

A very large part of the whole province of Tort is a proper field for the injunction. I should say that the only torts which lie outside the field of injunctions are assault and battery, false imprisonment, and malicious prosecution. I do not think that an injunction has been used or could be used to prevent these torts, which if they be torts will also at least in most cases be crimes. Here there are other remedies. If you go in fear of a man you can have him bound over to keep the peace, while if you are wrongfully imprisoned the writ of habeas corpus with its rapid procedure should serve your turn. A civil court, again, must not prohibit a man from instituting criminal proceedings. The Attorney-General's *Nolle prosequi* should be a sufficient preventive check on criminal proceedings of an obviously vexatious kind. But with these exceptions it would be hard to find a tort which might not in a given case be a proper subject for an injunction. Of libel I have already spoken, and something I have said of trespass and of waste. It was the Chancery's power of issuing injunctions against acts of waste that begot the doctrine of equitable waste. Sometimes the Chancery would give an injunction against waste for which a Court of Law would give no damages. Nuisance is a fertile field, so is the infringement of copyright, of patents, of trade marks. Indeed there are many rights which are chiefly, though not solely, protected by an injunction—the remedy by action for damages being but a poor one. Damages and injunction are not, you will understand, alternative remedies—in old times you could get the one from the Courts of Common Law, the other from the Court of Equity; now-a-days you may well get both from the same Court, the same division of the Court in the same action, damages to compensate you for wrong suffered, and an injunction to prevent a continuance of the wrong, it may be a mandatory injunction to prevent the continued existence of a wrongful state of things.

But while the remedy by damages is a matter of strict right, the remedy by injunction is not. This is best seen by referring to the cases in which a plaintiff can recover nominal damages. He has not really been hurt; he has not been made the poorer; but still his rights have been infringed and the Court pronounces a judgment in his favour. But the Court will not interfere by injunction where the tort complained of, though a tort, is one which does no real damage, and it will not interfere by injunction if damages will clearly be an adequate remedy.[1] Then again it may consider the plaintiff's conduct, and in particular any delay of his in bringing the action. To an action for damages delay is no defence unless the case has been brought within one of the Statutes of Limitation. Either the plaintiff still is entitled to the remedy or it has been taken from him by a Statute, and you can fix the precise moment of time at which the Statute takes effect —one moment he has a remedy, the next moment he has none. It is not so with the injunction; the Court may well hold for example that my neighbour must pay me damages for having blocked out light from my ancient windows, and yet, as I stood by and let him build, it would be inequitable to compel him to pull down his wall. Especially when a mandatory injunction is to be sought, the plaintiff must at once take action and prosecute his action diligently. The Court, it is said, in granting a mandatory injunction may look at the balance of convenience. The defendant is by supposition in the wrong, but on the whole and considering the conduct of both parties, shall we not be inflicting on him more harm than he deserves if we compel him to pull down his wall?[2]

Within the province of Contract the injunction plays a con-

---

[1] See *e.g. Llandudno U.D.C.* v. *Woods* [1899] 2 Ch. 705; *Behrens* v. *Richards* [1905] 2 Ch. 614; and see *Fielden* v. *Cox* (1906), 22 T.L.R. 411, where Buckley J. refused to grant an injunction against a Cambridge medical student and three young brothers who were alleged to have disturbed game by hunting for moths on a highway and on some adjoining lands near Whittlesea Mere. The plaintiff recovered a shilling as damages, which had been paid into Court, and he was ordered to pay the whole of the defendants' costs.

[2] See the cases collected in Seton on Judgments and Orders, pp. 518 *et seq.* (7th edition).

siderable part, but not so large as that which it plays in the field of Tort. Equity it will be remembered has here another weapon, namely the decree for specific performance. It has come to a body of doctrine about the use of that remedy, has decided that it is applicable to contracts of certain classes, in particular to contracts for the sale of land, and that it is not applicable to contracts of some other classes. However, for the enforcement of contract, it has used the injunction as well as the decree for specific performance. We must start with this principle that the injunction is only applicable to breaches of negative contracts, *i.e.* contracts not to do, as distinguished from positive contracts, *i.e.* contracts to do something. For the enforcement of negative contracts it is very largely employed, for example it has been the chief method of enforcing negative contracts contained in leases, covenants not to assign, not to use as a public house, not to sell hay or straw off the farm. You will remember how it was as an outcome of this power to grant injunctions that the doctrine about covenants which run with the land, not at law but in equity, made its appearance. And you will remember that that doctrine is confined to negative covenants, it goes no farther than the remedy by injunction will go.[1] Then again a common case for an injunction arises upon breach of a covenant against carrying on business of a certain kind. You will find that the decisions which have settled the limits between lawful and unlawful restraint of trade have been chiefly decisions of Courts of Equity given in suits for injunctions. These I mention as common cases. But I think that the rule is a very general one that the breach of a negative contract can be restrained by injunction. And applications for an injunction in these cases are treated somewhat differently from similar applications in actions founded on torts. We hear much less of 'the balance of convenience' when there is a contract, and the applicant is not bound to show that he has already suffered actual damage. When a man has definitely contracted not to do a certain thing, it is not for him to say that it will be greatly to his convenience, and not much to the inconvenience of the other party, that he should

[1] P. 163 above.

be allowed to do it. But this general rule seems to be limited by this, that you are not by means of an injunction to compel the specific performance of a positive contract which does not fall within one of those classes of contract of which the Court will decree the specific performance. Suppose that I agree to serve you as your clerk for ten years, no doubt this agreement will (at least in any common case) imply a term that I am not during that period of ten years to serve any other person. But a contract of hire and service is not one of those contracts of which the Court will decree the specific performance. Therefore you cannot directly compel me to serve you. Can you do so indirectly by obtaining an injunction to prevent me from breaking that negative but unexpressed term in the contract that I am not to enter the service of anybody else? No you can not. This seems well settled, that a merely implied negative term in a contract which is substantially positive can not be enforced by injunction. There has, however, been some difference of opinion as to cases in which an express negative covenant has been added as an accessory to an express positive covenant. In the famous case of *Lumley* v. *Wagner*, 1 De G.M. and G. 604, the defendant had agreed to sing at the plaintiff's theatre and not elsewhere without the plaintiff's permission; it was held that though she could not be compelled to fulfil the positive part of the agreement she could be restrained from breaking the negative part. In the well-known case, however, of *Whitwood Chemical Co.* v. *Hardman* [1891] 2 Ch. 416, Lindley L.J. said that he looked upon *Lumley* v. *Wagner* as an anomaly not to be extended. In that case the manager of a manufacturing company had agreed that during a specified term he would give all his time to the business. It was held by the Court of Appeal that the company could not have an injunction to prevent him giving part of his time to a rival company. The state of affairs seems to be this. You can not indirectly by means of an injunction enforce the specific performance of an agreement which is of such a kind that specific performance of it would not be directly decreed; but if you can separate from this positive agreement an express negative agreement that the defendant will not do certain specific things, then you may have an injunction to restrain a breach of that negative agreement.[1]

[1] A striking instance of the indirect enforcement by injunction of a positive agreement is to be found in *Lord Strathcona S.S. Co.* v. *Dominion Coal Co.* [1926] A.C. 108, a case which goes beyond the principle stated by Maitland and indeed beyond any of the earlier cases. As regards other aspects of this case see above, p. 177.

Where the covenant to be enforced is for personal service, as in *Lumley* v. *Wagner*, it must be remembered that such covenants are clearly in restraint of trade and the Court will, before granting an injunction, consider whether the restraint is reasonable, having regard to the interests of both parties and of the public. See *Rely-a-Bell Burglar Co.* v. *Eisler* [1926] Ch. 609 and the cases there cited.

NOTE.

For historical purposes a note is here reprinted which was written by the original editors in 1912 on the subject of Maitland's statements with regard to the doctrine of resulting trusts (page 77 of the present edition).

Both judges and text-book writers have differed upon this question, and it is desirable to draw the student's attention to this diversity of opinion. In support of Maitland's view that a resulting trust for the grantor is presumed on a voluntary conveyance of real estate in the absence of evidence of intent to give, may be cited decisions of Nottingham C.[1] and Somers L. K.[2] In more recent times the illustration given by Jessel M. R. in *Strong* v. *Bird*[3] is merely a dictum, but it shews that he accepted this view. Against this however there are very clear statements by Hardwicke C. in *Lloyd* v. *Spillet*[4] and *Young* v. *Peachey*[5]. The observations of Lord Hardwicke upon this point in the latter case are plainly dicta. The former case may be a decision upon the question, but it is to be observed that the conveyance in that case contained a power of revocation, and Lord Hardwicke having regard to common usage in conveyancing considered that the insertion of such a power made against a resulting trust.

In modern times James L. J. in an emphatic dictum denies that the implication of a resulting trust arises on a voluntary conveyance of land[6].

So far as the editors are aware, there are no expressions of judicial opinion bearing directly upon the point other than those cited.

A similar diversity of opinion is to be found in the text-books. Lewin[7] in a very carefully drawn general statement accepted the decisions of Lord Nottingham and Sir J. Somers; Sanders[8] following Lord Hardwicke argues very strongly against the implication of a resulting trust. Mr Joshua Williams[9] citing Sanders accepts his view, but in rewriting the portion of Williams' *Real Property* dealing with Trusts the present learned editor Mr T. Cyprian Williams adopted Lewin's position[10].

The authorities as to both real and personal estate are cited in the eighth edition of White and Tudor's *Leading Cases* (pp. 833–835), and it will be seen that a like diversity of opinion has existed in the case of personalty, and apparently the only point definitely covered by authority is that on a voluntary transfer of stocks or shares there is a resulting trust for the transferor, where he is not the father or husband of the transferee.

---

[1] *Elliot* v. *Elliot*, 2 Ch. Cas. 231, and see dicta in *Grey* v. *Grey* 2 Swans. at p. 598.

[2] *Duke of Norfolk* v. *Browne*, Pr. Ch. 80 and see *Rex* v. *Williams*, Bunb. 342.

[3] L.R. 18 Eq. 315 at p. 318.   [4] 2 Atk. 148.   [5] 2 Atk. 254.

[6] *Fowkes* v. *Pascoe*, L.R. 10 Ch. 343 at p. 348.

[7] See Lewin, 2nd Edit. p. 130 ; 6th Edit. p. 127 ; 12th Edit. p. 164. In his first edition at p. 170 Lewin had accepted Lord Hardwicke's statements in *Lloyd* v. *Spillet* (*supra*), and *Young* v. *Peachey* (*supra*), in all subsequent editions he and his editors followed Lord Nottingham.

[8] Sanders on Uses, 5th Edit. p. 365.

[9] See Williams' *Real Property*, 13th Edit. pp. 164, 165.

[10] 17th Edit. p. 172; 21st Edit. pp. 183, 184.

INDEX